Church in the Land of Desire

Church in the Land of Desire

Eastern Orthodox Encounter with
North American Consumer Culture

EDWARD ROMMEN

Foreword by Bradley Nassif

WIPF & STOCK · Eugene, Oregon

CHURCH IN THE LAND OF DESIRE
Eastern Orthodox Encounter with North American Consumer Culture

Copyright © 2021 Edward Rommen. All rights reserved. Except for brief quotations in critical publications or reviews, no part of this book may be reproduced in any manner without prior written permission from the publisher. Write: Permissions, Wipf and Stock Publishers, 199 W. 8th Ave., Suite 3, Eugene, OR 97401.

Wipf & Stock
An Imprint of Wipf and Stock Publishers
199 W. 8th Ave., Suite 3
Eugene, OR 97401

www.wipfandstock.com

PAPERBACK ISBN: 978-1-7252-7104-3
HARDCOVER ISBN: 978-1-7252-7105-0
EBOOK ISBN: 978-1-7252-7106-7

03/16/21

Contents

Foreword by Bradley Nassif   vii
Preface   xi

PART I: INTRODUCTION

1. External Threats to the Church   3
2. The Operating Principles of the Contemporary Social Imaginary   12

PART II: THE MARKETPLACE: THE CHURCH AND CONTEMPORARY COMMERCE

3. Introduction: Business in the Church   49
4. Management/Administration   58
5. Production/Preparation   89
6. Distribution/Presentation   110
7. Consumption/Participation   131

PART III: THE PUBLIC SQUARE: THE CHURCH AND CONTEMPORARY PUBLIC DISCOURSE

8. The Idea of the Public Sphere   147
9. Church as Topical and Metatopical Public Space   155
10. Challenges to Public Discourse   164
11. Influence of the Pubic Sphere on the Church   182

PART IV: A SELF-GOVERNING PEOPLE: THE CHURCH AND CONTEMPORARY POLITICAL STRUCTURE

12. A Self-Governing People   209
13. Democracy, Politics, and Self-Governance in the Church   217

PART V: CONCLUSIONS: EXTERNAL THREATS TO THE CHURCH REVISITED

14 Lessons and Principles	241
15 On the Possibility and Nature of an Ecclesial Imaginary	254
Appendix	267
Bibliography	283

Foreword

What is the role of orthodoxy in today's secular, godless, and materialist culture? That is the central question which guides the narrative of this volume. Its author, Edward Rommen, is eminently qualified as both a priest and professor of orthodox theology and missions. He is one of the very few Eastern Orthodox missiologists in the world today who is intellectually and experientially equipped to prescribe the remedy for the complex challenges facing the church today. In the following pages, he analyzes specific philosophical, scientific, ethical, and technological threats to the church's internal life and external witness. Sustained attention is given to the church's relationship to the marketplace of commerce, its witness in contemporary public discourse, and its response to the political realities of American democracy. The Appendix includes an intriguing area that is often overlooked by American scholars of religion, namely "The Special Challenges Faced by Orthodox Monasteries." Rommen shows how Orthodox monastic culture has the surprising potential to counter the secular affronts of American culture, but only if it can fulfill its prophetic role as the church's conscience, reminding us that the kingdom of God is not of this world.

The essential problem this book addresses is the reality that in many parts of the very wealthy and comfortable West there is a profound loss of spiritual consciousness. Too often the public mission of Christians has been characterized by fear, sectarianism, intellectual immaturity, and social conservatism or social progressivism. Why, then, should we be surprised if this clammy handshake has not worked? This is where a knowledge of orthodoxy can serve all Christians by making known the historic roots of their own spiritual tradition. It is one Protestants will recognize for its simplicity and personal faith, just as Roman Catholics will embrace it because of its richly Christocentric warmth. Both will be able to take as their own the ancient heritage of Christian wisdom that has been mediated through the Spirit-filled teachings of classical Christianity. That knowledge will enable all Christians, but especially the Orthodox, to navigate the temptations of contemporary life because the Orthodox tradition has kept this heritage alive across the centuries up to the present time.

In America, Orthodox Christianity is a minority religion comprising only about 2 percent of the total population (depending on the criteria one uses for church attendance). Unlike in traditional orthodox lands such as Russia, Romania, Serbia, and others, American orthodoxy lives in a sea of Protestant, Catholic, and non-Christian world religions. Perhaps that is what makes its voice all the more urgent. If true to itself, orthodoxy can speak eschatologically into a public forum which has successfully sterilized the gospel in a great many Christian churches. Modern culture has secularized the methods and content of the Christian faith, robbing it of its transformative power. Like John the Forerunner, the Orthodox Church can bear prophetic witness to the messianic age that is here and now among us. If true to its mission, orthodoxy in America may function as a remnant's witness to a historic faith that has been long forgotten, or even largely rejected by the modern church. Rommen believes orthodoxy needs to tell its own story with a spirit of mission rather than maintenance. It must speak afresh with passion, lived experience, and the courage to face marginalization with humility, without trumpeting the pomp of its past glories.

The famous Russian novel *The Way of a Pilgrim* features as its protagonist a simple Russian peasant who laments the fact that there is no one to teach him how to pray. This plea may also represent the pressing and powerful need to fill the void in modern men and women's souls that materialist reductionism has brought into their lives. Professor Rommen, therefore, sets the goal of his book to be nothing short of authentic orthodox existence. The ultimate point he makes might be summarized in a sentence: Genuine Christianity is a quest for the believer to become a human being, and in becoming a human being in Christ, the Christian becomes deified by the grace of the indwelling presence of God. Or to put it in the famous words of St. Athanasius, "God became man so that man might become god."[1] Rommen shows us the real problem today is not that men and women have become secularized (nonreligious, or whatever) and lost their sense of God, true though that is. The underlying problem is they have lost the sense of what it is to be *truly human*. The fundamental character of a true human being is the awareness that presses on all people that they are a *transcendent reality*. They are theocentric beings who cannot become fully themselves apart from the indwelling presence of God in their lives. This concept of communion with God, based upon a theocentric anthropology, liberates

---

1. St. Athanasius, *On the Incarnation of the Word*, §54.

humans from their slavery to materialism in all its forms, giving them a personal freedom that is recovered in the spiritual communion of the body of Christ. The catholicity of that communion with God, and other humans, make it the foundation of a universal mission to the world in which we live. Its theology is based on a theocentric understanding of humanity, the proclamation of the gospel, and on a sacramental understanding of baptism and the Eucharist. However, it also presupposes the church will provide the means for the proper experience of that which it is supposed to be. In that respect, the situation is tragic wherever the Orthodox Church fails to live out the existential realities of its own faith. This may happen when the gospel is not clearly preached or its worship has been reduced to the rote repetition of rites, or secular models of business administration and church growth have been adopted wholesale. All these too often exclude the liberating paschal character of public preaching and the Eucharist. Authentic communion with God, through Christ and the Spirit, leads us out of the world in order that we may return to it as the "new creation." The following pages demonstrate with uncommon skill that only Christ's resurrectional activity in the church can bring the kind of mission to America that will bear fruit in the winter season in which we now live.

Bradley Nassif
Professor of Biblical and Theological Studies, North Park University

Preface

The more the journey of the church continues through the centuries toward the end . . . the more the temptations and difficulties will increase.[1]

In volume I of his commentary on the book of Revelation, Archimandrite Athanasios Mitilianaios expounds on the implications of what he calls *the things that are*, that is, the dangers that were being faced by the churches in St. John's day as detailed in the warnings given to the seven churches of Asia Minor (Rev 1–3). In volume II, the Archimandrite turns his attention to St. John's description of the *things that will take place after this* (Rev 4–19). Mitilianaios points out that given the apostle's place in history, these *other things* would not take place until sometime after St. John's era, that is, not until sometime in his future, and because we are now living in that future, this could also mean at least some of these *other things* are taking place now. Accordingly, we "find ourselves not only in *the things which will take place after this*, but we may very well. . ." be facing dangers that are "part of the threshold that marks the very end of the future journey of the church."[2] Indeed, it seems reasonable to interpret contemporary endangerments of our secular, godless, materialistic, consumer-oriented culture in light of the apostle's warning. Moreover, having the advantage of divine forewarning, we should be able to identify and acknowledge the reality of these threats, anticipate the damage they can inflict, and actively develop an effective defense against them. Yet, because "we carry in ourselves a great deal of worldly thinking. . ." because "the world influences our life and our existence," we are, in spite of the warnings, often unable or unwilling to

---

1. Mitilinaios, *Revelation: Seven Seals*, 1–2.
2. Mitilinaios, *Revelation: Seven Seals*, 2 (emphasis his).

even acknowledge the threats.³ That may be why so few Orthodox faithful today speak openly about resisting these threats. For some Christians these dangerous forces appear to be irresistible or unavoidable. They argue that resisting is essentially futile, a losing battle⁴ not worth the effort. Others think we can tame and harness these powers for use within the church. Either way, it is this somnolent indifference to the dangers that allows them to infiltrate the church, to wreak havoc, and, like the savage wolves that St. Paul warned about, to "come in among you, not sparing the flock" (Acts 20:29).

God has used the divinely inspired book of the Revelation⁵ to warn us, and he has done so in order to "prepare [us] for [our] own personal struggle, to console [us], to strengthen [us], and to protect [us] from being scandalized and secularized."⁶ This essay is an expression of my desire to heed those warnings, to respond to them, and to deliberately enter the struggle against the forces threatening the church. Doing this has certainly been difficult, uncomfortable, and, above all, unpopular even with many in the church. But the alternative to not raising the alarm, not asking these questions, not raising our defenses, does not bear thinking. So, even now as we "witness [many] falling away from the church,"⁷ and while we see others using secular principles to change the very nature of the church, we must actively identify and resist these threats, knowing that if we do not, then we, too, could turn cold and lose our hope, if not the church herself.⁸

---

3. Mitilinaios, *Revelation: Seven Seals*, 3.

4. This pessimistic sentiment is eloquently captured in Tolkien et al., *Silmarillion*.

5. The Revelation is, of course, not the only place in Scripture where we find predictions of future challenges. In 2 Timothy 4:3–4, we are told "the time will come when they will not endure sound doctrine, but according to their own desires, because they have itching ears, they will heap up for themselves teachers; and they will turn their ears away from the truth, and be turned aside to fables."

6. Mitilinaios, *Revelation: Seven Seals*, 2.

7. Mitilinaios, *Revelation: Seven Seals*, 3.

8. Mitilinaios, *Revelation: Seven Seals*, 3.

PART I

Introduction

1

External Threats to the Church

Market capitalism was hostile; no immigrant culture—and, to a considerable degree, no religious tradition—had the power to resist it, as none can in our own time. Any group that has come to this country has had to learn to accept and to adjust to this elemental feature of American capitalist culture.[1]

Throughout my ministry, much of my attention has been focused on various aspects of ecclesial growth viewed mostly from a perspective within the church. I appealed to its theology, its tradition, its practices, and its God-given purpose in an effort to define the nature of church and what it might mean for a church to succeed. I asked what elements of church life can grow and how that growth can be measured. I explored ways in which we can use the resources already possessed by the church to encourage growth in the area of oneness, holiness, catholicity, and apostolicity. So, I was looking at growth factors that arise within the church and which are directly related to its own nature and God-given faculties.

There are, of course, growth factors that arise in the world outside the church. Because the church does not exist in a vacuum—that is, because it is embedded in the larger context of the prevailing culture—it will at times be required to engage that extraecclesial world, and that engagement can and will have an effect on its growth and well-being. For example, growth could

---

1. Leach, *Land of Desire*, 19–20.

come as a result of believers reaching beyond the confines of the church in order to engage the world by proclaiming the gospel, making disciples, or caring for those in need. But to effectively engage society in those ways, believers will need a working knowledge of the meanings, devices, and procedures of that culture, that is, they will have to speak the language and be acquainted with the general worldview and the rules of social interaction, as well as the means and technologies that make all of that possible. In the North American context, gaining that knowledge has not been all that difficult. In fact, with the help of almost constant exposure to the information conveyed by public education, advertising, and the mass media, most North American Christians have easily and thoroughly absorbed the defining elements of our culture. Without any real intentionality, they have embraced a cultural identity. They now know intuitively they are Americans and what that entails.

These same believers who, because they are citizens participate in the educational institutions, economic structures, moral order, legal code, and political foundations of the prevailing culture, can not only reach out and engage the world around them, they can just as easily bring the meanings, devices, and procedures of that culture, some of which are antithetical to the faith, back into the church. That, I submit, can alter, overwhelm, and even supplant the church's own internal meanings and practices. This ready flow of ideas and meanings into the church should not surprise us. Because their exposure to Christian teaching and practice constitutes only a tiny fraction of the overall amount of information these believers are exposed to, it takes a much more deliberate effort to acquire, call to mind, and exhibit the basic elements of a Christian identity. For that reason, it is usually this socially determined identity that dominates and effectively governs everyday life, including life in the church. This social identity and its underlying precepts are in the air we breathe and the water we drink, rendering the contours of our faith largely unintelligible, lost among the ubiquitous, quotidian details of simply being Americans in good standing. Societally engaged believers bringing the secular mindset of their culture into the church, intentionally or otherwise, is, I believe, the most serious threat to ecclesial well-being and growth we face today.

To be sure, I am not suggesting we should not actively engage the world around us. There is, as far as I can see, nothing fundamentally wrong with becoming constructive participants in society. But there are definitely some limits to, and—perhaps unintended—negative consequences of that kind of engagement. The prophet Jeremiah admonished the captives in Babylon to "Build houses and dwell in them; plant gardens and eat their fruit. Take wives and beget sons and daughters; and take wives for your sons and give your daughters to husbands, so that they may bear sons and daughters—that you may be increased there, and not diminished. And seek the peace of the city where I have caused you to be carried away captive . . ." (Jer 29:5–7). Moreover, Jesus encourages his disciples to "render to Caesar the things [taxes] that are Caesar's but give God the things that are God's (Matt 22:21),[2] that is, "give your material wealth to Caesar, but reserve for God the sole innocence of your conscience, where God is beheld."[3] In other words, serving God does not prevent us from participating in the workings of this world, for example, by paying taxes. Nevertheless, while we are taught to actively live in and engage our culture, we are to do so as sojourners whose basic identity and worldview are ultimately determined, not by the prevailing culture, but by intentional participation in another kingdom and by answering to an entirely different authority.

So, obviously some constraints will have to be placed on our involvement in this world. Jesus describes this limited participation by saying we are to be "in" the world and not "of" the world (John 17:16). He realized if we did engage, as we must, we would be exposing ourselves and the church to powerful, dangerous, and often corrupting meanings and devices— things that could and probably would damage the church, sicken it, and prevent its growth. Indeed, it would not be difficult to assemble a catalog of social inhibitors, that is, factors that impede the growth of the church. We would, no doubt, include things like consumerism, secularism, materialism, individual freedom, narcissism, unbelief, and so on. Ultimately, however, the most dangerous challenge to the church does not come from individual inhibitors taken in isolation but rather from the overwhelming power of an underlying set of secular principles that define, amplify, and intensify the effects of the individual threats. These principles act as a unified control mechanism that determines how the individual meanings, devices, and practices of our culture develop and are used. As such, this mechanism

---

2. While this passage definitely involves a question about taxes (at least that is the way Matthew reports the question being framed by the Pharisees), it was, of course, not an honest question but rather an attempt to trap Jesus in an either-or dilemma such that no matter what he said, they would be able to criticize him. Severus puts it this way: "Jesus' opponents expect that one of two outcomes must result for them from Jesus' response. They think they can show clearly that Jesus was acting wrongly against the law of Moses or against the power of the Romans. But Jesus does not fall into the trap and shifts the focus from the simple act of paying taxes to the question of the relationship between the image and its owner." According to Severus, "[t]he image of God is not depicted on gold but is imaged in humanity. The coin of Caesar is gold; that of God is humanity. Caesar is seen in his currency; God, however, is known through human beings" (Oden, *Ancient Christian Commentary*, 151).

3. Oden, *Ancient Christian Commentary*, 149.

effectively determines the outcomes of almost every social transaction and exchange by linking the disparate elements within an overall frame of reference, a social and intellectual environment in which we as Americans and as American believers interact.

As a result, any analysis of the dangers facing the church will involve much more than an examination of individual growth inhibitors but will have to begin with a consideration of this totalizing control mechanism which so effectively defines North American society. One way to describe such a system of thought would be to use Charles Taylor's idea of a social imaginary.[4] According to Taylor, a social imaginary is "the way people imagine their [entire] social existence, how they fit together with others, how things go on between them and their fellows, the expectations that are normally met, and the deeper normative notions and images that underlie these expectations."[5] It is what is at work when people speak of something being American or even Christian. In other words, it is an overlay that establishes what is normal and what is to be expected. It also includes moral order, notions of believability, and the practices associated with belief.

It is important to state at the outset that an imaginary is not simply a set of rules imposed on some population. It is rather a mindset, an overall worldview, an internal conceptual frame of reference that originated with formative ideas of an elite that slowly evolved through a process spanning centuries and continents. The North American imaginary, like other imaginaries,[6] began with seminal ideas developed by European philosophers of the early Enlightenment period—people like Descartes, Locke, Voltaire, Rousseau, and Kant. Their ideas were widely discussed, at first in academic circles, continually modified, popularized, and eventually adopted as established fact by the general population.

---

4. I have already considered this in my book *Get Real* in an attempt to define the overall mindset of the individuals to whom we are trying to present the gospel. How will it sound to them? How are they likely to react? Here, on the other hand, I am asking how this operating principle affects the meanings, devices, and technologies of our society and how they are used.

5. Taylor, *Modern Social Imaginaries*, 23.

6. I suppose we could speak of multiple imaginaries. Modern-day Europe's might be different, as would one developed within the history and tradition of the church. We can conceive of a process similar to that at work in the development of the social imaginary whereby the fundamental ideas seeded by those we could call the elites (fathers, mothers, saints, hierarchs) of the life in the church, the divinely inspired interpreters of Scripture and tradition, are evaluated and articulated, then disseminated throughout the membership where they are generally accepted as the sum total of that which constitutes a unique, internal, ecclesial vision (imaginary) which, like the social imaginary, governs the structures, devices, and practices of life—in this case, life within the church.

Knowing how these initial ideas were modified is critical to an understanding of the pervasive influence of the contemporary imaginary. Because they generally involved either human faculties as such or the procedures guiding the use of those faculties, we can identify two different mechanisms of change, s*anctioning* them *as rights* and *popularizing* them *by simplification*. On the one hand, the principles based on human faculties, such as the ability to reason, to criticize, to know, or to self-evaluate were gradually changed as a result of shifting the focus away from the faculty itself to the individual's right to use or express that ability. For example, the human ability to reason is a constituent aspect of human being. So, no one could be prevented from thinking, that is, from using their innate abilities to formulate their own private, internal, mental conceptualizations. Yet freely expressing that thought or criticism in public was, in fact, being resisted by governments and religious institutions alike by suppressing that liberty or by dictating what was to be believed. What was at stake here was not reasoning *per se*, but rather the autonomous use of that reasoning. For that reason, the focus of attention shifted away from the innate ability to reason and morphed into a demand for the freedom to use reason, that is, to express opinions or criticism in public.

The assertive character of these demands began to resonate with contemporaneous[7] discussions of natural *rights*, which led to further change. Hobbes[8] and Locke[9] had developed the idea of subjective individual rights which basically involved the idea that all individuals were equal, having been born with certain "inalienable" natural rights, including "life, liberty, and property." These rights of nature were said to constitute "a neutral sphere of personal choice, in which every citizen, as a private person, can egoistically follow goals of maximizing his own needs. Formal rights are in principle rights of freedom, because they must set free all acts which are not

---

7. Kant wrote about freedom sometime after Locke in 1784, but his ideas would certainly have found a place in the ongoing discussion initiated by Hobbes and Locke and which was carried on after Kant by Thomas Paine during the American Revolution. See Kant and Humphrey, *Perpetual Peace,* and Paine, *Common Sense.*

8. "The RIGHT OF NATURE, which Writers commonly call Jus Naturale, is the Liberty each man hath, to use his own power, as he will himselfe, for the preservation of his own Nature; that is to say, of his own Life; and consequently, of doing anything, which in his own Judgement, and Reason, hee shall conceive to be the aptest means thereunto" (Hobbes and Tuck, *Leviathan*, 63).

9. "To understand political power right, and derive it from its original, we must consider, what state all men are naturally in, and that is, a state of perfect freedom to order their actions, and dispose of their possessions and persons, as they think fit, within the bounds of the law of nature, without asking leave, or depending upon the will of any other man" (Locke and Macpherson, *Second Treatise*, 8).

explicitly prohibited according to externally specified criteria."[10] Once the Enlightenment concerns for freedom of thought and criticism were drawn into the context of the discussion of universal rights, they came to be seen as basic human rights and were aggressively promulgated as part of the rapidly spreading movement of rights revolutions that swept England,[11] France,[12] and America.[13] So, one way the seed ideas were changed was by shifting the focus of meaning away from human *faculties* themselves to the general *freedom* to exercise those faculties without any external constraints. That, in turn, led to the notion of the unassailable right of each *individual* to independently exercise and universally apply those faculties[14] to the irrepressible modern practice of autonomous opinionizing.

On the other hand, some of the changes to those early ideas had to do with reductionistic, mechanistic, empiricist, or scientific methodologies, that is, with procedures that were deemed necessary to effectively channeling and applying human faculties. The use of these methodologies in addressing the problems of human existence has, quite obviously, been very effective and has led to a host of important advancements. This has also led to increasingly complex techniques, as is obvious in medicine, physics, electronics, etc. Unfortunately, the actual processes involved in these endeavors have rarely been accessible to the nonexpert public. For that reason, a rigorous simplification of that information was required to achieve even a modicum of accessibility. But that distillation, which some have called the "easiness effect of science popularization. . .may lead to the risk of audiences relying overly strongly on their own epistemic capabilities when making judgments about scientific claims,"[15] leading to a divorce between the use of the devices developed by science and the science itself. In other words, end users know they have no real understanding of the science involved in, let us say, a computer or an internal combustion engine, but they know these devices work and deliver the desired "commodities." This effectiveness leads to the conclusion that "the science must be sound, even if I do not understand it." In this way a generalized faith in science replaces a real understanding of science or, to put it another way, the original meanings associated with the actual methodologies promoted by the Enlightenment elite have been transformed into a belief in science itself rather than an understanding

---

10. Habermas, *Theory and Practice*, 44.
11. "English Bill of Rights 1689."
12. "Declaration of the Rights of Man."
13. "U.S. Bill of Rights."
14. "Individualism."
15. Scharrer et al., "When Science Becomes Too Easy," 1003.

of particular methodology and its outcomes. This popularization by simplification[16] has created contemporary scientism—a blind belief in the omnipotence of science. This process of oversimplification transforms the actual complexity, analysis (reductionism), creativity (optimism), and self-evaluation of real science into a naïve belief in the inevitability of unabated progress and a simplistic assumption of the value neutrality of all scientific development.

So, this long process of modifying the original core ideas of the Enlightenment led to the basic content of the contemporary social imaginary, which, in turn, has facilitated the development of the meanings, devices, and technologies that dominate our culture. Moreover, those changes are now so widely accepted that the rate of change appears to have slowed to the point of a taken-for-granted steady state, and we are left with a set of convictions that no longer need to be discussed and now represent a near-automatic or reflexive take on practically every social, relational, philosophical, and religious topic of contemporary life. These basic dispositions constitute an omnipresent mental reservoir of unchallenged default positions, a foundation upon which we are able to dynamically construct our culturalisms without having to consciously reflect on the details of the foundation itself.

For that reason, we should also take note of the fact that some of the power this imaginary has over its participants is the result of aggregation. In other words, the individual principles have been linked together such that the impact of each one is multiplied or amplified and then added to a whole (the imaginary), the power of which is greater than the simple sum of its parts. The effect is similar to the dominance of an operating system on a computer. The individual segments of code, the routines and sub-routines that make up that system, collectively facilitate certain actions and restrict others, allowing some while disallowing others. None of the device's basic computational operations take place outside of and without the active direction of the operating system—no read/write operations, no input/output, no calculations, no communications. But because it is running in the background, that is, is being processed by the hardware, not the user, it is active in a realm almost beyond our awareness. As such, it is able to prevent, make possible, guide, or direct the operator with nearly imperceptible inexorability. As such, there is no unmediated, one-to-one correspondence between an operator's needs or desires and actual access to information or specific outcomes provided by the device. Clearly those needs or desires are shaped, limited, even determined by the already-existing physical constraints of

---

16. By way of illustration compare the papers given by actual scientists at a conference on Chaos Theory with the simplified version used to popularize these ideas. The original presentations are collected in Prigogine and Holte, *Chaos*.

the device and the operating system controlling them. These aspects of the computer are fixed and require no run-time redefinition or attention. In other words, the operator can, and probably does, use the computer without consciously thinking about the various elements of the operating system. In that sense he or she quite literally and without intentionality simply surrenders or submits to the dictates of the operating system.

Similarly, each one of society's imaginary-defining principles can be viewed, individually and collectively, as the outcomes or now-fixed conclusions of decades-long deliberation. They are now firmly established, beyond the need for further justification, are simply assumed, and require no further attention. Taken together, they function as the operating matrix of our society. They facilitate and dictate the shape of the meanings, devices, and technologies of our culture, such as consumerism or the Internet. Moreover, because these guiding forces are at work in the background, unseen, and rarely understood, we, for all intents and purposes, surrender our freedom to think and act independently of the power inherent in these principles.

It might seem unfair to suggest North Americans are not aware of principles operating in and shaping their lives. However, in keeping with the nature and the power of the North American imaginary, it is probably true most Americans have uncritically absorbed the substance of this social operating system, making it their own without any conscious decision to do so. Moreover, under the influence of easiness factors, many have developed a naïve, pragmatic, or even indifferent kind of optimism with regard not only to the operating principles themselves, but perhaps more importantly to the practices, devices, etc., they foster. But that cavalier attitude does not appear to be justified because most of these optimists have overestimated their own strength and underestimate the power of these social forces to change the way we live in practically every domain of social interaction.

Take as just one example the irresistible power of our imaginary-generated system of commerce. Of course, some have tried to resist. Some Christians, for example, have tried to replace commercial principles antithetical to the faith with Christian teaching. But in the end, all they have managed to accomplish is to "marginalize religion and doom it to irrelevance."[17] So, why has this happened? And indeed, it does seem to be the result of the efforts of most, even well-meaning believers. According to William Leach in *A Land of Desire*, this is quite simply the result of the overwhelming power of the imaginary-generated system. He claims no communities, not even religious ones, have been able to withstand the damaging influence of the secular, consumer-oriented society. It has subverted whatever custom, value, or folk

---

17. Leach, *Land of Desire*, 44.

idea came within its reach. While the science behind these developments might not have been intrinsically hostile to custom, or tradition, or religion, the resultant market capitalism definitely was hostile. "[N]o immigrant culture—and, to a considerable degree, no religious tradition—had the power to resist it, as none can in our own time. Any group that has come to this country has had to learn to accept and to adjust to this elemental feature of American capitalist culture."[18]

The cumulative effect of the operating principles that make up the North American social imaginary and, by extension, all of their facilitating structures and devices, has had an enormously negative effect on life in North America, including its religious life. But because these concepts have been uncritically and unconsciously absorbed, most individuals, including those in the church, are dominated and controlled by this prevailing vision of society (imaginary). Because many aspects of that vision are antithetical to basic teachings of the church, both the basic operating system (the imaginary) as well as the structures, devices, procedures, and technologies they give rise to represent grave threats to the church. Moreover, because these foundational convictions operate just beyond our conscious awareness, they are all but invisible. So we are likely to casually, even unintentionally, import the thought, practices, and products of the imaginary into the church without deliberately considering or even being aware of the underlying presuppositions and meanings, in which case we are in danger and don't even know it.

In light of this, the primary aim of this study is to expose these threats and initiate a conversation about the damage they can cause or are causing, what we can do to reverse the damage already done, and how we might protect the church in the future. Beginning in chapter 3 I will show how specific imaginary-related practices and products are damaging the church. This discussion of individual practices and devices will, however, only make sense if they can be related to the overall operating system or background which gives rise to them and provides the rationale for their use. So in chapter 2 I will describe more fully the genesis, nature, and function of the core operating principles of the contemporary North American social imaginary.

---

18. Leach, *Land of Desire*, 19–20.

2

The Operating Principles of the Contemporary Social Imaginary

Intentional states function only given a set of Background capacities that do not themselves consist in intentional phenomena.[1]

As stated above, an imaginary is not simply a set of rules imposed on and intentionally adhered to by some population. According to Taylor, it is

> something much broader and deeper than the intellectual schemes people may entertain when they think about social reality in a disengaged mode. I am thinking, rather, of the ways people imagine their social existence, how they fit together with others, how things go on between them and their fellows, the expectations that are normally met, and the deeper normative notions and images that underlie these expectations.[2]

An imaginary, then, is a mindset, an overall worldview, a conceptual frame of reference that constitutes an almost unchallenged, default position on practically every social, relational, philosophical, moral, and religious issue of contemporary life. Moreover, this mindset is not only uncontested, it can also affect social behavior without any obvious intentionality. It

---

1. Searle, *Construction of Social Reality*, 129.
2. Taylor, *Modern Social Imaginaries*, 21.

determines who we imagine ourselves to be as Americans without us having to give any conscious thought to the underlying opinions themselves.

It is similar to what John Searle calls the "Background," the "preconditions for the functioning of intentional contents,"[3] that is, a "set of non-intentional or pre-intentional capacities that enable intentional states of function."[4] These causal structures (abilities, tendencies, and dispositions)[5] enable linguistic and perceptual interpretation, shape and motivate the structure of experience, facilitate readiness, and dispose us to certain kinds of behavior.[6] So even though an imaginary is not a set of rules imposed and consciously followed, rules (of some kind) do play a role. So what may appear to be an intentional, rules-governed behavior is rather a near-automatic, reflexive take on an immediate situation. If, for example, a worshiper hears the priest's "peace be with you all," it is safe to say the person does not stop and rifle through a mental catalog of rules to find the right response—they intuitively know what to say. This person is not consciously or unconsciously applying liturgical rubrics; rather, they have developed a set of dispositions or capacities, that is, "a set of abilities that are sensitive to specific structures of intentionality without actually being constituted by that intentionality."[7] In other words, the individual just seems to know how to behave,

> but not because he is following the rules unconsciously nor because his behavior is caused by an undifferentiated mechanism that happens to look as if it were rule structured, but rather because the mechanism has evolved precisely so that it will be sensitive to the rules. The mechanism explains the behavior, and the mechanism is explained by the system of rules, but the mechanism need not itself be a system of rules. I am in short urging the addition of *another level*, a diachronic level, in the explanation of certain sorts of social behavior.[8]

So yes, an imaginary, the Background, contains rules or principles that enable a complex mechanism whereby the individual intuitively knows how to behave. Of course, the complexity of this mechanism is compounded by the fact that there may be competing sets of underlying rules each dictating divergent meanings and modes of behavior. For example, a believer routinely

---

3. Searle, *Construction of Social Reality*, 132.
4. Searle, *Construction of Social Reality*, 129.
5. Searle, *Construction of Social Reality*, 129.
6. Searle, *Construction of Social Reality*, 132–37.
7. Searle, *Construction of Social Reality*, 141.
8. Searle, *Construction of Social Reality*, 146 (emphasis mine).

giving a donation to a church might have developed a sensitivity to the biblical idea of stewardship as an expression of faith or to the commercial idea of payment for services rendered. Either way the act may not be intentional, but depending on which Background is in play, it could have very different meanings for the church and that person's spiritual state. So because some meanings and behaviors are antithetical to Christian teaching, we will, or at least should, ask ourselves which Background or imaginary is governing our action and how that affects its meaning. As I see it, most North American believers are so thoroughly immersed in the social imaginary that it will be that secular Background that has the most impact on their thought and behavior. But questioning and especially breaking with our Background takes enormous and deliberate intellectual effort.[9] Moreover, the degree of familiarity with one or the other Background could not only prevent alternative behavior but even the consideration of such. But not doing so will endanger the church since we will either mindlessly import damaging meanings and devices or refuse to examine our current practices. So before I turn to an examination of current ecclesial behaviors, I will examine the core operating principles of the contemporary North American social imaginary.

FREEDOM AND INDIVIDUALISM

The most fundamental of all Enlightenment principles is, of course, the idea of human freedom. For some thinkers, like Immanuel Kant, this concept was primarily associated with the free and public use of reason. His concern is not simply rationality as such, but its unfettered use, that is, the freedom to form and express one's own opinions. In a 1784 essay entitled "What is Enlightenment?" he states,

> Nothing is required for his enlightenment, however, except freedom; and the freedom in question is the least harmful of all, namely the freedom to use reason publicly in all matters. . . .The public use of one's reason must always be free, and it alone can bring about enlightenment among mankind; the private use of reason may, however, often be very narrowly restricted, without otherwise hindering the progress of enlightenment.[10]

The same idea is captured in 1859 by John Stuart Mill in chapter 3 of his work *On Liberty*:

---

9. Searle, *Construction of Social Reality*, 134.
10. Kant and H*umphrey, Perpetual Peace*, 42.

> Such being the reasons which make it imperative that human beings should be free to form opinions, and to express their opinions without reserve; and such the baneful consequences to the intellectual, and through that to the moral nature of man, unless this liberty is either conceded, or asserted in spite of prohibition . . . .[11]
>
> In my judgment, every human being should take a road of his own. Every mind should be true to itself—should think, investigate and conclude for itself.[12]

Peter Gay emphasizes the point, saying "[t]he men of the Enlightenment united on a vastly ambitious program, a program of secularism, humanity, cosmopolitanism, and freedom, above all, freedom . . ."[13] Indeed, during the intervening centuries, the idea of individual freedom was gradually embraced by the masses and is today so widely accepted, enthroned in so many constitutions and protected by such an array of institutions, that it is simply taken as a given, beyond discussion, already established. Because this idea is now so well established, that is, because there is no longer a need to argue the case for individual freedom, the focus of public attention has now shifted away from making the case for personal freedom to finding or devising new ways of conceiving of that freedom. Of particular interest to this study is the fact that this continued universalization of freedom has taken the concept way beyond Kant's "freedom to use reason" and transformed it into to an absolute right to choose or to have a personal opinion about anything in any area of human life or endeavor. Because this right also defines, in part, the personal identity of its agent, this sense of entitlement becomes so powerful that simply having an opinion, simply articulating, one makes it true. To deny this would be tantamount to calling into question the very personhood of the individual. This, of course, makes serious discussion difficult since this right masks or trumps the actual issues and disallows alternate opinions. In other words, as it has filtered down into the contemporary imaginary, freedom to think for one's self has morphed into an absolute right to choose between options that are assumed to be (or made to be) omnipresent or, to put it differently, the right to have a personal opinion, which is assumed to be true, on any topic whatsoever.

But of what practical use is freedom of thought and opinion if we cannot act upon it, freely express those convictions in our speech and, more importantly, our behavior? After defending the idea that human intellectual

---

11. Mill, "Of Individuality," loc. 523 of 2945.
12. Ingersoll, "Individuality," loc. 2335 of 2945.
13. Gay, *Enlightenment*, 17.

and moral freedom must never be ceded or limited by prohibitions, John Stuart Mill goes on to ask "whether the same reasons do not require that men should be free to *act* upon their opinions—to *carry these out* in their lives, without hindrance, either physical or moral, from their fellow-men, so long as it is at their own risk and peril."[14]

In 1872, the free-thinker George Jacob Holyoake added, "Without the reasonable action of opinion, thought is practically fruitless. We must be able to embody ideas in institutions. There must be fair play for thought as well as free play for thought as well as free play."[15] This free play is not to be limited either individually or collectively. What is being called for here is not simply a noble idea being imposed on human beings; it is rather a necessity that grows out of human existence itself. Holyoake justifies his stance by insisting

> [a]ll men love freedom naturally. It is an instinct of their nature. It is the condition of growth and development. There can be no progress without it. All art, all science, all improvement is owing to the use of it. Every new religion has been created by it. Christ and his Apostles employed it to a great extent. Men would have dwelt in ignorance and superstition without it. Freedom of thought is a necessity of progressive life.[16]

Yet it seems this is the very thing that is lost if freedom is suppressed or "comprised in obedience," which is what has happened to human beings at the hands of tyrants, in particular some forms of religion.[17] As a result of denying what is natural, "their human capacities are withered and starved: they become incapable of any strong wishes or native pleasures and are generally without either opinions or feelings of home growth, or properly their own."[18] But is that a natural or desirable condition of human being? Obviously not. If individuals actually and naturally possess "self-propriety,"[19] then this freedom is demanded because it is "necessarily driven by the desires and necessities of his own existence."[20] Thus it is that

> each and every person, from his cradle to his grave, must necessarily form his own conclusions; because no one else knows or

---

14. Mill, "Of Individuality," loc. 523 of 2945.
15. Holyoake, "Free Thought," loc. 2288 of 2945.
16. Holyoake, "Free Thought," loc. 2245 of 2945.
17. Mill, "Of Individuality," loc. 629 of 2945.
18. Mill, "Of Individuality," loc. 622 of 2945.
19. Overton, "Arrow against All Tyrants," loc. 1215 of 2945.
20. Spooner, "Vices are Not Crimes," loc. 1373 of 2945.

> feels, or can know or feel, as he knows and feels, the desires and necessities, the hopes, and fears, and impulses of his own nature, or the pressure of his own circumstances.[21]

What we are looking at here is a refusal to place any limits on individual thought, desire, or opinion. It amounts to an unfettered license to act on any desire an individual might have. We might be tempted to call this selfishness or some form of narcissism. But some, of course, would object to that negative assessment by suggesting there are always some constraints placed on individual action; basically, we do not harm others or interfere with their rights.[22] In fact, Mill argues that far from

> wearing down into uniformity all that is individual in themselves, but by cultivating it and calling it forth, within the limits imposed by the rights and interests of others, that human beings become a noble and beautiful object of contemplation; and as the works partake the character of those who do them, by the same process human life also becomes rich, diversified, and animating, furnishing more abundant aliment to high thoughts and elevating feelings, and strengthening the tie which binds every individual to the race.[23]

That notwithstanding, the Christian doctrine of sin recognizes the noble character given human beings by God has been damaged by their fall into sin, abandoning a love of God for a love of self.[24] In fact, the prophet Jeremiah proclaims "[t]he heart is deceitful above all things, and desperately wicked (17:9). Describing this dynamic, St. Theodorus writes "[s]elf-love, love of pleasure and love of praise banish remembrance of God from the

---

21. Spooner, "Vices are Not Crimes," loc. 1373 of 2945.

22. "Freedom of choice and self-determination are virtuous principles, but when selfish individual interests threaten to destroy the common good, the limits of individualism are exposed" (Callero, *Myth of Individualism*, 18).

23. Mill, "Of Individuality," loc. 643 of 2945.

24. Interestingly, even though most recognize that the Protestant Reformation facilitated rather than hindered the rise of individualism and free-thought, the implications of the teaching on sin were not lost on some of the free-thinkers. John Stuart Mill, for example, spoke of the theory of Calvinism: "According to that, the one great offence of man is Self-will. All the good of which humanity is capable, is comprised in Obedience. You have no choice; thus, you must do, and no otherwise: 'whatever is not a duty, is a sin.' Human nature being radically corrupt, there is no redemption for any one until human nature is killed within him. To one holding this theory of life, crushing out any of the human faculties, capacities, and susceptibilities, is no evil: man needs no capacity, but that of surrendering himself to the will of God: and if he uses any of his faculties for any other purpose but to do that supposed will more effectually, he is better without them" (Mill, "Of Individuality," loc. 629 of 2945).

soul. Self-love begets unimaginable evils. And when remembrance of God is absent, there is a tumult of the passions within us."[25] That is probably why we see so little that is noble and is why, in a world devoid of any limitations on individual freedoms, we are confronted with "the individual scramble for wealth, the cash nexus, and purely material relations, instead of sentiment between men."[26] That does sound rather selfish, and it is probably the case because "over time . . . individualism tends to degenerate into pure egoism, because it ignores the civic virtues on which society depends."[27] It seems then the prevailing desire for freedom is not just some vague inclination to promote one's self but, as it is implemented in our society, it amounts to a desire to express and act upon "unbounded self-love" and "there can be no doubt, of course, that in the language of the great writers of the eighteenth century, it was man's 'self-love,' or even his 'selfish interests,' which they represented as the 'universal mover . . .'"[28]

Whatever we may say about the origins and consequences of human self-love, there are, according to individualists, to be no external constraints on the expression of individual freedom. "No man hath power over my rights and liberties, and I over no man's."[29] Oscar Wilde's general statement is as good a summary of this belief as any:

> It is to be noted also that Individualism does not come to man with any sickly cant about duty, which merely means doing what other people want because they want it; or any hideous cant about self-sacrifice, which is merely a survival of savage mutilation. In fact, it does not come to man with any claims upon him at all. It comes naturally and inevitably out of man. It is the point to which all development tends. It is the differentiation to which all organisms grow. It is the perfection that is inherent in every mode of life, and towards which every mode of life quickens. And so, Individualism exercises no compulsion over man. On the contrary, it says to man that he should suffer no compulsion to be exercised over him. It does not try to force people to be good.[30]

This general talk of compulsion can easily be concretized by pointing to some of the things individualists felt constrained by. What they sought was release "from the ordinary restraints of family, church, and public opinion,

---

25. St. Theodorus, "Century," 92.
26. Wilson, "Archbishop Temple on Betting," loc. 2736 of 2945.
27. Smith, "Introduction," loc. 159 of 2945.
28. Hayek, *Individualism and Economic Order*, 13.
29. Overton, "Arrow against All Tyrants," loc. 1222 of 2945.
30. Wilde, "Soul of Man," loc. 845 of 2945.

even of the civil law, naturally and inevitably acquires a certain contempt for authority and impatience of it . . ."[31] It was, of course, the perceived tyranny of the church that reaped much of their displeasure. Ingersoll holds back nothing in his contempt for the supposed arrogance of the church. Insisting "[a]ll that is good in our civilization is the result of commerce, climate, soil, geographical position, industry, invention, discovery, art, and science,"[32] he brands the church an enemy of free-thinkers:

> The church has been the enemy of progress, for the reason that it has endeavored to prevent man thinking for himself. To prevent thought is to prevent all advancement except in the direction of faith. Who can imagine the infinite impudence of a church assuming to think for the human race? Who can imagine the infinite impudence of a church that pretends to be the mouthpiece of God, and in his name, threatens to inflict eternal punishment upon those who honestly reject its claims and scorn its pretensions?[33]
>
> The church has left nothing undone to prevent man following the logic of his brain. The plainest facts have been covered with the mantle of mystery. The grossest absurdities have been declared to be self-evident facts. The order of nature has been, as it were, reversed, that the hypocritical few might govern the honest many.[34]

So is there any room for common action, governance, organization, or instruction? Indeed, there is, but whatever cooperative or social arrangements the individual is to enter into have to be voluntary and for some obvious mutual benefit. They could under no circumstances be imposed without violating individual freedoms. For that reason, the rejection of any exclusive power ". . . is directed only against the use of coercion to bring about organization or association, and not against association as such."[35] As Hayek notes:

> Far from being opposed to voluntary association, the case of the individualist rests, on the contrary, on the contention that much of what in the opinion of many can be brought about only by conscious direction, can be better achieved by the voluntary and spontaneous collaboration of individuals.[36]

---

31. Smith, "Introduction," loc. 220 of 2945.
32. Ingersoll, "Individuality," loc. 2313 of 2945.
33. Ingersoll, "Individuality," locs. 2313–21 of 2945.
34. Ingersoll, "Individuality," loc. 2364 of 2945.
35. Hayek, *Individualism and Economic Order*, 16.
36. Hayek, *Individualism and Economic Order*, 16–17.

This basic approach is enshrined in the American Declaration of Independence (1776), which, while on the one hand, insists on certain unalienable, individual rights such as life, liberty, and the pursuit of happiness, does, on the other hand, call for government to secure those rights. But it is to be a government deriving its powers from the (voluntary) consent of those governed. This is also the basic premise of the United States' Constitution (1787), according to which government was formed in order to "establish justice, insure[sic] domestic tranquility, provide for the common defense, promote the general welfare, and secure the blessings of liberty for ourselves and our posterity." In the language of the day, "happiness" and "blessings of freedom" did, of course, not refer simply to some subjective emotional state, but rather to "prosperity or, perhaps better, well-being in the broader sense,"[37] the pursuit of which the government was to guarantee. But this was only acceptable if whatever governance was voluntarily accepted. Of course, this did (and does) facilitate self-interest, unrestrained in its origin (human desire) and unopposed by group-think, tradition, government, education, and especially the church, for it had become "the duty of each and every one to maintain his individuality."[38] For that reason, many came to see (fear) society and government "as nothing more than a voluntary association for the pursuit of self-interest, while relying upon their 'private stock of reason' to assess the desirability of traditional customs, values, and institutions . . ."[39]

It is this radical form of individualism that has become a basic characteristic of North American society. Godkin insists "individualism was a fundamental character trait of the American. It expressed itself in self-reliance,[40] abundant energy of action, ideals of unrestrained individual freedom, the capacity for organization and daring enterprise, and the belief in a free competitive economy."[41] Indeed, that does sound quite American, and why not? This has been our vision of ourselves since the very beginning. The intense commitment to this sentiment is hard to miss in the praise lavished on the new country in 1782 by one of its early defenders, J. Hector St. John de Crèvecoeur:

> I wish I could be acquainted with the feelings and thoughts which must agitate the heart and present themselves to the mind of an enlightened Englishman, when he first lands on

37. Rogers, "Meaning of 'the Pursuit of Happiness,'" para. 2.
38. Ingersoll, "Individuality," loc. 2371 of 2945.
39. Mill, "Of Individualism," locs. 127–34 of 2945.
40. Note the importance of this term in American thought, especially since the famous essay by Emerson. See Emerson, *Essay on Self-Reliance*.
41. Smith, "Introduction," locs. 233–41 of 2945.

this continent. . . . He is arrived on a new continent; a modern society offers itself to his contemplation, different from what he had hitherto seen. It is not composed, as in Europe, of great lords who possess everything, and of a herd of people who have nothing. Here are no aristocratical families, no courts, no kings, no bishops, no ecclesiastical dominion, no invisible power giving to a few a very visible one; no great manufacturers employing thousands, no great refinements of luxury. The rich and the poor are not so far removed from each other as they are in Europe. Some few towns excepted, we are all tillers of the earth, from Nova Scotia to Florida. We are a people of cultivators, scattered over an immense territory, communicating with each other by means of good roads and navigable rivers, united by the silken bands of mild government, all respecting the laws, without dreading their power, because they are equitable. We are all animated with the spirit of an industry which is unfettered and unrestrained, because each person works for himself. If he travels through our rural districts, he views not the hostile castle, and the haughty mansion, contrasted with the clay-built hut and miserable cabin, where cattle and men help to keep each other warm, and dwell in meanness, smoke, and indigence. A pleasing uniformity of decent competence appears throughout our habitations. The meanest of our log-houses is a dry and comfortable habitation. Lawyer or merchant are the fairest titles our towns afford; that of a farmer is the only appellation of the rural inhabitants of our country. It must take some time ere he can reconcile himself to our dictionary, which is but short in words of dignity, and names of honour. There, on a Sunday, he sees a congregation of respectable farmers and their wives, all clad in neat homespun, well mounted, or riding in their own humble wagons. There is not among them an esquire, saving the unlettered magistrate. There he sees a parson as simple as his flock, a farmer who does not riot on the labour of others. We have no princes, for whom we toil, starve, and bleed: we are the most perfect society now existing in the world. Here man is free as he ought to be.[42]

So the doctrine of freedom has become the operating principle of individualism (self-interest) and "amongst the Americans of our time it finds universal acceptance: it has become popular there; you may trace it at the bottom of all their actions, you will remark it in all they say. It is as often to be

---

42. de Crèvecoeur, "What is an American?," locs. 941–47 of 2945.

met with on the lips of the poor man as of the rich."[43] So individualism plays out, governs and directs our actions across all three of the areas of society we will be looking at. By way of anticipating the discussion below, it must be obvious by now that American individualism is a danger to the church and has already done a great deal of damage. On the surface it has caused many people to reject the teaching and the authority of the church and to move away from belief in God and practice in the church. For those who have remained in the church, individualism threatens the very nature of church itself by viewing it as a voluntary association for some mutual benefit, a completely free gathering in which no one has any particular authority over those participating. As one parishioner said to the priest, "Your job is not to tell me what to do or how to live, but to make me feel good about myself if and when I choose to come." It is of course true that active membership has its rewards, but it will serve to never satisfy all human desire for health, wealth, happiness, and whatever else we may want. Furthermore, individualism isolates each member from the others such that one individual comes to believe their thoughts, opinions, and actions are truly their own and cannot and do not affect, one way or the other, the other members of the body. A more detailed look at the many other ways in which individualism affects the church through the practices and opinions it governs will be taken up later in the study.

RATIONALISM AND SCIENTISM

Another prominent characteristic of Enlightenment thought had to do with the unfettered use of human reason. As Kant put it, *"Sapere Aude!* have courage to use your own understanding."[44] In this case, Kant is speaking not just of the *freedom* to use reason but rather of the *sufficiency* of human reason itself. As Bruce W. Hauptli summarizes it,

> Modern thinkers held that human beings, unaided by divine revelation or signs, could, through the application of their rational abilities, come to understand the basic structure of the world. This view holds both that the world has a fundamentally rational structure to it, and that we have sufficient rational ability to uncover this structure. [45]

---

43. de Tocqueville, "Democracy in America," loc. 9933 of 14266.
44. Kant and Humphrey, *Perpetual Peace*, 33.
45. Hauptli, "Enlightenment Project," para. 2.

This conviction has filtered down into the modern imaginary in several ways. First, the confidence in the human ratio translates into a widespread, naïve, unquestioned optimism. A kind of "we-can-do-this" (or, for that matter, "anything") attitude. Even though we have not, in fact, been able to solve every problem, North Americans, proud of our ingenuity, actually believe that if given enough time and resources, we can solve every problem, answer every question. Unfortunately, this spills over into the religious realm in the form of an unbridled pragmatism. There is the widespread notion that we can manage, do, and program anything we put our minds to, with or without God's help. I once heard of a visitor to the United States who, after visiting a number of megachurches, said that it was amazing what the Americans were able to do without the Holy Spirit.

Second, this faith in reason leads to the idea that human reason is omnipotent—that there is no need for any other agencies such as God and the supernatural. In fact, we have gotten so used to the exclusivity of our own thought that the possibility of divine agency is rarely even considered. To suggest we need supernatural help is considered irrational and an affront to our own natural potency.

Third, this leads to a world without any mystery. It is a world in which we claim to (or expect to be able to) understand everything. One recent expression of this might be the "medicalization" of most human problems. According to this therapeutic model, whatever ails us can be reduced to some disease or disorder that can be corrected with drugs or proper therapy, both the output of our rational abilities. It is a world in which little, if anything, lies beyond the reach of reason, in which there is nothing we cannot get our minds around. Thus, if we are going to speak of God and the supernatural, it has to make sense to us, and for many it doesn't. The enlightened *ratio* will brook no conundrum—no mystery.

As we have acted on these convictions, we have seen the application of a scientific orientation and methodology has brought rapid and real improvements in technology, medicine, psychology, communications, and many other areas of human life. These undeniable advances have convinced us the natural sciences provide an objective method of unlocking not only the mysteries of the physical world, but also "the secrets of both the human heart and the direction of social life."[46] As early as 1662, this belief that science and invention were the engines of progress was institutionalized in London's Royal Society.[47] As the pace of advancement increased, this naïve optimism grew and found "expression in a series of world's fairs

---

46. Postman, *Technopoly*, 139.
47. Nye, *Technology Matters*, 8.

on both sides of the Atlantic. All embodied the belief in material progress based on technology."[48] So there arose a widespread "belief that for every problem there is technological expertise which can take over the burden of solution."[49]

Interestingly, this faith in applied science, that is, in its technologies, has become a kind of second-order belief at some remove from the actual science involved. Very few who use these devices day in and day out really understand the actual science involved. The details of how and why televisions, stereo systems, or computers work seem to be beyond most of us. Even if we could understand, we tend not to even ask that question because "the machinery makes no demands on our skill, strength, or attention, and it is less demanding the less it makes its presence felt."[50] There was a time when we heated our homes with wood burned in a small stove. People who used them were usually very aware of the device and to use it they were burdened with any number of other tasks such as felling trees and splitting and hauling wood. Using it required some skill with tools and considerable knowledge of the forest. But as science advanced this technology, we arrived at the central heating unit which supplies a commodity, heat, and disburdens us of all other elements once associated with heating a home.[51] These have now been taken over by the machinery of the device. So as long as we are warm (or receive whatever commodity the technology promises) we do not even think about how that is happening. In a way, the technology has become almost invisible and yet its effect on the way we conduct our lives cannot be discounted. Borgman speaks of it as a "constraining pattern" underlying the "entire fabric of our lives . . . visible first and most of all in the countless inconspicuous objects and procedures of daily life in a technological society."[52] So this has become first a blind, thoughtless, or even uninterested faith in the technology, and second, an ignorant and therefore baseless, unjustified belief in the underlying science. All we need to know is it delivers the promised commodity.

It is also important to note this faith in science has crept into almost every area of human endeavor. Nothing, it seemed, lay outside the possibility of advancement through the application of science and technology. Typical of this technological optimism is Daniel Bell's description of possible advancements in education:

48. Nye, *Technology Matters*, 93.
49. Borgmann, *Technology and the Character*, 137.
50. Borgmann, *Technology and the Character*, 42.
51. Borgmann, *Technology and the Character*, 42.
52. Borgmann, *Technology and the Character*, 3.

> [A] rapidly increasing population, more literate and more educated, living in a vastly enlarged world that is now tied together, almost in real time, by cable, telephone and international satellite, whose inhabitants are made aware of each other by the vivid pictorial imagery of television, and that has at its disposal large data banks of computerized information.[53]

Of course, our confidence is not limited to answers that describe, explain, and even manipulate things based on the way things actually *are*. But now, given the success of that science-orientation, we hope its procedures will tell us not just how things are but also how things *should* or *ought* to be. Having, for the most part, abandoned any hope that God, the church, or Tradition might provide answers, we cast about for alternative sources and easily alight on science and technology:

> We need so desperately to find some source outside the frail and shaky judgments of mortals like ourselves to authorize our moral decisions and behavior. And outside of the authority of brute force, which can scarcely be called moral, we seem to have little left but the authority of procedures.[54]

All of this naïve optimism leads to a new object of our faith, a replacement for God: science itself. It is what Neil Postman calls "scientism," which he defines in terms of three interrelated ideas that, when taken together, constitute one of the primary operating principles of the modern imaginary.

> The first and indispensable idea is . . . that the methods of the natural sciences can be applied to the study of human behavior. The second idea is, as also noted, that social science generates specific principles which can be used to organize society on a rational and humane basis . . . The third idea is that faith in science can serve as a comprehensive belief system that gives meaning to life, as well as a sense of well-being, morality, and even immortality.[55]

Because we are now convinced applied science eliminates "complexity, doubt, and ambiguity,"[56] we can "believe" again, this time in the free, unfettered application of our own reason, in science itself.

---

53. Bell, quoted in Borgmann, *Technology and the Character*, 152.
54. Postman, *Technopoly*, 152.
55. Postman, *Technopoly*, 139.
56. Postman, *Technopoly*, 92.

> It is the desperate hope, and wish, and ultimately the illusory belief that some standardized set of procedures called "science" can provide us with an unimpeachable source of moral authority, a supra-human basis for answers to questions like "What is life, and when, and why?" "Why is death, and suffering?" "What is right and wrong to do?" "What are good and evil ends?" "How ought we to think and feel and behave?"[57]

Indeed, this belief in the sufficiency of human reason is applied to everyday life with the same conviction with which faith in God was once applied. Everything we do, build, devise, and develop is done in the name of, and on the basis of, this firm belief, this scientism. As such, it becomes one of the primary operating principles of the modern imaginary and dictates presuppositions, meanings, procedures, and outcomes in almost every sphere of human life. I have already hinted at some of the ways in which this view of the world might harm the church. But again, in anticipation of the more detailed discussion below, we see here the temptation to think anything and everything the church does or needs to do can be accomplished by applying our minds in a scientific way and developing the needed procedures and technologies. Scientism deceives us into thinking we can manage things on our own. If we need to raise money, for whatever purpose, we can always rely on the techniques and procedures developed by the business world. We are tricked into believing we can effectively bear witness to the faith by using modern (scientific) theories about persuasion, human nature, and communication, aided by the attendant technologies of cyberspace. But once we forget "the inevitable limits of human understanding and try to replace the ineffable Word of God with human logic and thus neglect the empowering of the Holy Spirit, all work in the church ceases to be *theologia* and sinks to the level of *technologia*."[58]

REDUCTIONISM AND A ONE-DIMENSIONAL WORLD

Obviously, the use of human reason was (would have to be) governed by certain methodological considerations. This has turned out to be a basically mechanistic, empiricist, and reductionistic method. Hauptli explains,

> this methodology carefully examines material or natural phenomena trying to break them down into (that is, to reduce them to) their simplest or most basic parts or units, and then it studies

---

57. Postman, *Technopoly*, 152–53.
58. Ware, "Theological Education in Scripture and the Fathers," para. 2.

how these units combine together to produce more complex phenomena (that is, it tries to synthesize the units).[59]

This basic methodology remains the standard in almost all areas of human endeavor. For all the good its legitimate use has done, this reductionism has been popularized into the modern imaginary with some less-than-helpful results. First, we seem to have developed a kind of analysis fever, a rage to dissect anything and everything. There is almost no aspect of late-modern life that has not attracted a cadre of experts willing to analyze and comment. Granted, sometimes it may be reasonable to analyze, as in the case of the scientist unraveling a chemical reaction or a physician examining an individual's state of health. But we have begun to obsessively analyze almost everything. We endlessly discuss the nonanswers of political spokespersons as if there was something of substance to analyze. We reduce to disjointed minutiae objects, which cannot be disassembled without robbing them of their sublime, spontaneous beauty, and thus rendering them boring, trivial, or even repulsive. In many cases, this deconstructive analysis is insulting, implying as it does that the listener is not quite up to the task of thinking for themselves and so it must be done for them. So in good Enlightenment fashion we are encouraged to think for ourselves, except when others think for us. This does lead to a general laziness of thought, evidenced in the ease with which politicians and advertisers manipulate their audiences. Nevertheless, on a very different plane, if everyone else can analyze, then so can we. So we analyze our diets, free time, relationships, moods, even our religion, and we do so until we are left with the disassembled remains of a life in which there is no more joy or love, and certainly no truth.

This penchant is obviously evident in the Church Growth Movement in which the sociological and statistical analysis of growth patterns is considered normal if not necessary, even urgent. The basic counting of worshipers or members is done in order to develop attendance patterns, calculate growth rates, etc.[60] The analyses of the social context of a church can reveal how political turmoil, opinion trends, external financial support, etc., have affected growth. An analysis of social structures can show whether or not the gospel has moved along the lines of kinship or if it has been readily accepted by certain social strata or subgroups. In the end, all this analysis is designed to reduce complex patterns into simple and more manageable bits of information. It has to do with control or at least the impression of control by promising insight into the past and the ability to manage (control) immediate and future circumstances.

59. Hauptli, "Enlightenment Project," para. 2.
60. See Ellas, *Measuring Church Growth*.

The second, and inevitable, result of reductionism is its tendency to fragment. We have indeed succeeded in breaking many things down into their smallest parts, but are having difficulty with the synthesis, putting the pieces back together in a coherent form. This is particularly true of religious principles. Pavel Florensky points out what happens when a religious principle is subjected to reductionistic analysis:

> The single and integral object of religious perception disintegrates in the domain of rationality into a multiplicity of aspects, into separate facets, into fragments of holiness, and there is no grace in these fragments. The precious alabaster has been smashed and the holy myrrh is greedily sucked in by the dry sands of the red-hot desert.[61]

Since reduction has become the default methodology, the contemporary social imaginary is now plagued by what we might call a loss of horizon, or better yet, a loss of metanarrative. We no longer have the traditional frameworks that once gave "a totalizing, comprehensive account [of] various historical events, experiences, and social, cultural phenomena based upon the appeal to universal truth or universal values."[62] As a result of the prevailing reductionist patterns of thought, some believe "meta narratives have lost their power to convince or legitimize various versions of "the truth"[63] and are being abandoned in favor of more modest and "localized narratives"[64] (fragments) with a multitude of possible interpretations or "truths."[65] Of course, this supposedly universal skepticism of a totalizing story could itself be considered a metanarrative. "If one is skeptical of universal narratives such as 'truth,' 'knowledge,' 'right,' or 'wrong,' then there is no basis for believing the 'truth' that metanarratives are being undermined."[66] More importantly, this contemporary abandonment of grand narratives leads to

---

61. Florensky, *Pillar and Ground of Truth*, 234.

62. "Metanarrative."

63. "Simplifying to the extreme, I define postmodern as incredulity toward meta narratives. This incredulity is undoubtedly a product of progress in the sciences: but that progress in turn presupposes it. To the obsolescence of the meta narrative apparatus of legitimation corresponds, most notably, the crisis of metaphysical philosophy and of the university institution which in the past relied on it. The narrative function is losing its functors, its great hero, its great dangers, its great voyages, its great goal. It is being dispersed in clouds of narrative language elements—narrative, but also denotative, prescriptive, descriptive, and so on [. . .] Where, after the meta narratives, can legitimacy reside?" (Lyotard, *Postmodern Condition*, xxiv).

64. "Metanarrative."

65. "Metanarrative."

66. "Metanarrative."

a level of fragmentation that makes it extremely difficult to maintain any grasp on any big picture. Without the grand narrative, on what basis could we insist Christ is the fulfillment of a divine promise made to the Old Testament saints? Without the framework, the stories of Abraham, Isaac, Jacob, and the rest of the Old Testament lose all meaning outside their immediate historical and social contexts even though they are clearly connected as co-bearers of the seed promised to Abraham. This is a heavy price to pay. For when we then do try to see the big picture, which we eventually will want to do, when we try to reassemble the fragments in our minds, to list and organize all the pieces, we will fail. It is like trying to reassemble the fragments of a broken mirror, which deny us a true reflection and cause us to misinterpret the "local" narratives.[67]

Of course, a reductionist approach to the world does not necessarily leave us with more fragments. As Wilson notes,

> behind the mere smashing of aggregates into smaller pieces lies a deeper agenda that also takes the name of reductionism: to fold the laws and principles of each level of organization into those at more general, hence more fundamental levels.[68]

Sometimes, this technique is used to reduce complexity, that is, flatten or homogenize multilayered or multidimensional objects, processes, and events into a single, and thus more manageable, object. The point of this, of course, is control, to reduce things to a single common denominator, as it were. One example of this reductionist approach can be seen in the now-common idea that there is only one sort of time: every day, every season, every moment, relentlessly ticking away in their monotonous uniformity, no one moment different or more valuable than another. What has been eliminated by this approach is the idea of a hierarchy of times rendering the concept of sacred time, of a feast day or of the Sabbath, incomprehensible. How could one day be any different than another? That is why it has become so difficult to distinguish between a work day and a Sunday, as evidenced by the growing number of businesses and trades that maintain full operations on Sundays. Indeed, if all time is the same, there is no reason to reserve one day, that is, no reason not to use Sunday for the same activities engaged in on the other days.[69]

This methodology is also used to reduce or eliminate diversity, to standardize, and to impose uniformity. This reductionism is at work in

---

67. ". . . the task is futile—similar to trying to reassemble the fragments of a broken mirror to see a true reflection. Thus, after a while we give up trying to see the whole altogether" (Senge, *Fifth Discipline*, 3).

68. Wilson, *Consilience*, 60.

69. Taylor, *Secular Age*, 271.

the widespread desire to eliminate gender diversity by reducing its natural multidimensionalism to a single interchangeable concept. This thinking is responsible for collapsing the God-given, multilayered, richly textured structure that defines personal being into a single, flat generalization. According to Berger, this same reductionism is at the heart of the many die-, fashion-, and gadget-based fads engineered by advertisers. These fads sweeping through consumer populations are destroying regional cultures and imposing a kind of cultural sameness. "For example, McDonald's has affected the eating habits of many Asian countries, [by using] advertising to attract patrons, [to a form of] cultural homogenization."[70]

Ironically, this imposed uniformity is sometimes adopted in the name of personal freedom, as when millions claim to express their individualism by wearing the now-ubiquitous torn and faded blue jeans promoted by big corporations. However, this prevailing urge to reduce all variation to a single, uniform system of thought and behavior is, according to Herbert Marcuse, "technological rationality colonizing everyday life, robbing individuals of freedom and individuality by imposing technological imperatives, rules, and structures upon their thought and behavior."[71] This one-dimensional thought is "systematically promoted by the makers of politics and their purveyors of mass information"[72] and leads to a loss of the very freedoms the modern imaginary envisions. Marcuse further notes,

> The distinguishing feature of advanced industrial society is its effective suffocation of those needs which demand liberation—liberation also from that which is tolerable and rewarding and comfortable—while it sustains and absolves the destructive power and repressive function of the affluent society. Here, the social controls exact the overwhelming need for the production and consumption of waste; the need for stupefying work where it is no longer a real necessity; the need for modes of relaxation which soothe and prolong this stupefaction; the need for maintaining such deceptive liberties as free competition at administered prices, a free press which censors itself, free choice between brands and gadgets.[73]

In other cases, this reductionism is referred to as rationalization, which has been defined as "the destruction or ignoring of information in order to

---

70. Berger, *Ads, Fads, and Consumer Culture*, 219.
71. Kellner, "Introduction to the Second Edition," loc. 92 of 5280.
72. Marcuse, *One-Dimensional Man*, 16.
73. Marcuse, *One-Dimensional Man*, 9.

facilitate its processing."[74] To take up the example of time again, consider the imposition of standardized time zones.

> Equally important to the rationalization of industrial society, at the most macro level, were the division of North America into five standardized time zones in 1883 and the establishment the following year of the Greenwich meridian and International Date Line, which organized world time into twenty-four zones. What was formerly a problem of information overload and hence control for railroads and other organizations that sustained the social system at its most macro level was solved by simply ignoring much of the information, namely that solar time is different at each node of a transportation or communication system. A more convincing demonstration of the power of rationalization or preprocessing as a control technology would be difficult to imagine.
>
> So commonplace has such preprocessing become that today we dismiss the alternative—that each node in a system might keep a slightly different time—as hopelessly cumbersome and primitive. With the continued proliferation of distributed computing, ironically enough, it might soon become feasible to return to a system based on local solar time, thereby shifting control from preprocessing back to processing—where it resided for centuries of human history until steam power pushed transportation beyond the pace of the sun across the sky.[75]

Obviously, this bent toward uniformity has invaded the church. In some cases, it is an internal necessity born of the necessity of common faith and practice. But in other cases, it is a damaging attempt to mimic the world, as in copying its music, imaging, business practices, and organization, an effort to reduce or eliminate the differences between the secular and sacred communities.

CRITICISM AND A FREE-FLOATING MORAL ORDER

As might have been expected, Enlightenment thought promoted more than the innocent use of reason. It turned into an insistence, a demand, for the freedom to criticize. According to Peter Gay, the Enlightenment's thinkers defined philosophy as the organized habit of criticism.

---

74. Beniger, *Control Revolution,* loc. 358 of 8020.
75. Beniger, *Control Revolution,* locs. 365–71 of 8020.

> The philosophes' glorification of criticism and their qualified repudiation of metaphysics make it obvious that the Enlightenment was not an Age of Reason but a Revolt against Rationalism. The claim for the omnicompetence of criticism was in no way a claim for the omnipotence of reason. It was a political demand for the right to question everything, rather than the assertion that all could be known or mastered by rationality.[76]

Well, it may not have started out that way, but this Enlightenment characteristic has been so widely and uncritically accepted that it too is now taken to be a basic human right. This insistence on criticism has been incorporated into the modern social imaginary in the form of argumentativeness and an elevated sense of the importance of individual opinion. This has resulted in a general decline in civility[77] and a questioning (usually followed by a rejection) of almost every metaphysical, religious, and moral principle.

The penchant for argument can be seen in the general loss of the art of conversation.[78] People used to get together for the expressed purpose of discussing different views on, let's say, politics or religion. This kind of conversation could last for hours and get rather intense. But it rarely led to confrontation, anger, or violence. Today's demand for the right to criticism is so intense it often leads to confrontation and has made many wary of discussions in which their ideas might be criticized. It seems we can no longer disagree without getting angry and resorting to verbal violence. The more closely an opinion is related to a person's own identity, as is often the case with our largely privatized religious opinions, the more likely a challenge will draw an angry, negative response.

As a corollary to the right to criticize others, there is the generally overstated importance of one's own opinion. A somewhat humorous example are the many online news outlets that include a sidebar entitled "Have Your Say" where the viewer is provided an opportunity to give their opinion on the news events of the day. This amounts to enabling anyone to have an opinion about anything (regardless of expertise). Indeed, if you read some of the comments that are made, you quickly realize there are very few people who are knowledgeable enough to make useful contributions. So the practice seems to be just another way to document the equivalidity of each and every opinion—of making everyone an expert. This is particularly evident in "less-than-scientific" domains such as religion. In these cases, everyone is an expert, and the truth and its validation gives way to the right of expression.

---

76. Gay, *Enlightenment*, 141.
77. See Brooks, *Road to Character*.
78. See Miller, *Conversation*.

It has been, I believe, this incessant, programmatic criticism of everything and anything that, at least functionally, establishes the individual as the primary locus of moral authority. This habit of criticism has challenged not only traditional values and institutions but has also altered the very context in which Western moral order operates. Referring to developments in the 1960s, Robert Bellah speaks of a "massive erosion of the legitimacy of American institutions—business, government, education, the churches, and the family."[79] He goes on to say, "This collective questioning of inherited values, beliefs and practices had long been devalued by the predominant culture which began to receive widespread consideration,"[80] undermining the prevailing moral order. What I am calling a moral order is a system of moral convictions and values organized around notions of authority and hierarchy, that is, "a hierarchy in society that expresses and corresponds to a hierarchy in the cosmos."[81] As such, this is not just a set of norms but rather notions of right and wrong embedded in an existing hierarchy. This is the ontic component that makes the norms realizable. Taylor suggests premodern moral orders existed in various modes of hierarchical complementarity, which include those that touch on human existence as well as God and the cosmos. In other words, society was made up of different orders arranged in a hierarchy of authorities. One example was the context created by medieval division of society into those who pray, those who fight, and those who work. As Taylor comments, "However, the modern order gives no ontological status to hierarchy or any particular structure of differentiation."[82] Now the only functioning norm/authority is each individual serves the needs of others and thus helps himself. For that, no hierarchy—cosmic or otherwise—and no particular social differentiation is needed. As Taylor puts it:

> In the premodern imaginary, the highest virtue was the service that the whole order, as it were, renders to all its members. But in the modern ideal, mutual respect and service is directed toward serving our ordinary goals: life, liberty, sustenance of self and family.[83]
>
> These two main ends, security and prosperity, are now the principal goals of organized society, which itself can come to be seen as something in the nature of a profitable exchange among

---

79. Lucas, *Odyssey of a New Religion*, 14. See also Stark and Bainbridge, *Future of Religion*.
80. Lucas, *Odyssey of a New Religion*, 14.
81. Taylor, *Modern Social Imaginaries*, 9.
82. Taylor, *Modern Social Imaginaries*, 12.
83. Taylor, *Modern Social Imaginaries*, 13.

its constituent members. The ideal social order is one in which our purposes mesh, and each in furthering himself helps others.[84]

The ongoing need to criticize all hierarchy, differentiation, and authority has left us with a moral order floating free in an undefined context. It has now become almost impossible to know right from wrong or make the case for any such discrimination. The moral order now operates without the benefit of either a transcendent or an immanent hierarchy. As a result, our ability to make moral choices is limited to whatever serves our own interests or purposes. The social aspect is governed only by the concept of participation contingent on a return on our investment.

CONSILIENCE AND THE PRIMACY OF INFORMATION

Another characteristic of Enlightenment thought, also related to the reductionistic methodology, is the notion of consilience. In essence, this is the conviction that all knowledge is unified, i.e., there is one single pool of interrelated knowledge that can be accessed by anyone using the right methodology. Wilson speaks of the strong form of this idea, namely

> total consilience, which holds that nature is organized by simple universal laws of physics to which all other laws and principles can eventually be reduced. This transcendental worldview is the light and way for many scientific materialists (I admit to being among them).[85]

In the modern imaginary, the idea of consilience leads to a kind of methodological arrogance, blind belief in what are called facts, the assured results of scientific study. According to this view, if there is only one kind of knowledge, then there is only one legitimate way of accessing it. This, in turn, leads to a general rejection of what might be called alternative sciences, or rather the rejection of the scientific status of anything other than the materialistic, reductionistic methodology. For example, one might argue there is such a thing as theological knowledge and that knowledge can be discovered using a methodology and a set of tools and rules appropriate to that method. One might even suggest if this kind of research were done in a consistent and systematic manner, it could be called a science.[86] Yet it is exactly this kind of latitude that is often eliminated in the name of consilience.

---

84. Taylor, *Modern Social Imaginaries*, 13.

85. Wilson, *Consilience*, 60.

86. This is the approach that the well-known theologian Wolfhart Pannenberg takes in *Theology and the Philosophy of Science of Science.*

If there is only one kind of knowledge, then there is only one legitimate methodology—science, the great engine of enlightened thinking—and it has to be applied to all areas of knowledge. Deceived by this oversimplification, some have sought to apply the scientific method to biblical and theological materials. The results of this methodological mismatch—the method does not correspond to the data being studied—are results that have little or nothing to do with the veracity or intended meanings of those texts. When these scientists are finished there is very little left of the original deposit left by Christ and the apostles. The reason for this is everything except what are thought to be actual facts have to be stripped away. A fact is something that is indisputably the case, that is, it has to demonstrably correspond with something in the unified pool of knowledge. If there is no such thing as knowledge of a metaphysical, miraculous, transcendent nature, then there can be no facts pertaining to those topics. If miracles cannot happen (because they violate the laws of nature), then any report or description of such events cannot be factual. So it is only the scientific method that can provide uncontested facts which give us information about, and thus control over, the world in which we live.

Ironically, it was the rapid, science-driven pace of technological advance that led "to a set of problems—in effect a crisis of control[87]—generated by the industrial revolution in manufacturing and transportation."[88] These rapidly developing technologies had to be controlled and that highlighted the need for ever more information.

> Before this time, control of government and markets had depended on personal relationships and face-to-face interactions; now control came to be reestablished by means of bureaucratic organization, the new infrastructures of transportation and telecommunications, and systemwide communication via the new mass media . . .[89]
>
> . . .the new societal transformations—rapid innovation in information and control technology, to regain control of functions once contained at much lower and more diffuse levels of society—constituted a true revolution in societal control.[90]

---

87. ". . .a period in which innovations in information-processing and communication technologies lagged behind those of energy and its application to manufacturing and transportation" (Beniger, *Control Revolution*, loc. 50 of 8020).

88. Beniger, *Control Revolution*, loc. 183 of 8020.

89. Beniger, *Control Revolution*, loc. 1639 of 8020.

90. Beniger, *Control Revolution*, loc. 210 of 8020.

Every area of our national economy developed technological responses to the crisis, to the need for control, by adapting aspects of information technology to suit its particular needs. "Transportation concentrated on the development of bureaucratic organization, production on the organization of material processing, including preprocessing, division of labor, and functional specialization; distribution concentrated on telecommunications, marketing on mass media."[91] As Beniger notes,

> Most bureaucratic innovation arose in response to the crisis of control in the railroads; by the late 1860s the large wholesale houses had fully exploited this form of control. Innovation in telecommunications (the telegraph, postal reforms, and the telephone) followed the movement of the crisis of control to distribution. Innovation in organizational technology and preprocessing (the shop-order system of accounts, routing slips, rate-fixing departments, cost control, uniform accounting procedures, factory timekeepers, and specialized factory clerks) followed the movement of the control crisis into the production sector in the 1870s. Most innovations in mass control (full-page newspaper advertising, a trademark law, print patents, corporate publicity departments, consumer packaging, and million-dollar advertising campaigns) came after the late 1870s with the advent of continuous-processing machinery and the resulting crisis in control of consumption. Along with these innovations came virtually all of the basic mass communications technologies still in use a century later: photography, rotary-power printing, motion pictures, the wireless, magnetic tape recording, and radio.[92]

So it is that we have become an information society. Information has become the most sought-after commodity in our economy. We pay for it; criminals steal it. We gather it by surveying, by spying. We store it and lock it away. We retrieve it and use it against those we intend to control and manipulate. Information about consumer behavior is used to micro-target advertising. "Advertisers are able to manipulate Americans 'into chasing ever-higher levels of consumption by means of 'motivational research,'"[93] which involves gathering information on, among other things, the fears of sexual inadequacy and low social status of potential consumers. Information is power. It gives those who wield it control, not only over transportation, industry, and distribution, but increasingly over the interpersonal

---

91. Beniger, *Control Revolution*, loc. 6526 of 8020.
92. Beniger, *Control Revolution*, locs. 6526–33 of 8020.
93. Berman, *Why America Failed*, 28.

relationships which can be regulated in terms of "a formal set of impersonal, quantifiable, and objective criteria, changes that greatly facilitate control by both government and business."[94] It is all rooted in our need for control, for which we need information, which consists of uncontestable facts, which are only available by means of one method—science—because there is but one type of, one unified pool of knowledge. Even the church, like any other business participating in the national economy, turns to information technologies, such as market research and statistical analysis, in order to acquire the information it needs to exercise control over its customers, members, its programs.

PROGRESS AND THE VALUE NEUTRALITY OF TECHNOLOGY

The modern mindset also holds that ". . . as our knowledge becomes both broader and more unified, we will experience continued progress (and they have in mind not only technological progress, but also social, political, and moral progress)."[95] Consider Condorcet's (1743–1794) optimistic *Sketch for A Historical Picture of the Progress of the Human Mind,* in which he declares

> the whole foundation for belief in the natural sciences is this idea, that the general laws directing the phenomena of the universe, known or unknown, are necessary and constant. Why should this principle be any less true for the development of the intellectual and moral faculties of man than for the other operations of nature?
>
> The time will therefore come when the sun will shine only on free men who know no other master but their reason; when tyrants and slaves, priests and their stupid or hypocritical instruments will exist only in works of history and on the stage; and when we shall think of them only. . .to learn how to recognize and so to destroy, by force of reason, the first seeds of tyranny and superstition, should they ever dare to reappear amongst us.[96]

The vision cast here by Kant and the other Enlightenment philosophers was an enlightened populace, perpetually at peace with other peoples and steadily advancing in every area experiencing continued progress. This was the promise of the Enlightenment.

---

94. Beniger, *Control Revolution,* loc. 6566 of 8020.
95. Hauptli, "Enlightenment Project," sec. 2.
96. Condorcet, cited by Hauptli, "Enlightenment Project," sec. 2.

In the modern imaginary, this expectation of relentless progress is reflected in a certain restlessness or dissatisfaction with the way things are. Having grown accustomed to the constant evolution of technology, the late-modern individual tends to generalize and project this movement on almost every area of life. Accordingly, the economy has to grow. Relationships, friendships, and allegiances have to change and evolve. Ideas (even truths) have to be developed. Speeds have to increase. Superstitions have to be overcome. This often takes the form of an outright rejection of the past. The beliefs, values, and aspirations of those who have gone on before us are thrown off simply because they are of the past. Like everything else, these things have been modernized and improved upon. Those no longer on the progressive side of life's curve are shunned and hidden away. The immanent obsolescence of just about everything leads to an idolization of the new and improved.

We come, then, to expect a steady stream of improvements, uninterrupted progress. We excitedly look for and buy every new software upgrade, every new gadget, the latest fashion, the newest cars. This expectation easily slips over into a kind of euphoria, that heady feeling of being on the cutting edge of progress. But as with all forms of euphoria, as expectations rise, our level of caution sinks. For the sheer joy of gadgetry, we fail to think about its implications, its meanings, the impact it may have on our lives, or the possible limits to progress itself.

Of course, some observers such as the Club of Rome and Herbert Marcuse have warned us:

> "Progress" is not a neutral term; it moves toward specific ends, and these ends are defined by the possibilities of ameliorating the human condition. Advanced industrial society is approaching the stage where continued progress would demand the radical subversion of the prevailing direction and organization of progress. This stage would be reached when material production (including the necessary services) becomes automated to the extent that all vital needs can be satisfied while necessary labor time is reduced to marginal time. From this point on, technical progress would transcend the realm of necessity, where it served as the instrument of domination and exploitation which thereby limited its rationality; technology would become subject to the free play of faculties in the struggle for the pacification of nature and of society.[97]

---

97. Marcuse, *One-Dimensional Man*, 18.

But most of us are not listening. Caught up in the delights of progress, we seek to preserve unfettered access to every advance either by not raising any objections to them at all or by unquestioningly accepting the assumption that all the elements, structures, devices, and technologies produced by society are value-neutral. The argument runs something like this: "The products of modern science are not in themselves good or bad; it is the way they are used that determines their value." We could say, "[a]pple pie is in itself neither good nor bad; it is the way it is used that determines its value" or "[t]he smallpox virus is in itself neither good nor bad; it is the way it is used that determines its value"; and again, "Firearms are in themselves neither good nor bad; it is the way they are used that determines their value,"[98] but to many this makes little sense. "For psychological and cultural reasons, it has been hard for people to grasp this. In particular, it would seem almost impossible for individuals living in societies such as ours to entertain the notion that technology is not neutral."[99] So most of us simply embrace, uncritically, the prevailing theory and remain naïvely convinced we, in using these tools, can decide to use them for good or evil, that we can guarantee positive outcomes and meanings. But as Morris Berman writes,

> [t]he only problem with this theory is that it is wrong. From Robert Redfield to Lewis Mumford to Marshall McLuhan to the Frankfurt School for Social Research (which includes Herbert Marcuse) to the techno-critics of today, the one thing they all agree upon, and have been able to substantiate in various ways, is that the "tool" theory of technology is hopelessly naïve. It ignores the fact that most technologies are not appropriate; rather, they carry with them a mindset, a way of life, that once introduced into a culture changes that culture forever.[100]

No wonder, then, that Marshal McLuhan refers to support for this idea as "the voice of the current somnambulism," as "the numb stance of the technological idiot."[101] It dangerously ignores the nature of the medium, of any and all media, namely, that each one brings with it presuppositions and meanings that simply cannot be separated from the medium itself and which inevitably alter our perceptions.

Some would agree modern technology and its devices bring some risks but find it hard to extend the potential of that danger to all elements of our society as I have done (economic structures, moral order, legal code,

---

98. McLuhan, *Understanding Media*, locs. 203–10 of 5353.
99. Berman, *Why America Failed*, 93.
100. Berman, *Why America Failed*, 93.
101. As quoted by Berman, *Why America Failed*, 94.

educational institutions, political foundations, etc.). Nonetheless, what we have learned is "what modern technology (and not just media technology) does is translate everything into mechanism (including cybermechanism)—people and human life included. If you live in a hustling society, everything is a commodity; if in a technological one, everything is a means, an instrument. There is nothing 'neutral' about this."[102]

To be fair to ourselves, don't we have to say that, at least in some cases, we have used the tools of culture for good? In spite of having become totally immersed in North American culture, in spite of (or perhaps because of) having accepted the value neutrality of technology, have we not been able to resist, deflect, and even correct for some of the negative meanings and consequences of these mechanisms? Haven't we done more good than harm? Hasn't the church been growing precisely because we have been using these technologies? One would certainly hope Christians of all people would be able to use some of these tools for good since they should be motivated and guided by the pure, noble, and pious motives of the faith. They certainly have done that in the form of email lists, Facebook accounts, and parish websites. Usually the only justification they need for deploying society's resources in the church is availability. If it is available to us, we get to use it. Of course, this takes place with very little thought and almost no theological reflection because we are so confident the tools are neutral and we can control them. For example, one parish website initiates the use of an online payment options with these words, "We live in a digital age, and sometimes it is hard to remember to bring (or mail) that check. We have had several requests for online giving options over the years, and we have now partnered with easyTithe[103] to offer secure, online giving . . ."[104] So the reasons given for using this technology are simply that it is available. Furthermore, some of our people have asked for this convenience. As I said, there is no evidence of any critical thought here, and there is an obvious absence of any theological/biblical input. What we have is rather an uncritical acquiescence to the twin business principles of availability and convenience. Obviously, that is no way to make such important decisions in the church.

The other justification for the use of these technologies is convenience, that is, making giving easy. But again, does this not change the very nature of giving, which is supposed to be a sacrifice, anything but easy? And does

---

102. Berman, *Why America Failed*, 94.

103. easyTithe is a secular company that provides the technology needed for online giving. Of course, it does so at a cost. Some (quite a bit, actually) of what is being tithed goes to the company. See "Plans and Pricing."

104. "Secure Online Giving at St. Basil."

it not violate the whole tenor of our teaching about life in Christ being a struggle, spiritual warfare?

There may be one other side-effect of the anticipated perpetuity of technological advance that has an impact on the church and that is the universal fear and loathing of what is referred to as boredom. This is an emotional state experienced when an individual is not sufficiently stimulated to activity, thought, or commitment. It most often occurs when a situation does not challenge the student, reader, viewer, or the worshiper with an adequate and, above all, enjoyable opportunity to interact with the latest gadgetry or the most up-to-the-minute information. Boredom is the underbelly of the expectation of inevitable progress. Because not all information or technology is meaningful, significant, or useful, we are sometimes at a loss for how to use it. The telegraph, for example, rendered much of the information it relayed irrelevant. What practical value in knowing the temperature in London is gained by the early-twentieth-century New Yorker? So "where people once sought information to manage the real contexts of their lives, now they had to invent contexts in which otherwise useless information might be put to some apparent use."[105] "'What am I to do with all these disconnected facts?' And in one form or another, the answer is the same: Why not use them for diversion? for entertainment? to amuse yourself, in a game?"[106] So it was that entertainment, the fascination with useless information, took on its dominant role in North American society, mediated primarily by radio, television, and movies:

> Together, this ensemble of electronic techniques called into being a new world—a peek-a-boo world, where now this event, now that, pops into view for a moment, then vanishes again. It is a world without much coherence or sense; a world that does not ask us, indeed, does not permit us to do anything; a world that is, like the child's game of peek-a-boo, entirely self-contained. But like peek-a-boo, it is also endlessly entertaining.[107]

Unfortunately, the malaise caused by the absence of the exciting, the contemporary, and the progressive has crept into the church, and there one often hears of a desire to alleviate the boredom experienced by some during the services by tweaking the traditional formats and practices in such a way as to make them more tolerable, attractive, and, yes exciting. Some now make a distinction between traditional and contemporary services. In a spoof of this trend a group of young people calling themselves "Blimey Cow" suggested a

105. Postman, *Amusing Ourselves to Death*, 90.
106. Postman, *Amusing Ourselves to Death*, 90.
107. Postman, *Amusing Ourselves to Death*, 91.

number of ways of making the Sunday liturgy more appealing. In their YouTube clip, they propose the use of fog, lights, volume, blue jeans, iPads, and the like.[108] It seems then we have to provide perpetual technological progress or, at a very minimum, boredom-dispelling adjustments to traditional practice.

REFLEXIVITY, SELF-LOVE, AND THE PURSUIT OF HAPPINESS

The concern for one's own opinion is also indicative of the Enlightenment's turn inward. This first-person perspective, while anticipated by Plato and Aristotle, is rooted in the work of Augustine. His was a turn to the self. According to Taylor, "[i]t was Augustine who introduced the inwardness of radical reflexivity and bequeathed it to the Western tradition of thought. The step was a fateful one, because we have certainly made a big thing of the first-person standpoint."[109]

But it was surely Descartes who gave this turn its most recognizable form with his maxim, "I think, therefore I am." "This new conception of inwardness, an inwardness of self-sufficiency, of autonomous powers of ordering by reason, also prepared the ground for modern unbelief."[110] This turn inward was adopted by the Enlightenment and has come into the modern imaginary in the form of a radical self-centeredness. This is more than a simple fascination with the self; there is a sense in which the entire late-modern project can be viewed as reflexive. This project is ontologically reflexive in that it seeks to ground being in a tautological reference to itself. "I exist because I exist." It is morally reflexive since it situates morality in the self by deriving moral principles from within. And it is practically reflexive in that its primary concern is the well-being of the individual. As the Enlightenment took hold, people lost interest in the supernatural, the higher order of time, the hierarchy of the church and its mysteries. What came to dominate was a concern for an "affirmation of ordinary life"[111]—basically happiness and a satisfaction with the realities of everyday personal living. As a result, the individual becomes preoccupied with a constant monitoring of itself in order to secure its being, its own desires, that which it perceives to be good, its own happiness. This happiness is so closely related to our understanding of individual freedom that it is, as noted above, institutionalized and enshrined as an inalienable human right in the US Constitution.

108. Blimey Cow, "How to Get Millennials Back."
109. Taylor, *Sources of the Self*, 130.
110. Taylor, *Sources of the Self*, 158.
111. Taylor, *Modern Social Imaginaries*, 74.

In the church, this focus on the self is often referred to as self-love. Much of the work on the idea was developed by St. Maximus the Confessor. He began with the standard division of the human being into three parts: the mind, the will, and the emotions. According to him, if the mind is in communion with God, then the will is directed toward God and others. If the mind is disconnected, then the will will focus exclusively on itself. It was this reversal of the divine order, this turn inward that St. Maximus called self-love, and he calls it the root or source of all human sin. What is of particular interest for me here is "[s]elf-love, love of pleasure and love of praise banish remembrance of God from the soul . . . And when remembrance of God is absent, there is a tumult of the passions within us."[112] Those passions include the insatiable demand (greed) to satisfy every desire. In every sense God is replaced by the self and its wants, which leaves the individual vulnerable to the very worst forms of manipulation—marketers playing to their love of self. So those seeking to promote their products, probed "people's subsurface desires, needs, and drives . . . in order to find their points of vulnerability."[113] In doing so they studied "human motivations and desires and developed a need for goods with which the public has at one time been unfamiliar—perhaps even undesirous of purchasing."[114] The advertisers shamelessly used human selfishness and discovered

> narcissism indicated that nothing appeals more to people than themselves; so why not help people buy a projection of themselves? That way the images would preselect their audiences, select out of a consuming public people with personalities having an affinity for the image. By building in traits known to be widely dispersed among the consuming public the image builders reasoned that they could spark love affairs by the millions.[115]

The church is, of course, not exempt from such manipulation. Because self-love is not limited to the world outside the church, its members and leaders were equally easy prey for the advertisers. "Public-relations experts [began] advising churchmen how they can become more effective manipulators of their congregations,"[116] using marketing "research to fill churches and sharpen sermons,"[117] market and brand their congregations, and sell Jesus.[118]

---

112. Theodore, quoted in Nicodemus et al., *Philokalia*, 2:32.
113. Packard, *Hidden Persuaders*, 57.
114. Packard, *Hidden Persuaders*, 48.
115. Packard, *Hidden Persuaders*, 67.
116. Packard, *Hidden Persuaders*, 33.
117. Packard, *Hidden Persuaders*, 24.
118. See Webster, *Selling Jesus*.

◆◆◆

These, then, are the principles which define the shape of the contemporary North American social imaginary. Taken together they both limit and empower the ways we live together, the things we value and consider worthy of pursuing. They are like the components of a language that make possible the expression of individual self-understanding within the common life of the mutual give-and-take of our entire population. This language also governs the structure and inner workings of organizations and institutions that unite groups of individuals in the pursuit of common interests. On the one hand, the activities of an organization's members are coordinated or structured in order to most efficiently achieve a goal or set of goals that lie outside the entity itself. For example, a business is organized and structured for the purpose of making a profit. As such, an organization will be largely governed by the rules of the prevailing social imaginary. On the other hand, an institution, which is a special form of organization that comes into being to meet some social need, is usually established to provide knowledge or service. An academic institution, for example, provides education, and thus adds value to the general public, rather than taking away said value from it. For this reason, at least some of the rules that govern the ways in which an institution generates, preserves, and presents that knowledge are governed by a specialized set of principles. In other words, an institution will have its own internal imaginary that supplements, often takes precedence over, but does not fundamentally conflict with, the prevailing social imaginary. The challenge, of course, is not to let the social imaginary supplant the academic one as happens when commercial interests override those of scholarship. Given the power of the imaginary, that sadly does happen. In the case of the church, we are dealing with a special type of institution that does not arise specifically from any social need. It is rather the direct result of divine intervention at Pentecost, where the Father sends the Holy Spirit into the world in order to validate and continue the ministry and presence of the incarnate, resurrected, and ascended Son. As such, it has been given its own unique, completely sufficient, and internal imaginary, which is governed by Holy Scripture and Tradition. As indicated above, the challenge here is the church and its members, being embedded in the larger context of society, run the risk of allowing the social imaginary to influence, distort, or even override crucial elements of their own ecclesial imaginary. So when Jesus tells us to be *in* but not *of* the world, he is warning us not to replace the ecclesial imaginary, or even parts of it, with the social imaginary, and not to allow the operating principles of the prevailing imaginary to govern the way we do things in the church. That would, after all, constitute being *of* rather than just *in* the world.

So if, as stated above, the aim of this study is to consider the degree to which that imaginary-substitution might be happening in the church, assess danger, and identify threats, what are we to look for? How will we know if, how, and where the operating principles of society are active in the ecclesial setting? What aspects of church life do we examine? Going back to the basic idea that the imaginary and its operating principles govern the way people interact, engage one another, or share their lives together, we could seek to identify behaviors, meanings, devices, and technologies produced by the social imaginary and ask if those same behaviors and principles are evident in the church. But because the sharing of life is such an enormously complex, dynamic, and variegated accretion of phenomena, it almost defies that kind of systematic analysis. Obviously, we will not be able to cover every facet of our culture, but we can certainly identify a few patterns or interaction groupings related to specific needs or purposes. Three of the most obvious forms of this social interaction are *commerce, public discourse,* and *self-governance*. These are definitely not the only areas of social interaction we could look at, but they are the most common.

The significance of the last of these fields of interactivity, *governance,* is easily seen since for us to effectively function as a society, we need to agree on norms that will balance the needs and rights of each individual with those of others. But governance is not simply defending the individual, it is also an attempt to facilitate joining forces, banding together for the greater good, which no individual can accomplish alone. This certainly affects the first area of social interaction, *commerce,* which is the collective expression of individual desire for wealth, that is, continual progress and accumulation, everyone buying and/or selling something, which obviously needs to be regulated or controlled. In turn, that need for regulation explains the importance of the second area, *discourse,* which serves as a bridge between commerce and governance, that is, as the forum for discussing both the ethical basis for and the actual details of commerce as regulated by self-governance. Each one of the three areas of social interaction articulates its own objectives and establishes its own meanings, devices, structures, and techniques, which are used to achieve their stated goals.

This three-fold division of society (commerce, discourse, governance) gives us an overall framework for systematically identifying and evaluating the use of nonecclesial practices and for assessing the extent of the damage their use might be doing to the church. Thus, we could ask: Are the accepted practices of these three fields of societal interaction being used in corresponding areas of ecclesial life? Moreover, we need to ask if those activities are being governed by the operating principles of the social imaginary or the church. Is it the societal operating principles that are governing the use of commercial meanings, devices, and techniques as they are being applied in the ecclesial setting? Or is an ecclesial imaginary informed by Scripture and Tradition which are establishing the meanings, devices, and practices needed to address both individual and collective needs within the church and govern its interaction with the world? I am not suggesting we reject secular structures and technologies out of hand. Rather, I want to ask if they actually enhance the ministry and life of the church, if they need to be avoided because they pose a danger, or if they can be modified for effective use in the church. My goal here is to initiate some level of ecclesial discourse that will allow us to collectively explore the conditions for the use of (even the potentially positive use of) some of these secular structures, and to develop or highlight already-existing ecclesial alternatives. Parsing this interface between church and society lies at the heart of this study. I will do that by looking at the ways in which the church has implemented the practices of the marketplace (Part II), mimicked social discourse (Part III), and adopted democratic self-rule (Part IV). Finally, I would like to assess any damage that may have been done to the church and consider a way forward by offering guidelines for the ongoing interaction between the church and the secular, technological world by rearticulating the nature of the ecclesial imaginary and its operating principles (Part V).

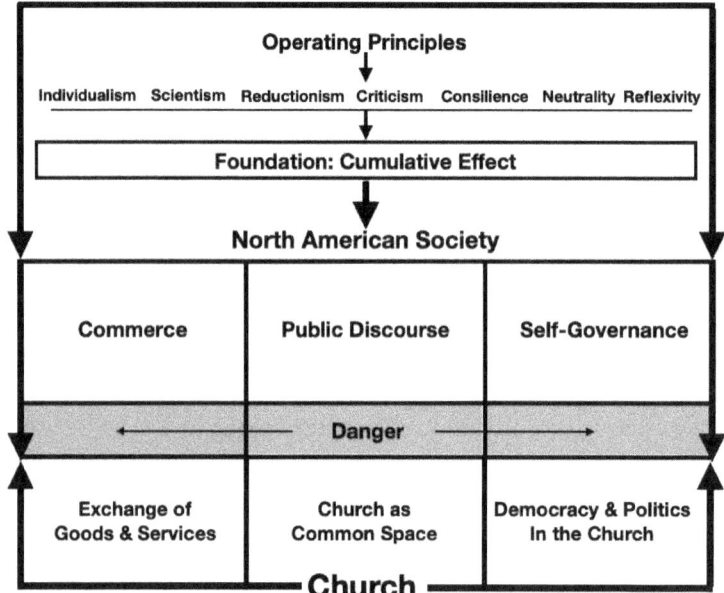

The Social Imaginary

PART II

The Marketplace

The Church and Contemporary Commerce

3

Introduction: Business in the Church

As one digs deeper into the national character of the Americans, one sees that they have sought the value of everything in this world only in the answer to this single question: how much money will it bring in?[1]

Buying and selling are probably the most readily observable aspects of North American social interaction. One of the practices unleashed by the Enlightenment and guaranteed by our Constitution was the individual pursuit of wealth. At its most basic this involves the freedom to exchange goods and services for what is sometimes called mutual benefit, but more often, simply, profit. This activity, which has been with us since the inception of the nation, is so prevalent, so dominant, that it is often the first thing visitors notice, and it has even been viewed as an essential aspect of the North American[2] psyche or character. "This commercial orientation became our trademark. The principal goal of North American civilization, and of its inhabitants, is and always has been an ever-expanding economy—

---

1. de Tocqueville, cited by Berman, *Why America Failed*, 2.

2. The same criticism was also leveled at Russia by the Slavophiles of the Silver age of Russian Philosophy. "Ancient Rome as the triumph of naked and pure reason relying on itself alone and recognizing nothing above or outside itself. This pernicious rationalism led to excellence in jurisprudence and the development of a society that was merely an aggregation of rationally thinking individuals motivated by personal advantage and knowing no other social bond than that of common business" (Walicki, *History of Russian Thought*, 92).

affluence—and endless technological innovation—'progress.'"[3] On a somewhat negative note, Herman Melville portrayed all Americans as hustlers "in the sense of self-promoters, scofflaws, occasional frauds, and peripatetic self-reinventers."[4] Of course, there is more to Americans than just that. "They are also hustlers in the positive sense: builders, doers, go-getters, dreamers, hard workers, inventors, organizers, engineers, and a people supremely generous. Needless to say, those qualities, not their baser ones, were what justified Americans' faith in themselves, their nation, and their nation's destiny among nations."[5]

In any case, as these "entrepreneurs and their supporters acquired influence they began to bend political and social institutions to meet their own demands," and so "a whole new ethic or way of looking at the world developed."[6] The pursuit of wealth, according to Bushman,[7] was so avid in the eighteenth century that it managed to rupture traditional bonds and boundaries. "The prospect of getting rich unleashed a rapacity rarely seen before in human society."[8] In the process, transcendent values were left behind in the dust.

> While these new ways of looking at the world of work had to coexist for a long time with the older values that stressed status, stasis, and communal obligations, the ideal of productivity finally did become dominant. Where earlier, talented young men might have aspired to be courtiers or even clergymen, as the eighteenth century opened, careers in manufacturing, finance, retailing, and foreign trade beckoned. There can be no capitalism, as distinguished from select capitalist practices, without a culture of capitalism, and there is no culture of capitalism until the principal forms of traditional society have been challenged and overcome.[9]

So this capitalistic, commercialized, profit driven orientation became "above all a culture, a mindset."[10] In other words, it is not just something a few of the elite think about in the isolation of one privileged segment of the social context; it is rather an integral part of our national being, part of

---

3. Berman, *Why America Failed*, xiii.
4. McDougall, paraphrasing Melville in *Freedom Just around the Corner*, 7.
5. McDougall, *Freedom Just around the Corner*, 7.
6. Appleby, *Relentless Revolution*, locs. 2013–14 of 8323.
7. See Bushman, *From Puritan to Yankee*.
8. Appleby, *Relentless Revolution*, locs. 7116–17 of 8323.
9. Appleby, *Relentless Revolution*, locs. 2016–21 of 8323.
10. Appleby, cited in Berman, *Why America Failed*, 28.

the overall social imaginary. Profit came to define what it means to be an American, and it guided and dictated the terms of social interaction across the whole spectrum of society, for the rich as well as the poor. As Samuel Gompers once observed, even "the poor in America have never wanted a fundamentally different type of society; they just wanted a larger cut of the pie. But a poor hustler is still a hustler; the social vision (if so, it can be called) remains the same."[11]

> Capitalism, then, has never been just an economic system. It impinged on every facet of life and was itself influenced by every institution or identity that shaped its participants. It created new cultural forms, stimulated new tastes, and introduced a whole new vocabulary for discussing the impact of private enterprise on the welfare of the society as a whole.[12]

So embedded in this culture, we are all, to one extent or another, driven by the desire to get rich quickly.[13] We have absorbed the dominant characteristics of the culture's consumerist mindset, and it may not surprise us to find this commercialized thinking and its attendant devices and practices are being brought into the church. However, what should surprise us is the ease with which and the extent to which this is happening. On the one hand, the demands of secular employment (business, medicine, education, etc.) in a consumer-oriented society often require we master and make regular use of these technologies. That sustained involvement causes us to become intimately acquainted with and accustomed to both the devices themselves and the ends they pursue. Our familiarity with those practices makes it understandable, quite natural for us to transpose readily available methodologies from the secular world into sacred space with little or no forethought, even when they pose a danger to the church. On the other hand, the ecclesial use of these commercial practices is, in some cases, actually justified since there is a degree of *correspondence* between the problems business methods have been designed to solve and the challenges faced by the church. In other cases, the church may even be required to comply with the structures and practices established by civil authorities to promote the greater good. These shared challenges might involve the rules that govern taxes, banking, basic human rights, or even the consequences of social distancing imposed during a health crisis, such as the one we experienced during the Coronavirus

---

11. Berman, *Why America Failed*, 28.
12. Appleby, *Relentless Revolution*, loc. 231 of 8323.
13. Hence, the popularity of the lotto, where the already poor waste what little they have for an astronomically small chance of getting rich quickly.

pandemic of 2020. All of these circumstances may, in turn, encourage, justify, or even compel the occasional use of familiar technologies.

FAMILIARITY AND ACCEPTANCE

It is not surprising that many of our members, who have been raised in the contemporary environment, who work and live in it every day, quite naturally bring the mercenary ways of the secular world into the church simply as a consequence of having to live and work in both contexts. While this may be done without any specific *intentionality*, it is almost impossible for these commercialized individuals to look at the presentation of the gospel as anything other than the sale, marketing, and distribution of a product. They are likely to see the services offered by the church as commodities that have to be paid for in some way. They will be tempted to look at their own relationship to Christ and their own involvement in the local parish in terms of some imagined bottom line, that is, gaining some return on whatever investment they think they have made. As this culture of commerce infiltrates the community of faith, just about everything the church teaches and does will be run through the filter of commerce and adjusted to fit the profit/loss paradigm.

What happens, then, when church income fails to meet its needs? In that case, those familiar with apparently more effective commercial methodologies will feel compelled to deploy those technologies (online giving, buying, selling) in the church in order to generate the needed income.[14] At this point the reculturation[15] of the church becomes quite *intentional,* and it is justified by the belief these secular devices, structures, or procedures will help the church more effectively fulfill its mission. This might mean thinking that background checks done by secular companies are more effective than pastoral leadership, that parish management software is more efficient than the divinely given charismatic structures of ministries, that a certified and paid spiritual director can replace the spiritual fathers and mothers of Tradition, or that parish web sites, networks, and Facebook accounts will be effective alternatives to the hard work of real-time interpersonal relationships.

---

14. This was the reason given by one of our hierarchs when defending Orthodox monasteries (and I am sure it is true of parishes as well) who sell the used-up detritus of the rich at flea markets and market a host of products that have nothing to do with the spiritual life, such as soap and coffee. In the absence of tithes, they have to do what they need to do to survive. Understandable, but at what cost?

15. I say "re"-culturation because I believe just as Leach has already discovered in non-Orthodox settings, the values, customs, and practices of the Orthodox Church are being subverted. See Leach, *Land of Desire*, introduction.

In fact, the intentional use of these familiar business structures, devices, and technologies is occasionally given *official endorsement*[16] by both official position statements, recommendations, public commendations,[17] and the transparently consumerist lifestyle of many of our priests. With some clergy demanding ever-larger compensation packages, displaying copies of *Fortune Magazine* and books like *Money: Master the Game*[18] around their upper-class homes,[19] and owning and operating luxury automobiles, it is hard to deny these representatives of Christ are communicating a full-throated endorsement of the entrepreneurial materialism of commerce to the parishioners they serve.

For example, while it is in some cases certainly necessary for priests to engage in secular employment, some of the clergy have actually transformed the extraecclesial sphere of their lives into for-profit businesses in the pursuit of personal wealth. In one case, a priest established a consulting firm[20] in which he offered to give motivational talks on "Crafting Your Own Professional Success." In a post on his website entitled "Building a Startup?," he describes how he worked to "up-class" his modest starter house in order to turn a profit. That return on his investment enabled him to move into a 4000-sq.-ft. mansion now valued at just under a million dollars, in what he calls a "sexy" neighborhood,[21] something the old neighborhood was apparently not, but something which was nevertheless important because success is often seen as a series of ever bigger and more expensive houses.[22] In addition to exemplifying this mindset, this priest/businessman has also recommended it in a small book, *Stop Climbing that Ladder*, describing his own journey. He starts out by saying, "I started my career as most people do with

---

16. For example, one national church officially promotes the use of Facebook, project management software (Asana.com), as well as a church management system from ACS Technologies called Realm in an article by Andre Paez called "Planting Grant Missions: Digital Tools for the 'Modern Fishermen,'" posted on the website of its seminary.

17. The use of commercial software for parish management was endorsed in an article that appeared on the OCA's national website (see OCA, "Planting Grant Missions"). The Greek Orthodox Archdiocese directly endorses the use of software for use with Apple TV, which allows live video streaming and on-demand viewing.

18. See Robbins, *Money*.

19. Here is a sampling of other titles from one priest's personal library: Metaxas, *Seven Men*; Warrillow, *Automatic Customer*; Brunson, *Expert Secrets*; Gardner et al., *Motley Fool Million-Dollar Portfolio*; Galloway, *Four*; Clifton and Badal, *Entrepreneurial Strengths Finder*; and Rath, *Strengths Finder 2.0*.

20. See "Author, Speaker, Consultant. Peter Robichau" at https://robichau.com.

21. Robichau, "Building a Startup?," para. 2.

22. See Osteen, *Become a Better You*.

a series of entry level jobs . . ."[23] He criticizes people who start out in life getting the "wrong" or no education, and then, giving himself as an example, he says, "I pursued graduate theological studies after college (which led to a master's degree), and I now make my living in the technology world."[24] Here he seems to imply his theological education and work as a priest were mistakes, or perhaps just rungs on the ladder of success, because now he is finally doing what he really wants to do: work with modern technology.[25] Of course, what this is all really about is revealed when he quotes Dave Ramsey, saying, "'With modern technology, if you have a good idea, and you are willing to work hard, then there is no reason why you can't make a million dollars.'"[26] I can imagine the faithful members of his parish, already familiar with the world of commerce, will view his behavior as an official affirmation of the complete compatibility of entrepreneurial materialism with the ecclesial, which will embolden them to, in their own ways, bring similar devices and principles into the church.

SACRED/SECULAR CORRESPONDENCE

The ease with which we bring commercialized thinking into the church can also be explained in terms of the commonalities of human existence. At a minimum that existence entails three primary or fundamental aspirations: love, order, and security. Each of these ends is undergirded by the God-given capabilities or faculties required for their attainment. For example, the need for order is facilitated by humanity's rational capabilities and the resultant ability to impose order and discipline. Security is made possible by the human ability to meet the many challenges and threats of life, such as housing, food, illness, etc. These aspirations and faculties taken together reflect the God-given logic across the whole breadth of human existence. For that reason, the desire for love, order, and security will be just as evident in the ecclesial realm as they are in our secular lives. In other words, individuals remain human beings created in the image of God wherever they happen to be, and thus the basic aspirations remain the same as do the God-given faculties needed to achieve those ends. This, I believe, explains the apparent correspondence between the secular world of business and the sacred realm

---

23. Robichau, *Stop Climbing*, 27 of 334.

24. Robichau, *Stop Climbing*, loc. 40 of 334.

25. This individual is apparently capable and very well known in the medical technology field, has made positive contributions to the lives of many others, and certainly has the right to work in the field of his choosing.

26. Robichau, *Stop Climbing*, locs. 53–60 of 334.

of the church. The need for order, planning, etc., is no less pronounced in one than it is in the other.

So given these shared aspirations, it is easy to see why and how many secular practices make their way so easily into the church. If, for example, a secular company develops an effective tool (strategic planning) designed to meet the challenge of defining goals and allocating resources, then a church, facing the same challenge, could reasonably consider borrowing that tool to address its own needs. If the universal need for human interaction has been facilitated using social media developed outside the church, we will be likely to use that device to meet the same need within the church. If, during a government-imposed lockdown, a university turns to video conferencing in order to maintain instruction in the absence of in-person classes, then perhaps the church can use the same technology as a substitute for its in-person liturgies.

In any case, whether because of our familiarity with them, their availability, official sanction, or because they address shared challenges, the devices, technologies, and procedures of the secular world of commerce are being brought into the church. While it may seem reasonable to simply transfer the solutions to concerns we share with others, we must be aware of different sets of desires or motives fueling these shared aspirations, interests which result in very different applications and developments of the underlying human faculties. In an ecclesial setting, love, for example, will be motivated by a self-sacrificing commitment to the well-being of others and the glory of God. As a result, every attempt to impose order or provide security will be self-transcending. That, in turn, will have a pronounced effect on the devices, structures, and techniques devised to reach those ends. These tools could, for example, under no circumstances violate the dignity of others or the sanctity of creation. They could never be self-serving or dishonoring to God or alter the meaning of the church, its teachings, and its practices. In other words, tools developed in the ecclesial realm would be undergirded by certain meanings.

By way of contrast, love in a secular environment is generally focused on the self, with profit and the accumulation of wealth being the chief expression of this self-love. The tools developed to further that self-interest, to maximize profit and gain, will quite naturally assume a character or meanings that could indeed violate the dignity of others, the sanctity of the world, either ignore or offend God, and do damage to the life of the church. For that reason, it is incumbent on us to systematically evaluate the impact the use of commercial thought and practice is having in the church.

I will start by identifying prominent aspects of the commercial landscape and attempting to map them onto the corresponding needs within the church. This mapping will serve as a guide for identifying those areas of church life most notably impacted by commercial thought, as well as the specific technologies being used in those areas. There are four general challenges faced by every commercial enterprise: management, production, distribution, and consumption. These correspond roughly to administration, preparation, presentation, and participation in the church. *Management*, that is, organizing, planning, developing, offering, and distributing, is a crucial element of any business venture. Even though the church is not a business, its activities do need to be organized, overseen, and planned. These similarities and the sheer effectiveness of secular practices appear to render thinking of ecclesial activities in commercial management terms quite reasonable. However, since we believe it is God himself who animates and guides the church, we might want to stay away from the term *management*, which seems to imply we are somehow in control, the primary agents. Taking that into account, we could call this category of ecclesial activity church *administration,* or better yet, *stewardship*.

The *production* of the products to be sold is the second aspect of the commercial process. Since the church is not selling anything, we have no products to develop or produce. However, we do offer an array of services, and they have to be prepared for use. So here we could call it the *preparation* of those services. If you have products to sell, they will, of course, have to made available.

Distribution, then, is the next major focus of commercial enterprise. But again, since the church has no products, it cannot really speak of distribution. However, the services it offers do have to be made available. This process could be referred to as *presentation* and would include making these offerings known (advertising?) and providing instructions on how to use or participate in those services.

Finally, if a business is to succeed, its products will have to be bought and used, that is, consumed. The idea of *consumption* makes little sense in the absence of products. Nevertheless, the church will have to teach members and potential members how to make use of the services offered. This might be called *participation*. Obviously, I will not be able to cover every occurrence of technological transfer and some overlap between categories will be inevitable. Nevertheless, this scheme may help identify those aspects of ecclesial life that have been affected the most.

Finally, let me remind the reader my goal here is not some kind of primer on commerce; it is rather, on the one hand, an inquiry into the degree to which the church has itself become involved in commerce and whether or not it has been damaged by that participation, and, on the other hand, an effort to extrapolate principles that may have and could again protect the church from such damage.

Table 1 Commerce in the Church			
Secular World	Church	Ministry Area	Imported Tools
Management	Administration	Planning	Strategic Planning
		Finances	Digital Giving
		Legal	Incorporation
		Record Keeping	Software
Production	Preparation	Clergy	Educational Structures
		Liturgical Services	Online Resources
		Physical Plant	Architectural Expertise
Distribution	Presentation	Publicity	Advertising
		Education	Church School
Consumption	Participation	Liturgy/Eucharist	Online

4

Management/Administration

Our first premise is that everything done in the church, including the actions of our leaders, must be in accordance with God's will.[1]

IN THE WORLD OF commerce Frederick Winslow Taylor's *The Principles of Scientific Management* is said to have influenced almost all subsequent thinking on management.[2] According to him, "The principal object of management should be to secure the maximum prosperity for the employer, coupled with the maximum prosperity for each employee."[3] After bemoaning the fact that early-twentieth-century American industry was suffering from defective systems of management and rampant inefficiency, he concludes the next generation will have four essential tasks:

1. To develop a science for each element of a man's work;
2. to scientifically select and then train, teach, and develop the workman;
3. to heartily cooperate with the workmen so as to insure all of the work being done in accordance with the principles of the science which has been developed;

---

1. Danilchick, *Thy Will Be Done*, loc. 333 of 6469.
2. Note the similarities in the recent Blanchard and Woren, *New One Minute Manager*.
3. Taylor, *Principles of Scientific Management*, 4.

4. to take over that work for which they are better fitted than the workmen.⁴

Thus conceived, "all of the planning which under the old system was done by the workman, as a result of his personal experience, must of necessity under the new system be done by the management in accordance with the laws of the science."⁵ This planning will include a series of related activities: defining mission and strategy and coordinating efforts to accomplish those goals by marshaling available resources, such as financial, natural, technological, and human resources.

In the context of the church, we should, as mentioned above, avoid the term "management" as it places undo emphasis on human agency apart from the work of God. Instead I have considered using the word *stewardship* to express a synergy created by the faithful overseeing, with divine help, of the use of the gifts (tools) given to the church by God. However, not everything we do in the church is simply a matter of oversight. Certain aspects of the life of the church have to be actively managed and creatively planned. For that reason, it might be better to use the term *administration* as it allows us to recognize that even though we in the church will have to respond to some of the same challenges faced by secular organizations, and even though we may occasionally make ecclesial use of their devices and methods, we will still need to avoid the implication of exclusive control associated with the term *management*. We do not, for example, manage a divine liturgy, but we do preside over it. We do not strategically plan our liturgical cycle, but we do organize it according to the rubrics we have received. We do not engage in "Customer Relationship Management"⁶ in order to drive up loyalty, but we do teach about the nature and importance of commitment. We do not evaluate our work using "Benchmarking"⁷ or "Balance Scorecard"⁸ techniques, but we do measure ourselves in the light

---

4. Taylor, *Principles of Scientific Management*, 26.

5. Taylor, *Principles of Scientific Management*, 27.

6. "Customer Relationship Management (CRM) is a process companies use to understand their customer groups and respond quickly—and at times, instantly—to shifting customer desires. CRM technology allows firms to collect and manage large amounts of customer data and then carry out strategies based on that information" (Rigby, *Management Tools 2015*, 26).

7. "Benchmarking improves performance by identifying and applying best demonstrated practices to operations and sales. Managers compare the performance of their products or processes externally with those of competitors and best-in-class companies, and internally with other operations that perform similar activities in their own firms" (Rigby, *Management Tools 2015*, 14).

8. "A Balanced Scorecard defines an organization's performance and measures

of divine commandments. Notwithstanding that distinction, some of what takes place in the church does have to be planned, organized, and managed. Moreover, given our familiarity with and the availability of apparently effective commercial mechanisms, we are probably going to be making use of tools developed in the business world. Because these devices and methods could bring implications, meanings, and consequences that could damage the church, we really do need to evaluate the practice. Obviously, we cannot examine every management tool being used in or by the church. However, we could look at the direct use of one business practice, strategic planning, which is being widely used in the church today. We could also look at several areas in which the church makes indirect use of secular practices by seeking professional help with financial matters, legal issues, and record keeping. While this approach is somewhat limited, it will provide insight into the issues and dangers involved in using these devices in the church, and it will highlight the kinds of questions we need to be asking ourselves about their use.

PLANNING

In order to achieve their commercial ends, business leaders have developed an impressive array of management tools. One of the most well-known of these is the now-ubiquitous practice of strategic planning. Indeed, business-related literature is full of

> coverage on the topic of strategic planning. Every nuance, every variance, every view, and every possible issue associated with strategic planning—purposes, definitions, methods, and implementation—are covered in seemingly endless ways and detail.[9]

Annual surveys conducted by Bain & Company consistently point to the predominance of strategic planning.[10] Describing the tool, Bain's 2017 summary states "strategic planning is a comprehensive process for determining what a business should become and how it can best achieve that goal."[11] It offers managers a systematic process for asking and answering the most critical questions facing their businesses. The actual procedure will, of

---

whether management is achieving desired results. The Balanced Scorecard translates Mission and Vision Statements into a comprehensive set of objectives and performance measures that can be quantified and appraised" (Rigby, *Management Tools 2015*, 12).

9. Young, "Perspectives on Strategic Planning," 1.
10. See Rigby and Bilodeau, "Management Tools & Trends."
11. Rigby and Bilodeau, "Management Tools & Trends," para. 4.

course, differ from business to business, but it will inevitably include: describing the organization's mission, vision and fundamental values; targeting potential markets; analyzing the company's strengths and weaknesses;[12] developing strategies; allocating resources; and monitoring performance.[13] According to Bain, companies use this tool in order to predict and respond to market changes, and, most importantly, to increase confidence in the business's direction.[14] Part of the device's usefulness is it seems to alleviate some of the anxiety associated with the unpredictability of the future and gives us the impression we are in control of at least some of it.[15]

This promise of predictability, precision, and security may help explain its popularity, and there can be no doubt its application in the business and institutional worlds has been extraordinarily successful. Perhaps it is the commercial effectiveness and the ready availability of this tool that have piqued the interest of so many in the church, many who are now hoping it will give them a way of exerting some measure of control over the fluid life of the church.[16] Indeed, strategic planning is now being openly and enthusiastically used by the church at both the national and local levels. For example, strategic planning is being promoted by the Orthodox Church in America,[17] the Greek Orthodox Metropolis of Atlanta,[18] the Ukrainian

---

12. Sometimes a SWOT exercise is used. This is an aspect of strategic planning whereby an organization's Strengths and Weaknesses, Opportunities and Threats are assessed.

13. Rigby, *Management Tools 2015*, 54.

14. Rigby, *Management Tools 2015*, 54–55.

15. Martin, "Big Lie of Strategic Planning," 1.

16. Looking at the dates of ecclesial examples of the use of this tool in the orthodox world, we might speak of a "rage to strategize" that spans the last two or three decades.

17. "As the Body of Christ, the Orthodox Church in America is committed to bringing the Gospel to all the people of North America–embracing all languages, cultures and races. This is Christ's commandment to 'Go into all the world and make disciples of all nations, baptizing them in the Name of the Father, and of the Son, and of the Holy Spirit, teaching them to observe all things that [He has commanded us]' (Matt. 28:19–20). This Strategic Plan for the Orthodox Church in America is a guide to help the Church in better fulfilling this mission in North America" ("Strategic Plan for the Orthodox Church in America," 4).

18. "Holy Scripture teaches us that 'Where there is no vision, the people will perish.' (Proverbs 29:18) It is in that spirit, that I am pleased to present to you a new and exciting vision for our Holy Metropolis and its Parishes. For over a year, a dedicated group of faithful that reflect the great and rich diversity of our Metropolis and Archdiocese have diligently toiled together to identify such a vision. It is a vision that reflects on our significant challenges, and yet is motivated by our great and holy opportunities to serve our Lord in his vineyard here in the beautiful Southeastern United States. After a wonderful and enormous effort, we are honored to present this Strategic Plan to you. It's primary focus and purpose is to strengthen our Parishes and parishioners. We have

Orthodox Church in the USA,[19] and St. John the Divine Greek Orthodox Parish.[20] There is even a specifically orthodox book on the topic by Peter M. Danilchick, *Thy Will Be Done: Strategic Leadership, Planning, and Management for Christians*. The book seeks to enable the reader to "understand the fundamental goal of Christian *strategic leadership*."[21] It "outlines a specific

---

fully researched and identified a comprehensive step-by-step process and action plan to achieve 34 very critical and strategic goals. We have also recruited an incredibly capable team from throughout our Metropolis to achieve these important goals" ("Strategic Plan for the Greek Orthodox Metropolis of Atlanta," 3).

19. "Holy Scripture admonishes us that 'Where there is no vision, the people will perish.' (Proverbs 29:18) With that powerful guidance, we are pleased to present to you a new and exciting vision for our Holy Ukrainian Orthodox Church of the USA (UOC of USA) and its Parishes. A faithful and devoted group of your peers that reflect the great and rich diversity of our Church have diligently toiled together for over a year to identify such a vision. With the prayerful guidance of the Holy Spirit, we pursued a strategy that acknowledges our significant challenges yet focuses on our many blessings and opportunities to serve our Lord in His Vineyard here in the United States. After an invigorating and comprehensive effort, we are honored to present this Strategic Plan to you. Its primary focus and purpose are to strengthen our Parishes and parishioners. We fully researched our challenges and weaknesses and identified a comprehensive step-by-step process and action plan to achieve 25 very critical and strategic goals. We have also recruited an incredibly capable team from the membership of our UOC of USA to achieve these important goals" ("Strategic Plan for Ukrainian Orthodox Church in the USA," 2).

20. "The Mission of St. John The Divine is to proclaim the Holy Gospel by teaching and spreading the Orthodox Christian Faith in a dynamic and welcoming community devoted to serving all people who seek a growing relationship with Jesus Christ. . .St. John the Divine will be a SPARK that proclaims and witnesses the Good News of Jesus Christ and the Orthodox Church by: Serving, Praying, Accepting, Relating, Knowing" ("GPS," 4).

21. Emphasis mine. Note the change in the expression. This shift to strategic leadership illustrates the fact that the overall concept has undergone considerable development in the last few decades. "Over the years, the practice of strategy has evolved through five phases (each phase generally involved the perceived failure of the previous phase): 1. Basic Financial Planning (Budgeting), 2. Long-range Planning (Extrapolation), 3. Strategic (Externally Oriented), Planning, 4. Strategic Management, 5. Complex Systems Strategy: Complex Static Systems or Emergence and Complex Dynamic Systems or Strategic Balance" ("Strategic Management," 1). The reason for this evolution of the concept was that "experience with strategic planning led to mixed results. In a minority of firms, strategic planning restored their profitability and became an established part of the management process. However, a substantial majority encountered a phenomenon, which was named "paralysis by analysis": strategic plans were made but remained unimplemented, and profits/growth continued to stagnate" ("Strategic Management," 6–7). In 1972, Ansoff developed the concept of strategic management in which he asserted "the importance of strategic planning as a major pillar of strategic management but added a second pillar—the capability of a firm to convert written plans into market reality. The third pillar—the skill in managing resistance to change—was to be added in the 1980s" ("Strategic Management," 7).

process for strategic planning that can be used in personal, Church, community, and corporate situations," and "provides specific Christian leadership guidance and principles synthesized from Scripture, the writings of the church fathers, and Church tradition as well as practical experience gained by the author over more than four decades."[22]

In any case, it is rather obvious this tool is being brought into the church. However, what is not as obvious is whether or not there has been any serious discussion or even awareness of the limitations and potential dangers of using this tool in the church. Although, as if anticipating this question, all of the strategic studies mentioned above do try to put the activity on a biblical or spiritual footing and to qualify or even limit its use. The OCA plan, for example, begins with the words

> This Strategic Plan does not reflect traditional corporate strategic plans with numbers, statistics, membership numbers or budgets. The church is not an institution. It is a sacramental mystery that unites us to Christ to transform our lives and by our witness to transform those around us. It is this inner spiritual transformation and the resulting efforts to reach out to others that are the focus of this Plan. If we follow Christ in this, then everything will follow[23]

The plan developed by the Greek Orthodox Metropolis of Atlanta shows an awareness of the danger and expresses the hope that "This comprehensive Strategic Plan will help all of us manage the 'business' of our Parishes without turning our Parishes into a 'business.'"[24]

So much to their credit, the framers of these documents appear to be aware of the secular meanings associated with strategic planning. It is, as I see it, nothing short of an acknowledgment that these meanings could be problematic, that they might not be appropriate in an ecclesial setting, and that they could lead to faulty decisions and even damage the church. But alas, that seems to be the only indication of any serious discussion of how this technology will be used in the church. In general, church leaders apply the tool with the same enthusiasm and in much the same way as their secular business-world counterparts. While I do not want to in any way disparage the well-intentioned work of so many faithful individuals, I would like to take a closer look at the ecclesial use of this device by asking several questions: 1) Are there any presuppositions or underlying principles associated with this tool that are not consistent with theological underpinnings of

---

22. Danilchick, *Thy Will Be Done*, locs. 68 of 6469.
23. "Strategic Plan for the Orthodox Church in America," 5.
24. "Strategic Plan for the Greek Orthodox Metropolis of Atlanta," 6.

our faith? If so, what are they? 2) Have the meanings, weaknesses, and limitations inherent in this device damaged or changed the nature or practice of the church? 3) Are there acceptable alternatives or principles that could help us meet the administrative needs of the church without subjecting ourselves to possible harm?

1) Presuppositions. Although it is, no doubt, an oversimplification, strategic planning is built on two basic premises.[25] In order to be successful, leaders need to develop and implement a strategy that a) *defines* the vision, mission, values, tasks, and outcomes of their organizations, and b) takes *control* by anticipating future developments, allocating resources, and meeting constituents' needs, thus facilitating the desired outcomes. The implication here seems to be that by using our rational faculties, our reductionistic mode of thinking, and our own resources, we can control the process and achieve whatever objectives we have defined. So how do these foundational presuppositions line up with Christian teaching?

The presuppositions associated with these premises become apparent during the initial stages of the strategic planning process. After some consideration of preliminary issues[26] such as engaging leadership, motivating stakeholders, etc., the planning itself actually begins an attempt to define a *mission*, which is essentially "an expression of strategic intent."[27] This is followed by an articulation of a *vision,* which "provides a picture of what the mission will look like as it is realized in the life of the community."[28] Next, strategic planners move on to the question "why is this being done?" by establishing a set of *values* which "speak to what is most important in the life of an organization."[29] This leads to a statement of desired *outcomes*, that is, setting immediate and long-term goals,[30] including a list of *tasks* or the specific action steps needed to achieve the goals. This answers the question of how we intend to accomplish our goals. It usually results in a formal

---

25. "Strategic planning. . . is based on the premise that leaders and managers of public and nonprofit organizations must be effective strategists if their organizations are to fulfill their missions, meet their mandates, and satisfy constituents in the years ahead" (Bryson, cited in Young, "Perspectives on Strategic Planning," 1.

26. Allison and Kaye, *Strategic Planning for Nonprofit Organizations*, 29–58.

27. Malphurs, *Advanced Strategic Planning*, 107.

28. Malphurs, *Advanced Strategic Planning*, 128.

29. Malphurs, *Advanced Strategic Planning*, 146.

30. "The planning, monitoring, and evaluation of an organization's strategies and plans is known in many circles as Results Based Management. On the positive side, this type of management system has constant feedback built in so that organizational leaders can continuously learn and improve its plans and strategies" ("Process of Developing," para. 1).

document, which summarizes the results of these initial steps and also provides the details for a plan of implementation.[31]

In most cases a significant amount of time, expense, and resources will have to be invested in the effort to produce such a strategic plan. In some cases, it is done by a committee of localized individuals. In other cases, the committee members are broken up into task forces scattered all over the country and contribute their ideas by email, phone, Skype, etc. Often, the process involves a number of exercises or activities or techniques. For example, in a *top-down* model, owners or CEOs write and present it to their team. But it could also be done *face to face* around the table together, debating each word and nuance. It might take the form of a *round-robin* gathering. After much discussion, an editor circulates a draft for comment, with the owners or CEO having the last word. Or it could even take place in a retreat-like atmosphere with participants *away from the office,* key players seeking a consensus at an inspiring place. In addition to these physical arrangements, a whole host of discussion schematics can be used, such as the *snowflake exercise,* during which all ideas produced by the group are pinned to the wall on small pieces of paper, dropped to the floor when they are rejected, leaving the accepted ideas to serve as the basis for a vision/mission statement.

The strategic plans of the national churches mentioned above all followed this general procedure. In the OCA, for example, work began in July of 2009 when the "Strategic Planning Committee" met for the first time.[32] It then reached out into the broader church for input from a variety of sources, including: The Holy Synod, the Metropolitan Council, Department Heads, Diocesan Assemblies, theological schools, working groups established for each of the stated goals, and workshops at the 16th All-American Council (2011).[33] So after several years of input, a draft of the strategic plan was finally presented to the All-American Council, where it was discussed, revised, and adopted as the comprehensive action plan of action for the next decade. By January 2012, full implementation teams were to be in place. By the spring of 2012, the Metropolitan Council was to receive a detailed plan for implementation, a budget, and a funding strategy for each goal.[34]

---

31. "An effective operating plan states the strategic goal to be addressed, clearly breaks out the activities or action steps required to accomplish the goal, establishes time frames and who is responsible" (Allison and Kaye, *Strategic Planning for Nonprofit Organizations,* 215).

32. "OCA Strategic Planning Committee Holds First Meeting," para. 1.

33. See "Strategic Planning Workshop #1."

34. See "Minutes of the Joint Meeting."

Obviously, the OCA, like the Greek and the Ukrainian Churches, spent a great deal of time, money, and other resources in multiyear efforts to define the vision, mission, values, tasks, and outcomes of its respective national strategic plans. In other words, it took years just to get to the point of concrete action and implementation. For national organizations with members and institutions spread all over the country, this costly and lengthy procedure might be expected or even necessary, but is that same investment of time and resources needed when using this tool in a local parish?

Using the example of St. John the Divine Greek Orthodox Parish cited above, we see the same basic pattern does, in fact, apply to local parishes. Although their documents do not indicate how much time was spent, the care and detail that went into producing the materials used to present the process to the parish are impressive and must have involved a considerable investment. In the case of St. John's, we see they used some of the ideas and handouts developed though Bill Marianes's ministry "Stewardship Calling."[35] While the tools used in this program of parish development are by no means limited to strategic planning, that particular tool does play an important role, and its use mirrors the significant commitment of time and resources we have been observing at the national level. In particular, it envisions the process taking place in six steps: an initial planning retreat (SWOT, Why, Mission, Vision, Core Values, Strategic Areas of Focus); strategic task force conference calls; a second planning retreat (finalize Strategic SMART Goals and detailed action plans); presentation of an initial plan to the whole community; writing and communicating the finalized strategic plan; and the implementation of the strategic plan.[36]

Again, we see that even in a local setting it takes a significant investment of time and resources to define the vision, mission, values, tasks, and outcomes of a strategic plan before getting to the point where it can begin to be implemented. It is clear, then, that the fundamental presuppositions of strategic planning have had a profound, practical, and quite costly effect on the life and work of the churches. These believers seem to be convinced that before making any attempt to fulfill their mission to the world, they first have to take the time, sometimes years, to carefully define that mission, secure the necessary resources, and assure certain results. So does this

---

35. Bill Marianes is a partner in the Atlanta office of a 900-plus-lawyer international law firm and practices in the areas of corporate law, mergers and acquisitions, intellectual property, business succession planning, and church matters, and for the past 35 years has been working with individual church communities, clergy, and faithful to better understand and implement true stewardship in their Parishes and lives. He has a blog at Ancient Faith. See Marianes, "It's Not about Me," paras. 7–10

36. See Marianes, "Igniting the Flame."

enormous expenditure actually lead to valid definitions that, in turn, give control, thus facilitating the desired outcomes?

As I see it, orthodox theology makes it clear that we created beings are not in need of, authorized to, or even capable of (re)defining the divine givens of ecclesial life (mission, vision, values, outcomes). Furthermore, trying to do so does not give us the control we hope for. I say we do not need to define mission, vision, tasks, and outcomes of the church because the church is an entity created by God, and as such it is not member-defined but has already been defined at the time of its inception. Actually, the essence of the church, what it is, had been established in the mind of God even before it was created. For that reason, we can say the church is brought into existence with its key attributes, that is, its nature, identity, purpose, and responsibilities are already determined. Fortunately, these basic elements of ecclesial life have been clearly spelled out for us in the Scriptures. We are told the church established by Christ at the mystical supper (Mattt 26:26–29) was actualized on the day of Pentecost (Acts 2:46) when the disciples celebrated the first Eucharist.[37] For that reason, we say it is the gathering of the faithful for the purpose of worship and Eucharist. This eucharistic community is the church. Thus, defined or constituted, you might expect the church's mission, vision, values, and outcomes to grow naturally out of its nature as a eucharistic community. Indeed, Jesus specifically commands the apostles to take the message of his coming kingdom into the whole world (Matt 28:19–20), presupposing the presence of a eucharistic community from which this mission emanates and into which the new believers are incorporated, in which the sacraments the disciples were told to work toward bring others to the point of personal faith in Christ, and then make baptism, ongoing teaching, and the whole sacramental context of the church available to them. Based on these Scriptures we can say the *mission* (strategic intent) of the church is to make disciples. Its *vision* (its mission realized) is the eucharistic community. The basic *values* (why this is being done) are obedience to God and love of neighbor. The *outcomes* can be thought of in terms of new disciples added to existing and newly formed communities. Finally, the *tasks* are proclamation, baptism, providing the sacraments, and teaching.

So we do not need to redefine what has already been given, but even if we wanted to, we are not authorized to do so because that would amount to a human redefinition of something divinely given. This, I submit, would also violate the orthodox understanding of what Tradition is and how it works. St. Paul urges us to hold fast to (not redefine but preserve) the traditions they had received (2 Thess 2:15). The idea is based on three particular

---

37. Afanasiev and Plekon, *Church of the Holy Spirit*, 1.

words: that which has been *received* from the Lord (1 Cor 11:23); that which the apostles (and their successors) have *given* (1 Cor 11:23); and that which is to be *kept* just as it has been delivered to you (1 Cor 11:2; see also 1 Cor 15:1–3 and 2 Tim 2:2). So not only do we not need to (re)define our mission, values, etc., but we are not meant to do that. We are, however, tasked with guarding, that is, not changing, our common inheritance. "The apostle hands down the doctrine of faith to the churches where it must be kept unharmed through the succession and continuance (*diadoche*) of individuals entrusted with the guarding of the doctrine."[38]

Moreover, even if we invest time and resources in (re)definition, which is not necessary in the first place, it does not render us capable of *independently controlling* future developments and facilitating outcomes. The idea that we have control over our lives violates our understanding of the relationship between divine providence and human agency. Because the world was created by God out of nothing, it has a positive power, divinity, as its foundation. As such it is indestructible (Ps 93:1)[39] and its continued existence, its preservation, is already given in creation. However, God's relation to the world is not exhausted by his calling it into being. His continued guidance is necessary, and it is God's constant intervention that actually controls and facilitates future outcomes. Yet because human beings still have an albeit-limited free will, the nature of God's dealings with the world are of necessity a kind of interaction, or *synergism*:

> Divine providence does not destroy human freedom but responds to it, acting with absolute wisdom. *God cooperates with creatures according to an infallible purposiveness, while preserving their freedom.* The principle of *synergism* signifies that creatures are never deprived of the protection of divine providence, whatever may be their proper self-determinations, toward good or toward evil. The synergism here is a mutual self-determination that has an element of novelty, actualized in different modes for the two sides in the interaction.[40]

---

38. Afanasiev and Plekon, *Church of the Holy Spirit*, 242.

39. "This positive foundation gives indestructibility to the world: 'The world also is stablished, that it cannot be moved' (Ps. 93:1). God's creative words, with the blessing 'let there be,' resound for all God's creative words, with the blessing 'let there be,' resound for all times in the universe. The world was created once, but the creative act continues supra-temporally and all-temporally: 'My Father worketh hitherto, and I work' (John 5:17). In this sense, the preservation of the world's being with its indestructibility is already included in the creation of the world and does not require a special providence for itself" (Bulgakov, *Bride of the Lamb*, 193).

40. Bulgakov, *Bride of the Lamb*, 239 (emphasis in the second sentence is original; emphasis on "synergism" is mine).

Providence is not the imposition of extracreational force but rather a kind of interaction that takes place within the world, according to its God-given laws. "God answers the needs of creation with absolute infallibility and purposefulness while preserving freedom within the limits of the world's entelechy."[41] Strategic planning, then, cannot be seen as creating or defining the givens of this world but rather as an acknowledgment of and a submission to divinely mandated givens, coupled with a humble effort to participate in, not dictate, the fulfilling of God's plans for the world. This we do using whatever means are at our disposal, while always remaining aware of the necessity of and determinateness of divine involvement.

2) Damage Assessment. With its widespread use of strategic planning, the church has uncritically adopted a set of practices based on principles that are at odds with its own teaching. Moreover, in spite of its popularity, it almost never delivers the anticipated benefits. It is in the light of this disconnect, or rather this context of contradiction, that some of the potential dangers to the church become apparent.

First, the widely recognized problem of nonimplementation means in many cases a great deal of time and money is wasted. Even in the business world, strategic planning seldom brings an adequate return on the investments made, and even when a coherent plan does emerge, it often remains unimplemented, simply abandoned in light of unanticipated changes. In tracing the history and development of strategic management, Vijaykumar Bhatia points out

> Strategic planning was initially accepted as a plausible invention and received an enthusiastic reception from the business community. But subsequent experience with strategic planning led to mixed results. In a minority of firms, strategic planning restored their profitability and became an established part of the management process. However, a substantial majority encountered a phenomenon, which was named "paralysis by analysis": strategic plans were made but remained unimplemented, and profits/growth continued to stagnate.[42]

It is obvious the strategic planning initiatives undertaken by the ecclesial bodies cited above have involved years of effort by hundreds of people consuming untold financial resources. But if you talk with the participants of those programs, they will tell you it was a mostly "fruitless endeavor" because "nothing has changed," and "the plan has simply not

---

41. Bulgakov, *Bride of the Lamb*, 233.
42. "Strategic Management," 6–7.

been implemented."[43] A number of years ago, a local pastor participated in a church growth seminar[44] put on by the national church. He came back enthused and full of ideas, chief among them was the need for strategic planning. Accordingly, he assembled a working group of parishioners (of which I was a member), and we spent weeks and weeks trying to hammer out vison and mission statements using all of the above-mentioned techniques. In the end it proved to be a colossal waste of time and even caused dissention and discord in the parish since we could not even agree on the basics. In this we were not alone. I have heard the same thing from others who were involved at the national, diocesan, and parish levels. Lots of time is spent making plans that were not or could not even be implemented. Nothing changed!

Now, in the case of a giant corporation with almost unlimited resources, such a waste might be more easily absorbed. Investing its own surplus profit in such a venture might even be seen as a risk worth taking especially if there is the promise of increased earnings. In any case, given adequate assets, the planning project would probably not keep the company from doing all the other things it is supposed to do. So while this waste of effort might tweak the bottom line, the exercise in strategic planning will not do any permanent damage to the company, and it will certainly not change its basic nature.

However, in a local parish, and even in a national church organization, both funds and personnel are strictly limited. This raises the question of sound stewardship. The resources invested in strategic planning are not owned or earned by the church and its members but rather are freely given by God and are to be used to implement divine, not human, goals. The faithful are called to be good stewards of the resources given to them. It follows then that anything that wastes these resources and prevents the church from fulfilling its God-given tasks would have to be considered damaging to the church.

This points to another danger posed by the uncritical use of strategic planning in the church: a loss of focus. What is so tragic about this waste is resources are expended in order to redefine what has already been given to the church. To their credit the framers of the OCA's strategic plan do specifically mention Jesus' statement of the mission at the very beginning of their report, citing Matthew 28:19–20. The Greek plan begins by declaring

---

43. I report this on the basis of an interview with a member of the OCA's Metropolitan Council (May 2018).

44. See "AAC Delegates Pass Funding Resolution," and Simerick, "New Era of Evangelistic Fervor."

its intention of welcoming "all people seeking salvation, love, truth and fulfillment,"[45] and the Ukrainian statement indicates its desire to "embrace those who hunger for love, comfort, fulfillment and hope."[46] All three cite Jesus' words of commission, and one would think this by itself would narrow or limit the desired outcomes of such plans to the results of implementing the twin tasks of making disciples by baptizing and teaching. However, in spite of these direct and indirect acknowledgments of the mission defined by Christ, that awareness does not translate into concrete evidence that the mission, values, and tasks envisioned by Jesus have been prioritized. Judging by their own lists of "top goals," these planners envision a "diversification" of activity that includes almost every imaginable aspect of contemporary ecclesial life and practice.[47] They include things like empirical metrics, skills matching, comprehensive communications platforms, and cohesive branding, things that go way beyond and have little to do with fulfilling Christ's commission. Moreover, these diverse goals multiply and become so numerous that the church, standing before this veritable mountain of tasks, doesn't know where to begin and so often does nothing as a result. Interestingly, both the Greek and Ukrainian plans mentioned above state the commission Jesus "gave his apostles *[is] a clear strategic plan* as to how they were to achieve his vision."[48] If the biblical text already provides a vision, spells out its goals, and specifies tasks, then why are they wasting time and losing their focus in a costly effort to (re)define what has already been defined?

This brings us to another danger, namely, by using this tool we create the impression of security and of control but only the illusion of control. Actually, we fall into a dangerous trap recognized even in the business world. In his brief article, *The Big Lie of Strategic Planning*, Roger L. Martin notes

45. "Strategic Plan for the Greek Orthodox Metropolis of Atlanta," 3.

46. "Strategic Plan for Ukrainian Orthodox Church in the USA," 2.

47. The following list of goals is found in the Strategic Plan of the Ukrainian Church and is similar to what is found in all the plans cited above: "1. Administration: Empirical Metrics, Skills Matching, Operational and Personnel Needs. 2. Clergy: Clergy Development Program, Clergy Compensation and Wellness, U.S. Clergy Recruitment. 3. Communications: Welcoming Ministry, Comprehensive Communications Platform, Cohesive Brand. 4. Education: Orthodox Education Lifelong Learning Program, Orthodox Leadership Development Program. 5. Family & Youth: Family Lifecycle Program, College Student Outreach Program, Adolescent Outreach Program. 6. Healthy Parishes: Healthy Parishes Program, Caring Ministry Program. 7. Outreach and Evangelism: Outreach & Evangelism Ministry, New Successful Mission Parishes, Philanthropic Outreach" (UOC of USA, "Strategic Plan for Ukrainian Orthodox Church in the USA," 14).

48. OCA, "Strategic Plan for the Orthodox Church in America," 10 (emphasis original); UOC of USA, "Strategic Plan for Ukrainian Orthodox Church in the USA," 6.

> All executives know that strategy is important. But almost all also find it scary, because it forces them to confront a future they can only guess at. Worse, actually choosing a strategy entails making decisions that explicitly cut off possibilities and options. An executive may well fear that getting those decisions wrong will wreck his or her career.
>
> The natural reaction is to make the challenge less daunting by turning it into a problem that can be solved with tried and tested tools. That nearly always means spending weeks or even months preparing a comprehensive plan for how the company will invest in existing and new assets and capabilities in order to achieve a target—an increased share of the market, say, or a share in some new one. The plan is typically supported with detailed spreadsheets that project costs and revenue quite far into the future. By the end of the process, everyone feels a lot less scared.
>
> This is a truly terrible way to make strategy. It may be an excellent way to cope with fear of the unknown, but fear and discomfort are an essential part of strategy making. In fact, if you are entirely comfortable with your strategy, there's a strong chance it isn't very good.[49]

Like so many in the secular world, church leaders are tempted to insulate themselves and their ministries from the unknowable aspects of an ever-changing world by seeking some degree of control over future outcomes. We want to alleviate our anxiety and make ourselves feel better by creating our own zones of comfort outside the providence of God. But this selfish and perhaps arrogant desire to do it ourselves weakens our faith in God's involvement and obviates the guidance, equipping, and empowering of the Holy Spirit. If we, in keeping with the operating principles of the contemporary social imaginary, claim for ourselves the freedom to define our mission, the unfettered ability to use our rational ability to solve challenges we face, and make use of the supposed neutrality of all technologies and resources, then what need is there of divine assistance? Here there is no synergy but rather human beings defining, planning, and executing that strategy on their own and for their own benefit. In another place[50] I have suggested this amounts to shifting the mode of ecclesial life from *being* church to *doing* church and that shift is damaging the very foundations of our faith.

---

49. Martin, "Big Lie of Strategic Planning," 1.
50. See Rommen, *Being the Church*.

3) An Alternative: Dynamic Discernment. I believe, then, that the uncritical use of this business tool, strategic planning, has damaged the church and is actually preventing the church from fulfilling its mission in the world. This tool developed in the business world is not neutral, and it cannot be transferred directly to the nonbusiness environment of the church. We do need to rearticulate, develop, and implement the mission we have been given, but, given the nature of that mission, we need planning procedures of a fundamentally different character. Again, to their credit, the faithful who developed the plans referred to above recognize and try to express this sentiment. The Greek and Ukrainian models state "strategic planning is first and foremost Biblical and Christ-centered."[51] That, of course, is not quite true. This device is not biblical, it is commercial, but I suppose what they are trying to express is their desire to be biblical and Christ-centered in whatever it is they are going to do. The OCA plan makes a much stronger point by observing thusly:

> The church is not an institution. It is a sacramental mystery that unites us to Christ to transform our lives and by our witness to transform those around us. It is this inner spiritual transformation and the resulting efforts to reach out to others that are the focus of this Plan. If we follow Christ in this, then everything will follow.[52]

That is probably why they feel compelled to qualify their work. "This Strategic Plan does not reflect traditional corporate strategic plans with numbers, statistics, membership numbers or budgets."[53] And yet, as these plans unfold, they adhere, almost to the letter, to common business procedures. Everything from the executive summaries, to the basic sequence of topics/questions, to the techniques used to gather input are standard business practice. They reflect little or nothing of the exegetical, theological, and historical treasures of orthodox tradition. We can clearly see the hand of business executives, lawyers, and financiers, but what marks have the biblical scholars, theologians, and canon law experts left on these reports? So while these ecclesial planners indicate an awareness of the factors and sources that define Christian content, there is little evidence of anything other than a passing nod of acknowledgment. They say one thing and do another. Perhaps they feel this business tool is neutral, that it is the most effective or even the only option. Perhaps they are unaware of viable alternatives.

51. OCA, "Strategic Plan for the Orthodox Church in America," 10; UOC of USA, "Strategic Plan for Ukrainian Orthodox Church in the USA," 6.
52. OCA, "Strategic Plan for the Orthodox Church in America," 5.
53. OCA, "Strategic Plan for the Orthodox Church in America," 5.

Or perhaps they just uncritically do in the church what they do every day at their secular places of work.

So is there a truly biblical and Christ-centered way of implementing the church's mission? I believe there is, and, for lack of a better designation, I will call it *Dynamic Discernment*. This approach is based on the conviction that to effectively fulfill its mission in the world, the church will have to intentionally participate in God's constantly evolving strategy which will be a) *established* on the unchanging givens (mission, vision, values, tasks) provided by God, b) *structured* applying the charismatic resources and abilities given by the Holy Spirit, and c) *directed* by the continual guidance of the Holy Spirit.

Mission is *established* on unchanging givens. In the New Testament we are told Christ is the author and the finisher of our faith (Heb 12:2). One of the implications is his life, practice, and teaching collectively constitute the initial definition of the divine mission in the world. At the end of his earthly ministry, Christ transferred everything the church needed to continue his work to his apostles. That included all his teaching, commandments, and instructions for the practice of the faith, most of which are preserved in the New Testament and the tradition of the early church. So the obvious way to articulate our understanding of this divine strategy is to distill the givens (mission, vision, values, tasks) from these sources. This, of course, cannot be done using methodologies that assume it is the participants who establish these givens. In the church we begin with the notion that Christ alone defines these goals and values. For that reason, we begin our journey, not with the top-down, face-to-face, round-robin, or snowflake exercises of the business world, but with exegetical studies, theological and historical reflection designed to help us discern, not define, the givens.

This initial deposit was not a static collection of doctrines and rubrics but rather a living, dynamic baseline for engaging the world under the guidance of the Holy Spirit. We see this at work in the Jerusalem Council (Acts 15). The decisions of the council made with the help of the Holy Spirit were added to the apostolic deposit. Therefore, we have the possibility particularizing but not altering the baseline. Anything that is added will be the church's Spirit-guided attempt to address changes in its encounter with the world, but it will in every case conform to the original deposit. So over time this deposit developed, became, and continues to become what we call the collective consciousness or mind of the church. In this sense the process is a dynamic and active reality, synergistically enacted by God and his people in the church.

Mission is *structured* by charismatic resources. In addition to establishing this baseline of departure, the Holy Spirit equips the believers for ministry within and outside of the church (Eph 4:12) by giving the charism or gift to perform a particular ministry to each and every member of the body (Eph 4:7). This gifting provides everything that is needed for the church to fulfill its mission in the world, but it adds nothing extraneous, nothing that is not directly related to that mission. So there is no need to import devices, techniques, and principles from the world of business and politics. The church is not a business, not a secular corporation, not a democracy, and must not be managed as if it were one. By committing themselves to a structure generated by the ministries of prophets, apostles, teachers, evangelists, and pastors (Eph 4:11), the church will have rejected an order generated by the expertise of accountants, advertisers, and executives and will have preserved its own character. So the next step on the journey will be discerning what spiritual gifts and resources have been given in a particular setting and offering them back to God for his use.

Mission is *directed* by divine guidance. Not only does God tell us what our mission is, and not only does he give us the motivation, resources, and ability to implement that plan, he also provides constant (real-time) direction as we seek to respond to an ever-changing world. By way of example, we see the Holy Spirit actively determined and directed the geographic movement of early church missionaries. Note that it is the Holy Spirit who is presented as the initiator of outreach (Acts 13:1–4). They were not doing strategic planning but rather praying together, seeking the will of God, and he answered, telling them whom to choose for the task and then later where they should go. What we see here is the selection of an area of missionary responsibility is not just a matter of sociodemographic research but an explicit instruction from the Holy Spirit. It seems every time the church moved into a new geographic area, the Spirit was there, directing and confirming the advance, validating the message of the church. You see this beginning with Jerusalem (chs. 2–7), then on to Samaria (8), Damascus (9), Caesarea (10–11), Antioch (12), and throughout the travel of St. Paul (13–28). This clearly indicates we should not simply be targeting areas we or our data-gathering sociologists deem needy, but rather asking the Holy Spirit to show us where we should be working.

Dynamic Discernment, then, means discovering and acknowledging God's own definitions as revealed in the holy Scriptures, establishing and matching God-given resources with God-defined tasks, and allowing God to direct our path and our words toward the desired outcomes. This can be done by small groups under the direction of local priests or by participants scattered across the country led by a central agency of the national church. Because this plan is dynamically evolving as the world changes around us, it is not limited to a specific time frame, or number of sessions, and it will only be completed when Christ returns.

FINANCES

In this section I will address the part of the church's finances which involves monies donated. At this point I am not concerned with questions of accounting or the expenditure of funds, just giving. In the past we have often referred to this as stewardship or tithes and offerings.[54] These gifts were brought to the church and physically offered during a divine service as an expression of faith and an act of worship. Today, that direct link between the giver and the church is being challenged, and the disconnect is being intensified as we continue to deploy ever more commercial devices and methods. The main justification for using these technologies seems to be a desire to provide the members with a more pleasant and satisfying experience by making it increasingly easy and convenient for them, especially by eliminating the need for an actual physical presence at the church. These new methods include mailed-in, direct deposit (EFT), online, credit card, and, more recently, crowd-sourced donations.

One of the first steps in this direction was the use of regular mail, sometimes in combination with special dated offering envelopes, to send money to the church. One company, for example, Church Budget Envelope & Mailing, "offers boxed sets of all Sunday, special collection or monthly collection offering envelopes for the entire year . . . Each set of envelopes are numbered and dated . . . [and] may be numbered with your current system's numbers."[55] It may seem plausible to suggest this envelope system did increase the regularity of giving and thus increase the amount given, but there is little evidence to support this. However, the practice does represent an initial step in the process of decoupling giving and worship.

Today, "60% are willing to give to their church digitally."[56] Some of this takes place by setting up regular automatic withdrawals form the giver's bank account which are then transferred (EFT)[57] directly to the parish ac-

---

54. Unfortunately, "[t]ithers make up only 10–25 percent of a normal congregation" ("Ultimate List of Online Giving Statistics," para. 4).

55. Church Budget, "Boxed Set Envelopes," para. 1.

56. "Ultimate List of Online Giving Statistics," para. 4.

57. According to the Federal Trade Commission, "Electronic banking, also known as electronic fund transfer (EFT), uses computer and electronic technology in place of checks and other paper transactions. EFTs are initiated through devices like cards or codes that let you, or those you authorize, access your account. Many financial institutions use ATM or debit cards and Personal Identification Numbers (PINs) for this purpose. Some

count. This certainly is convenient for the parishioners, and once it is set up, they never have to give it another thought, and so the act of giving fades into the background. Another digital means of giving is the online donation. According to Non-Profit Source, a marketing consulting firm, two-thirds of nonprofit agencies surveyed were accepting online donations.[58] They recommend implementing this technology because

> [g]iving your members the option of donating online or on the go is a huge benefit to your church—the more available and simpl[er] you make the giving process, the more donations you will get. This is because when you accept donations online, you give your busy and impulsive donors the speed and simplicity they need, you make it possible for them to set up recurring donations, and also your church can start to build relationships with the younger generation of donors, as younger people are more likely to donate online.[59]

A link marked "donation tools" on the Capterra page takes you to a list (with descriptions and additional links) of 159 donation management programs. One example is "easyTithe,"[60] which claims it is being used by over 15,000 churches, including a number of Orthodox parishes.[61] In many cases this type of online giving involves the use of a credit card. According to Non-Profit Source, "49% of all church giving transactions are made with a card."[62] This option is seen to be so attractive that some have suggested installing credit card readers in the church. That way you can give simply by swiping the card. In a more recent variation on this idea, online giving can now be tied into the purchases you make at other retailers. For example, one parish in Pennsylvania recently offered its members a new way to contribute.

> St Philip's is a participant in the Amazon Services LLC Associates Program, an affiliate advertising program designed to provide a means for sites to earn advertising fees by advertising and linking to amazon.com.

---

use other types of debit cards that require your signature or a scan. For example, some use radio frequency identification (RFID) or other forms of 'contactless' technology that scan your information without direct contact with you. The federal Electronic Fund Transfer Act (EFT Act) covers some electronic consumer transactions" ("Electronic Banking," 1).

58. "Ultimate List of Online Giving Statistics," 9.
59. Readings, "Online Giving," para. 2.
60. See software *easyTithe*.
61. Seven of the fourteen parishes in the Carolina Deanery of the OCA's Diocese of the South have online giving options shown on their web sites.
62. "Ultimate List of Online Giving Statistics," 1.

> If you'd like to purchase one of these books, you can click the title, if it is a link, and it will take you to that book's listing on Amazon.com. Whatever you purchase during that session on Amazon, St Philip's will get a small commission. (Your price is not affected.).[63]

This allows the member to seamlessly contribute a percentage of the purchases they were already going to make on Amazon to the parish. While this may be convenient, it does mean the church website is actually advertising for Amazon. In other words, the church is now working for Amazon, yet another member in its marketing network, which, of course, Amazon recognizes and is willing to pay for. In addition, through this association the church is actually affirming and encouraging the materialistic tendencies of its members by giving them a readily available justification for their purchases; after all, the more they buy, the more money comes to the church. Since their extravagances will now trigger fewer and less intense pangs of conscience, they will, as is Amazon's sole intention, buy even more. At the same time, this practice fundamentally changes the meaning of Christian stewardship, that is, the money that comes to the church is no longer a conscious, deliberate expression of faith but rather a mindless, painless, and unreflected byproduct of our own greed.

Now, if you don't really want Amazon present on your parish website, you can participate in a similar arrangement by joining Amazon Smile. In this case, Amazon "will donate 0.5% of the purchase price from your eligible AmazonSmile purchases . . .the purchase price is the amount paid for the item minus any rebates and excluding shipping & handling, gift-wrapping fees, taxes, or service charges."[64] This amounts to an amazing five cents on the purchase of a $10 book. Would it not be more in keeping with the church's understanding of giving for the individual to forego (sacrifice) buying the book and give the whole $10 to the church? Once again, it is obvious this is a marketing ploy offered by Amazon, under the guise of philanthropy, for the sole purpose of increasing its own profit.

Another form of this indirect giving is called "Shop with Scripts"[65] which enables you to purchase gift cards "for your everyday needs, like groceries, gas, clothing, entertainment," and in the process the church earns money on every purchase.[66] All of these devices obviously raise the level of consumer convenience, but at the same time they widen the physical,

---

63. "Fr Noah's Suggested Reading List."
64. "About AmazonSmile," para. 1.
65. "Learn More."
66. "What is Scrip?"

personal, and spiritual disconnect between the act of giving and its place in the church.

One more note on giving: not everything that comes into a parish is considered tithes and offerings. There is, for example, on the occasion of a major building project, the need to raise significant sums over and above the regular giving. These are often referred to as capital fund campaigns. These efforts "require coordination and cooperation from the organization and community. Without the support of board members, staff, and individuals within the area, a capital campaign has little to no chance of succeeding."[67] Managing these multiyear projects is no easy feat, and for that reason many parishes turn to expert fundraisers. Once again, there are all manner of companies offering hands-on help, software, or both. Here is just a small sampling: Jeffrey Byrne and Associates,[68] Averill Fundraising Solutions,[69] Aly Sterling Philanthropy,[70] Donor Search,[71] and Double the Donation.[72] These firms use a combination of the above-mentioned technologies, as well as seminars and advertising, to research and target a specific group of potential donors. This appeal can range way beyond the limit of local parish membership and include what some call crowd-sourcing.[73]

Most of the above-mentioned opportunities for online giving are offered with the conviction that tithing online increases overall donations. Some have claimed that "churches that accept tithing online increase overall donations by 32%."[74] If that is the reason given by a particular parish for using this technology, doesn't that amount to arguing that the ends justify the means (something we have shied away from in the church)? But even if giving were to increase, we still have to ask what the costs to the church are. None of the services mentioned above are free. They all involve fees on a software package, on every transaction, as well as monthly and/or yearly membership fees. So some of that increased giving is going to pay for these services. What the actual cost in dollars might be is simply a matter of a cost-benefit analysis.[75] One firm, WebServes, concluded "While software does pose challenges to its users, most of the research respondents agreed that

67. "Capital Campaigns," para. 1.
68. https://byrnepelofsky.com.
69. https://averillsolutions.com.
70. https://alysterling.com.
71. https://www.donorsearch.net/capital-campaigns-guide.
72. https://doublethedonation.com/capital-campaigns.
73. https://www.gofundme.com.
74. "Ultimate List of Online Giving Statistics," para. 4.
75. See Ahmed and Lorenz, "Understanding the Costs."

Fundraising software has mostly had a positive impact on their fundraising activities . . . ."[76] But another study showed "[t]he largest donations tend to come by wire transfers and checks, and then by cash, digital wallet, card, and finally third party platforms (in descending order)."[77] In other words, much of the giving still comes through traditional, nondigital channels. Of course, none of this can hide the fact that today overall giving to the church is down. In 2017, "Christians are giving at 2.5% of income; during the Great Depression it was 3.3%," and "37% of regular church attendees and Evangelicals don't give [any] money to church."[78] In light of these patterns, it does not seem likely that the problem is the church does not make giving convenient or monetary technologies are not modern enough, but rather the whole idea of giving-as-worship has been lost. Still, we keep trying ever-new technologies in the hope of somehow increasing giving. But this approach assumes the only issue here is the amount of money that eventually lands in the parish's coffers. If that is our perspective, then we have indeed fallen completely under the spell of commercialism and have forgotten the spiritual aspects of tithing, sacrifice, and almsgiving.

So have these giving technologies informed and changed the biblical meaning of giving? What messages come with using online giving and credit card readers? Giving has always been a part of the liturgical context. Separating it from its natural ecclesial context encourages or even requires a redefinition of this sacrificial act of worship.[79] As we know from Scripture and Tradition,

> [t]he paying of the tithe was first and foremost an act of worship, not merely a duty. When it comes to finances, we often tend to think in secular, rather than religious concepts. We owe our *money* to the bank, the credit card company, or the IRS. God, on the other hand, gets the spiritual stuff—or at least it often plays out that way. The perspective of the Mosaic Covenant was much more holistic when it came to such matters. Rather than a nagging debt to be settled over and over again, year after year, the payment of the tithe was seen to be a privilege—an act of worship, a reasonable sacrifice, a giving back to God of a portion of that which He has given to his people.[80]

---

76. "Cost-Benefit Analysis of Nonprofit Fundraising Software," para. 4.
77. Ahmed and Lorenz, "Understanding the Costs," 9.
78. "Ultimate List of Online Giving Statistics," para. 4
79. See Zell, "Trail of the Tithe."
80. Zell, "Trail of the Tithe," 3–4 (emphasis original).

It was also assumed, as mentioned above, this act of worship, tithing, would take place in a special, sacred space. In other words, the act of a believer bringing an offering to God presupposes a special place of God's particular presence. We see this clearly taught in the Old Testament. For example, in Deuteronomy 12:5–6 we read

> [b]ut you shall seek the place where the Lord your God chooses, out of all your tribes, to put his name for his dwelling place; and there you shall go. There you shall take your burnt offerings, your sacrifices, your tithes, the heave offerings of your hand, your vowed offerings, your freewill offerings, and the firstborn of your herds and flocks.

The Israelites were forbidden from worshiping in any of the places frequented by the nonbelieving pagans. Instead, there was to be a special place chosen by God himself and the "choice of one common place for the solemn rites of religion was an act of divine wisdom, for the security of the true religion."[81] So it began in the moveable tabernacle in the wilderness and then, after they entered the promised land, it moved successively from Mizpeh, to Shiloh, and then finally to the temple in Jerusalem. So it was to this special place of divine presence that tithes and offerings were to be brought (Neh 12:44; 13:5: Mal 3:10). That same practice is reflected in Jesus' teaching. In Matthew 5:23–24 he says, "Therefore if you bring your gift to the altar, and there remember that your brother has something against you, leave your gift there before the altar, and go your way. First be reconciled to your brother, and then come and offer your gift" (See also 1 Cor 9:13; 10:18). He also commends the poor woman for bringing an offering, which was truly a sacrifice, to the temple (Mark 12:41–44; Luke 21:1–4). As might be expected, this practice of bringing offerings was continued in the early church. In Acts 4:34–35 we read "all who were possessors of lands or houses sold them and brought the proceeds of the things that were sold and laid them at the apostles' feet." Not long after that the practice of a weekly offering brought to the church was established. In 1 Corinthians 16:1–3 St. Paul tells the Corinthians and the Galatians, "On the first day of the week let each one of you lay something aside, storing up as he may prosper, that there be no collections when I come." The reference to Sunday seems to imply the church as the context for the sacred space of giving.

Taking giving out of the worship setting causes it to morph into something akin to a payment for services rendered. Moreover, if we tie donations to our own buying habits, giving recedes even further and is comingled with our already materialistic desires. Perhaps that will somehow justify our

---

81. Jamieson et al., *Commentary, Critical and Explanatory*, "Deuteronomy 12.5."

indulgence, but it is in no way the desired spiritual act of giving. So if you no longer need to actually go to the liturgy and worship in order to give your tithe, and if giving becomes a common financial transaction, as mindless as paying for a book online or swiping a card in order to buy gasoline, then what remains of the sacrificial purposefulness of the act of giving? Surely, this technology changes the nature of giving into something that is not recognizable as a spiritual offering in any biblical sense of the word.

LEGAL MATTERS

As we have seen, the basic character of the North American psyche is, to a large extent, determined by an essentially mercenary mindset. In other words, it is a context within which everyone can and does freely engage in an exchange of goods and services, doing whatever they deem necessary to turn some form of personal profit. Shaped by our particular brand of every-person-for-themselves individualism, this freedom creates a competitive context in which the potential for chaos, abuse, and conflict is incalculable. Indeed, as U.S. Supreme Court Justice Felix Frankfurter put it, "If one man can be allowed to determine for himself what is law, every man can. That means first chaos, then tyranny."[82] So because not all men are angels,[83] some form of governance or imposed order becomes necessary, a set of publicly disclosed legal codes and processes that serve as a constraint on individual and institutional behavior and to which all members of a society are subject,[84] including the church and its members.

In order for the church and its members to take advantage of the benefits of this rule of law, it will not only have to comply with the laws that pertain to them but also deliberately establish its legal identity within the system. One way to do this is to incorporate the parish in keeping with the laws of the state it is in. In essence this allows the state to recognize the parish as a formal legal entity which is doing business in that state as a nonprofit corporation and which it views as a corporation, that is, a group

---

82. "What is the Rule of Law?," 5.

83. "What is the Rule of Law?," 4.

84. "The World Justice Project has proposed a working definition of the rule of law that comprises four principles: 1. A system of self-government in which all persons, including the government, are accountable under the law 2. A system based on fair, publicized, broadly understood and stable laws 3. A fair, robust, and accessible legal process in which rights and responsibilities based in law are evenly enforced 4. Diverse, competent, and independent lawyers and judges" ("What is the Rule of Law?," 6). See also Lautenbach, *Concept of the Rule of Law*.

of individuals acting as one, rather than individually, and thus subject to certain laws.

This idea is, of course, not without some controversy. Some argue it is not necessary to formally incorporate since churches are automatically classified as tax-exempt 501(c)(3) organizations, so donations to an unregistered, unincorporated church are automatically tax-deductible. However,

> [a]lthough there is no requirement to do so, many churches seek recognition of tax-exempt status from the IRS because this recognition assures church leaders, members and contributors that the church is recognized as exempt and qualifies for related tax benefits. For example, contributors to a church that has been recognized as tax-exempt would know that their contributions generally are tax-deductible.[85]

But even if financial donations to an unincorporated entity are tax-deductible, incorporation helps prove tax-exempt status and makes it easier to get the benefits of an IRS determination:

> An IRS determination letter can aid the church in proving it qualifies for certain exemptions from local real estate transfer taxes, property taxes, or sales and use taxes. A determination letter can also be very useful to a member of the congregation who is being audited and must prove that his contributions to the church were in fact deductible. It is also necessary to receive gifts from donor advised funds.[86]

Others argue incorporation causes the church to cede sovereignty to the state, that is, it places itself under the control of the state. However, as David Gibbs points out,

> [w]hile it is true that incorporation places the church under those laws which govern corporations, it does not mean that the state has licensed you to preach. *You may form a church and preach the gospel regardless of whether your church is incorporated.* What it does mean is your church is now recognized by the state as a separate legal entity. The laws of the state leave it up to the discretion of the not-for-profit corporation to determine what officers it will have and what internal rules will govern its operation. These laws also leave it up to the corporation to determine how best to fulfill the purpose for which it was organized, so long as there is no breach of the law. Incorporating

---

85. "501(c)(3) Tax Guide," 2.
86. Bea, "Should Churches Incorporate?," 3.

> simply allows the church to enjoy the convenience of holding property in the church's name, allows the church members to enjoy freedom from personal liability, and allows the church organization to continue in existence in spite of large fluctuations in membership and internal church disputes.[87]

It seems, then, that we are, as a matter of fact, subject to the laws of the country and being incorporated under those laws brings a number of advantages and safeguards to the church. So it is probably something we should be doing. But how can we justify participating in a secular legal system? On the one hand, we have little choice. On the other hand, doing so does not necessarily impact the nature or practices of the church. So perhaps it comes down to avoiding a passive participation by developing constant awareness of what incorporation means, why we are doing it, and, based on that informed understanding, being prepared to recognize and deal with any violations of the church that may arise.

Another now-common practice impacting the parish legal situation is the use of criminal background checks. Due to the rise in the number of sex-related crimes in and by the churches of our country, many Orthodox churches have felt the need to secure a more effective legal footing by establishing churchwide, binding policies. This is certainly being done to protect members of the congregation from this kind of misconduct, but it is also being done to protect the churches from the growing number and skyrocketing costs of lawsuits brought by those thus abused. For example, in just one church, the Roman Catholic Church in America, "between 2004 and 2013, the church spent a total of $2,744,876,843 in costs related to abuse allegations, which includes settlements, therapy for victims, support for offenders, attorneys' fees, and other costs."[88] Understandably, then, in 2014 the Holy Synod of the Orthodox Church in America revised and reissued its "Policies, Standards, and Procedures on Sexual Misconduct"[89] thusly:

> It is the goal of the entire Church to provide a safe and healthy environment for all of the faithful of the Orthodox Church in America. The church laments the sin of sexual misconduct and will not tolerate sexual misconduct by its clergy or any layperson. To further the prevention of sexual abuse of children, the Holy Synod has approved a training program by the nonprofit

---

87. Gibbs, "5 Questions on Church Incorporation," para. 5 (emphasis original).

88. Hafiz, "Sex Abuse Cost the U.S. Catholic Church," para. 8.

89. See Holy Synod of Bishops of the Orthodox Church in America, "Policies, Standards, and Procedures."

organization "Darkness to Light"[90] Their training program, "Stewards of the Children" [SOC], is available for free to all those who are required to take the training.[91]

This program also includes the mandatory screening of all current clergy as well as "potential clergy, church employees, and volunteers."[92] The screening process involves an application, interview, references, criminal history background check,[93] and training on sexual abuse prevention.[94] Part of this process involves hiring a company to run triannual criminal background checks[95] on those working in the church. The OCA is now using a company called "Protect My Ministry,"[96] which promises to reduce both costs and risks to organizations and children, thus protecting both. The argument seems to be the screening will prevent sexual misconduct, but if something were to happen, the church, if sued, would be able to mount an effective defense by claiming it did everything humanly possible (due diligence) to prevent it.

It would appear the general lack of moral integrity both in and outside the church, combined with the litigious tendencies of a mercenary culture, make screening of one form or the other necessary. Still, one might argue that by using these intrusive technologies, we lose a very precious aspect of church life, namely, arch-pastoral oversight. Traditionally, it was the bishop who knew his clergy so intimately, the pastor who knew his parishioners so well, any actual or even potential misconduct would be identified. But does the present practice mean ceding those pastoral functions to secular companies with no interest in or involvement in church other than providing a service for profit? Not necessarily. We insist we are not abdicating our

90. "Background Check," *Definitions*.

91. Holy Synod of Bishops of the Orthodox Church in America, "Resources for the Prevention of Sexual Misconduct," para. 1.

92. Holy Synod of the Orthodox Church in America, "Guidelines on Background Checks," 2.

93. "A background check is a 'records' screening of an individual which can be as little as a one-county check or as in-depth as a Security clearance investigation. Public and private records can be searched once applicant consent is given" ("What is a Background Check?)"

94. See Holy Synod of the Orthodox Church in America, "Guidelines on Background Checks."

95. "A background check must be obtained, and renewed every three years for all readers, subdeacons, deacons, priests, and bishops in the Orthodox Church in America, as well as for all laypersons who have more than incidental contact with children in the course of their work in the Church." Holy Synod of the Orthodox Church in America, "Guidelines on Background Checks," para. 4.

96. https://www.protectmyministry.com.

shepherding responsibilities, we are simply making use of more efficient, modern tools. Obviously, the argument is based on the idea the technology is itself neutral and using it will not affect the church negatively.

But is that the case? Questions of confidentiality and privacy aside, I fear the use of criminal background checks may have two negative outcomes. On the one hand, they give a false sense of confidence and security which, if relied on, could further erode true pastoral oversight. Perhaps we assume a proper screening regimen will prevent sexual abuse. But these things still can and do happen. In the study of the Roman Catholic Church mentioned above, researchers found that in 2013 99.6% of all priests had been screened yet in that same year 730 clerics[97] were accused of misconduct. So screening alone will not suffice but will rather have to be but one component in a dynamic continuation and intensification of the traditional shepherding functions.

On the other hand, background checks could alter, that is, narrow, the scope of our definition of life in Christ. There will certainly be a temptation to focus on and be satisfied with the overall evaluation provided by background checks, the criminal aspects of screening, while neglecting the more immediate and intimate spiritual qualities. If a person is not listed in some national register, if he has no record, will we still feel compelled to instill in him the essentials of radical discipleship? Or will we conclude some lawyers have done our work for us and this is a good person, that this is simply good enough? In any case, I do not think, given today's challenges, we have much choice but to make use of these secular screening technologies. But they must not be accepted uncritically. They can damage the church. So we should embed these techniques in larger discussions about the nature and scope of true pastoral oversight. The very need for background checks should trigger a deliberate reactivation of the full role of a shepherd in keeping with holy tradition.

RECORD KEEPING

Now on to one last area of ecclesial administration: record keeping. Because there is a certain amount of procedural overlap at points where the church touches the world around it, handling church records, especially financial records, will have to be governed by orderly procedures that will be

---

97. "538 of those accused were priests, of which 382 were diocesan priests, 110 belonged to a religious order, and forty-six had been incardinated elsewhere. Eleven deacons were accused, and 175 accused were of an unknown clerical status" (Hafiz, "Sex Abuse Cost the U.S. Catholic Church," para. 4).

recognized as such by the secular institutions we have to deal with, such as banks and taxing agencies. Today, there are any number of software offerings that can help the parish with these administrative tasks. One example is the church management program "Realm"[98] from ACS Technologies. According to one priest using this product, "Realm is a very effective tool for monitoring church attendance and other metrics, creating a private online community and collecting tithe contributions online . . ."[99] Of course, if you have access to computer technology, much of this can be done inexpensively, that is, without the high cost of commercial software packages, by using a simple spreadsheet. Nevertheless, the use of digital tools can certainly facilitate the difficult and often tedious task of record keeping. Still, a hard-copy, handwritten record in the form of entries in a metrical book used to record parish sacramental celebrations, including registries for baptisms, receptions into the church, marriages, and funerals, has much to commend it. Throughout history these written records of the church have included hard evidence of the lines of apostolic succession, as well as the lives of the many generations of believers. There is something comforting and uplifting about holding and paging through these written records: the frayed bindings, the faded and multicolored ink, the many and varied styles of writing, the succession of dates and ecclesial events stretching back before our time. All this in a series of physical volumes collectively assuring us we are not alone, that others have gone before us. As such, they should be explained, made available, and occasionally explored by everyone in the parish. Keeping and being mindful of such records allows the priest and the parish to participate directly and physically in an ancient practice and offset the lifelessness of the narrow fixation of modern society with the contemporary moment. So using software might be convenient, but an overreliance on digital technology, leading to neglect of and disinterest in the permanent written metrical books, could cause the parish to lose a small but very tactile part of its connection to the past. That continuity assures us we are part of something much larger than ourselves, something that needs constant reinforcement in this day of the perpetually new and unique.

In addition to the tools we might use, there is also the question of who might do this work. There are times when the church needs the input of experts, lawyers for example. I know of a church that hired itself a business manager who, while a qualified accountant, did not participate otherwise in the life of the group, being neither a member nor a believer. In what sense could he be in communion with the parishioners he was to serve?

---

98. See "Realm Church Management Software."
99. Paez, "Planting Grant Missions," para. 2.

How could he participate in the oneness of mind and Spirit generated by the eucharistic assembly? How could he possibly know the mind of Christ with respect to the use of their resources? Obviously, he could not. In fact, his attempt to do the ministry of financial administration without the grace of an appropriate divine gifting radically undermined the unity of the church since he could not possibly be of one mind and one heart with the assembly. In all likelihood he brought with him assumptions and principles that were at cross-purposes with the mind of the church. Things like the profit motive, matching clergy compensation to secular standards, building ever bigger and better buildings, financial security by saving as much as possible rather than giving it to the needy, and so on. This is not to say a church cannot take advantage of skills and abilities just because they are also being used outside the church. However, in a church these skills are ideally exercised by someone who already participates in the priestly ministry common to the assembly and is enabled by the Spirit to own the shared needs and purposes of a finite group of believers unified in their response to the infinite presence of God in the eucharistic assembly. That is, the use of these skills will have to directly contribute to the spiritual well-being of the group. Since the Holy Spirit has given the church everything it needs to be a church, there is no need to import insights and principles from the world of business and politics. Since the exercise of the gifts of the Spirit implies and builds the essential unity of the church, it would be counterproductive to incorporate noncharismatic activities into its life. The church is not a business and must not be run as one. It is not to be set up like a secular corporation with a CEO and officers. The church is not a democracy and must not operate as one. By committing themselves to a structure generated by the ministries of prophets, apostles, teachers, evangelists, and pastors (Eph 4:11), the church will have rejected an order generated by the expertise of accountants and advertisers, and executives and will have preserved its character and unity.

5

Production/Preparation

Today the living temple, the temple of the Great King, enters the Temple, to prepare a Divine Abode. Wherefore, O ye nations, rejoice.[1]

THE NEXT ASPECT OF the commercial process I would like to consider is the *production* of the commodities businesses sell. Of course, since the church is not selling anything, that is, since we have no products, either to develop or to produce, one might be tempted to think commercially oriented production practices are not likely to have been brought into the church. Nevertheless, we do offer an array of services which have to be prepared to be made available. According to the traditional definition, a church is constituted when believers come together to celebrate the Eucharist under the leadership of a priest ordained for that purpose by a canonically consecrated bishop. From that it can be seen that, at the very least, we need to train clergy to develop guidelines (rubrics) for celebrating the liturgy and make ready a space suited for that celebration. But none of this can be understood in terms of the production of products offered for sale. Moreover, this in-house preparation requires nothing the church does not already possess. Nevertheless, I fear our attraction to commercial thought, coupled with the vague similarities between ecclesial and commercial notions of preparation/production, have, in spite of the absence of products, tempted us to apply businesslike approaches and methods to the preparation of the services we

---

1. "Post-Gospel Stichera," lines 2–4.

do offer. While the preparation for ecclesial ministry involves hundreds, if not thousands, of elements, I will concentrate on just three: clergy, worship, and worship space.

PREPARATION OF CLERGY

There are, of course, many elements involved in preparing the clergy for service, things like appropriate experience, an assessment of spiritual maturity, required background screening, psychological profiling, and so on. However, I think most of us today would see theological education as the most prominent aspect of training for the priesthood. Ordinarily, this training takes place at a theological school such as St. Vladimir's Orthodox Theological Seminary[2] or Holy Cross Greek Orthodox School of Theology.[3] What is striking about the names of these schools is one is called a Graduate School of Theology while the other designates itself as a Seminary. The difference, even if it is not born out in the reality of these institutions, is significant.

According to contemporary Catholic Canon law, "[t]he Church has the duty and the proper and exclusive right to form those who are designated for the sacred ministries."[4] In other words, the training of priests was the sole responsibility of the community of faith and not some secular or state agency. For that purpose, special schools of theology, that is, seminaries, were established that had but one purpose—the preparation of clergy. Interestingly, there is little or no mention of education. The priests were rather to be provided with spiritual formation during which

> students are to become equipped to exercise the pastoral ministry fruitfully and are to be formed in a missionary spirit; they are to learn that ministry always carried out in living faith and charity fosters their own sanctification. They also are to learn to cultivate those virtues which are valued highly in human relations so that they are able to achieve an appropriate integration between human and supernatural goods.[5]

This formation was to take place in a communelike context in which a single rule governed all aspects of daily life: the seminarians would eat

---

2. https://www.svots.edu.
3. https://www.hchc.edu/holy-cross/.
4. Catholic Church et al., *Code of Canon Law*, can. 232. I have not found anything like this in the Canons of the Eastern Church, but I am sure they would agree.
5. Catholic Church et al., *Code of Canon Law*, can. 245 para. 1.

together, attend classes together, and worship together. At the heart of this common life was the Eucharist.

> The eucharistic celebration is to be the center of the entire life of a seminary in such a way that, sharing in the very love of Christ, the students daily draw strength of spirit for apostolic work and for their spiritual life especially from this richest of sources.[6]

This formation also included instruction in doctrine, philosophy, theology, and the holy Scriptures.

> The *doctrinal* instruction given is to be directed so that students acquire an extensive and solid learning in the sacred disciplines along with a general culture appropriate to the necessities of place and time, in such way that, grounded in their own faith and nourished thereby, they are able to announce in a suitable way the teaching of the gospel to the people of their own time in a manner adapted to their understanding.[7]
>
> *Philosophical* instruction must be grounded in the perennially valid philosophical heritage and also consider philosophical investigation over the course of time. It is to be taught in such a way that it perfects the human development of the students, sharpens their minds, and makes them better able to pursue theological studies.[8]
>
> *Theological* instruction is to be imparted in the light of faith and under the leadership of the magisterium in such a way that the students understand the entire Catholic doctrine grounded in divine revelation, gain nourishment for their own spiritual life, and are able properly to announce and safeguard it in the exercise of the ministry.[9]
>
> Students are to be instructed in sacred *scripture* with special diligence in such a way that they acquire a comprehensive view of the whole of sacred scripture.[10]

All of this was to be "grounded in the written word of God together with sacred tradition," and taught "only [to] those who are outstanding in virtue and have obtained a doctorate or licentiate from a university or faculty recognized by the [Church].[11]

6. Catholic Church et al., *Code of Canon Law*, can. 246 para. 1.
7. Catholic Church et al., *Code of Canon Law*, can. 248.
8. Catholic Church et al., *Code of Canon Law*, can. 251.
9. Catholic Church et al., *Code of Canon Law*, can. 252 para. 1.
10. Catholic Church et al., *Code of Canon Law*, can. 252 para. 2.
11. Catholic Church et al., *Code of Canon Law*, can. 253 para. 1 (emphasis mine).

So it was that the church envisioned and then established seminaries, specialized schools independent of the state university system,[12] which had only one purpose: the spiritual formation and not the academic preparation of the priest. They were not in the business of granting degrees, they did not charge tuitions, they did not seek to gain accreditation, but simply answered to the mandate given by the church. Indeed, this is the way most seminaries[13] started, but alas, much has changed under the pressure of the scientific university model of education and our descent into the world of commerce.

The secular or scientific university model was created by Wilhelm von Humboldt at the University of Berlin in 1810. His model of education was based on the humanistic conviction that "schools and universities be fundamentally 'neutral'—free from ideological influences and private interests such as those seen, for example, in feudal or clerical tutelage."[14] This implied freedom of scientific inquiry and the unity of teaching and research. As Muller notes,

> When von Humboldt put forward the idea of freedom of teaching and study, he meant above all, freedom from religious orthodoxy. And the notion that scientific knowledge could be discovered rather than learned as revealed in the past . . .[15]

This approach to higher education "effectively overthrew the hegemony of theology, [which had been considered the queen of all sciences] leaving the matter very unclear as to what, if any, place it would have in higher

---

12. Of course, all manner of schools and academies have existed since ancient times. But, the first true university is said to have been established in Bologna, Italy in 1088. Some of these institutions were initially affiliated with the Catholic Church. However, they also developed as independent entities and were at times in conflict with the church. This is illustrated by the University of Naples, founded in 1224 as a "public institution dedicated by a king rather than the pope or Catholic church. Some see this as the beginning of developing the concept of secular education, although virtually all higher education institutions had religious curriculum as part of their broader education." So, while they often gave philosophy and theology a place of privilege, they were not primarily in the business of preparing individuals for pastoral service (Nicholas, cited in "How Did Universities Develop?," para. 2).

13. This is not only true of the Roman Catholic seminaries. The Orthodox St. Vladimir's Theological Seminary was established (1925) because the hierarchy "recognized the need for American-born-and-raised clergy and decided to establish a permanent seminary" ("Our History," para. 1). Similarly, a free church in Germany established (1912) a Predigerschule (preacher school), that is, its own "Ausbildungsstätte (place of training) 'für Diener des Wortes'" ("Geschichte der Hochschule," para. 2).

14. Kern, "Humboldt's Educational Ideal," 1.

15. Muller, "Wilhelm von Humboldt," 254.

education."[16] This meant that "[t]heology's place in a research university was in doubt because theology had traditionally rested on 'revelation,' on authorities whose authoritative status could not itself be examined in an orderly, disciplined, and critical [that is scientific[17]] way."[18] There were some at the time who sought to preserve theology's place in the university curriculum by trying to establish it as a subject of scientific inquiry. For example, in his *Kurze Darstellung des theologischen Studiums*, published in 1811, F. D. Schleiermacher developed the science[19] of theology as an integrated whole, the primary value of which is to be seen in its relationship to the practical needs of the church. He refers to theology as the "collective embodiment of those branches of scientific knowledge and those rules of art without the possessions and application of which a harmonious guidance of the church is not possible."[20] As he conceived of it, theology could be divided into three major areas: philosophical, historical, and practical. With this the "the seed of specialized scholarship had been sown."[21] From there it was a short step to establishing chairs and departments of divinity at the universities. This had already begun in Europe as early as Edinburgh in 1620 and 1694. The freedom-loving, scientific-minded, and mercenary Americans were not far behind with their own chairs of theology at Harvard (1721) and Yale (1755). This specialization quickly led to the idea of graduate-level instruction,[22] along with the granting of masters and doctoral degrees.[23]

16. Conniry, "Reducing the Identity Crisis," 139..

17. In the German sense of Wissenschaft, a particular epistemology, research methodology involving orderly, disciplined, critical inquiry.

18. Kelsey, *Between Athens and Berlin*, 15.

19. According to Schleiermacher's scheme, theology is to be viewed as a positive science (Scholz, *Schleiermachers Kurze Darstellung*; compare with Pannenberg, *Theology and the Philosophy of Science*.

20. Scholz, *Schleiermachers Kurze Darstellung*, 2.

21. Farley, *Theologia*, 335.

22. "Shortly after, by an irrepressible inherent logic influenced by the German universities, particularly that at Halle, a graduate component appeared" (Cahill, "Theological Education," 355).

23. ". . . the University of Berlin became the vanguard of modern 'research universities'—and the first institution to confer the (modern) Doctor of Philosophy degree. Other German universities quickly followed suit, attracting many students from other countries, including the USA. By 1884, for example, thirteen of Johns Hopkins' faculty had earned German doctorates. Accordingly, even though in 1861 Yale University was the first American institution to confer the Ph.D., scholars of American higher education typically cite the founding in 1876 of Johns Hopkins University as the decisive moment when the 'Berlin' model made its debut *tour de force* in the American Academy" (Cahill, "Theological Education," 138).

As these programs proliferated in the commercial context of North America, a kind of competition developed. But that in turn led to the question of the relative value or worth of the individual degrees. Did these degrees all represent the same level of education? In order to establish the quality of their own programs (degrees) and establish the value returned on the investment made by students, the vast majority of these schools turned to the notion of accreditation, a means by which a supposedly independent agency, such as the Association of Theological Schools, examines and confirms the integrity of a given program. According to their handbook, the ATS accrediting process is "a primary means of quality assurance" in North American higher education.[24] The agency's standards for degree programs is "intended to ensure a common understanding of the academic work involved in degree programs at member schools and to provide common public meaning for a degree."[25] Initially, accreditation meant "a school had adequate library resources, facilities, and faculties appropriate in skill and education for graduate, professional theological education."[26] In this way, the Humboldtian vison[27] of education was disseminated, if not imposed, on various schools in order to insure a uniform standard[28] for judging the adequacy of professional training.

All of this became enormously expensive, and soon state and national church funding was insufficient and a new source of revenue, fees, and tuition was established. The reasoning seems to be the student is provided with a service (education) whose quality is certified by a resume-enhancing, accredited degree, which increases the likelihood[29] of employment, can be used

24. *Self-Study Handbook*, 1.
25. "Preface to the Standards of Accreditation," 2.
26. *Self-Study Handbook*, 1–2.
27. According to ATS standards, "Faculty are expected to engage in research, and each school shall articulate clearly its expectations and requirements for faculty research and shall have explicit criteria and procedures for the evaluation of research that are congruent with the purpose of the school and with commonly accepted standards in higher education" ("Standards of Acreditation," 15).
28. "Commission accreditation is based on Standards of Accreditation ("Standards") and Policies and Procedures ("Procedures") that have been adopted by the Commission's membership." This includes "specific Standards for each type of degree program offered by accredited schools that define an agreed-upon understanding of their purpose, content, location, duration, resources, and admission requirements" (*Self-Study Handbook*, 4).
29. In 2019, the employment rate was higher for those with higher levels of educational attainment. For example, the employment rate was highest for 25- to 34-year-olds with a bachelor's or higher degree (87 percent). The employment rate for those with some college (80 percent) was higher than the rate for those who had completed high school (74 percent), which was higher than the employment rate for those who

as a benchmark by potential employers, and is a justification for demanding increased levels of compensation. For all this the students themselves should bear some of the cost. And so, "The cost of obtaining a U.S. degree is among the highest in the world and rising . . . ."[30] Yet those costs seem to be justified since a higher education (a degree) generally leads to higher earning power.[31] With tuition the main source of income, there was a constant struggle to increase the number of paying students and reduce the cost of the services provided, that is, develop a new business model.[32] One approach was to diversify the schools' offerings by introducing additional degree programs (MA, ThM, etc.) for those who do not seek full-time work in the church. Modern technology, such as online and distance learning, was also introduced on the basis of cost/benefit considerations. In fact, the use of this technology was widely required as a result of the COVID-19-related shutdown of in-person classes beginning in late winter 2020. Even though the use of video conferencing technologies such as Skype and Zoom in education had been somewhat tentative, we are now being forced to explore it as an alternative or supplement to in-person teaching. Our experiences during the winter semester of the 2019–2020 school year are still being processed, but the actual effectiveness of this medium for teaching remains a matter of some doubt.[33] But even if some of its limitations could be overcome, it remains clear there is something profoundly unsatisfying about this methodology, and I think it is safe to say something as intimate and personal as spiritual formation cannot possibly be done in this way.

Whatever technologies are being used, there can be no question Orthodox theological schools have wholeheartedly adopted these Humboldtian (scientific, humanistic) and commercialized devices and structures. Today, they are selling a product (education/degree) which has to be bought and paid for, which "assures" the potential "employers" (parishes) of its quality ("guarantees" the graduate's ability to do the work of a pastor), and justifies

---

had not completed high school (57 percent). The same pattern was observed among both sexes" (Employment and Unemployment Rates by Educational Attainment").

30. Hau, "World's Most Expensive Universities," 4.

31. "A large body of research focusing on identical twins routinely shows that the twin with more education earns more than the twin with less" (Simkovic "Value Added Perspective," 4).

32. One administrator of St. Vladimir's Seminary Press uses exactly that phrase. Speaking of special donors, "they have also helped us complete one of the short-term goals of our new business model" ("SVS Press Receives Major Gift," para. 3).

33. See "Pros and Cons of Online Education," and Tom, "5 Disadvantages to Consider about Online Education."

the candidate's demand for a substantially higher benefits package.[34] These, then, are some of the developments that have moved the original concept of the seminary away from *theologia* as pious learning and have transformed it into degree-granting institutes of graduate education and professionalized[35] its graduates rather than forming them spiritually for their pastoral duties.

It is understandable that secular universities embedded in the North American consumer context have chosen to take this path. But given the original goal of spiritual formation, one has to wonder why the seminaries have given in so easily. But have they really? Is there anything left of the ideals of seminary training? To their credit, I believe the administrators of both St. Vladimir's Theological Seminary and Holy Cross Graduate School of Theology have, in fact, sought to maintain some of those original values and outcomes. While not a prominent feature, you will find numerous references to spiritual formation throughout their websites and catalogues. Holy Cross defines itself as an "intellectual, educational, and spiritual formation center of the Greek Orthodox Archdiocese of America . . . ."[36] Both schools invest a lot into developing an on-campus social, academic, and worship community. This includes on-campus living arrangements, common meals, and daily liturgical cycle. These schools still seek to maintain something of that original seminary vision. This is evident in the way they describe themselves:

> Holy Cross Greek Orthodox School of Theology is an Orthodox Christian seminary and graduate school of theology centered on the Trinitarian faith as revealed by Jesus Christ and as preserved in its fullness, genuineness, and integrity by the one, holy, catholic, and apostolic Church. The School embodies the historic and specific educational mission of the Ecumenical Patriarchate of Constantinople and its archdiocese in the United States. Holy Cross educates its students to articulate and understand the biblical, historical, dogmatic, ethical, and liturgical traditions of the Orthodox Church. Students are prepared to become future

---

34. In a conversation with an OCA diocesan administrator, that priest expressed his frustration at the fact that he could no longer find seminary graduates willing to be assigned to places that did not meet their financial expectation. "All they want is more money." Interview with Fr. Thomas Moore, dean of the Carolinas' Deanery of the OCA Diocese of the South, in person, July 11, 2018.

35. "It would be but a short step to conceiving the minister as a professional, one prepared to undertake certain tasks. Farley even suggests—and I think quite correctly—that the ladder of ecclesiastical promotions was not constructed by intellectual or even pious acquaintance with theologia. Promotion, if this is the proper name, occurs because of abilities that have only a remote connection with theologia" (Cahill, "Theological Education," 335).

36. "Mission and Vision Statements," para. 2.

Orthodox clergy and lay leaders who demonstrate faith, sensitivity, and compassion as they cultivate an attitude of offering a service of truth and love in the world. Through its graduate degree programs, Holy Cross offers men and women the opportunity to become spiritually mature persons through immersion in worship, theological studies, and service to community.[37]

St. Vladimir's Orthodox Theological Seminary serves Christ, his Church, and the world through Orthodox Christian theological education, research,[38] and scholarship, and the promotion of inter-Orthodox cooperation. In this way, the Seminary prepares students for ministry as bishops, priests, deacons, lay leaders, and scholars so that they may build up Orthodox communities, foster Church growth through mission and evangelism, teach the Orthodox faith, and care for those in need.[39]

Yet much damage has already been done by the twin dangers of an academic view imposed by extraecclesial agencies and a professionalization of the priesthood. For those reasons these schools live and operate in a no-man's land between an ancient vision and contemporary realities. The tension is evident when St. Vladimir's reconstitutes itself in primarily business terms, replete with CEO, in order to better preserve the true purpose of a seminary.[40] Whether this structural reorganization or, for that matter, any of the other advancements (degrees, accreditation, tuition, etc.) will help or continue to bring further damage may well depend on the administrators' ability to remain committed to the very clear and focused understanding of theological education set out in the Canons and to evaluate every proposed innovation in light of that ultimate purpose: the spiritual formation of future priests.

I wonder if Archbishop Dmitri's[41] vision of a diocesan-level program of priestly formation conducted in local parishes by qualified senior clergy, without tuition, degrees, or accreditation, might not have been a step back in the right direction. But alas, a minor program like that would have brought competition and loss of revenue to the major schools. So the idea never got off the ground. Another promising approach is the Neighborhood Seminary

---

37. "Mission and Vision Statements," para. 3.
38. Hence the "publish or perish" maxim for faculty.
39. St. Vladimir's Theological Seminary, "Mission, Vision, & Values," para. 1.
40. See "St. Vladimir's Trustees Implement."
41. Dmitri was archbishop of Dallas and the South (OCA), and just after 2000 he began floating this idea with some of us (his clergy) who shared an interest in such a project. It quickly became apparent his suggestion would not resonate in the higher echelons of OCA leadership.

initiated by Duke Divinity School in September 2017. The program provides theological, spiritual, and missional formation to equip laypeople to engage in their home, neighborhood, workplace, and community. It is a nondegree program providing in-depth theological knowledge for interested laypersons and those transitioning into ministry. It is team-taught by a group of Duke scholars, community practitioners, and spiritual directors. The participants meet monthly over two years for classroom work, community practicums, and spiritual direction.[42]

PREPARATION FOR WORSHIP

Today, as I have noted, we are under ever-increasing pressure to incorporate elements of modern technology into the life of the church. This prevailing business model dictates that in order to succeed, the church, even though it does not have products to produce, needs to diligently prepare its services for consumption by potential consumers. This, of course, puts pressure[43] on us to somehow improve, that is, make more attractive and enjoyable, our primary offering to the world, namely, our Sunday worship service, the divine liturgy. The Protestant rage for user-friendliness has allowed them to create totally new and, as they call it, contemporary forms of Sunday worship by abandoning traditional elements like the creed and the Lord's Prayer and by incorporating countless innovations like worship bands, video clips, special lighting, stages, cinema seating, etc. We cannot, of course, follow the lead of our Protestant friends since the Orthodox cannot technologically tweak their worship service. We are convinced these forms have been handed down to us and we are to faithfully preserve them. It is not that the liturgy can't be change—it certainly has been modified over the centuries[44]—but there is in the church a clear understanding that its worship forms have been given for one reason alone: to provide a context for our communion with Christ. For that reason, anything that would trivialize, distract from, or alter that basic premise has to be and has been rejected. Most Orthodox would intuitively agree certain devices such as musical instruments, video clips, and, in many cases, even pews, cannot have a place in Orthodox worship. I believe it is this innate sense of the mystical as opposed to the

---

42. See Lacy, "Teach the People."

43. Some of this pressure comes in very subtle ways. An orthodox version of church-growth thinking suggests "one of the things that leads to growth is what they call 'Inspiring worship,'" thus implying the need for some kind of improvement (Schwarz, *ABC's of Natural Church Development*, 14–15).

44. See Dix, *Shape of the Liturgy*.

entertainment-like character of worship that has led the faithful to quite successfully resist the pressure to modernize their worship. In other words, I think they recognize the true nature of the liturgical event. It is unique, which means it cannot be modified without becoming something other than liturgy. Moreover, it is a celebration, which means it is not done by us, or done to us, but is rather constituted as we participate in the synergistic divine-human act of communion.

Every time Orthodox believers gather to celebrate the Eucharist, they are initiating a unique, one-time, nonrepeatable event that, for lack of a better term, I will call a "happening." So this week's liturgy is not simply repeated next Sunday. In fact, that is not even possible since each event is a completely separate occurrence or instance of the liturgy. Now, what is happening during the liturgy is that ordinary time is being suspended and the participants enter into the temporal space of the eternal kingdom of God. When we speak of God's kingdom, we are not referring to some specific geographic space but rather to the space, any space, where God's absolute authority or dominion reigns completely. That this is the case during the divine liturgy is guaranteed by the very real presence of Christ, our King and our Lord, in the Eucharist. The other thing that is happening is that communion, a total interpersonal engagement, is established among those who partake of the sacred mysteries.

Because of its nature as a happening, anything that is integral to the celebration of the liturgy takes on that same character of uniqueness, one-timeness, that is, it can only be what it truly is within the context of the liturgy. We see this clearly in the Eucharist itself. The church, which is not constituted by a building but by the actual, physical gathering of the faithful, is the only God-appointed place for that to take place. It is the special place of God's special self-manifestation.

The same thing applies to all other aspects or practices of the church. The music, for example, sung as part of the celebration, is unique and can only be truly liturgical music if it is sung during and for the liturgy. For that reason, the church has always frowned on presenting its music as concerts for the pleasure of listeners outside the services of the church. A sermon can only be a sermon within the context of the happening. Outside of that it is only a text, a powerless representation of what was delivered, empowered, and guided by the Holy Spirit active during the service. It is something like the difference between a musician's practice sessions and the concert itself. Tithing, that is, the bringing of offerings to the church, which in the ancient church took place during the liturgy, can only really be tithing, a deliberate act of faith, if done within the context of the happening.

So what would it mean, for example, if we added something extraneous such as video clips or computer projections during the liturgy? We might argue this would enhance our singing, supplement our sermons, and even keep the attention of our worshipers. But what messages come with this technology? First and foremost, it affects the way we view the use of images in the church. It would mean, at its worst, an outright rejection of the church's teaching that only certain images, namely icons, are to be used in the church (which is what makes them sacred), and, at best, it would mean abandoning our understanding that icons are the only holy images, that is, the only images that can be filled with the sanctifying power of the Holy Spirit and can thus transcend the boundary between the created and the uncreated worlds. I suppose we could consider the possibility of blessing or sanctifying a video projector or a computerized PowerPoint presentation, but the church certainly has not authorized and probably never will authorize us to do that. So what we see with this example is there are some technologies that cannot be incorporated into the liturgical happening without actually violating the very nature of the liturgical event, the liturgy.

It is clear, then, that preparation of or for worship does not involve incorporating modern improvements but rather doing everything we can to preserve and participate in its unique character. Since most of what we need to do in the service has already been given, the liturgy itself is fixed and with the exception of some movable (seasonable) parts, does not require much preparation. However, because the liturgy is the common work of the faithful and the clergy, we do need to prepare both the participants and the celebrant. So what would this purposeful preparation look like?

There are some basic rules of preparation that apply to everyone who intends to participate. These vary from tradition to tradition, but in general it means each individual is expected to have had recent confession, fast from the evening before, participate in the vespers and/or matins preceding the liturgy, to be at peace with all others, and, perhaps more importantly, to read the precommunion prayers.[45] This minimal preparation leads to a quiet conscience, a peaceful heart that is full of anticipation as it moves toward meeting the living Christ in the Eucharist. Thus prepared, the faithful can be fully attentive, completely engaged in the prayers, hymns, Scriptures of the service, and actively contribute to the life of the happening. This preparation transforms the passive, mercenary consumer from being a mere spectator into a dynamic co-celebrant.[46]

45. See "Guidelines for Clergy Compiled." The pre-communion prayers are available in most prayer books as well as some service books. For example, Coniaris, *My Daily Orthodox Prayer Book*.

46. In today's parlance, we have gotten used to referring to the presider as the

Obviously, this applies equally to the clergy and those serving with them. It is essential that the clergy and the servers know why we are doing what we are doing and what difference that makes. Have we taught the servers or the clergy, for that matter, more than the mechanics of the services? Have we shown them how this mystical happening is a spiritual exercise and an expression of our faith? Have we insisted on a correspondence between their lives and serving? Should they be serving if they are openly sinning? This awareness in addition to the preparation mentioned above will enable the clergy to consciously experience, to taste each and every line of the liturgy, every petition, every exclamation, every blessing, making every petition a real, deliberate, and genuine request to the Lord, making every blessing an intense wish for the well-being of the people and so on. Is this level of engagement even possible? Yes, it is, but it takes effort, practice, time, and above all, preparation. But more than that, it takes an intentional and deliberate determination to live the liturgy and not just sell it, as it were, to a group of consumers or spectators. This renewed consciousness of the nature of the liturgy, coupled with proper preparation, is the only way to reverse and prevent the damage that has been done to worship by the market mentality we have brought into the church.

PREPARATION OF THE WORSHIP SPACE

From the aforementioned vision of properly prepared worship, it becomes clear we need a suitable place in which to celebrate the liturgy. Being able to prepare that venue involves our understanding of sacred space, beauty, and the language of architecture. If all the world has been created by God and exists in him, then all of created space is in some sense sacred. There is no part of it that does not reflect the divine will and prototype and, as such, it can all serve as a place of worship, prayer, and Christian fellowship. God is omnipresent! Nevertheless, we do notice in the Scriptures, in addition to this general presence of God, there are specific manifestations of the divine person which create an especially sacred space and which occur under temporally and spatially limited circumstances which are occasionally repeated,

---

celebrant as though the priest alone served the Eucharist. Similarly, if more than one priest serves, we speak of concelebration, as if only those two or three priests were serving. This usage, however, violates the idea of the priestly function of the whole people of God. We seem to have lost sight of the fact that it is not just the priest but also the whole people who share in the priestly function of the eucharistic assembly. Throughout the divine Liturgy, the people are to collectively participate and affirm that which is being done by the presider.

lending the divine presence a degree of permanence or predictability. Consider the example of the burning bush:

> And the Angel of the LORD appeared to him in a flame of fire from the midst of a bush. So he looked, and behold, the bush was burning with fire, but the bush was not consumed. Then Moses said, "I will now turn aside and see this great sight, why the bush does not burn." So when the LORD saw that he turned aside to look, God called to him from the midst of the bush and said, "Moses, Moses!" And he said, "Here I am." Then He said, "Do not draw near this place. Take your sandals off your feet, for the place where you stand is holy ground." (Exod 3:2–5).

What makes the space around the bush sacred is the special presence of God, not the setting, the architecture, the lighting, etc. Moses' experience on the mountain while receiving the law must have been similar. Note the physical effects of having been in the presence of God (Exod 20). This is, of course, repeated in the lives of the saints and the prophets, through whom God spoke. The same can be said of the tabernacle and the temple, each of which had a most holy (holy of holy) place where God was said to meet with the priests (Exod 30:36). This space was to be carefully honored, adorned with oils, implements, the ark of the covenant, an altar, and vestments—all of which were said to be holy by virtue of their proximity to the dwelling place of God. Simply touching the holy oil of the tabernacle could make both objects and persons holy (Exod 30:29). So this was the focal point of God's manifestation to the Old Testament community. Here, the Lamb was slain, atonement made; here, the community met God. Notice how often God is referred to as being in the sanctuary (Ps 68:24; 73:17; 77:13; 150:1). Finally, there is the most obvious manifestation of God's presence in the incarnation: Emmanuel, God with us. The all-holy one was with us, sanctifying everything he came into contact with.

The Idea of Sacred Space

Today, God comes to us in the Eucharist. There, we have that spatial manifestation of the real presence of God. This presence of God is embedded in several layers of spatial dimension that makes the church itself a sacred space.

First, in the holy gifts of bread and wine, given by the people, returned, sanctified by the presence of the living Christ. The fact that we take these elements seriously is institutionalized in the role of the presider (pastor, priest) who is the only one who can call down the Spirit upon the gifts. Now, if we take that presence seriously, then we should think in terms of a sanctification of the other elements, layers of the eucharistic event. And here, there are some distinct parallels to the Old Testament via the early church.

Second, the holy vessels/altar, those implements that contain and bear the gifts, take on special significance through their contact with the holy mysteries. As such, they should be handled with care and respect and not just by anyone (cleaning the holy vessels is not done in the kitchen sink, but by the priest at a special place of preparation; the altar, not touched, not used to support weary servers, but a sacred space touched only when necessary, and only by those so ordained).

Third, the sanctuary, that space around the altar, set apart for the celebration of the holy mysteries, is not to become a thoroughfare for those seeking a shortcut, or the promenade of the curious, but rather a space reserved for those administering the sacrament, a place of quiet awe.

Fourth, the nave of the church, the place of the faithful who have gathered to worship, a place of quiet preparation for the service, a place of repentance, a place of anticipation and not a meeting hall, gossip forum, or the home of a pep rally.

If we acknowledge the sanctity of these spaces, what should our response be? How should we treat these sacred places? To begin with, it should be observed that the operating principles of the contemporary social imaginary put us at a distinct disadvantage when it comes to thinking in these terms. According to Charles Taylor (*A Secular Age*), there has been a monumental shift in thinking since the Reformation/Enlightenment, a shift he calls desacralization. As he sees it, we have gradually dismantled the hierarchies of temporality and spatiality that are characteristic of the becoming of creation. He speaks of a homogenization of time and space, a compressing of the various layers into one. In the case of time, there is no longer any sacred time as in the liturgy, the feast days of the church year, as in the Sabbath. Now, we are simply dealing with one kind of time that ticks on relentlessly, irrespective of the divine presence. Thus, it has become impossible to distinguish between a work day and a Sunday (since many work on Sunday), between an ordinary Monday and a feast day. Similarly, the hierarchies of space have been flattened into the one plane of common space, leaving us bereft of holy objects, altars, and sanctuaries. I have noticed with some alarm the casual (disrespectful) way in which the spaces in our own chapel are treated. People leaning on the communion table as if it were just another piece of office furniture, transforming the high place (apse) into a utility space amidst jokes and laughter. We live in a world in which almost nothing is sacred, and this attitude has bled over into and damaged the church.

What I find so tragic about these developments is that it is precisely in the two areas that indicate the becoming, the potential of humanity, that humankind has mounted its assault against God. Temporality and spatiality are the markers of becoming, a movement of human beings toward their divinely appointed destiny. And it is to remind us of that end, that both time and space are (were) hierarchical—the suspension of ordinary time during the liturgy in order to give us a foretaste of the coming kingdom, and the real presence of the risen Lord in the holy gifts on the altar to emphasize the hope of personal communion between the human and the divine. By destroying the hierarchies, we have transformed the divinely inspired becoming of humanity into a mere existence. By removing sacred space, we have condemned ourselves to an endless circling of life rather than movement toward our entelechy.

How, then, should we treat sacred space, or should I say, rediscover the importance of a divine hierarchy of space? We could begin by reintroducing an emphasis on human becoming in Christ. Bring back the idea of dynamic movement instead of the sometimes-static view we take of our worship spaces. The church is a place where something happens, where the Spirit moves. The communion table/altar is not a familiar object that we simply use uniformly. No, it repeatedly hosts the divine presence and each time it comes with new force to further our becoming. It is, like the sanctuary and the nave, a dynamic, living receptacle of divine, personal presence.

This reorientation will allow us to view the church as a place set apart for the special manifestation of God. If it is indeed a sacred space, then it has its own hierarchy, something which should be bathed in respect and careful practice. We need to teach our people that when they enter the church, they have a right to expect something to happen, something to move them. If this is a place of divine manifestation, how sad it would be if we came away having experienced nothing? If you are going to enter into a sacred space, you will, like Moses before the burning bush, have to remove the dirty shoes of your own sinfulness. At the very least you will have to repent as you enter the space, appealing, as did the publican, to God's mercy. Without this personal investment, I fear we blind ourselves to what God is doing in the church. Finally, we need to find ways of preserving a sense of mystery. Our callous disregard for our own inability to understand divinity robs us of the awe, the *tremendum*, that should overcome us in the presence of God. He is not our playmate, our private intellectual hobby. He is the Lord of the universe, Creator of all that there is; he is our Savior and Redeemer. I am quite convinced if we would cultivate an environment of sacredness in our church, we would never enter a church the same way again.

Beauty

Having established the idea of sacred space, this pattern of localized divine presence, God commanded Moses to prepare a place for his abiding presence among his people. So the Lord spoke to Moses, saying, "And let them make me a sanctuary, that I may dwell among them" (Exod 25:8). But this was not supposed to be just any ordinary space. God gave them a specific pattern for constructing the tabernacle and asked that the people gather their most precious items in order to build and beautify that space (Exod 25:2–9). So objective criteria were established to indicate exactly what it is that constitutes ecclesial beauty. Everything from the ark of the covenant and the vestments of the priests were to be made from gold, precious stones, the finest woods, and skins, all "for glory and for beauty" (Exod 28:2, 40). Later, when the people of Israel transitioned from their moveable tabernacle into the permanent temple, it was built with the same concern for creating a space of beauty. Solomon "decorated the house with precious stones for beauty, and the gold was gold from Parvaim. He also overlaid the house—the beams and doorposts, its walls and doors—with gold; and he carved cherubim on the walls" (2 Chr 3:6–7).

So these special, sacred spaces created by God's people as a place for his enduring manifestation were to be made beautiful by fashioning them out of the finest materials and at some great cost to the people. Obviously, the ways in which these precious materials are used have varied throughout time and space, in keeping with the cultural diversity of the world. So the objective standard here is not a particular artistic expression but rather the effort to create a special and beautiful space using the finest materials and the most gifted artisans. In other words, these were not ordinary spaces but were viewed as splendid alternatives to the spaces of everyday life, places set aside for the special purpose of worship, and they were to reflect the beauty of God himself. Entering into the temple was to be awed by his brilliance. It was like entering another world, a world set apart in which the space itself was meant to raise the human spirit to the contemplation of absolute beauty.

Of course, the beauty of these sacred spaces is not just a function of their finite glory but of the infinite, spiritual beauty of God himself. As mentioned above, what made both the tabernacle and the temple glorious was each contained a most holy (holy of holy) place where God was said to meet with the priests (Exod 30:36). As noted above, this space was to be carefully beautified, adorned with oils, implements, the ark of the covenant, an altar, and vestments, all of which were said to be holy by virtue of their proximity to the dwelling place of God. Simply touching the holy oil of the tabernacle could make both objects and persons holy (Exod 30:29). So this became the focal point of God's manifestation to the Old Testament community—here the Lamb was slain, atonement made, here the community met God. Notice how often God is referred to as being in the sanctuary (Ps 68:24, 73:17, 77:13, 150:1). This is the very same idea expressed by Solomon upon completing the temple: "I have surely built you an exalted house, and a place for you to dwell in forever" (2 Chr 6:2). And God did respond so that "the glory of the Lord filled the house of God" (2 Chr 5:14). Elsewhere:

> Then, at the dedication of the temple, when Solomon had finished praying, fire came down from heaven and consumed the burnt offering and the sacrifices; and the glory of the Lord filled the temple. And the priests could not enter the house of the Lord because the glory of the Lord had filled the Lord's house. When all the children of Israel saw how the fire came down, and saw the glory of the Lord on the temple, they bowed their faces to the ground on the pavement, and worshiped and praised the Lord, saying: "For He is good, For his mercy endures forever." (2 Chr 7:1–3)

So God comes to us, dwells with us, and makes holy and beautiful the space we have created for him in the church. What, then, is more wondrous than divine beauty?

But again, I fear the modern social imaginary limits our ability to recognize beauty, but more importantly for the church, it prevents us from consistently implementing the basic ideas involved in God's command to beautify our sacred spaces. Acting like pragmatic consumers in a vast marketplace, we now see the availability, the supposed neutrality, and the utility of a particular technology as sufficient justification for mindlessly bringing it into sacred space no matter what other messages it may bring with it. Not long ago I was at a monastery where the monastics were erecting an enormous new building that was to contain their main chapel. Even though it was still under construction, services were held, and some care was given to ensuring the beauty of the space. There were truly magnificent stained-glass windows, beautiful icons, an altar made of purest marble, etc. But being unfinished, lighting was a bit of a problem, and one day I came to the service and discovered the nave and part of the sanctuary had been festooned with crisscrossing strings of party or carnival lights. Obviously, this type of lighting is not neutral, but carries with it a host of meanings, mostly antithetical to the sanctity and beauty of the sacred space of a chapel. Those meanings include partying, eating, drinking, etc., enjoyed in a casual, frivolous, party-like, pleasure-oriented setting, and may even imply overindulgence, extravagance, self-centeredness, and moral laxity. These associations were, in fact, the first thing that another attendee expressed by saying, "all we need now are a bunch of round tables with red checkered tablecloths." Indeed, these are meanings we cannot separate from this technology, not even from their temporary or provisional use, and they are meanings which we should not bring into the sacred realm of the church, especially during the divine services. This was an obvious departure from "decorating the house for beauty," (2 Cor 3:6) which did indeed undo or debeautify what was already in place. As might be expected, the church was damaged. There were quite a few of us who took offense at this inappropriate lighting and found it difficult to worship under them. But alas, they were kept. They were, it was said, in good mercenary fashion, just lights, neutral, and, above all, they worked! But at what cost?[47]

The Language of Architecture

Everything I have said about sacred space and its beautification is actually implemented in the architecture of the church buildings we construct. Clearly, we will have to engage various experts, contractors, lawyers, engineers, and architects in order to meet government codes and make effective use of contemporary building materials and techniques. I don't think we need to insist these people be part of our parish community since they are not directly involved in the translation of theological principles into form but are just implementing an already-developed concept. However, one expert, the architect or designer, does need to be a person who does understand, from personal experience and conviction, the spiritual and liturgical needs of the church. So designing a church is not simply a matter of plugging in a series of supposedly orthodox elements, domes, cupulas, etc. We know the elements used in the building can and do have an effect on the very nature of worship. "In describing the late medieval introduction of pews into worship, he likens it to the placement of bleachers directly on the basketball court, writing that 'it changes the event into something entirely different.'"[48] Designing a church is also not simply a matter of copying the architectural styles of other orthodox cultures.[49]:

---

47. Interestingly, these inappropriate lights had wide-ranging consequences, causing a great deal of distress. Many were no longer able to worship there, relationships were broken, a priest was dismissed because he objected, and young people were driven to consider leaving the church they now considered badly damaged.

48. Kavanagh, as cited in Vinogradov, "Vernacular in Church Architecture," 25.

49. According to Nicholas Denysenko, "American Orthodox communities surely attempt to construct clichés of past models" (Denysenko, *Theology and Form*, 12).

> The age of the immigrant ghetto in America is over. That means that the national styles of Russia, Greece, Macedonia, and Romania no longer need to be enlisted to hold together a transplanted culture in a foreign land. In America at least, while Christians can indeed remain eschatological "strangers" and aliens, they are commissioned to transform the "flesh" of their own historical context just as Christ labored within the flesh of Palestinian culture.[50]

So designing a church is rather "an experiment—one whose success will not be measured in architectural critiques but by the fruit of a genuine life in Christ that is facilitated within it."[51] For that reason, we should "avoid architectural firms that offer a hybrid[52] composed of elements you choose from a pictorial buffet and then throw into a computer,"[53] and choose a faithful orthodox architect who will be able to transform the principles of our faith and liturgical requirements into a sacred space, using the architectural language of the culture in which we live.[54]

> The purpose of both church architecture and iconography, as they combine with music and aromas and light, consists not in bringing us to an exalted perception of external delights, but rather in a transformation within the hearts of the assembled faithful. The question for architecture is how it can serve its own iconic purpose. In the icon we must pass through the paints and lines to the prototype, just as the pieces of a parable must move us beyond the immediate story towards its central revelation. Architecture cannot satisfy participants by dazzling with formal and technical gymnastics. The forms themselves must move us toward their hidden content, bringing us to Paul's affirmation of "Christ who lives in me" (Gal. 2:20).[55]

---

50. Vinogradov, "Vernacular in Church Architecture," 30.

51. Vinogradov, "Vernacular in Church Architecture," 30.

52. As for contemporary Orthodox architecture, Denysenko "proposes that contemporary Orthodox architecture has evolved beyond the form/function paradigm and shows how architecture has become a synthetic repository of immigrant cultural identity, modern liturgical theology, and mission" (Denysenko, *Theology and Form*, 8).

53. Vinogradov, "Vernacular in Church Architecture," 28.

54. But defining just what an Orthodox architectural style might look like may not be as straightforward as it seems. Research done by Denysenko suggests at least three models: "These models represent the landscape of Orthodoxy in America, which is a collection of churches with varying ecclesiologies, liturgical styles, and approaches to mission. Three groups define the collections of churches: the immigrant model, the liturgical renewal model, and the American Church model" (Denysenko, *Theology and Form*, 224).

55. Vinogradov, "Vernacular in Church Architecture," 25.

In contrast to the glitzy expectations of a consumer-oriented culture, the process of beautifying a sacred space where God can dwell involves facilitating the engagement of the worshiping body with the divine. In the end, we have to ask, will the newly constructed or newly beautified temple "promote the glory of the community, the glory of its designer, the glory of its builder? Or will it show forth the glory of God's kingdom, spilling from its walls into the heart of the neighbor and travelling stranger?"[56]

---

56. Vinogradov, "Vernacular in Church Architecture," 30.

6

Distribution/Presentation

Those who live always according to the Spirit of Christ are, without the use of words, the best preachers of Christ and the most convincing apostles of Christianity.[1]

In the world of the marketplace, if you have products to sell, you will, of course, have to make them known and available to potential customers. Commercial enterprise refers to this as *Distribution*. It is marketing proper, and it involves advertising, branding, and a variety of other tools used to disseminate information about the products being made available. A brand, for example, is a combination of visual (logo), verbal (catchphrase), and personal (the CEO) information that allows a prospective customer to immediately recognize your business and, hopefully, associate it with a certain level of quality. Your brand is, as one author put it, "your promise to your customer. It tells them what they can expect from your products and services, and it differentiates your offering from your competitors."[2] The reason for this is "these days, everyone will Google you before they visit your restaurant, buy your products, hire you to perform a service, loan money to you or invest capital in your new or existing venture. Any time you interact with people—online or off—your brand will matter."[3] Presumably, then, a

---

1. Saint Theophan the Recluse, *Thoughts for Each Day*, 53.
2. Williams, "Basics of Branding," para. 1.
3. Martin, "Why Your Brand Plan," para. 1.

prospective visitor will look your church up on the Internet, recognize the OCA, the GOA, or the Antiochian Church as a respectable brand, and, as a result, visit the parish. Of course, you could also brand the local parish itself (e.g., St Basil's, All-Saints, Saddleback) or, if you are more into personality cults, you could brand the priest or pastor himself (e.g., Joel Osteen). According to some, for this to happen effectively today, one also needs what is now called a digital footprint, that is, a presence in cyberspace. The concept is nicely summarized by one business who writes, "The foundation of your brand is your logo. Your website, packaging, and promotional materials–all of which should integrate your logo–communicate your brand."[4]

When it comes to advertising in general, of which branding is just a small part, the logic seems to be that in order for people to buy your product, they have to know about it and, perhaps more importantly, you have to help them develop a desire for it and then convince them to buy your version of it. There are already numerous studies that reveal the dark side of this manipulative and often unethical activity. Vance Packard, for example, speaks of disquieting

> large-scale effort[s] being made, often with impressive success, to channel our unthinking habits, our purchasing decisions, and our thought processes by the use of insights gleaned from psychiatry and the social sciences. Typically, these efforts take place beneath our level of awareness, so that the appeals which move us are often, in a sense, "hidden." The result is that many of us are being influenced and manipulated, far more than we realize, in the patterns of our everyday lives.[5]

For what I hope are obvious reasons, the church cannot engage in any activity designed to deliberately manipulate or even disable human free will/choice in order to then encourage a particular decision. But what about a presence in the cyber world? That might be useful, if for no other reason than name recognition and simply providing information about our parishes. Moreover, since the church has no products, it really does not have to speak of distributing anything in the ordinary sense of commodities. What we are offering to the world is rather an introduction to the person of Christ and not our parishes or clergy. So I suppose we could brand Jesus, as in certain Jesus-only groups, but I think that diminishes or reduces him to an object for sale, and it completely violates who he is and what he has done for us. Nevertheless, if we wish to serve others, the church will have to, in some way, promote those services by not only making others aware of what

4. Williams, "Basics of Branding," para. 1
5. Packard, *Hidden Persuaders*, 31.

is available but also how to use and participate in those services. Given the nature of who and what we are offering, that information will have to be disseminated without manipulation or self-aggrandizement. For that reason, I suggest we avoid the term *advertising* and describe this activity in terms of *publicity* and *education,* considering how the church can best *present* its offerings to the world it desires to serve.

PUBLICITY

When I think of publicizing a parish, what I think ought to happen is its members and clergy, so excited by what they experience in the church, will go out and spontaneously talk to some their neighbors, colleagues, and friends about what they have seen and heard. They won't be able to help themselves. Some have called this "The Spontaneous Expansion of the Church."[6] Believe it or not, this is exactly how the early church spread the gospel throughout the Mediterranean region. It did not happen because of any organized missionary outreach and not because of programs, advertising campaigns, websites, concerts, lectures, and the like, but quite simply because everyday Christians talked about their faith in the market, at school, and at work. Along those lines, Michael Green claims early evangelism was not

> formal preaching, but the informal chattering to friends and chance acquaintances, in homes and wine shops, on walks, and around market stalls. They went everywhere gossiping the gospel; they did it naturally, enthusiastically, and with the conviction of those who are not paid to say that sort of thing. Consequently, they were taken seriously, and the movement spread, notably among the lower classes.[7]

Green's descriptions make it "abundantly clear that in contrast to the present day, when Christianity is highly intellectualized and dispensed by a professional clergy to a constituency increasingly confined to the middle class, in the early days the faith was spontaneously spread by informal evangelists and had its greatest appeal among the working classes."[8] As Paul Little put it, "[w]itnessing is that deep-seated conviction that the greatest favor I can do for others is to introduce them to Jesus Christ."[9] So in order for you to spontaneously shine the light of Christ through your life out into the

---

6. See Allen, *Spontaneous Expansion.*
7. Green, *Evangelism in the Early Church,* loc. 2731 of 5531.
8. Green, *Evangelism in the Early Church,* loc. 2748 of 5531.
9. Little, *Witnessing,* loc. 118 of 433.

world, you will have to be in the world, that is, have face-to-face contact with and access to other human beings.

However, today's social context makes this personal and spontaneous expansion of the church rather difficult for two reasons. *First*, there is the trend "toward giving up face-to-face for virtual contact—and, in some cases, a preference for the latter."[10] It seems our "desire to sustain and develop *online* friendships" may come

> at the cost of our availability to engage with our families, our neighbors and those we meet in the daily reality of our places of work, education and recreation. If the desire for virtual connectedness becomes obsessive, it may in fact function to isolate individuals from real social interaction while also disrupting the patterns of rest, silence and reflection that are necessary for healthy human development.[11]

So since we have now lost the art of direct personal interaction, we have to find some new alternative, and are thus under a great deal of pressure to make use of the very tools that have robbed us of that ability in the first place.

The second difficulty in communicating our faith has to do with the way in which the operating principle, individual freedom, has evolved in our culture. The basic Enlightenment insistence on the freedom to choose is no longer the simple impulse to freely fulfill desires. It has become a demand for unlimited choices in every area of life, as if the reality of our own freedom to choose depended on the proliferation of options. This rage for choice has in turn led to an extreme personalization. It is not just a matter of having unlimited choices but a kind of macro-choice, choosing which choices I am exposed to. According to Sunstein, "emerging technologies" are providing consumers with striking power to "'filter what they see.'"[12] They can now not only choose to visit some new outlets and avoid others, they can personalize their own personal news feed, avoiding anything that irritates them and limiting what they see exclusively to items like American, international, or sports news. With the digital tools of cyberspace,

> You need not come across topics and views that you have not sought out. Without any difficulty, you are able to see exactly what you want to see, no more, no less. You can easily find out

---

10. Rosen, "Virtual Friendship," 15 (emphasis his).
11. Benedict XVI, "New Technologies," para. 6.
12. Sunstein, *#Republic*, 5.

what "people like you" tend to like and dislike. You can avoid what they dislike. You can take a close look at what they like.[13]

This is a kind of filtering[14] along the lines of "I get to choose what I choose" is the ultimate expression of consumer sovereignty. The consumers apply multiple filters based on personality, geography, political orientation, etc., and define in advance what they choose to be exposed to. This consumer sovereignty forces businesses to target their advertising so it corresponds with those filters. Again, we observe that the digital tools of the modern cyberscape render this easily done. Since these firms know or can find out where you live and work, what you buy, the measure of your finances, your political orientation, your gender, email address, and so on, it is a small thing for them to target their messages in such a way as to match your filters. They know what you want to see, and they show it to you. For example, the sponsored sections of a news outlet's web page is now able to include advertising geared to the viewer's city and state because they know where she lives. This kind of targeted advertising played a significant role in the outside efforts to swing voter opinion during the 2016 election. A company called Cambridge Analytica developed a technique called "microtargeting," in which

> They collect data from Facebook and Twitter (which is perfectly legal) and have purchased an array of other data—about television preferences, airline travel, shopping habits, church attendance, what books you buy, what magazines you subscribe to—from third-party organizations and so-called data brokers.
> They take all this information and use it for what Nix calls "behavioral microtargeting"—basically individualized advertising.[15]

In other words, by gathering information on the kinds of filters being used by customers, they are able to "nuance" their message to "resonate more effectively with those key groups."[16] Hardly anyone can contest the convenience and effectiveness of these cybertechnologies.

So if a priest asks how he is to present his parish and the gospel to a world almost devoid of personal relationships and dominated by the extremes of consumer sovereignty, he will quite naturally turn to the tools that are readily available, which are, ironically, the very same tools that have

---

13. Sunstein, *#Republic*, 1.
14. For more on this idea of filtering, see Negroponte, *Being Digital*.
15. Illing, "Cambridge Analytica," paras. 31–32.
16. Illing, "Cambridge Analytica," para. 25.

created the depersonalization and extreme filtering. We have gotten so accustomed to these devices and structures, and so convinced of their supposedly neutral effectivity, that using them in the church requires, and is in fact given, little thought. We seem to have immersed ourselves and the church in the jargon and principles of a consumer culture. Church leaders now refer to their parishes as franchises, church polity as a business model, the senior priest as CEO, and outreach as development and marketing departments.[17] There seem, then, to be few objections to bringing the parish into the cyberworld and thus under the influence of its operational model. This can be seen in the following excerpts from an article entitled "Digital Tools for the Modern Fishermen."

> "One of the first administrative tasks I accomplished at Saint John's was to get set up Google Apps," said Father Andre. "Google Apps offers users access to Google's robust suite of cloud-based tools, like Gmail, Google calendar, Google docs, YouTube, and more. It is very important for the priest's church e-mail address to match the church web site domain, which helps to 'brand' the church and build awareness in the local community."

Father Andre adds that maintaining an up-to-date parish web site is also important.

> "In 2015, we updated our mission's web site by purchasing the #1 WordPress template called 'X Theme' from Themco," Father Andre continued. "The template was very easy to customize and included a one-time $64.00 charge. Saint John's new WordPress site is hosted by Go daddy, which is also the company we used to purchase our domain name. For those who are less tech-savvy, professional freelancers to help with web site and other projects can be found on Fiverr.com and Upwork.com. . . . An active web site and a Facebook presence with videos and images of church life helps people experience the community before they make their initial visit," Father Andre stated. "Ultimately we pray that what they see will encourage them to discover Jesus Christ in the life of his Orthodox Church."[18]

In light of the challenges created by digital technologies, I wonder if this optimistic endorsement of their use is justified. Are these tools as effective as they seem to be? Or are they actually doing damage to the church and the parishes that use them uncritically? Let's take a critical look at a couple

---

17. See "OCMC Seeks Development."
18. Paez, "Planting Grant Missions," paras. 3–4, 10.

of the tools mentioned in the previous quote (Google, Facebook, websites) and ask if their use in ministry settings raises any questions.

Google has been known primarily for its search engine and its free email service, Gmail. More recently it has evolved as a major marketing service. It uses a form of targeting to place ads and deliver them to all of the tools offered by Google. Many of these ads are generated automatically (targeted) based on ad-creative elements from the advertiser and location extensions. Google automatically optimizes ad delivery across Search, YouTube, Maps websites, and apps in its ad networks.[19] In other words, anytime you use one of these tools, two things will be happening: Google will be mining data on you, and you will be exposed to customized, targeted ads (YouTube videos interrupted by adverts, composing emails amidst flashing ads, etc.). In any case, ads seem to be what is driving the whole thing. By using their "free" services you are making money for Google. To that end, the most recent tools[20] are "designed to draw [even] more spending from e-commerce businesses and drive offline sales . . . to drive foot traffic to stores."[21] It is clear, then, that

> [t}he business model of social-media companies is based on advertising. Their true customers are the advertisers. But gradually, a new business model is emerging, based not only on advertising but on selling products and services directly to users. They exploit the data they control, bundle the services they offer, and use discriminatory pricing to keep for themselves more of the benefits that otherwise they would have to share with consumers.
>
> Social-media companies deceive their users by manipulating their attention and directing it towards their own commercial purposes. They deliberately engineer addiction to the services they provide.[22]

In other words, we are being used, tricked into focusing on our own ministry, thinking we are getting some useful service for free when we have actually become active and integral parts of a vast commercial enterprise that uses every participant to make money for itself. Do we not compromise our integrity, the very foundation of the gospel, by mindlessly participating in the grand deception? Are we not in danger of losing our freedom of mind, our autonomy? Are we not quite literally becoming pawns in the

---

19. See Marvin, "Google Marketing Live."
20. See Marvin, "Google Marketing Live."
21. Stambor, "Google Doubles Down," paras. 1, 13.
22. Price, "George Soros," 7.

game of desire, servants of mammon? Have we not sold our souls to the devil of convenience?

In addition to this general question of endorsing by participating, we should also ask if what we are getting from Google is worth the price? How effective are these tools? In and of themselves, they are indeed very effective in disseminating information. But in light of the limits created by extreme customization and individual filtering, one has to wonder how many people will actually google an Orthodox church? A traveling believer, perhaps? An occasional seeker? Chances are there will not be many cyber cascades[23] or trending videos to draw interest to the everyday offerings of these parishes.

This and several other concerns are highlighted by Google Search. If you sign up for this service, you are added to their network of businesses and advertisers. Actually, you don't even have to sign up for it. Google is so sure you will want this service that it creates, without your knowledge or permission, a window next to the search results list that is dedicated to your business. That window, usually at the right side of the screen, will contain the name, address, phone numbers, etc., of your business, a few pictures, and a link to Google Maps. In addition, the searcher provides an opportunity to ask questions of the business and even leave a review of the business. The reviews are posted and translated into a score of so-and-so many stars out of five. For example, one local Orthodox parish was given a five-star rating while the local monastery was only given one star. This is coupled with the ability to like and dislike the business (this is a Facebook knock-off and provides a bit of ego stroking). Finally, there is a row of small spaces at the bottom of the window that show other businesses that have been searched for by the persons who have also searched for you. In the case of a search for an Orthodox church, these windows showed pictures of and contained links to Baptist, Lutheran, Catholic, and Anglican churches. Here, the enquirer can compare the churches' respective ratings and see their geographic proximity to one another. These, then, are the competitors, and this service helps the seeker choose which one to patronize. The fact Google created the sidebar without being requested to do clearly reveals the manipulative nature of this so-called service. Moreover, Google retains control over this service and grants the owners only minimal editorial ability to Google accountholders. For example, you can correct the name, address, phone number, and

---

23. Speaking of Cybercascades in terms of information as wildfire and tipping points, Sunstein states that the phenomenon of group polarization is closely related to the widespread phenomenon of "social cascades" in which "information, including false information, can be spread to hundreds, thousands, or even millions by the simple press of a button" (Sunstein, *#Republic*, 98).

pictures. But you cannot turn off or control whether reviews, ratings, and competitors are displayed, or what the reviews say.

As already mentioned, the extreme fragmentation and polarization fostered by the Internet in general renders this particular tool relatively ineffective. Anecdotal evidence supports the impression that, with rare exceptions, the only people who search for a church online are people who are already believers or at least interested. My own experience and that of the priests that I have spoken with confirms the fact very few people are coming to the church as a result of a web search. So no, in terms of the benefit to the parish, this tool is not very effective. However, Google Search is extraordinarily effective in shifting public perception about church. By deliberately inserting churches (with or without its consent) into the vast cauldron of the North American marketplace, the parish is reduced to just one of thousands of competing enterprises., abusiness that can be rated like any commodity based on the whims of customers, liked and disliked according to individual taste, and selected from a list of competing companies. I am sure in the mind of the average American citizen there is a distinction between a for-profit-business and a church, but as those individuals and millions like them continue to subject themselves to Google's massive monopoly on information and its presentation, they (even church members) will gradually and uncritically absorb the prevailing business model. Even if they eschew that specific description, they will eventually transfer the dominant cybermediated conception onto the church, altering their understanding of its nature and their expectations of it. Google is doing the church a disservice by redefining it against our will. As Price comments, "This is particularly nefarious because social-media companies influence how people think and behave without them even being aware of it."[24]

Facebook. Everything I have said about the manipulative, unethical, and addictive activities of Google can also be applied to Facebook. This company mines data from its users (with and without their knowledge) and sells that information for profit to better position itself among its competitors and to manipulate public opinion with a finely tuned approach to "digital mass persuasion."[25] Most recently, the "UK Information Commissioner's Office (ICO), the country's data protection watchdog, has slapped Facebook with fines to the tune of $660,000—the maximum allowed by law—after an investigation concluded that 'Facebook contravened the law by failing to safeguard people's information.'"[26] In the sociopolitical realm, "trust and

---

24. Price, "George Soros," 5.
25. "UK Hits Facebook," para. 8
26. "UK Hits Facebook," para. 1.

confidence in the integrity of our democratic processes risk being disrupted because the average voter has little idea of what is going on behind the scenes."[27] So every time a parish sets up a Facebook account, it is unwittingly buying into this manipulative scheme. The data it willingly offers Facebook is used for purposes that are not only unethical and illegal, but decidedly anti-Christian. This makes me wonder why our churches would want to be associated in any way with such a corrupt and corrupting business. Is it just because we want to be seen as up-to-date? If so, we need to ask ourselves if the damage done to the church is worth whatever benefits we think we derive from being seen as "with it."

Another danger posed by Facebook is rooted in what we could call its addictive character. According to George Soros, these companies "deliberately engineer addiction to the services they provide."[28] How that is done was recently revealed by a now contrite founder of Facebook, Sean Parker:

> "The thought process that went into building these applications, Facebook being the first of them, was all about: 'How do we consume as much of your time and conscious attention as possible?' That means that we need to sort of give you a little dopamine hit every once in a while, because someone liked or commented on a photo or a post or whatever. And that's going to get you to contribute more content, and that's going to get you. . . more likes and comments."[29]

This "social-validation feedback loop"[30] is the root of this addiction, and it is nothing short of a deliberate exploitation of "a vulnerability in human psychology."[31] Recent research shows "people's psychological characteristics can be accurately predicted from their digital footprints, such as their Facebook Likes or Tweets."[32] So is the church luring its members into this addictive behavior by officially endorsing the service by establishing a Facebook page for the parish? Do we thereby encourage members to spend hours checking on "friends" rather than being with their families, feeding their children, investing in their spiritual life? I fear this addictive behavior is very much present in our parishes and is spreading rapidly.

For all of its drawbacks, Facebook supporters claim it gives believers an unprecedented opportunity to create a more intimate and meaningful

27. "UK Hits Facebook," para. 11.
28. Price, "George Soros," 3.
29. Lee, "Facebook Founding President Sounds Alarm," para. 3.
30. Allen, "Sean Parker Unloads on Facebook," para. 3.
31. Allen, "Sean Parker Unloads on Facebook," para. 2.
32. Matz et al., "Psychological Targeting," 1.

community. That raises the interesting question of whether or not community is even possible in cyberspace. Let's start by asking if intimacy and/or friendship, both constitutive elements of community, can be sustained in the cybersphere. Historically, we have thought of intimacy in terms of a closeness that involves the exclusivity of personal knowledge. On a social network your best friend and your other fifty "friends" (mere acquaintances) will share posted information on an equal basis. So this more-or-less public nature of the information posted on Facebook seems to make this exclusivity difficult at best. Nevertheless, there is talk of online intimacy. For example, Lisa Reichelt introduced the concept of "ambient intimacy" which she said "is about being able to keep in touch with people with a level of regularity and intimacy that you wouldn't usually have access to, because time and space conspire to make it impossible."[33] She goes on to claim knowing these details actually creates intimacy.[34] But is simply having knowledge, even intimate detailed knowledge, of a person in whose life we do not otherwise participate, to whom I am not fully present, the same thing as personal, face-to-face intimacy? Does ambient intimacy provide enough strength of personal presence to constitute a truly intimate interpersonal relationship, or does it provide just enough connection to keep us from pursuing real intimacy? If we insist on using the idea of cyberintimacy, we must recognize it is something very different than the traditional concept. Now it has to

> conceptualize ambient intimacy as a feeling of closeness that is developed in a peripheral way (through constant and regular reception and/or interaction through social media). Intimacy refers to a feeling of closeness, and ambient refers to the peripheral process of developing intimacy by aimless browsing and spontaneous interactions on social media.[35]

The same kind of redefinition is required if we use the term "friendship" in the context of cyberspace. Until recently the ideas of intimacy and close friendship have been associated with a relatively small number of acquaintances. The reason is

> to be someone's best friend requires a minimum investment of time. More than that, though, it takes emotional energy. Caring about someone deeply is exhausting. At a certain point, at somewhere between 10 and 15 people, we begin to overload, just as

---

33. Reichelt, "Ambient Intimacy," para. 3.
34. Lin et al., "Ambient Intimacy on Twitter," 10.
35. Lin et al., "Ambient Intimacy on Twitter," 2.

we begin to overload when we have to distinguish between too many tones.[36]

Yet the speed and the resources of Computer-Mediated Communication (CMC) seem to be altering these conceptions of intimacy and friendship. Today we claim thousands of friends on various social networking sites. Can we really call these online connections friendships? At the very least, online social networking seems to have changed the way we understand friendship. Christine Rosen suggests we are dealing with a new taxonomy of friendship:

> "Friendship" in these virtual spaces is thoroughly different from real-world friendship. In its traditional sense, friendship is a relationship which, broadly speaking, involves the sharing of mutual interests, reciprocity, trust, and the revelation of intimate details over time and within specific social (and cultural) contexts. Because friendship depends on mutual revelations that are concealed from the rest of the world, it can only flourish within the boundaries of privacy; the idea of public friendship is an oxymoron.
>
> The hypertext link called "friendship" on social networking sites is very different: public, fluid, and promiscuous, yet oddly bureaucratized. Friendship on these sites focuses a great deal on collecting, managing, and ranking the people you know. Everything about MySpace, for example, is designed to encourage users to gather as many friends as possible, as though friendship were philately.[37]

So cyberfriendship is a mixed and fluid concept that is being redefined. As Rosen notes, "The use of the word 'friend' on social networking sites is a dilution and a debasement. . .it is not an expression of the human need for companionship, but of a different need no less profound and pressing: the need for status."[38] So what does all of this say about the possibility of community? If the ideas of both friendship and intimacy are fundamentally altered, what are we to say about the larger concept of community? Here again we encounter a redefinition of terminology. Recent research indicates "virtual communities differ from real-life communities on the basis upon which participants perceive their relationships to be intimate."[39] In cyberspace there is a tendency to base feelings of closeness on shared interests

---

36. Gladwell, *Tipping Point*, 177.
37. Rosen, "Virtual Friendship," 11.
38. Rosen, "Virtual Friendship," 12.
39. Smith and Kollock, *Communities in Cyberspace*, 185.

rather than shared social characteristics such as gender, age, and race. But because racism, ethnocentrism, and stereotyping flourish in cyberspace, some have suggested the idea of true community online is a fantasy, an illusion. Or is it just a matter of redefinition? Rheingold, for example, argues these communities "are social aggregations that emerge from the Net when enough people carry on . . . public discussions long enough, with sufficient human feeling, to form webs of personal relationships in cyberspace."[40]

If participating in social media platforms exposes the church to unethical and addictive practices, and if those practices cannot provide community in the sense of an intimate fellowship of believers, then we can only conclude that Facebook is doing the church a disservice and robbing it of the very things it promises.[41] The naïve hope that "An active web site and a Facebook presence with videos and images of church life helps people experience the community before they make their initial visit"[42] is at best nothing more than wishful thinking and at its worst a form of self-deception, that is, an excuse for projecting the believer's own responsibility for initiating contact with the church onto the nonbelieving, mostly uninterested segments of our society.

One final note on Facebook: it seems the users of this medium are convinced almost everyone will use the service. This is evident in the fact that the company itself has created Facebook pages for companies that have not asked for it and without their knowledge or consent. Our church in Raleigh, North Carolina was provided with a page even though we had decided as a parish not to use the service. But this assumption of irresistibility also affects Facebook users who effectively eliminate anyone not using the service from any information they want to share. So we who do not use the service never found out about the birth of children, the death of friends, the surgeries of acquaintances. I don't think this contributes positively to overall communication in the parish.

Web Pages. That leaves us to evaluate the last of these digital tools, the parish website. Most church websites can be classified either as presenting information about the parish or as inviting the visitor to participate in some form of religious practice. In the literature this distinction is captured in the phrase "religion online" as opposed to "online religion." The first category is clear and unproblematic. Examples would include the websites of any

---

40. Cited by Dawson and Cowan, *Religion Online*, loc. 83 of 4045.

41. "Although these attributes have the potential to bridge gaps and unite communities, they also have the potential to fragment interaction and divide groups by leading people to spend more time on special interests and by screening out less preferred contact" (Van Alstyne and Brynjolfsson, "Electronic Communities," 2).

42. Paez, "Planting Grant Missions" para. 13.

number of parishes. These are exclusively informative. One potential difficulty arises from the fact many of these informative sites are also commercialized by association with the companies that are paid to help create the sites. For example, one such company, Squarespace, is the all-in-one platform to build a beautiful online presence, from websites and online stores to marketing tools and analytics. They claim to offer all you need to create a website, all you need to sell online, all you need to market yourself, all you need to measure success.[43] So we are again faced with the question of how much of this commercial thinking is transferred to the church and to what extent the church compromises its own integrity by becoming indebted to such a for-profit company. We also have to ask about the implications of using tools like Google Calendar to post scheduling information. True, it is only information, but using this service allows the Google logo to appear on the parish website and, more importantly, ties the parish into the Google network with all of its nefarious schemes.

The second category is what interests me most since they give the appearance of simulating real-world activities. In many cases, the websites of Christian churches offer a section on prayer. The simplest form offers an opportunity to type in a prayer request, which is then forwarded to some prayer groups within the church or organization. This can be taken a step further. In some cases, you are not only asked to write a request, you are offered a prayerful "environment" (music, visuals, instructions) and asked to pray while in a virtual chapel.

Another way in which participation is encouraged is through links to ongoing projects the visitor can engage in. For example, one site (UMC) offers a link to a clean energy initiative, with several ways of participating. Of course, it is not really clear whether this is online participation or just the implementation in the real world of suggestions made online.

The most ambitious of these sites offer a worship experience, communion, baptism, and even confession online. Worship amounts to viewing an actual service via video stream or joining other gaming characters in a virtual church or a guided session through various parts of a liturgy with text, prayers, sermons, music, and, of course, visuals. This, of course, raises the question of whether the corporate worship of the church can be practiced in this way. In what sense is being there a requirement? In what sense is the individual on the Net actually being there? If we should conclude, as some have (see below), the sacraments are among the givens that predetermine the shape of worship, then we are forced to ask: Are those who are offering them in cyberspace proclaiming or violating the gospel?

---

43. https://www.squarespace.com.

EDUCATION

As I have argued elsewhere, the gospel is not simply information about Christ but rather the person of Christ himself. Our basic task is to personally introduce him and not simply transfer information about him. However, we do know that as the fulfillment of the ancient promise, Jesus was born into and ministered within the flow of a concrete historical context. The evangelist Matthew goes to extraordinary lengths to establish that human context by beginning his gospel account with a detailed genealogy of Jesus, and this is certainly information about Jesus. This historical context established by that information serves as a unified, totalizing backdrop for our encounter with the person of Christ. Without this overarching narrative, we simply cannot understand Jesus' place or role in the redemptive plan of God. So teaching all that Christ commanded (Matt 28:19–20) involves telling the whole grand narrative of the history of God's provision of salvation.

While almost no one in the church would deny it is our responsibility to teach and thus prepare people for life in Christ, there is considerable discussion on just how we should fulfill that charge. Again, there is evidence we are importing secular devices and structures we think we can redefine for ecclesial use but that are actually redefining us. Fortunately, the Canons give us some practical instructions, a few basic principles that are to govern just how that teaching is to take place.[44]

First, this teaching is to be gentle and devoid of coercion and manipulation.

> As for a Bishop, or Priest, or Deacon that strikes believers for sinning, or unbelievers for wrongdoing, with the idea of making them afraid, we command that he be deposed. For the Lord has nowhere taught that; on the contrary, he himself when struck did not strike back; when reviled, he did not revile his revilers; when suffering, he did not threaten.[45]

---

44. In each one of the following examples, we see the authors of the Canons simply assumed it was their Christ-given responsibility to teach everything Christ had taught them. This is affirmed in the Canon of St. Gennadios, the Patriarch of Constantinople: "Our Lord and God and Savior Jesus Christ, after handing over the preaching of the Gospel to His holy disciples and sending them forth over the whole inhabited earth as teachers, gave an express command that what they had received from Him freely they were to impart the same to men freely, without charging therefore any copper, or silver, or gold, or any other thing of material or earthly value whatever" (Orthodox Eastern Church and Cummings, *Rudder*, 179).

45. Canon 27 from the 85 Canons of the Holy Apostles. Compare Canon IX of the 1st and 2nd Synod; Canon V of Antioch; Canons LVII, LXII, LXXVI, CVI, CVII of Carthage; and 1 Pet 2:23. See Orthodox Eastern Church and Cummings, *Rudder*.

In his explanation of the Canon, Nicodemus adds,

> In teaching his disciples his divine commandments the Lord used to say, "Whatever I say to you, I say also to all." (Mark 13:37). One of his commandments is to turn our left cheek to anyone that strikes our right cheek (Matthew 5:39). If, therefore, this commandment ought to be kept by all Christians, it ought much more to be obeyed by those in Holy Orders, and especially by bishops, regarding whom divine Paul wrote to Timothy that a bishop ought not to be a striker (I Timothy 3:3).
>
> That is what the present Canon says also. If any bishop, or priest, or deacon strikes those Christians who disappoint him, or unbelievers that do wrong to others, with a view to making others afraid of him with such blows, we command that he be deposed. For in no part of the gospel has the Lord taught to do such a thing as that. In fact, he has taught us quite the contrary with his example, since when beaten by the soldiers and Jews, at the time of his Passion, he did not lift a hand to beat them in return. When accused and insulted, he did not insult others, nor did he accuse them. Even when suffering on the Cross, he did not threaten to chastise them, but begged his Father to pardon them.[46]

Second, this teaching is to be based solely on the Holy Scriptures. After giving careful instructions to the clergy on how they are to discharge their duties, Canon 85 legislates which books are to be used as sources for teaching in the church. Canon 9 speaks negatively of those heretical books, which were banned (which would have included the so-called "Gospel according to St. Thomas," "Revelations" of Abraham, Isaac, Jacob, and of the "The Alphabet of Alphabets"):

> If anyone reads to the public in churches, the books of impious writers bearing false inscriptions and purporting to be holy, to the injury of laity and clergy, let him be deposed.[47]
>
> To all you Clergymen and Laymen let the following books be venerable and holy: Of the Old Covenant, the five of Moses, namely, Genesis, Exodus, Leviticus, Numbers, and Deuteronomy; the one of Jesus of Nave (commonly called Joshua in English); the one of Judges; the one of Ruth; the four of the kingdoms; two Chronicles of the Book of Days; two of Esdras; one of

---

46. Orthodox Eastern Church and Cummings, *Rudder*, 140.

47. Canons 62 and 85 from the 85 Canons of the Holy Apostles. See also Canons II and LXIII of the 6th Ecumenical Synod; Canon IX of the 7th Ecumenical Synod; and Canon LI of Laodicea. Orthodox Eastern Church and Cummings, *Rudder*, 140.

> Esther; three of the Maccabees; one of Job; one Psalter (Psalms); three of Solomon, namely, Proverbs, Ecclesiastes, and the Song of Songs; twelve of the Prophets; one of Isaiah; one of Jeremiah; one of Ezekiel; one of Daniel; outside of these it is permissible for you to recount in addition thereto also the Wisdom of very learned Sirach by way of teaching your younger folks. Our own books, that is to say, those of the New Covenant, comprising four Gospels, namely, that of Matthew, of Mark, of Luke, and of John; fourteen Epistles of Paul; two Epistles of Peter, three Epistles of John; one of James; one of Jude; two Epistles of Clement; and the Injunctions addressed to you Bishops through me, Clement, in eight books, which ought not to be divulged to all on account of the secret matters they contain) and the Acts of us apostles.[48]

Both Canons give clear statements on the books that are allowed for teaching. Since they are limited to the recognized books of the Holy Scriptures, these Canons clearly concentrate the content of our teaching all things on the story told by the Bible. I take this to mean that in the church we will not be using materials generated by secular philosophers, pop-psychologists, or businesspeople, no matter how good they might be, to fulfill this part of our missiological responsibility. I am not suggesting there is no place in the church for considering other sources, but I am saying in the formal exercise of our commission to teach all things, we rely exclusively on the grand narrative of the Bible. So until that work is done, there should be no book studies in the church, but only Bible studies.

Third, the Canons describe the overall procedure for this teaching ministry and show how other sources of information (the fathers) are to be used:

> We declare that the deans of churches, on every day, but more especially on the Lord's Days, must teach all the Clergy and the laity words of truth out of the Holy Bible, analyzing the meanings and judgments of the truth, and not deviating from the definitions already laid down, or the teaching derived from the God-bearing Fathers; but also, if the discourse be one concerning a passage of Scripture, not to interpret it otherwise than the luminaries and teachers of the church in their own written works have presented it; and let them rather content themselves with these discourses than attempt to produce discourses of their own, lest, at times being resourceless, they overstep the bounds of propriety. For by means of the teaching afforded by

---

48. Orthodox Eastern Church and Cummings, *Rudder*, 194.

the aforesaid Fathers, the laity, being apprized of the important and preferred things, and of the disadvantageous and rejectable, are enabled to adjust their lives for the better, and do not become a prey to the ailment of ignorance, but, by paying due attention to what is taught, they sharpen their wits so as to avoid suffering wrongly, and for fear of impending punishments they work out their own salvation.[49]

So according to our Tradition, teaching the fundamentals of the faith, which includes all Christ taught, everything he passed down to his apostles, should involve all educational ministries (opportunities) of the church. This teaching will have to take place according to the requirements laid down in the canons of the church and be gentle, nonviolent, and complete. In keeping with these principles, the church has, over the years, developed catechetical materials and methods appropriate to and adequate for the task.

However, today, under the pressures of the contemporary social imaginary, many in the church are abandoning as outdated the traditional materials and are looking outside the church for, and in some cases using, methods they consider more effective and interesting. Consider the popular Montessori philosophy of education as just one example of what is at stake for the church.

The Montessori Method is founded on an educational philosophy developed by a late-nineteenth-century physician, Maria Montessori. It is "a child-centered educational approach based on scientific observations of children from birth to adulthood."[50] Based on these observations,

> Her basic principle was to "follow the child." A Montessori classroom is carefully prepared to allow the child to work independently and allow for the joy of self-discovery. Teachers introduce materials and children are free to choose them, again and again, working and discovering, and ultimately mastering ideas. Lessons are given, but the goal is for children to discover the answers by using the "auto-didactic," or "self-correcting" materials that are found only in Montessori classrooms.[51]

In the United States interest in this philosophy is concentrated in the The American Montessori Society which sees itself as "the foremost

---

49. Canon 19 of the sixth Ecumenical Council. See also Apostolic Canon LVI; Canons II, XVI of the 1st Ecumenical Synod; Canon XIX of Laodicea; Canons LXXIX, CXXXI, CXXXLI, CXXXIII of Carthage; Canon X of Peter; and Canon VI of John the Faster. Orthodox Eastern Church and Cummings, *Rudder*, 240–41.

50. "What is Montessori?," para. 1, cited from the American Montessori Association.

51. "Montessori Philosophy," para. 1.

advocate for quality Montessori education, an innovative, child-centered approach to learning."⁵² Because the teacher is the very foundation of the methodology, the AMS offers training and to teach children in age levels: birth through 3, 2–6, 6–12, and 12–18.

> Appropriately prepared teachers are the foundation of Montessori education. AMS offers nearly 100 affiliated programs, providing education for prospective teachers of children and youth birth through age 18, as well as for Montessori administrators.⁵³

It should not surprise us that this now-commercialized methodology has been brought into the church. Much of the movement has been the result of deliberate efforts by The National Association of Catechesis of the Good Shepherd. This association was established in 1983 in order to "support catechists, parents, and others in the church and beyond, as they grow in their understanding of the religious potential of children."⁵⁴ All of this was an attempt to give a thoroughly Montessori dependent methodology some religious or even Christian content. Committed to the child-centered approach, the association's founder reminds us "constantly to look to the child for that sign of a deeply religious life—joy—and to always ask the question: 'What face of God is the child telling us he or she needs to see?'"⁵⁵ Although it is a primarily Roman Catholic-developed organization, it did eventually attract the attention of the Orthodox, and the methodology is now "actively implemented in many Orthodox parishes in the USA. It first came to Orthodoxy in 2003 at St Athanasius Orthodox Church in Goleta, California. In 2010, the first Orthodox Formation Leader, Seraphima Sierra Butler, offered two courses, Santa Barbara, California and Franklin, Tennessee."⁵⁶ In the meantime it has been endorsed by bishops,⁵⁷ educators,⁵⁸ and theologians.⁵⁹ It now provides Montessori teacher training and certification and is aimed at establishing programs to nurture a child's spirituality.⁶⁰ One school claims the program benefits the parish:

---

52. "About the American Montessori Society," para. 1.
53. Purnell, "AMS Seeks Assistant Manager of Membership," line 1.
54. "Catechesis of the Good Shepherd," para. 3.
55. "History of the Catechesis of the Good Shepherd," para. 1.
56. "CGS in the Orthodox Tradition," para. 1.
57. See Mahaffey, "Endorsement Letter"; Bishop, "Beloved in Christ."
58. See Vrame, "Endorsement from Rev. Anton C. Vrame."
59. See Ford, "Catechesis of the Good Shepherd."
60. See Mooney, "Nurturing Spirituality."

Children experience and grow in their faith while participating in the Children's Room. As children share their experience parent interest peaks. Some parents, who had stopped coming to church, returned in order to enroll their children in the hands-on style Sunday school. The day school generates income for the parish, as it makes use of classroom space, during the week and community is built as parishioners become involved in the program.[61]

However, the main attraction seems to be the promise of it completely avoiding "that kind of religious training that many of us may have received [which] was too intellectual and too moralistic, providing only information about God."[62] It is instead a way of "helping the children to 'be in love with God in a manner that creates harmony and happiness within them, with others, and their world.'"[63]

This methodology has much that commends it. It would appear to be an improvement over the dry and dusty texts sometimes used in the past. It is certainly gentle and loving in keeping with the guidelines of the Canons. It appears to be, at least in part, based on Holy Scripture, and it does cover a few important aspects of Orthodox practice and Tradition. But then again, much of it seems to be simple common sense, or at least ideas and principles that have long been part of the Orthodox tradition of spiritual formation. So it causes me to wonder why we need to look outside the church for educational principles when we already have them. Why this rage to have new, up-to-date, scientifically-proven, and thus legitimate, programs, when God has already given us everything we need? Why should we get our church schools tangled up in the expensive process of training teachers in a method essentially foreign to the church, grasping after legitimacy through a secular certification process? Aside from the questionable practices of using this approach to earn money for the parish, that is, transforming it into a for-profit educational institution, there remains one fundamental concern: Can an educational program that is directed by the learner, in this case children, provide a context for genuine teaching and learning, or does it not leave us open to the whims and desires of the natural, sinful predilections of all human beings? It sounds somewhat unrealistic and naïve to suggest so much will be achieved if only the child himself is the teacher.[64] Yet, that is exactly

---

61. "Saints Constantine and Helene Academy: A Montesorri School." https://www.schacademypreschool.com.
62. Cavalletti, *Good Shepherd and the Child*, 11.
63. Ford, "Catechesis of the Good Shepherd," 1.
64. Ford, "Catechesis of the Good Shepherd," 2.

what Montessori advocates hope to achieve by following the child, which to them means

> *carefully observing* what really works, what makes a deep positive impression, what leads to peace, prayer, serious reflection, great concentration, and focused attention; and observing what the children love—what leads them to experience a tranquil, "joyful satisfaction," what helps them "fall in love with God.[65]

In many cases what makes one happy, tranquil, etc., has nothing whatsoever to do with God or his word. This sounds like we are treating those learning as though they were customers and that a measure of their satisfaction is the key to measuring our own effectiveness. It seems even here we cannot escape the pervasive influence of a commercialized society. It is so deeply engrained in our psyche that we even see our children as customers who have to be satisfied and thus determine how effective our marketing of truth has been. But is it not the church that is to direct the formation of its members? Is it not basic to our understanding of the faith that we are all learners, followers, in need of submitting to God rather than telling God what makes us happy? Can a method of religious instruction be sound and true to Christian principles if its fundamental premise is false? Is this not a case of allowing the structures and devices of our commercialized culture to infiltrate the church, redefining our relationship to God, our teachings, while causing us to neglect our own Tradition?

---

65. Ford, "Catechesis of the Good Shepherd," 2 (emphasis original).

7

Consumption/Participation

The real consumer has become a consumer of illusions. The commodity is this materialized illusion, and the spectacle is its general expression.[1]
The spectacle is the material reconstruction of the religious illusion.[2]

IF A BUSINESS IS to succeed, its products will not only have to be produced and sold but also bought and used, that is, consumed. Of course, this idea of *consumption* makes little sense in the absence of products, and as we have seen, the church has no products, no commodities it is selling. However, it does offer a number of services such as liturgical gatherings and sacraments such as the Eucharist and Confession. So what do the potential users of these ecclesial offerings do with them? Does one acquire and then use a liturgy? Are the beneficiaries of the sacraments autonomously making use of some service? Are they what commerce would call end-users or consumers? No, I think a more appropriate way of expressing the ecclesial analog to the business world's idea of consumption is to speak of intentional *participation*. What the recipient of sacramental offerings does is personally engage by giving themselves over to, surrendering to, the happening, and receiving the benefits afforded. So how can the church facilitate that kind of mindful participation in the services it offers? By way of illustration, consider the challenge of enabling participation in the liturgy/Eucharist and in the rite of Confession.

1. Debord, *Society of the Spectacle*, 40.
2. Debord, *Society of the Spectacle*, 28.

LITURGY/EUCHARIST

In the case of the divine liturgy, the church brings individuals together in one place and celebrates the service together with them. It is not done to them or even for them but together with them as a multiindividual, collaborative exercise of faith. Here, there are no bystanders, no spectators, but only participants. According to Orthodox teaching, the celebration of the liturgy is to take place within a specific spatially, temporally, and personally defined context, created by the gathering of the faithful, under the administration of a priest duly ordained by a canonical bishop, according to the rubrics of Scripture and Tradition, and by the power and descent of the Holy Spirit. In other words, an instance of the church is constituted by the actual, physical *gathering (sunaxij)*[3] of the faithful for the celebration of the Eucharist. That this gathering is of a personal nature is clear from the fact the thus-constituted group of faithful is also called the body of Christ, that is, they are unified by the person of the fully present Christ. By partaking of one cup and of one bread (1 Cor 10:16, 17), the many become one. In order for that to happen, the faithful have to be physically present in the place where one eucharistic Lamb (bread) is being offered and received. This presence, this gathering, is taken so seriously that the Eucharist cannot be celebrated unless some of the faithful have come together. A priest may not celebrate alone. In other words, the faithful have to be physically, personally present to one another and to Christ.

Moreover, the reality of the sacrament is tied to the actual presence of the gifts prepared, consecrated, fractured, and distributed by the priest in a particular place, that is, in the context of the gathering. We also have exact instructions, rubrics, as to what kind of bread (leavened wheat bread, not crackers) and wine (pure red wine with no additives, not water or some other liquid) we are to use, how to cut the Lamb,[4] pierce the Lamb, pour wine and water into the chalice, and so on. These actions are not context-neutral but are to be done in the actual presence of believers gathered in a particular physical place, bound not only by time and space but by the dictates of holy Tradition.

For these reasons, the Orthodox Church has consistently insisted that its services be offered in the actual places set aside for the gathering of believers. But what happens when, because of natural disasters, wars, or epidemics, we are unable to gather, or are even forbidden from gathering, in those designated spaces? This has of course happened, but for most of us

---

3. Schmemann, *Eucharist*, 15–16.

4. The cube-shaped piece of bread which symbolizes the body of Christ throughout the Liturgy.

those are occurrences of a distant past that have not directly affected us until now. Beginning in late winter 2020, government agencies around the world issued stay-at-home orders in an effort to slow the spread of the deadly Coronavirus.[5] Suddenly, deprived of access to our worship spaces, we all asked how we could, in spite of that, retain some semblance of our religious practices. Some asked if it might be possible to create the conditions for our services and peoples' participation in them in some other, perhaps nonspatially bound places such as cyberspace. Others wondered if Zoom, Skype, or live video feeds of actual services might serve as a temporary substitute for the in-person participation in the life of the church. Indeed, almost overnight, the vast majority of parishes and churches were actively gearing up to do just that—video stream their services. This nearly universal decision was hardly unexpected. Many had already been using this technology. Our familiarity with it, our love affair with modern technology, its immediate availability, and the fact that many others, such as those in higher education, were rapidly turning to these technologies, all contributed to the impression that streaming was the obvious solution. Admittedly, there were very few alternatives, yet the move was made with almost no public discussion, no careful reflection, no consideration of the theological implications, potential dangers, or unintended consequences of which the main body of parishioners were made aware. To be fair these decisions were made under duress, if not a sense of panic, and there certainly was considerable discussion of the proposed measures behind the scenes. For example, Archbishop Elpidophoros of America reports:

> Having discussed the situation with the Sacred Center of Orthodoxy, at length, and having inquired specifically about the United States, I received his All Holiness Ecumenical Patriarch Bartholomew's reply, namely, that we should allow for the divine services, including Divine Liturgies, to be celebrated in our Holy churches behind closed doors . . . In this way we may be able to keep our liturgical tradition alive, even in this minimal way . . .[6]

For all those who were forced to stay at home, the archbishop went on to suggest "we may broadcast through streaming and other means the aforementioned services for the spiritual benefit of our faithful."[7] I realize the church had to do something to meet the spiritual needs of the people in the absence of being able to physically attend church and that there was little time to respond. Under the circumstances, this move to what is thought to

---

5. See Kokkinidis, "Greece Overrules Church."
6. Kampouris, "Ecumenical Patriarch Announces Halt," para. 5.
7. Kampouris, "Ecumenical Patriarch Announces Halt," para. 6.

be neutral[8] is understandable, and this turn to technology came to dominate the church's response to many aspects of the crisis.[9] But in the case of the liturgy/Eucharist, almost overnight the church, collectively and mindlessly, surrendered itself to the most immediately available solution.

Reflection and reservations came later. After just a few weeks of video-streamed services, one seminary student lamented, "This doesn't seem right. I'm not sure what this is, but it is certainly not worship."[10] We heard this sentiment from many of the faithful. The feeling was clearly expressed by many who resisted and even protested against not being allowed to physically attend the service.[11] They knew something essential was missing. They were not satisfied by what they experienced as inadequate, a counterfeit. These questions were and are boiling up from the ranks of the dissatisfied faithful. So yes, we should be asking questions even now after the fact. Does this technology even deliver on its claim to provide a worship experience? Have we offered the people a false bill of goods? Are the presuppositions upon which this technology is built at odds with the teaching of the church? Has using it changed us or damaged the very nature of worship? Did we have any other alternatives? What will we do which this practice and these devices once the lockdown eventually ends? In the hope of stimulating some needed discussion, let me make four observations about the nature and the use of live-feed video streaming of a divine liturgy.

First, on a conceptual level, this practice redefines both the participants in and the nature of the liturgical event. On the one hand, the faithful watching at home are no longer participants but simply observers or, better yet, spectators. In the absence of actual personal presence, there can be no corporate affirmation of, for example, the petitions of the litanies, no unified singing, reading, chanting the creed, the hymns, or the Scriptures. Even if the observers do sing, read, etc., that is being done in isolation

---

8. "On the contrary, the society of the spectacle is a form that chooses its own technological content. If the spectacle, considered in the limited sense of the "mass media" that are its most glaring superficial manifestation, seems to be invading society in the form of a mere technical apparatus, it should be understood that this apparatus is in no way neutral and that it has been developed in accordance with the spectacle's internal dynamics" (Debord, *Society of the Spectacle*, para. 24).

9. See "COVID-19 Digital Toolkit for Parishes." I have no doubt some of these tools can be effective in transmitting information as in the case with prayers, service texts, church school lessons, and the like. My concern here is whether or not digital technology can be used effectively in the case of the Liturgy, the Eucharist, and the other Sacraments.

10. Conversation with a student at Duke Divinity School, March 2020.

11. See Kokkinidis, "Greek Faithful Defy Coronovirus Scare," and Synovitz, "Coronavirus vs. the Church."

with no immediate awareness of any others that might be doing the same.[12] Here, there is no together, no gathering. On the other hand, this practice transforms the clergy into performers who are essentially going through the motions, executing the rite in order to be seen or observed by others. I am not suggesting they see themselves as actors—that impression exists mainly in the minds of the spectators—however, I do think knowing they have a digital audience does weigh on their minds and does affect their execution the liturgy. As if to prove that point, when the technology disappoints and the clergy cannot be seen or heard as desired, the observers simply send text messages during the service demanding the necessary corrections. Focusing on the external evidence (sight and sound) that something is being presented obviously transforms by definition the video-streamed liturgy into a kind of spectacle[13] or theater, that is, into the mere appearance of something which those external markers cannot possibly cause it to be. Accepting such a redefinition or substitution is obviously at odds with the teaching of the church. I am sure what the clergy and servers do and experience in the church is indeed liturgy for them, but it is not and cannot be that for those watching a video representation.

Second, what a video-streamed liturgy does do is allow the clergy to be informationally present to others. The video feed is transmitting data, information about, among other things, the clergy in the form of images of the priest, not the person of the priest himself. Actually, this involves digitally mediating multiple images in order to enable a number of individuals to simultaneously form mental images of the priest. However, each one of those mental images is formed in isolation, that is, in the absence of the unifying presence of the person depicted in the image. You might argue that fifty people standing in the nave of the church will also see the priest in the sanctuary as fifty separate mental images. But that is not the same thing as fifty people in their respective homes all looking at a picture of the priest. The difference is the fifty visual images in the minds of the actual worshipers are generated directly, without mediation, by the presence of

---

12. It might be argued that similar to our belief that the angels and departed faithful who make up the invisible church are always present, always sing with us, togetherness can be achieved in "spirit" apart from any particular physical space. However, it must be noted that the Saints have moved on from this time/space-bound realm and have a kind of mobility we earth-bound believers do not yet have. It seems that to achieve that mutual presence we have to actually come together in one place.

13. "Spectacle" is a term used by modern philosophers to indicate something is not what it purports or appears to be. The classic example is professional wrestling which, while it appears to be a form of that sport, is in reality a staged piece of theater. So, in our case we have something that looks like but is not really a Liturgy. See Barthes, *Mythologies,* and Debord, *Society of the Spectacle.*

the person whose image is formed in their minds. For that reason, these immediate images, which depend on and coalesce in the actual presence of a person, can and do serve as a vehicle of direct interpersonal communion. It seems obvious you can have communion (fellowship) with the celebrant of the service you are actually present at but cannot have communion, cannot interact personally, with a picture at home. I am not suggesting seeing the images of the clergy and the church in this way is without any benefit. I am sure it does help the faithful deflect the distress of not being able to be at church. I suppose it does keep memories alive, give some hope, and does provide some kind of warm, fuzzy (spiritual?) feeling, which we may think is the best we can do right now.

Nevertheless, whatever it is, the video-streamed liturgy does not offer the kind of intimate, personal presence and community required for the constitution of the body or for the unity established by actual participation, and it precludes the very possibility of eucharistic communion. Still, some have argued that participation in the sacrament, the Eucharist itself, could be mediated through cyber channels by having those viewing a live video stream of an actual liturgy place bread and wine before the video monitor, allowing them to be consecrated along with the Lamb in the service. Apparently, the idea is the Holy Spirit who sanctifies the gifts and is not limited by place could simultaneously sanctify the remote bread.[14] A priest may be represented or depicted in cyberspace, but a video link cannot mediate the real presence of the celebrant nor can it actualize his concrete liturgical movements. It can picture but cannot affect the consecration of the gifts. Furthermore, the representation of the gifts being consecrated is symbolically removed from the actual signifier/signified[15] unity that exists in a real celebration of the Eucharist. A representation of the signifier cannot signify, cannot do anything. A picture of a piece of bread cannot become, cannot represent the actual body of Christ. That is, the depiction cannot participate in the sacred act of consecration, cannot be the object of the Holy Spirit's power and descent, and is thus sacramentally powerless. Because the cyber representation is only pictured and not actually done in the participants' presence, it effectively excludes the observer from all active, sacramental participation in the liturgy shown. What we have done is destroyed the Spirit-enacted harmony between Signified and Signifier that is at the core of sacramental symbolism.

---

14. See Neal, "Holy Communion over the Internet."

15. For more on the Orthodox understanding of eucharistic symbolism, see the appendix in Schmemann, *For the Life of the World*.

It seems, then, that in our haste to provide a solution, we have actually offered our people a counterfeit, an illusion that has tricked some of them into thinking they are actually contributing to the maintenance of their spiritual lives. Thus, satisfied with the illusion, they become lazy and do nothing else. I was surprised to hear this insight forcefully expressed by a student pastor who said, "We are going to stop video streaming because we are deceiving the people, giving them the false impression that they have been worshiping when, in fact, they have been engaged in a harmless but useless exercise. This has done little or nothing to help maintain their spiritual lives and growth during this crisis." So did we have any other options? Is there a more spiritually effective way of responding to being barred from our own churches?

Third, one of the most damaging aspects of this ill-advised use of technology is it gives us the impression of having done something (even though it is not being done) and prevents us from facing the truth of our situation. Consider the children of Israel forcibly taken off into Babylonian captivity. Separated from Jerusalem and the temple, they were literally unable to bring sacrifice, to worship, and "by the rivers of Babylon, [they] sat down, yea, [they] wept when [they] remembered Zion" (Ps 137:1). What I find remarkable here is they are said to have acknowledged their loss, faced up to their grief, and found ways of processing it. They tried to nurture the remembrance of Jerusalem, but they did not devise false substitutes and pretend they were still there. Instead of accepting some ineffectual counterfeit, they focused their attention on what they did have and what they hoped to someday have again. "If I forget you, O Jerusalem, let my right hand forget its skill! If I do not remember you, let my tongue cling to the roof of my mouth—If I do not exalt Jerusalem above my chief joy" (Ps 137:5–6).

But we moderns are not usually willing to take no for an answer. We do not like to feel pain or be uncomfortable. We find it hard to admit something just cannot be done and prefer to take matters into our own hands. We rush to do something, anything, even if it is not the thing we have lost, as long as it satisfies our atavistic desire to be active. Yet would it not have been better for us in the long run if we had accepted the reality of our situation, felt and even savored the pain, used it and allowed it to nurture spiritual growth? In the tradition of Orthodox spirituality, we have often been told pain, suffering, and illness are often allowed by God to help us mature. We fast, for among other reasons, to feel the discomfort of hunger and to learn from it. Of course, in the case of fasting we often get around the dietary restrictions by consuming all manner of substitutes such as soy, almond milk, etc., and wind up consuming so much of it we never really feel the pain of hunger. So we can fast without fasting just as we are now worshiping without worshiping. This kind of intentional reflection on loss and hope could have been prepared and guided by the clergy and practiced by the faithful in their homes, and it would no doubt have been more spiritually beneficial than pretending, than simulating the worship that cannot now take place.

Fourth, I have the impression that providing live video-streamed liturgies deceives the faithful into thinking they have done everything—in fact, the only thing—that can be done under the circumstances. But there does actually appear to be an alternative to this pretending that preserves the connection to liturgy and would involve us in a real and genuinely spiritual activity. Consider the words of Azariah's prayer offered during the time of Israel's exile (Dan 3:26–45 LXX). This prayer was offered just as God was demonstrating his mercy in response to the obedience of his people. Having been saved from the fiery furnace, "Azariah stood up in the midst of the fire and prayed aloud: Blessed are you, and praiseworthy, O Lord, the God of our ancestors, and glorious forever is your name" (3:26). He immediately goes on to acknowledge their dire situation was at least in part divine judgment for their own sinfulness. "For we are reduced, O Lord, beyond any other nation, brought low everywhere in the world this day because of our sins" (3:28). Part of that punishment was being deprived of their ability to worship. Azariah laments the loss: "We have in our day no prince, prophet, or leader, no burnt offering, sacrifice, oblation, or incense, no place to offer first fruits, to find favor with you" (3:38). In other words, they did not have access to the sacred place of the temple; it was physically impossible for them to bring sacrifices and to worship in Jerusalem. But rather than trying to retain the semblance of true worship by means of some contrived form of pseudo-sacrifice, Azariah said they would sacrifice, that is, offer up, the one thing they did have left, a broken life:

> But with contrite heart and humble spirit let us be received; as though it were burnt offerings of rams and bulls, or tens of thousands of fat lambs, so let our sacrifice be in your presence today and find favor before you; for those who trust in you cannot be put to shame. And now we follow you with our whole heart, we fear you and we seek your face. Do not put us to shame . . . (3:39–41)

Indeed, a contrite heart is considered an acceptable sacrifice by God. What God requires of us is not what we do not have but rather the things we have left. He will not demand nor fault us for not bringing the "official burnt offering" when that is simply not possible. But he will accept the sacrifices of a broken spirit, of "a broken and a contrite heart" (Ps 51:16–17). Our divine liturgy is all about participating, through the Eucharist, in the unrepeatable, unique sacrifice made by Christ. This may well be what Archbishop Elpidophoros was suggesting when he called the faithful to "a different kind of communion," one in which we ourselves "become Eucharist, become thanksgiving, become gratitude . . ."[16] So like the ancient Israelites we who are to offer that sacrifice have now been prevented from doing so; it is now impossible. In that case, would it not have been more appropriate for the church to have led its people in the kinds of actions modeled by Azariah? We have many services (Akathists) of praise that could be done by families in their homes. We could have been guided through exercises of repentance (Canons) knowing some of what has transpired is, indeed, the result of our own unfaithfulness. Again, in fairness, it must be said some instructions to this end were given, both nationally and locally.[17] We were, in fact, asked to allow our hearts to be broken, and I think there was a desire on the part of at least some of the ecclesial leadership to encourage and lead the people in an offering of their own contrite hearts as an act of real and true worship. But I fear that because we were offered an easy and convenient option, an illusion, a counterfeit, many were deceived, distracted, and prevented from offering anything at all. By offering a cyber substitute for the liturgy/Eucharist, the church is doing its observers a disservice since the service is not real and the supposed participation is a mere illusion. But as "the real world is transformed into mere images, mere images become real beings . . . " and thus a new sense of reality emerges.[18] As that transformation of ecclesial reality begins to take hold, I fear many will not be willing to give up the convenient fantasy of spectacle. They will be tempted to make streaming their preferred mode of worship. It is, after all, the real thing.

INTERIM CONCLUSIONS

In this section I have tried to show consumerism has become the dominant view of life in our society. I have also suggested that because this worldview has been so thoroughly owned, even by the faithful, and because it is now a constituent element of our national identity, it seems quite natural to view the church in these terms. We have seen, then, a combination of these pressures is being brought to bear on the church. Pressures that are allowing the North American spirit of consumerism to gain a foothold and spread throughout our parishes. Even though technology is not neutral, in spite of the fact the church is not a business, has no product, and no consumer

16. Elpidophoros, "Different Communion in 2020," 0:42—0:49.
17. See "COVID-19 Digital Toolkit for Parishes."
18. Debord, *Society of the Spectacle,* para. 18.

base, we insist on using the meanings, devices, structures, and techniques of the prevailing, commercialized social imaginary. We have so thoroughly imbibed this spirit we will use any technology that is available and deemed to be effective. We view our services as commodities, Christ (the gospel) as a product to sell, ourselves as entrepreneurs, our children as consumers, and concern ourselves with customer satisfaction. In this intellectually and spiritually somnolent state, we are damaging the church and weakening its witness in the world while neglecting the very God-given tools needed to grow the church. But then, familiarity, amazing effectivity, and good-old American pragmatism makes transforming the church into a business the most natural of all possible moves:

> After all, the chief business of the American people is business. They are profoundly concerned with producing, buying, selling, investing and prospering in the world. I am strongly of the opinion that the great majority of people will always find these the moving impulses of our life.[19]

For the church this amounts to a major paradigm shift. We have moved away from the biblical and Traditional idea that the church is a living organism, the very body of Christ, filled with and directed by the Holy Spirit, fully equipped by that same divine Spirit, a foretaste of the coming kingdom of God, and a living alternative to the world around it. This framework has been supplanted, replaced by the worldview of commerce, which sees the church as a business selling some commodity to customers whose desires need to be satisfied. We come to view "the entire world (including the church) as a venue for self-gratification."[20] In everything we do and think, in our programs and our language, we reveal we have reduced the church to nothing more than an active participant in the great expanse of the North American marketplace. This is the basic orientation, the default position, that now pervades every aspect of ecclesial life.

This paradigm shift has made it quite easy for the faithful to apply to the church any and every tool, device, and structure deemed effective in the marketplace. Doing this seems to raise few if any concerns. These things are brought into the church without any critical discussion simply because they are available, and without fear because these devices are considered neutral. But

> [b]ecause church marketers assume that marketing is neutral, they conveniently sidestep any discussion about whether using

---

19. Coolidge, "Address to the American Society of Newspaper Editors," para. 9.
20. Kenneson and Street, *Selling Out the Church*, 75.

marketing as a means is appropriate to the church's goals or ends.[21]

Yet we have to have this discussion precisely because marketing is not neutral. It is a "value-laden enterprise rooted in specific sets of convictions,"[22] and it threatens to change the very character of the church. "The convictions that are at marketing's heart don't seem to be those at the heart of the gospel . . . As a result, marketing threatens to refashion the church in its own image."[23]

What would, or should I say *what does*, this transformed "church" look like? Consider the effects of just a few of marketing's primary axioms:

- *The Commodification of All Goods and Services.* This transforms the gospel into an item for sale rather than the living person of the resurrected Christ. It causes our services to be offered as performances for the audience and to be viewed as rendered for a price. Are we really in the business of selling Jesus, promoting the performing arts? Are the liturgy, sacred mysteries of the Eucharist, the sacraments of baptism and confession just commodities we offer to satisfy the needs of consumers? What else can they be if we accept the next axiom of commerce?

- *The Centrality of Transaction (the mechanism of exchange).* Every liturgical act, every offering, every presentation becomes a transaction, an exchange in which something is given in exchange for something else. What then happens to concepts like gifts, grace, offering, etc.? If we abandon the idea of giving as a selfless act of faith and replace it with the concept of self-interested exchange, our relationship with God and others is corrupted.[24] Is eternal life what we get in exchange for attending a liturgy? Is an MDiv what I get in exchange for my tuition payments? Is it what I use to negotiate with a prospective parish for a higher compensation package?

- *Consumer Sovereignty.* The entire focus of commerce is concentrated on the customer and the effort to provide what they demand. One question dominates our discussions: "are consumers getting what they want?"[25] But if you treat people like customers, they will act like it and "inquire incessantly how any given activity or program meets their

21. Kenneson and Street, *Selling Out the Church*, 31.
22. Kenneson and Street, *Selling Out the Church*, 33.
23. Kenneson and Street, *Selling Out the Church*, 34.
24. Kenneson and Street, *Selling Out the Church*, 49.
25. Sunstein, *#Republic*, 41.

always changing list of needs."²⁶ So it is attendees who dictate what has to happen in order for them to have a rich and rewarding worship experience. It is the students, not teachers, who determine if and when they have learned what they need to learn. The uncontested sovereignty of the consumer completely undermines and supplants the basic idea that the church has been built on "the foundation of the apostles and prophets, Jesus Christ himself being the chief cornerstone" (Eph 2:20). The church is to be guided by the dictates, the eternal givens of Scripture and Tradition. Yet that has been largely ignored, and many (most) believe in consumer sovereignty and "are likely to think that that freedom consists in the satisfaction of private preferences—in an absence of restrictions on individual choices."²⁷

- *Felt-Need Satisfaction as the Ultimate Goal.* The commercial paradigm envisions business enterprises evaluating their success in terms of ever-increasing profits and, above all, customer satisfaction. Deprived of an actual profit motive, church marketers have pegged their measure of success to customer satisfaction, that is, making sure the parishioners get exactly what they want to be given. As Kenneson and Street note, "A view of the church's ministry and service that revolves around and is synonymous with meeting felt needs operates with the explicit dogma that all felt needs, by virtue of being felt, are legitimate."²⁸ But traditional Christian anthropology clearly teaches that people do not know what is best for them, that their desires are corrupted by sin and morph into a kind of self-love. Kenneson and Street go on to say, "By making self-interested exchanges central to the church's identity, a marketing orientation corrupts the church's embodied witness to the mercy and grace of the triune God."²⁹

So marketing and its related devices and techniques represent a real danger to the church because they involve meanings that will fundamentally change the very identity of the church. Kenneson and Street capture this conclusion nicely:

> We believe that placing a marketing orientation at the center of the church's life radically alters the shape and the character of the Christian faith by redefining the character and mission of the church in terms of manageable exchanges between

---

26. Kenneson and Street, *Selling Out the Church*, 75.
27. Sunstein, *#Republic*, 45.
28. Kenneson and Street, *Selling Out the Church*, 73.
29. Kenneson and Street, *Selling Out the Church*, 59.

producers and consumers. Much that is central to the Christian life will not fit neatly into the management/marketing scheme, and, not surprisingly, these matters are neglected in a marketing paradigm.[30]

What are we, who live in this mercenary world, who work in a church which has largely capitulated to these corrupting forces, to do? To begin with, we need to recognize the danger, name it, discuss it, and expose it. There is for each one of the tools and structures examined in this chapter an alternative that grows out of the biblical and dogmatic tradition of the church. We need to rediscover, reaffirm, but above all deliberately reapply those principles and procedures to the life and work of the church. In doing so we will begin to undo the commercial disfigurement of the church and start the process of restoring it to its God-intended state of beauty.

---

30. Kenneson and Street, *Selling Out the Church*, 62.

PART III

The Public Square

The Church and Contemporary Public Discourse

8

The Idea of the Public Sphere

How do we live with our deepest differences, especially when those differences are religious and ideological, and very especially when those differences concern matters of our common public life? In short, how do we create a global public square and make the world safer for diversity?[1]

As we have seen, the operating principles discussed in chapter 1 have had a pronounced effect on social interaction in the realm of commerce. The same thing holds true for the second area of social interaction which I will be calling the Public Sphere. According to Charles Taylor, this aspect of a society is considered to be

> a common space in which the members of society are deemed to meet through a variety of media: print, electronic, and also face-to-face encounters; to discuss matters of common interest; and thus to be able to form a common mind about these. I say "a common space" because although the media are multiple, as are the exchanges that take place in them, they are deemed to be in principle intercommunicating.[2]

---

1. Guinness, *Global Public Square*, 13.
2. Taylor, *Modern Social Imaginaries*, 83.

TOPICAL COMMON SPACES

The most basic expression of this type of discourse is called into being "when people are assembled for some purpose, be it on an intimate level for conversation or on a larger, more public scale for a deliberative assembly, a ritual, a celebration, or the enjoyment of a football match or an opera."[3] Taylor calls this localized form of common space a "topical common space."[4] This is what is created when friends gather at the local pub for a discussion on a particular topic, book, news item, etc. In this case, there is a direct, face-to-face exchange of information and positions that involves an open meeting of the minds, often resulting in shared or common convictions, and which always ends amicably. Although the common space is initiated simply by the coming together of the participants, its noble purposes are only achieved when it is established on prior and active commitment to three conditions: soul freedom, civility, and self-transcendence.

Soul Freedom describes the absolute freedom of thought possessed by every human being and thus every participant in a common space. Os Guinness defines it as

> the inviolable freedom of thought, conscience, religion and belief that alone does full justice to the dictates of our humanity. As we shall see, it best expresses human dignity and agency; it promotes freedom and justice for all; it fosters healthy giving, caring, peaceful and stable societies; and it acts as a bulwark against the countless current abuses of power and the equally countless brutal oppressions of human dignity.
>
> As such, soul freedom concerns the foundational freedom to be human. It is both the expression of a high view of human worth and the answer to a human yearning for freedom that is universal and enduring, as well as the surest bulwark against the darker angels of our nature. Soul freedom rises to the challenge of the dictates of our humanity because it is about nothing less than our freedom and responsibility to be fully human and to live together in thriving and beneficial communities, and at the same time to know how to lean against the crooked timber that is also at the heart of our humanity.[5]

In other words, each participant is free to take any stance he or she may choose. No positions are categorically ruled out, none are illegitimate. This does not mean all of them are factually correct, equally useful, or worthy.

---

3. Taylor, *Modern Social Imaginaries*, 85.
4. Taylor, *Modern Social Imaginaries*, 85.
5. Guinness, *Global Public Square*, 14.

But processing that diversity and reconciling such differences is precisely what a common space is intended to do. If the existence of diversity is disallowed, then the discourse of common space ceases to function.

Civility. If we are going to discuss, even rigorously, our differences, then we will need some basic rules of engagement. Each participant will need to believe in some things with enough conviction to say no, as a matter of principle, to some ideas and yes to others. But in order for that kind of exchange to function, it will have to be governed by some basic rules of civility. But what is civility? According to Pier Massimo Forni, "Whatever civility might be, it has to do with courtesy, politeness, and good manners."[6] Forni states:

> Courtesy is connected to court and evoked in the past the superior qualities of character and bearing expected in those close to royalty. Etymologically, when we are courteous we are courtier-like. Although today we seldom make this connection, courtesy still suggests excellence and elegance in bestowing respect and attention. It can also suggest deference and formality.[7]
>
> To understand politeness, we must think of polish. The polite are those who have polished their behavior. They have put some effort into bettering themselves, but they are sometimes looked upon with suspicion. Expressions such as "polite reply," "polite lie," and "polite applause" connect politeness to hypocrisy. It is true that the polite are inclined to veil their own feelings to spare someone else's. Self-serving lying, however, is always beyond the pale of politeness. If politeness is a quality of character (alongside courtesy, good manners, and civility), it cannot become a flaw. A suave manipulator may appear to be polite but is not.[8]

Self-Transcendence. What has just been described is, of course, rooted in the very character of the participants. Speaking of people of character, David Brooks notes

> [t]hey radiate a sort of moral joy. They answer softly when challenged harshly. They are silent when unfairly abused. They are dignified when others try to humiliate them, restrained when others try to provoke them. But they get things done. They perform acts of sacrificial service with the same modest everyday spirit they would display if they were just getting the groceries.

---

6. Forni, *Choosing Civility*, locs. 251–59 of 2601.
7. Forni, *Choosing Civility*, locs. 243–50 of 2601.
8. Forni, *Choosing Civility*, loc. 250 of 2601.

> They are not thinking about what impressive work they are doing. They are not thinking about themselves at all. They just seem delighted by the flawed people around them. They just recognize what needs doing and they do it.[9]

Self-transcendence, then, means laying aside self-absorption and becoming actively aware of others by "weaving restraint, respect, and consideration into the very fabric of this awareness."[10]

METATOPICAL SPACES

Under these conditions (soul freedom, civility, self-transcendence), any localized gathering for dialogue could constitute a safe space for airing and addressing differences, that is, a topical common space. From the seventeenth century onward, these spaces developed among the lettered portion of the population which met in parlors, pubs, coffee and tea shops to discuss issues of common interest. Increasingly, these deliberations were facilitated by the spread of print media, newspapers, tracts, and books, giving access to a broader strata of the general population.[11] So it was that the number of topical common spaces grew and morphed into what might be called public discussions, which often led to a general consensus or public opinion. But according to Taylor this now-public sphere is something different:

> It transcends such topical spaces. We might say that it knits together a plurality of such spaces into one larger space of nonassembly. The same public discussion is deemed to pass through our debate today, and someone else's earnest conversation tomorrow, and the newspaper interview Thursday, and so on. I call this larger kind of nonlocal common space "metatopical." The public sphere that emerges in the eighteenth century is a metatopical common space.[12]

This *metatopical* public sphere is *extrapolitical,* and it is *secular.* On the one hand, neither the opinions nor their underlying questions were imposed on the populace by force of class, education, real estate, law, the church, or government, but gradually developed independently of those influences. As Habermas describes the transformation, the emerging public sphere was no longer the exclusive revere of the ruling classes, whose power had until

---

9. Brooks, *Road to Character,* loc. 147 of 5605.
10. Forni, *Choosing Civility,* loc. 227 of 2601.
11. See Habermas, *Structural Transformation of the Public Sphere.*
12. Taylor, *Modern Social Imaginaries,* 86.

then determined both the questions and the outcomes of discourse. This defeudalization of the public sphere opened it up to the growing bourgeoisie and repurposed public debate as a "social and political force [that could] articulate collective political demands against the old estates and the states."[13] Even though the public had become an essentially extrapolitical dynamic, it was, perhaps because of its independence, now in a position to exert the force of public opinion on government which was "wise to follow [public] opinion [and] morally bound to do so.[14] This modern iteration of the public sphere was no longer the vehicle for disseminating the wishes of an elite but had become a dynamic cauldron in which a much wider, reasoning public formed opinions "that governments ought [now] to legislate."[15]

Even though this renewed space is, at least in theory, a "virtual stage"[16] on which everybody can participate as well as spectate, there is a strong hierarchy in which the "national quality press"[17] is awarded the role of opinion leader. Unfortunately, the political public sphere is now "dominated by the kind of mediated [mass-]communication that lacks the defining features of deliberation,"[18] hence,

> it is the mass media professionals that have the power to select, shape and *mediate* opinions (originating either from the political system or from the civil society) towards the broad and general public(s).[19]

Thus, even in the absence of feudal constraints, discourse can and often is constrained by another hierarchy of powers. The issues deliberated by the new public are chosen for them by power brokers. These, as we shall see below (chapter 10), are affected by the communications technologies themselves, inequity of access, the media, and above all, the commercialization of culture. Nevertheless, "with an independence of the mass media and with the help of an inclusive civil society, deliberative democracy could still function properly, in spite of the unequal distribution of power to influence public opinion construction."[20]

---

13. Szabó, "Impact of the Internet," 13.
14. Taylor, *Modern Social Imaginaries*, 88.
15. Taylor, *Modern Social Imaginaries*, 88.
16. Habermas, "Political Communication," 415.
17. Habermas, "Political Communication," 419.
18 Habermas, "Political Communication," 414.
19. Szabó, "Impact of the Internet," 22.
20. Szabó, "Impact of the Internet," 22.

On the other hand, this public opinion is radically secular "because it stands in contrast not only with a divine foundation for society but with any idea of society as constituted in something that transcends contemporary common action."[21] In other words, it is its own authority, its own standard of truth. Seen in this way,

> The public sphere is an association that is constituted by nothing outside of the common action we carry out in it: coming to a common mind, where possible, through the exchange of ideas. Its existence as an association is just our acting together in this way. This common action is not made possible by a framework that needs to be established in some action-transcendent dimension, either by an act of God or in a Great Chain or by a law that comes down to us since time out of mind. This is what makes it radically secular.[22]

Here, we see the obvious influence of several of the *operating principles* mentioned in chapter 1, namely, rationalism, scientism, etc. This reasoning power is defined as autonomous and self-sufficient . . . Proper reason takes nothing on faith in any sense of the word. We might call this the principle of "self-sufficient reason,"[23] that is, a secular-nonreligious, scientific reason. Some have suggested in a diverse society we will need to "deliberate in a language of reason alone, leaving [our] religious views in the vestibule of the public sphere."[24] This, it was thought, would promote the use of a language that everyone could agree with:

> The idea seems to be something like this. Secular reason is a language that everyone speaks and can argue and be convinced in. Religious languages operate outside this discourse by introducing extraneous premises that only believers can accept. So let's all talk the common language.[25]

This "secular reason is the basis on which the public arrives at "the normative conclusions it needs, such as establishing the legitimacy of the democratic state and defining our political ethic."[26] But if this interaction is not guided by any force or standard external to it, how does this communicatively shaped and discursively clarified common mind acquire anything

---

21. Taylor, *Modern Social Imaginaries*, 93.
22. Taylor, *Modern Social Imaginaries*, 93.
23. Butler et al., *Power of Religion*, 56.
24. Butler et al., *Power of Religion*, 49.
25. Butler et al., *Power of Religion*, 49.
26. Butler et al., *Power of Religion*, 49.

like a normative character? One suggestion is the normative force of public opinion is derived from a combination of consensus and rationality. That is, it is a common mind arrived at by means of rational discourse, "established and maintained as a "unity of a *communication community*."[27] According to Habermas, what makes that consensus possible is the fact that

> speech acts are always potentially (even if implicitly) rational. This rationality means that whoever is communicating is capable of arguing for their best interest. Every act of meaningful social interaction in an undistorted situation could be described as steps of communicative action in order to establish a mutual understanding (intersubjectivity) between the participants, with rational claims about their respective best interests.[28]

So in the context of public discourse, rationality does not refer to the nature of the thought process itself, that is, not to human rational faculty, but rather to presuppositions, frameworks, and outcomes which, in the final analysis, are acceptable to "the public of citizens as authors of the legal order."[29] The public sphere, then, is best described as a network for communicating information and points of view (i.e., opinions expressing affirmative or negative attitudes); and in the process the streams of communication are "filtered and synthesized in such a way that they coalesce into bundles of topically specified public opinions."[30]

As good as all this might sound, this metapolitical, reasoned approach leaves several issues unresolved. How, for example, do we resolve the inconsistencies involved in saying there are no political, or for that matter religious, forces posing the questions or imposing solutions, while at the same time admitting other powers, such as an independent press, can and do affect which questions we take up and what positions we develop? Who determines which questions we deliberate? Will we not have to at least identify these forces and ask what right they have to inform our discussion? Is it reasonable to think public discourse free of all external standards can by reason alone arrive at principles that will be applied universally to a diverse populace? According to Taylor, "the problem with this is that there is no such set of timeless principles that can be determined, at least in the detail they must be for a given political system, by pure reason alone."[31] It seems, then, we may need some external authority after all. Some will suggest we

27. Haberman, quoted in Szabó, "Impact of the Internet," 16.
28. Szabó, "Impact of the Internet," 16–17.
29. Habermas, *Between Facts and Norms*, 414.
30. Habermas, *Between Facts and Norms*, 360.
31. Taylor, "Why We Need a Radical Redefinition," 35.

look to Scripture as a standard of truth. But how do we decide how much of a normative character to ascribe to the holy Scriptures as over a major newspaper, a blogger, or some internet expert? The public sphere is not well served by simply excluding certain authorities or languages, but rather in finding ways to use them to evaluate both the source of our questions as well as the proposed solutions.

> But as long as religious communities play a vital role in civil society and the public sphere, deliberative politics is as much a product of the public use of reason on the part of religious citizens as on that of nonreligious citizens.

Admittedly, secular public debate is not to be seen "primarily [as] bulwarks against religion but as good faith attempts to shape their institutional arrangements . . . to maximize the basic goals of liberty and equality between basic beliefs."[32] In other words, "what the public sphere does is enable the society to come to a common mind, without the mediation of the political sphere, in a discourse of reason outside power, which is, itself, normative for power."[33]

---

32. Taylor, "Why We Need a Radical Redefinition," 56.
33. Taylor, *Modern Social Imaginaries*, 91.

9

Church as Topical and Metatopical Public Space

The Church, which was established by Christ at the Mystical Supper, was actualized on the day of Pentecost when the Disciples celebrated the first Eucharist.On the day of Pentecost, the Disciples were filled by the Spirit and formed "into one body" (I Cor 12:13) which they became in the Eucharist, accomplished by the Spirit and through the Spirit.[1]

TOPICAL ECCLESIAL COMMON SPACE

IF A LOCAL PARISH meets the above-mentioned conditions (soul freedom, civility, self-transcendence), it could be viewed as a localized or topical common space. It can easily be seen in the context of deliberations designed to reach a common mind. This would certainly be true of Bible studies, book study groups, catechesis, etc., since we are engaging differences (if only in the form of ignorance) and seeking to provide new information which could contribute to a shared position. In this sense, a local Bible study, for example, approximates the dynamic and purpose of a pub discussion. This might also apply to the general context of evangelism or mission in which

---

1. Afanasiev and Plekon, *Church of the Holy Spirit*, 1–2.

we engage different opinions in the form of unbelief and seek through dialogue to move toward some common ground of belief. If done with courtesy, politeness, and good manners, evangelism could be seen not as polemic or apologetic but rather as a means of acknowledging and processing differences in the hope of reaching a shared understanding.

However, unlike the secular public sphere, the common space of the church cannot, from the outset, claim it reaches its common mind without the mediation of outside powers or solely on the basis of human reason. In an ecclesial setting, we are, rather, dealing with several factors—history/tradition, scripture, hierarchy, and celebration—which determine what this common space is like and how it works. In other words, these forces are givens, and they define the space, set the agenda, and determine what the questions are and how they are to be answered.

Unlike the immediacy or timelessness created by the nearly instantaneous exchanges in cyberspace, and unlike the uniform character of having all time flattened into ordinary time, the common space of a parish is embedded in a richly layered 2000-year history. As such it moves not only at a much slower pace but also in many different directions at once. The church's beliefs and practices have been developed and universally[2] agreed upon within a continuously unfolding flow of time often referred to as Tradition, that is, a body of information which evolved slowly under the guidance of the Holy Spirit. This content serves as a starting point for all ecclesial discussion and because it is considered to be the product of divine intervention and guidance it is not something we are free to revise at will but rather to rearticulate, when required, by the immediate cultural context. In other words, the common mind that results from ecclesial discourse is a shared understanding of everything that has been passed down to us by the church.

Scripture, perhaps the most important part of Tradition, is considered to be the very word of God, and as such, true and authoritative. So the dialogue of ecclesial common space is not directed at imposing individual interpretations on the Scriptures but rather coming to a shared understanding

---

2. A principle articulated by St. Vincent of Lerins in the fifth century: "Moreover, in the Catholic Church itself, all possible care must be taken, that we hold that faith which has been believed everywhere, always, by all. For that is truly and in the strictest sense Catholic, which, as the name itself and the reason of the thing declare, comprehends all universally. This rule we shall observe if we follow universality, antiquity, consent. We shall follow universality if we confess that one faith to be true, which the whole Church throughout the world confesses; antiquity, if we in no wise depart from those interpretations which it is manifest were notoriously held by our holy ancestors and fathers; consent, in like manner, if in antiquity itself we adhere to the consentient definitions and determinations of all, or at the least of almost all priests and doctors" (Lerins, "Commonitory," para. 2).

of exactly what the holy texts mean and how they are to be applied. This understanding is ascertained not by appealing to contemporary experts but rather to the writings of the early fathers and the saints of the church. In that regard, we are not trying to be clever or inventive but are rather trying to take our place in the ongoing flow of church history. It is clear from this that ecclesial discussion is not an open-ended free-for-all in which every opinion is considered equally valid. This form of discourse is, rather, guided by the idea that some interpretations are true and others false and that the differences are adjudicated by appealing to the standard of Tradition and Scripture. This limits the field of things that can be openly disputed and directs our attention to the implications and implementation of those truths. To put it differently, some of the voices being heard in an ecclesial discussion are going to be ancient and are going to have more credibility than others.

Another constraint can be seen in the organizational structure of the church, that is, its hierarchy. The clergy are given a privileged position in the local church and are de facto participants in all discussions. Although they do not possess the unquestioned authority or veracity of Scripture and Tradition, the Holy Spirit working to make up for individual clerical limitations through the sacrament of ordination gives their voices some added weight, or better, supernatural insight.

This presence and working of the Holy Spirit guiding the church is yet another factor that defines ecclesial public space. It is not just about overcoming our differences; it is the process of coming to a consensus with the help of the divine Spirit, as, for example, during the very first assembly at Jerusalem. According to the book of Acts, the announcement of the consensus was introduced with the words "it seemed good to the Holy Spirit, and to us" (Acts 15:27). The actual goal is a form of communion. When I speak of communion, I am referring to a self-transcendent, intersubjective interpenetration of two or more personal beings that takes place in complete freedom and kenotic love. It is "I," driven by self-emptying love for the Other, overcoming the boundaries of its own personhood in order to share in the I-ness of the Other, a sharing that can be so complete it is possible to speak of a multihypostatic "I," that is, a "We." Communion involves a free, unhindered flow of information, emotions, and desires, and an unmediated participation in every aspect of the Other's being. The characteristics of healthy communion are a) mutual acknowledgment and engagement of non-I as subject; b) an interpenetration/participation or sharing of thoughts, emotions, physical presence, and desires, all without fear; and c) complete freedom of thought, movement, and speech. Communion, then, is not a static given, but rather a dynamic, living reality that can both grow and diminish. This is unity in a very different sense than implied in the common term "consensus."

A final constraint is seen in the concept of celebration. Here, I am thinking of the fact that we are not simply discussing some content (as in the various classes we conduct) but are rather collectively celebrating an inherited form of liturgy which prescribes much of what we do during the service. This multiindividual celebration only works because there is prior agreement active during the celebration as to what is to be done by whom and when. Those rubrics, as we call them, represent a body of already-agreed-upon information that directs the discourse and limits individual contributions to affirming and participating in what the group as a whole is doing, and joining themselves to the unity that is established by the Eucharist, them all partaking of one bread:

> The cup of blessing which we bless, is it not the communion of the blood of Christ? The bread which we break, is it not the communion of the body of Christ? For we *being* many are one bread, *and* one body: for we are all partakers of that one bread. (1 Cor 10:16–17)

So in a local church a topical common space is generated when its members join their voices to those of Scripture, Tradition, and the hierarchy in order to reach a consensus of belief and practice. Seen this way, a local parish is in reality a collection of common spaces brought together in the Sunday liturgy. And this unity, this oneness, is

> the culminating moment of the whole eucharistic assembly . . . [is] communion, which . . .[can] not [be] torn away to become a self-standing act. Everyone who [participates] at the eucharistic assembly from the beginning . . . [is] a partaker, and only those who . . . [are] partakers participat[ing] in the eucharistic assembly.[3]

Nevertheless, the parish remains a topical as opposed to a metatopical space since those involved at all levels tend to know one another directly. They assemble in one place to celebrate their unity in Christ.

METATOPICAL ECCLESIAL SPACES

It is the notion of a diocese or a national church uniting a multitude of local parishes that brings us to a metatopical space. In some respects, a national

---

3. Afanasiev, *Lord's Supper*, 61.

church organization, such as the OCA, functions much like any metatopical space. It is there that a common mind is sought. However, in this case that is not achieved exclusively through face-to-face encounters but by sharing information in the form of print and electronic media. This information is often generated in submetatopical spaces like the Holy Synod, the Metropolitan council, and deanery meetings, and then passed up to the quintessential expression of the metatopical space, the All-American Assembly, a deliberative body that through delegates and clergy represents each one of the parishes. The consensus reached at the assembly is then considered normative for all parishes. For example, for years the question of tithing has been discussed in local parishes and by study groups. However, it was not until the proposals for proportional giving were accepted at an assembly that this approach to giving became the official and generally accepted position of the Orthodox Church in America.

Unlike its societal counterpart, an ecclesial metatopical sphere is neither radically secular nor is it entirely extrapolitical. It does not stand outside or apart from a divine foundation for society, and it does indeed transcend immediate common action of the participants. It inherits from its topical members the four constraints mentioned above. For that reason, it too is subject to Tradition, Scripture, Hierarchy, and Celebration, all of which can be expressed in the metatopical setting, where delegates deliberate under the direction of their bishops and join in the celebration of the liturgy. This space is also not extrapolitical. In ordinary parlance, the government does not exert pressure on the deliberations in the public sphere. However, public opinion is supposed to influence and guide the political process. In the church, it is the national church, in essence the Synod of Bishops, which in dialogue with the parishes and their members guides the discussion but simultaneously allows itself to be informed and moved by the public discourse. In this sense the church is a self-directing and self-correcting entity that relies on its own common space for input as it develops a common mind.

Concerning this common mind, St. Paul does in fact refer to it as the "mind" which is in Christ (Phil 2:5), that is, a pattern of thinking that conforms to his understanding and love of the world. Some Christians have extended this idea to include this pattern of thinking as it had dynamically developed in the church under the guidance of the Holy Spirit. It is sometimes referred to as the catholic consciousness of the church and at other times simply as the mind of the church. The truths transmitted individually by each element of Tradition and Scripture are harmoniously fused together into a unified whole which defines the catholic consciousness or mind of the church, a consciousness that is guided by the Holy Spirit. In other words, the service performed by Scripture cannot be accomplished by any of the other instruments. Similarly, the benefits of apostolic succession cannot be achieved through liturgical structures or iconography. Yet taken together under the guidance of the Holy Spirit, they constitute a unity—the fullness of life in Christ. Thus, there is no dogma that is not supported by Scripture, preserved by apostolic succession, reflected in icons, lived out by the saints, facilitated by liturgical structures, defended by the councils, and proclaimed by missionaries. This represents the church's own mechanism for processing diversity. The inner-church differences in hymnography, architecture, and iconography are evidence of the church being able to incorporate local cultures while maintaining its deposit of common belief and practice. In fact, this mechanism, discussion in a common space, has allowed this dynamic interchange to remove fear and distrust and has led to a celebration of human diversity.

PUBLIC OR PRIVATE SPACE?

What we have discussed so far indicates members or citizens of a given public, whether secular or religious, bear certain responsibilities for developing the opinions that lead to effective governance and order. To fulfill that responsibility, each individual has to focus his or her attention on the well-being of others, in particular the health and prospering of the larger groups to which they belong. This idea of a unit based on self-transcendence is particularly pronounced in the Christian church. St. Paul uses the image of the many members of a body joined together in a spiritual and physical unity. He begins by referring to the individual believer's body as a member of Christ's body and the temple of the Holy Spirit (1 Cor 6:12–20). It is an extremely intense expression (Eph 5:30–31) and implies unity (1 Cor 6:17). In 1 Corinthians 10:16–17, the image of a body is broadened to include the entire believing community and its head, Christ (1 Cor 11:29). St. Paul goes on to state we, being many, are *one* body (1 Cor 10:17) in Christ (Rom 12:5). In 1 Corinthians 12:12, this unified body is referred to as Christ himself, the members being joined to him through the baptism, reconciled to God in *one* body (Eph 2:16). There is *one* body and one Spirit. "The apostle speaks precisely about one body (Eph 4:4–6) in direct relation with the unity of God."[4] The oneness of the eucharistic assembly depends, of course, on everyone partaking, that is, on every member fulfilling his or her responsibility to the larger group:

---

4. Bulgakov, *Bride of the Lamb*, 258.

As the very term "communion" suggests, through communion they become partakers of the body and blood of Christ. The other faithful are merely present during communion. By not communing, they do not participate in the eucharistic mystery since in the words of Metropolitan Makarii, "The Eucharist is that mystery through which the Christian partakes of the real body and blood of his Savior." The fundamental principle of the ancient church life became atomized: "Always everyone and always together" turned into the opposite "not everyone and not together" but each one for himself and each one separately.[5]

In any case, the members of a local parish are citizens in the sense that they individually bear responsibility for creating by participation the unity of which St. Paul speaks. There is thus no place for observers or spectators among the faithful. Put differently, there is no room for consumers, those who are intent on getting some benefit for themselves. The public space of the parish is, above all, a matter of participation (celebration) in a centuries-old discourse on belief and practice. It has nothing whatsoever to do with the self-serving sovereignty of the consumer. There are no products to be bought and sold. There is only life, which is freely offered to those who cocelebrate, who participate as citizens.

This idea of citizenship and responsibility underscores the public nature of these common spaces. In contemporary usage, the term "public" has at least four distinct meanings:

> First, we speak of physical spaces, such as city squares and parks, as being public when they are open to all and part of a shared "commons." Extending this metaphor, we think of information and cultural resources as public when they are freely accessible and communicable and therefore potentially "common."
>
> Second, we distinguish between public and private concerns. We identify the former with issues that are of common interest to all members of a polity and therefore the legitimate concern of governmental institutions and the latter with areas of life that should be left to people's private discretion and remain their personal secrets . . .
>
> Third, we employ the term public as a social category. We use it in both a relatively restricted sense, to describe everyone who participates in particular public events or forms of expression, as in the phrase "reading public," and in a more general sense to characterize the collective of citizens.

---

5. Afanasiev, *Lord's Supper*, 61.

Fourth, we describe the aggregate of individual views that emerge among a public of citizens on issues of the day as "public opinion." The contestations involved in the formation of public opinions are often called "public discourses."[6]

As I have suggested, there are three fields of modern society in which human interaction takes place: commerce, the public sphere, and government. What is important for our understanding of the second of these areas, the public sphere, is that the first, commerce, is largely private. Taylor, referencing Habermas, notes the new public sphere "brought together people who had already carved out a 'private' space as economic agents and owners of property, as well as an 'intimate' sphere that was the locus of their family life."[7]

So in the world of commerce, people do interact with one another commercially in what at first glance appears to be a public space. However, the commercial engagement itself cannot be public except in the most general sense that it is "a metatopical common space, a space in which people come together and contact each other."[8] But it is in reality very private in the sense that almost all of its activity is predicated on individual or private ownership of the devices, structures, practices, and technologies required for the exchange. Above all else, the ultimate goal of this activity, profit, is supremely private, individually owned. Moreover, commercial activity is not seen as having an effect on or being affected by matters of general societal concern. Nor is it conceived of in terms of fulfilling some responsibility to the institutions of self-governance. Its only purpose is the acquisition of personal, that is, private, wealth.

So a common space, whether secular or ecclesial, can be either public or private depending on the behavior of its members. If the individuals are participating primarily as *consumers,* then the space becomes private. If the participants are deliberately living as *citizens,* the common space takes on a public nature. Yet the boundary between citizen and consumer, between public and private, is neither fixed nor always self-evident, and I suggest it is precisely this dual orientation, compounded by modern communication technologies (filtering), that actually threatens real public dialogue both in and outside the church. Perhaps it is more accurate to speak of this dual-mindedness in terms of a conflict of competing interests. The concerns of a citizen will, for example, be directed toward the common good, order and general safety, the guarantee of basic freedoms, the limitation of other

---

6. Gripsrud and Eide, *Idea of the Public Sphere,* xiv.
7. Taylor, *Modern Social Imaginaries,* 101.
8. Taylor, *Modern Social Imaginaries,* 103.

freedoms by means of laws, and so on, and will result in active participation in this process (voting) and responsibility (observing the laws, etc.). This is what St. Paul seeks to describe with his many images (body, house, temple) of the church. Unfortunately, the power of commerce is such that, even in the church the consumer has become sovereign and biblical "laws and policies are 'bought,' in the same way that soap and cereal are bought,"[9] causing the public space of the church to devolve into a company of isolated individuals, each competing to defend their own interests in a depressingly private place.

Summing up, local churches have (should have) topical public spaces generated by members joining their voices to those of Scripture, Tradition, and the Hierarchy in order to reach a consensus of belief and practice. Likewise, a collection of such parishes creates an ecclesial metatopical common space.

---

9. Helberger, *Digital Consumers*, loc. 591 of 1201.

10

Challenges to Public Discourse

The computer has become the new cultural symbol of the things that Rousseau feared from the pen: loss of direct contact with other people, the construction of a private world, a flight from real things to their representations.[1]

AIDED BY THE WIDESPREAD use of print media and print-related technologies, participation in public discourse has increased exponentially and has positively transformed basic aspects of the public sphere. These technologies have made it possible to easily disseminate vast amounts of information, clearly identify and articulate a multitude of differing opinions, and, to some extent, facilitate an effective processing of those differences. As a result, we as a people are in a position to reach consensus on many of our common concerns and see the public's opinion inform those responsible for developing and enacting public policies. In spite of these advances, it has become obvious to most of us that contemporary public dialogue is not living up to its new potential. Today, we are experiencing increased levels of anger, isolation, and polarization. There is a lack of civility, a lack of freedom to express and entertain differing positions. As a result, we can rarely speak of public consensus, and for that reason few, if any, policies that benefit the many are being developed and implemented. These failings could, as with the down sides of commerce, rightly be ascribed to fallen human nature, to greed, and to self-love. But what concerns me here is my suspicion that the

---

1. Turkle, *Second Self,* loc. 1332 of 5322. See Rousseau, *Essay on the Origin of Writing.*

very same technologies which drove the transformation of public discourse are also amplifying the negative effects of human nature, making that desired dialogue nearly impossible.

This dialogue, we must remember, was and often is an actual exchange of spoken words, that is, people talking face to face. The question here is, what happens to that oral word when it is put into the many forms of writing and then transmitted using available computerized technology (CMC)? On the one hand, these devices and structures multiply the impact of an individual's words by making them available to a much wider audience. This availability alone should and, in a way, does enhance and broaden public discourse. But on the other hand, these technologies also appear to fundamentally alter the ways in which words are or can be received and processed. For example, a verbally presented lecture would unite all the members of the audience in the act of listening and provide a context for immediate discussion. The same information could, of course, be presented in the form of a printed document such as a handout, book, or blog. Given the effectiveness of modern technology, that text could then be made available to vastly larger groups of individuals (listeners?) than those physically present at the lecture. Yet the very technology that makes the text so widely available is the very thing that makes public dialogue concerning that information so difficult. Since reading is a private, primarily individualistic activity,

> [w]riting and print isolate. There is no collective noun or concept for readers corresponding to 'audience'. The collective 'readership'—this magazine has a readership of two million—is a far-gone abstraction.[2]

If groups of readers are abstractions or in some way illusory, then so is the discourse that might have taken place in these imaginary units. Print technologies, moreover, enhance the reader's ability to freely choose what they expose themselves to without having to face the various social pressures that might require one to attend or not leave a particular lecture. Nor would they have to deal with the dialogue-generated curiosity that would impel them to seek out views other than their own. Print technologies then, especially those propagated in cyberspace, may actually hinder the dialogue we had hoped they would facilitate. Since my goal here is to facilitate (recover) effective public dialogue by mindfully using all appropriate technologies, it behooves me to identify and understand the impact those same technologies are having on discourse in our public space. What happens to public dialogue when the words we use are 1) mediated (writing, print) rather

---

2. Ong, *Orality and Literacy*, loc. 1457 of 4721.

than presented directly (verbally, orally), 2) confined to the echo chambers of user preference, 3) divorced from authority structures and expertise, 4) made vacuous in the alternate, pseudo-realities of social media, and 5) fragmented by the pressures of globalism and multiculturalism?

DISCOURSE AND MEDIATED COMMUNICATION (CMC)

There is nothing in spoken language that necessitates the invention of writing or print. We know "oral expression can exist and mostly has existed without any writing at all . . . "[3] Indeed,

> language is so overwhelmingly oral that of all the many thousands of languages—possibly tens of thousands—spoken in the course of human history only around 106 have ever been committed to writing to a degree sufficient to have produced literature, and most have never been written at all. Of the some 3000 languages spoken that exist today only some 78 have a literature[4]

One reason for this might be the intersubjectivity of natural human communication. When we speak, we are generally talking to someone and expecting immediate feedback. In other words, it is never one-way. The speaker always expects a response, and the form and content of the message are determined, in part, by the anticipated response:

> This is not to say that I am sure how the other will respond to what I say. But I have to be able to conjecture a possible range of responses at least in some vague way. I have to be somehow inside the mind of the other in advance in order to enter with my message, and he or she must be inside my mind. To formulate anything I must have another person or other persons already 'in mind'.[5]

In this sense spoken communication is a uniquely human activity "which signals the capacity of human beings to form true communities wherein person shares with person interiorly, inter-subjectively."[6] This dynamic process is captured in Saussure's model of oral, interpersonal communication, his "speech circuit," originally published in 1915, which

---

3. Ong, *Orality and Literacy*, loc. 286 of 4721.
4. Ong, *Orality and Literacy*, loc. 263 of 4721.
5. Ong, *Orality and Literacy*, locs. 3229–37 of 4721.
6. Ong, *Orality and Literacy*, loc. 3237 of 4721.

famously represented in the form of two facing heads with what look like telephone wires slung between them and connecting their brains, mouths, and ears. Unlike most transmission models, it has directional arrows indicating not only feedback but the equal participation of both participants. It is sender-oriented insofar as comprehension on the part of the listener is presented as a kind of mirror of the speaker's initial process of expressing a thought. The textual commentary refers only briefly to the speaker's use of 'the code provided by the language' (a code which is assumed to be shared), but at each end of the process in the diagram there is a representation of a process of mental decoding or encoding to or from the 'sound pattern' (or signifier) and the concept (or signified).[7]

One of the difficulties with this is the sounds that carry the words being exchanged are "essentially evanescent," that is, they only exist when they are going out of existence. To use one of Ong's examples, "when I say 'existence', by the time I get to the '-tence', the 'exis-' is gone."[8] That being the case, it was not the best vehicle for remembering exchanges such as contracts, inventories, trade agreements, and the like. Oral exchanges do not effectively address "human beings' fundamental need to store [remember] information in order to communicate, whether to themselves or to others, at a distance in time or space."[9]

As a result, human beings developed a whole series of "graphic mnemonics" such as knot records, notches, and simple markings.[10] But these simple memory tools were limited to a small subset of everything that could be expressed by articulate speech. In order to convey more content, the writing system would have to coordinate sounds and symbols to create a "sign" of a writing system.[11] This led to the development of the alphabet which "operates more directly on sound as sound than the other scripts, reducing sound directly to spatial equivalents, and in smaller, more analytic, more manageable units than a syllabary: instead of one symbol for the sound ba, you have two, b plus a."[12] Cast into an alphabet as written or printed, words become objects, not events; they are present all at once. You no longer have bits of it disappearing as they are spoken.

7. "Speech Circuit."
8. Ong, *Orality and Literacy*, loc. 1746 of 4721.
9. Fischer, *History of Writing*, loc. 97 of 6365.
10. Fischer, *History of Writing*, loc. 148 of 6365.
11. See Ong, *Orality and Literacy*, loc. 1698 of 4721.
12. Ong, *Orality and Literacy*, loc. 1746 of 4721.

Put in terms of Saussure's speech, circuit print is a channel, a carrier, a medium inserted between the sender and the receiver which is used to convey the content that had been carried by verbalization. One might say the information the sender intended to convey is now mediated by a text. This mediation of content fundamentally changes the nature of human communication.

First, mediated communication creates *the illusion of dialogue* by introducing a kind of unreality or artificiality. Plato criticized writing as "inhuman, pretending to establish outside the mind what in reality can be only in the mind."[13] The illusory nature of print media lies in the fact that text is a secondary modeling system removed by at least one degree from the realities it seeks to represent. Letters are only simulacra of a living reality presented in the form of text, pictures, and, in some cases, audio and video clips. Some of these representations could be said to possess a degree of quasi-reality if they correspond to actual objects existing in the real world, as in the descriptions of an item actually sold and delivered via e-commerce. Other objects are completely unreal in that there is no correspondence to actual things—they are purely imaginary or fictional as in the case of gaming characters (avatars); we are dealing with pure simulation, an unreal character in the form of symbols. Put simply, what you see on a printed page or in an image (however presented) is merely a representation of an actual word, object, place, or person. So if a mediated message requires the recipient to imagine the true state of the source based on a representation and if true dialogue is actively *communal,* that is, requires the participation of at least two individuals, then any interaction involving a mediated message is at best only an illusion.

Second, mediation creates what has been called *autonomous discourse* in which the sender, the message, and the recipient are each divorced from each other. With no attachment to the recipient, the sender can formulate and deliver the message without any anticipated reference to a respondent. Thus, the author cannot be directly questioned or contested, effectively eliminating the feedback loop. This also renders the disagreeing recipient incapable of effectively refuting the author's position. He may vehemently disagree, but if the message has been mediated by print, a book for example, then the author cannot be reached in the book and the reader's refutation is powerless to change the printed message. As for the mediated message itself, it is forced to play a completely inert role, passive and unresponsive, unable to alter or defend itself. This autonomous discourse is hardly dialogue at all.

---

13. Ong, *Orality and Literacy*, loc. 1535 of 4721.

Third, mediated messages disrupt the natural timing or rhythm of human discourse. The speech circuit rightly posits an immediate feedback loop. Obviously, that immediacy is lost when messages are mediated by print technologies. One can still respond, refute, or affirm, but it happens at some chronological distance. The answer to a handwritten letter could take months to arrive. It is probably the natural immediacy of human dialogue that pressures us to expect instantaneous responses to emails, tweets, and especially texts. Yet being mediated, there is always a delay.

Fourth, mediated communication *replaces dialogue with monologue* by shifting much of the responsibility for interaction to the recipient. Any active anticipation of recipient response ceases to exist once the message is picked up by the medium carrying it. Once dispatched, it falls to the recipient to choose which message to engage and possibly respond to. Since a mediated message is no longer evanescent, every message ever encoded can, with help of modern technology, be made permanently available. This fits in nicely with the social imaginary's conception of our demand for unlimited choice, but recipient sovereignty has, at least in this case, one serious downside. Once the choice is made, the only dialogue the recipient can have is with him or herself.

DISCOURSE AND INTERNET FILTERING

We have been talking about dialogue in a public space. Obviously, these public discussions presuppose the participants have at least some shared or common experiences. In order for dialogue to be genuine, that is, to reach its intended goal of managing and processing differences, all of the participants will have to willingly expose themselves to various opposing views, that is, "to materials that they would not have chosen in advance."[14] These encounters with views that differ from one's own help avoid the narrow and predictable outcomes that are generated when people only talk with those who are likeminded. It is this ability or willingness to be exposed to, to acknowledge, and to interact with opposing views that makes the dialogue in these forums public. Being exposed to a variety of people and positions and then processing those differences is precisely what makes the development of a common mind possible. Christians interacting with Muslims are challenged to rethink and more effectively articulate their own beliefs while at the same time acquiring new information. As John Stewart Mill once noted,

14. Sunstein, *#Republic*, 6.

> It is hardly possible to overrate the value ... of placing human beings in contact with persons dissimilar to themselves, and with modes of thought and action unlike those with which they are familiar. ... Such communication has always been, and is peculiarly in the present age, one of the primary sources of progress.[15]

Unfortunately, at least from the perspective of genuine dialogue, the increased capability of computer-mediated communication has made it easier for participants to filter out any unwanted content, that is, to avoid anything that does not square with their own position. As Bartlett points out, there are now thousands of Internet news sources each vying for our attention[16]:

> the average person is overwhelmed by the cacophony of information. Many simply tune out altogether and have become less informed about the news that affects them, while others consume only the sliver of news that interests them, whether it be sports, entertainment, or the stock market. When it comes to politics, there is a growing tendency to obtain news only from sources favorable to one's ideological or partisan point of view.[17]

But as Sunstein observes, "People with identifiable leanings are consulting sources, including websites, that match their predilections, and are avoiding sources that do not cater to those predilections."[18] This customization is illustrated by the now-popular internet practices of social bookmarking and social news sites. The basic idea is the individual members of these communities, the receivers and not the transmitters, "act as editors of the flows of information available online." It is as if

> *The New York Times* were publishing a single newspaper tailored to your interests. In this first example, a small subset of bits has been selected especially for you. The bits are filtered, prepared, and delivered to you, perhaps to be printed in the home, perhaps to be viewed more interactively with an electronic display.[19]

The technology makes available a whole range of filtering options:

---

15. Mill, cited in Sunstein, *#Republic*, v.
16. Bartlett, *Truth Matters*, 1.
17. Bartlett, *Truth Matters*, 1–2.
18. Sunstein, *#Republic*, 53.
19. Negroponte, *Being Digital*, 18.

Social bookmarking means saving the address of interesting websites, or pieces of websites (e.g. pictures or other individual files) and describing these websites with the help of freely chosen keywords (tags). The resulting package of information is simply called a bookmark: it tells you where to find a particular site and what you can expect to find there. Since the bookmarks are stored on the web server that powers the bookmarking site, they can be accessed from any computer that is connected to the internet.[20]

Social news sites such as Digg (http://www.digg.com) or Reddit (http://www.reddit.com) are also based on user-submitted content, decidedly focusing on news items and putting a more pronounced emphasis on the discussion about the submitted news items. Importantly, the users of social news sites can express both their like as well as their dislike for an article. In the case of Digg, one can see the list and a brief summary of the submitted articles, and can decide whether to "digg" (vote for) or "bury" (vote against) a particular item.[21]

Everything is now made to order; it is personalized in the extreme, based on the assumption that the recipient is an individual and not part of some group.[22] Information becomes a private commodity, owned, evaluated, and managed by the individual, in which case discourse becomes difficult, if not impossible. This failure is down to a technology-enabled filtering which

> artificially limits the size of our "solution horizon"—the mental space in which we search for solutions to problems . . . lack[s] some of the key traits that spur creativity . . . [and]encourages a more passive approach to acquiring information, which is at odds with the kind of exploration that leads to discovery.[23]

So in spite of its tremendous potential, electronic media may in fact be hindering public discourse by isolating individuals into fragments of the overall social construct. Many users are now able to exclude other ideas and avoid any information they do not already agree with. Clint Watts has called this self-imposed blocking of ideas a preference bubble.[24]

20. Szabó, "Impact of the Internet," 81.
21. Szabó, "Impact of the Internet," 82.
22. Negroponte, *Being Digital*, 162.
23. Pariser, *Filter Bubble*, 93.
24. See Watts, *Messing with the Enemy*.

> In a preference bubble, users create an alternative reality, built around values shared with a tribe, which can focus on politics, religion, or something else. They stop interacting with people with whom they disagree, reinforcing the power of the bubble. They go to war against any threat to their bubble, which for some users means going to war against democracy and legal norms. They disregard expertise in favor of voices from their tribe. They refuse to accept uncomfortable facts, even ones that are incontrovertible.[25]

As we observed, every communicative act involves a transmitter sending information to a receiver. Filtering is obviously the result of the recipient making certain choices that determine what the recipient is exposed to. But what if the intelligence that determined content resided not with the recipient but with the sender?

The prospect of sender-generated personalization, already possible in preference bubbles, was given a new twist in December 2009 when Google announced its plans for what it called the "Personalized Search." Google proposed using

> fifty-seven signals—everything from where you were logging in from to what browser you were using to what you had searched for before—to make guesses about who you were and what kinds of sites you'd like. Even if you were logged out, it would customize its results, showing you the pages it predicted you were most likely to click on.[26]

This type of personalization is now a "core strategy for the top five sites on the Internet—Yahoo, Google, Facebook, YouTube, and Microsoft Live . . . ."[27] This "new generation of Internet filters looks at the things you seem to like—the actual things you've done, or the things people like you like—and tries to extrapolate."[28] Using what they know about you, they become

> prediction engines, constantly creating and refining a theory of who you are and what you'll do and want next. Together, these engines create a unique universe of information for each of us—what I've come to call a *filter bubble*—which fundamentally alters the way we encounter ideas and information.[29]

---

25. McNamee, *Zucked*, 93.
26. Pariser, *Filter Bubble*, 2.
27. Pariser, *Filter Bubble*, 7.
28. Pariser, *Filter Bubble*, 9.
29. Pariser, *Filter Bubble*, 9 (emphasis mine).

The frightening thing about these filter bubbles is we are not alone in it since the sender groups us with other recipients of a similar profile. The bubble is also invisible:

> Google's agenda is opaque. Google doesn't tell you who it thinks you are or why it's showing you the results you're seeing. You don't know if its assumptions about you are right or wrong—and you might not even know it's making assumptions about you in the first place.[30]

Moreover, joining the bubble is not the recipient's choice. Unlike the individual filtering, "you don't make the same kind of choice with personalized filters. They come to you—and because they drive up profits for the Web sites that use them, they'll become harder and harder to avoid."[31]

The exponential increase in diversity actually gives us the ability to satisfy our desire for a multitude of choices and at the same time never stray beyond our own intellectual backyard. Taken together with profit-based personalization, genuine public dialogue becomes impossible since the participants "sort themselves [or are sorted] into echo chambers of their own design,"[32] grouped into what might be called digital tribes, sacrificing their individual responsibility and making "decisions based on groupthink, blocking out alternative viewpoints, new information, and ideas."[33] Obviously, this makes genuine discourse difficult since,

> left to their own devices, personalization filters serve up a kind of invisible autopropaganda, indoctrinating us with our own ideas, amplifying our desire for things that are familiar and leaving us oblivious to the dangers lurking in the dark territory of the unknown.
>
> By definition, a world constructed from the familiar is a world in which there's nothing to learn. If personalization is too acute, it could prevent us from coming into contact with the mind-blowing, preconception-shattering experiences and ideas that change how we think about the world and ourselves.[34]

So we are now faced with the self-imposed blocking of ideas called a *preference bubble* as well as the *filter bubbles* imposed by others based on user choices, "algorithms feeding people more of what they want, but also

---

30. Pariser, *Filter Bubble*, 9.
31. Pariser, *Filter Bubble*, 10.
32. Sunstein, *#Republic*, 6.
33. Watts, *Messing with the Enemy*, 217.
34. Pariser, *Filter Bubble*, 14.

people choosing more of what they like in the virtual world, leading to physical changes in the real world."[35] As mMcNamee states, "Filter bubbles and preference bubbles undermine democracy by eliminating the last vestiges of common ground among a huge percentage of Americans."[36] All of this changes the nature of public information and effectively eliminates the possibility of genuine dialogue by leaving us with an audience the size of one.[37]

DISCOURSE AND THE DEATH OF AUTHORITY AND EXPERTISE

Not long ago I was giving a lecture at a major university. During my talk some of the students were logged into the school's wifi network and were checking the details of my presentation. Even though that net search proved me correct, it was a rather unsettling experience. This now-commonplace practice of "fact checking"[38] points to several paradoxical consequences of the Internet, namely "instant experts"[39] and the "death of expertise."[40] In each case the possibility of public discourse and perhaps democracy itself is greatly reduced.

The reason cyberspace facilitates instant expertise is "the Internet is a magnificent repository of knowledge"[41] to which users have almost unlimited access. However, since

> no mechanism by which information posted to or claims made on the Internet may be vetted beforehand, the World Wide Web produces what some have either lauded or deplored as the phenomenon of "instant experts."[42]

However, the traditional idea of an expert as one with comprehensive and authoritative knowledge of some discipline hardly applies to these new cyberexperts. Obviously, instantly googling an answer to a question does provide some information but hardly the comprehensive knowledge that

---

35. Watts, *Messing with the Enemy*, 216.
36. McNamee, *Zucked*, 93.
37. Negroponte, *Being Digital*, 161.
38. Determining what is true is not a new problem, but the rise of CMC-mediated competing claims has made it increasingly important. See Graves, *Deciding What's True*.
39. Dawson and Cowan, *Religion Online*, loc. 50 of 4045.
40. Nichols, *Death of Expertise*, 3.
41. Nichols, *Death of Expertise*, 9.
42. Dawson and Cowan, *Religion Online*, locs. 50–55 of 4045.

usually takes a lifetime to acquire. This superficial "knowledge" is deceptive because it is actually making many of us intellectually lazy. Today, we no longer need to or want to invest time and resources in learning another language. We simply allow some online translator to offer us fragments of the other language. We don't bother learning geography, history, or logic. But it is more than mere laziness—we now face outright resistance to learning anything:

> Not only do increasing numbers of laypeople lack basic knowledge, they reject fundamental rules of evidence and refuse to learn how to make a logical argument. In doing so, they risk throwing away centuries of accumulated knowledge and undermining the practices and habits that allow us to develop new knowledge.[43]

Taken together with filter and preference bubbles, the internet is actually making "many of us dumber, it's making us meaner: alone behind their keyboards, people argue rather than discuss, and insult rather than listen."[44] Yet proud of their own "googled knowledge" or relying on the strongest voices in their digital tribes, these very limited experts are actually rejecting established knowledge as well as the comprehensive expertise normally associated with that knowledge. We have gotten to the point where many now reject the advice of experts in order to assert their own freedom or autonomy. It is "a way for Americans to insulate their increasingly fragile egos from ever being told they're wrong about anything."[45] Nichols fears we are now

> witnessing the death of the ideal of expertise itself, a Google-fueled, Wikipedia-based, blog-sodden collapse of any division between professionals and laypeople, students and teachers, knowers and wonderers—in other words, between those of any achievement in an area and those with none at all.[46]

Some of this is exacerbated by the social imaginary's insistence on the equivalidity of all opinion. "Americans now believe that having equal rights in a political system also means that each person's opinion about anything must be accepted as equal to anyone else's,"[47] but this is to misunderstand both expertise and democracy. On the one hand, "the relationship between

---

43. Nichols, *Death of Expertise*, 3.
44. Nichols, *Death of Expertise*, 9.
45. Nichols, *Death of Expertise*, 1.
46. Nichols, *Death of Expertise*, 2.
47. Nichols, *Death of Expertise*, 5.

experts and citizens is not 'democratic.' All people are not, and can never be, equally talented or intelligent."[48] Not everyone can do brain surgery, design a car, or put a satellite in orbit. On the other hand, democracy is not a state of actual equality in which every opinion is as good as any other. Yet individual beliefs or feelings now seem to be more important than facts: "if people think vaccines are harmful, or if they believe that half of the US budget is going to foreign aid, then it is 'undemocratic' and 'elitist' to contradict them."[49] But if, as we have already seen, "principled, informed arguments are a sign of intellectual health and vitality in a democracy,"[50] then genuine dialogue in the absence of these values is impossible.

DISCOURSE AND THE PSEUDOREALITIES OF SOCIAL MEDIA

As noted above, social interaction requires the participation of at least two individuals. If they are physically present, actually verbalizing, then the exchange will encompass not only the reality of the participants but of the whole context generated by the encounter:

> The word in its natural, oral habitat is a part of a real, existential present. Spoken utterance is addressed by a real, living person to another real, living person or real, living persons, at a specific time in a real setting which includes always much more than mere words. Spoken words are always modifications of a total situation which is more than verbal. They never occur alone, in a context simply of words.[51]

However, if a message is not spoken but rather mediated in some way, it is detached from the reality of its source and original context and is thus unreal. If those mediated messages are being transmitted by digital devices, then the entire exchange is possessed of an increased degree of unreality. William Gibson, in his novel *Necromancer,* goes so far as to suggest cyberspace is

> a consensual hallucination experienced by billions of operators, in every nation. . . a graphic representation of data extracted from every computer in the human system. Unthinkable

---

48. Nichols, *Death of Expertise*, 251.
49. Nichols, *Death of Expertise*, 252.
50. Nichols, *Death of Expertise*, 1.
51. Ong, *Orality and Literacy*, locs. 1925–33 of 4721.

complexity. Lines of light arranged in the nonspace of the mind, cluster and combinations of data. Like city lights receding.[52]

Social interaction in cyberspace is at best an indirect representation of reality. Expanding on C. Wright Mills's idea of "second-hand worlds,"[53] Gabriel Weinmann constructs a model of reality in which we have to distinguish between "(a) reality, (b) constructed mediated reality (or CMR), and (c) perceived mediated reality (or PMR)."[54] This model suggests certain aspects of real-life events are used by a communicator to form CMR, such as news stories, fictional drama, newspaper reports, pictures, or music. Even though it is based on reality, the "CMR is more dramatic, more colorful, more intense, more active, and faster than real life."[55] Once the constructed reality is in place, the recipients select or adopt certain aspects of the CMR as if they were real. The information is then gleaned from mediated reality and then applied as the recipient's reconstruction of their own actual life[56] *ad infinitum*. This cyclical dynamic leaves the recipients

> uncertain of who we are or how we should act. In the aggregate, it erodes the foundations of society. We don't bond with others; we 'team' with them. We don't have friends; we have contacts. We're not members of enduring, nurturing communities; we're nodes in ever-shifting, coldly utilitarian networks. . . . But every time we reinvent ourselves, we erase the meaning that our past experiences granted us. In place of an ethical sense of ourselves as people with clear attachments, we are left with an ironic sense of ourselves as fabrications. We become unreal, virtual.[57]

Of course, the phrase *virtual reality* is a contradiction in terms. "Virtual means not in fact; reality means in fact. VR, then, means not in fact fact."[58] This concept of social media unreality is easily seen in terms of the absence of personal presence and the masking of true intent. Physical presence is, of course, the hallmark of all natural human interaction. It involves a physical presence and the opportunity to converse orally. One might say "traditional media such as television, film, and many others offer a lesser

---

52. Cited by Wood and Smith, *Online Communication*, 18.
53. Weinmann, *Communicating Unreality*, 10.
54. Weinmann, *Communicating Unreality*, 12.
55. Weinmann, *Communicating Unreality*, 12.
56. Weinmann, *Communicating Unreality*, 13.
57. Friedman, *Lexus and thre Olive Tree*, 399.
58. Weinmann, *Communicating Unreality*, 330.

degree of presence as well."[59] In the case of social media, personal presence is reduced to a merely digital depiction of presence completely divorced from that reality. Once I post something, that message can and does exist without my active presence, but more importantly, completely without reference to the time, the moment, of its inception. The synthetic nature of social media is clearly evident in almost everything it purports to provide. As mentioned above (ch. 7), even though it claims to do so, it does not and cannot facilitate anything that depends on personal presence such as genuine intimacy, friendship, or community. At its very best social media can only offer a diluted version of the personal interaction we can all have naturally. This is why I have suggested it is artificial, unreal. In other words, what you are getting is not what you think it is.

Moreover, the unreality of social media is shown in the way it conceals its true intent. Purporting to provide a tool for social interaction, pretending to care about the well-being of its users, social media tools are actually designed in a way that actively undermines social discourse by convincing us "to talk at each other instead of talking with each other."[60] They favor broadcasting over engagements, posts over discussions, shallow comments over deep conversations.[61] Individual isolation is further amplified by the sheer volume of personalized content that is provided, assessed, and shared. But why? To inform the users? No, getting likes, etc., simply gives users "an incentive to spend more time on the site and join photo tagging as a trigger for addiction to Facebook."[62] The real purpose of this deliberate addiction is, of course, financial:

> The artificial intelligences of companies like Facebook (and Google) now include behavioral prediction engines that anticipate our thoughts and emotions, based on patterns found in the reservoir of data they have accumulated about users. Years of Likes, posts, shares, comments, and Groups have taught Facebook's AI how to monopolize our attention. Thanks to all this data, Facebook can offer advertisers exceptionally high-quality targeting.[63]

So if social media is devoid of personal presence and is not what it claims to be, how can any real discourse take place? Obviously, this synthetic environment does not encourage public discussion. In fact it has

59. Weinmann, *Communicating Unreality*, 329–30.
60. Taplin, *Move Fast*, 222–23.
61. Nichols, *Death of Expertise*, 217.
62. McNamee, *Zucked*, 63.
63. McNamee, *Zucked*, 85.

"contributed to our conversion from citizens to consumers" to a "collapse of functional citizenship."[64] Social media tends to "absolve citizens of their responsibilities to learn about issues that matter."[65] But "there is only one group of people who must bear the ultimate responsibility for this current state of affairs, and only they can change any of it: the citizens of the United States of America."[66] From this perspective it is easy to accept Watts's contention that

> [t]he internet brought the world together, but, over time, social media has torn the world apart. There are many reasons why this has happened, but one factor stands above the rest: preference. Unbridled preference—man's ability to make nearly endless selections on social media—when accumulated on a global scale, *has torn the fabric of societies, crippled democratic institutions, and polarized audiences into virtual and physical bubbles.*[67]

MULTICULTURALISM, TRANSNATIONALISM, AND PUBLIC DISCOURSE

Another set of contemporary developments bringing pressure on public dialogue grows out of the increasingly pluralistic character of our society. Traditionally the public sphere has been conceived of as a "phenomenon inside a nation state. But economic and political developments across state borders and around the globe have . . . [led to] new forms of cooperation, conflict, and communication [which] are being established at various inter- and trans-and supranational levels."[68] Many have welcomed these developments and the rise of digital technologies, especially the Internet, "with its promise of openness and universality as the basis for a new and inclusive public sphere."[69] My primary concern here is the in-nation plurality best described as multiculturalism. This involves an energetic interplay between multiple religions and a multiplicity of cultures all within the bounds of one nation state and the attempt to manage their competing claims. Do the members of each group have the right to transplant, propagate, and maintain their own cultures and religions?

64. Nichols, *Death of Expertise*, 217.
65. Nichols, *Death of Expertise*, 215.
66. Nichols, *Death of Expertise*, 225.
67. Watts, *Messing with the Enemy*, 214 (emphasis mine).
68. Gripsrud and Eide, *Idea of the Public Sphere*, 235.
69. Gripsrud and Eide, *Idea of the Public Sphere*, 235.

The challenge to public discourse is twofold. On the one hand, the increased exposure to human diversity means we have even *more differences to process* if we are to live together in one society. On the other hand, this diversity can lead to *intense fragmentation*, that is, loss of identity and the sense of belonging. Human diversity is an undeniable fact of contemporary social existence and while it does increase social tension, it has been successfully managed in a number of countries (Switzerland, Canada, England, the United States). These examples demonstrate

> a political culture in which constitutional principles can take root need by no means depend on all citizens sharing the same language or the same ethnic and cultural origins. A liberal political culture is only the common denominator for a constitutional patriotism (*Verfassungspatriotismus*) that heightens an awareness of both the diversity and the integrity of the different forms of life coexisting in a multicultural society.[70]

This multicultural response to diversity is based on the "the coexistence within the same political society of a number of sizeable [sic] cultural groups wishing and in principle able to maintain their distinct identity."[71] Its intention is to ensure "all citizens can keep their identities, can take pride in their ancestry and have a sense of belonging."[72] The benefits of belonging have been established by psychological studies which indicate belonging is one of our basic human needs. This is generally satisfied by sharing thoughts and feelings, acceptance, confirmation, understanding, and influence with others we deem to be significant. When this need for belonging is left unsatisfied, a person will feel its absence in the form of loneliness, ostracism, rejection, friendlessness, and rootlessness. But what can it mean to belong when membership is electronic and the members never even see each other, never get to know one another? For some this means turning to what have been called imaginary communities, ethnic and actual cultural enclaves (China Town, Little Italy), in which shared language, history, foods, etc., offer a basis for personal identity, a sense of belonging conceived of as deep, horizontal comradeship.[73]

However, in cyberspace there is a tendency to base those feelings of closeness on shared interests rather than shared social characteristics such as gender, age, race, etc. Yet cyberspace is not the great leveler we once thought it would be: "Far from being a site where race, racism, ethnocentrism, or

---

70. Habermas, *Between Facts and Norms*, 500.
71. Raz, "Multiculturalism," 197.
72. "Multiculturalism," line 1.
73. Anderson, *Imagined Communities*, 6–7.

stereotyping are banished, these phenomena flourish in newsgroups."[74] Perhaps one of the reasons for the confusing mix of coarseness, vulgarity, and intimacy commonplace on social networking sites is we are dealing with a dislocation of mind and body. Uninhibited by the conventions of everyday embodied life, users are "both more intimate and more hostile with each other than would be socially acceptable in everyday life. Today, cyberspace, in spite of its potential, is actually causing widespread fear and rejection of diversity. In their desire to force belonging, many have used the Internet to spawn nationalistic, ethnically based, countermovements. These movements support the idea that each distinct cultural/linguistic/religious group (assuming, at least in the US, it is not white, Caucasian, English-speaking, and Protestant) will be forcibly incorporated into the common culture or simply not allowed to be here. Here, we see "Internet innovations . . . widen inequalities . . . How did something so promising go so wrong?[75]

---

74. Smith and Kollock, *Communities in Cyberspace*, 72.
75. Taplin, *Move Fast*, 20.

11

Influence of the Public Sphere on the Church

The central question [is] who can place issues on the agenda and determine what direction the lines of communication take?[1]

As we have seen, public dialogue has been threatened by a number of perhaps unintended consequences of the contemporary digitization of print technologies. Taken together with the differentiation of multiculturalism, the personalization promoted by digital technologies that results in filter and preference bubbles, the erosion of expertise and authority, the pseudo-reality of online relationships, and the general use of computer-mediated communication have caused cultural isolation and led to a fragmentation of the public sphere. These forces have hindered the circulation of ideas between members of the public,[2] and effectively eliminated genuine public discourse.

The question I now turn to is whether or not these same influences have altered or even damaged discourse in the public spaces of the church. I have already stated discourse in the public space of the church differs from its secular counterpart in that it is constrained or directed by Scripture, Tradition, and Hierarchy. Obviously, the presence of normative givens,

---

1. Habermas, *Between Facts and Norms*, 379.
2. Gripsrud and Eide, *Idea of the Public Sphere*, 237.

which are not outcomes of dialogue proper, change both the purpose of and the form of discourse in the church. On the one hand, dialogue will not be about building a consensus in the sense of a compromise that fuses a number of competing, equivalid positions, to create something new. It is rather more like the process of growth, individuals all moving from their initial positions toward a common mind, that is, a collective acceptance of or submission to the position provided by the aforementioned constraints. It will certainly involve the hard work of rearticulating the received position in light of the contemporary moment. But it will be a melding of the immediate positions with the those of the catholic consciousness of the church in a way that does not violate but rather affirms that which is given.

On the other hand, these constraints will change the ways and the settings in which that dialogue will be expressed, as well as the nature of the outcomes. As I see it, there are at least five types of such discourse. 1) *Administrative* discourse involves elements of church life that have to be organized and planned. This could be what takes place in a parish council meeting or an annual parish meeting during which the faithful deliberate to find outcomes that are not pre-dialogue givens but Spirit-guided and -enabled consensus upon which they base corporate policies and actions. 2) *Liturgical* discourse involves the faithful believers interacting with one another and God for the purpose of moving individuals from a state of nononeness to the oneness of body offered in and around the Eucharist. It is a collective negotiation for mystical unity. 3) *Didactic* discourse has to do with all the teaching ministries of the church. In this case dialogue has the individuals negotiating the path from nonknowing to knowing. It involves repeated cycles of clarifications and explanations which lead to understanding. 4) *Communal* dialogue refers to all the interaction that leads to the biblical notion of fellowship. This, too, is a cycle of mutual, gradual trust-building through which we seek to navigate the path from mere acquaintance to genuine communion. 5) *Transformational* dialogue, which takes place between the faithful, the clergy, and the divine presence, is not limited to any particular space (as is the liturgy) and ultimately leads to sanctification. It is the activity of negotiating the path from carnality to holiness, from a passion-filled life to one of deification.

Taking up the basic question of the previous chapter—What happens when the words we use are subjected to certain pressures?—let me now reframe that question and ask what happens to these different types of ecclesial dialogue at both the topical and the metatopical levels when they are mediated (writing, print) rather than presented directly (verbally, orally); confined to the echo chambers of user preference; divorced from authority structures and expertise; made vacuous in the alternate, pseudorealities of social media; and fragmented by the pressures of globalism and multiculturalism. Finally, we will also need to consider a sixth type of discourse, ecclesial agenda building, that is, how the questions we discuss are put on the agenda. Presumably, we are discussing issues that arise out of some common interests or problems. But how are these questions or issues identified? Who is posing the questions and why?

ADMINISTRATIVE DISCOURSE

When it comes to the dialogue involved in the administrative tasks of the church, it is probably true that outside the actual meetings (parish council, etc.) in which oral discourse is a necessity, *mediated* communication provides a most effective means of discriminating, recording, and preserving the information generated during those meetings. These technologies do not appear to hinder this type of dialogue. In fact, they may well enhance it by assuring all participants have the same data and the same recollections. That information becomes the basis for the real and necessarily verbal discourse. Accordingly, whatever *filtering* might be done will have to be expressed contemporaneously and will be visible to the other participants and subject to immediate acceptance or rejection. Of course, the information disseminated before or after the oral exchange could be filtered turning the whole group into a filter bubbler or an echo chamber. The loss of *expertise* and authority will have only limited impact since the positions of pastoral and administrative positions will have to have already been allocated for the meeting to be convened. Any expert information or advice will have to be presented by an already-recognized member of the group and/or vetted by that member. In all likelihood that vetting will not be done via instant internet fact-checking during the meeting. Similarly, the *unrealities* of social media will not affect this kind of dialogue since it will probably not be conducted using a social media platform. Finally, *multiculturalism* might have some impact if individual members of the group represent particular cultural or linguistic concerns. In general, then, if we treat administrative dialogue in the church as a search for Spirit-guided consensus, we will avoid most of the negative constraints being exerted on public discourse today.

LITURGICAL DISCOURSE

In light of the requirement for catholic participation, it is easy to conceive of liturgy as a form of *ecclesial discourse*. When the faithful gather to celebrate the Eucharist, they participate in what Afanasiev calls the "sacrament of the assembly."[3] It is a group activity, a corporate undertaking during which each participant interacts with the others in order to negotiate a path that transcends individuality and culminates in the quintessential expression of Christian unity, the one body of Christ. Earlier I suggested this dialogue, this activity, could be thought of as celebration, in which case everyone present is concelebrating. Sometimes this term is used to indicate that more than one priest is participating in overseeing the Eucharist. The one presiding is called the celebrant, the others are called concelebrants. However, this usage seems to overlook the priestly function of all the people. So it is not just the priest, but all the people gathered who share in the priestly function of the eucharistic assembly. This idea captures the assumption of shared responsibility, that is, a responsibility that is expressed as an action of or by the whole assembly. It is not just a matter of attending or observing but deliberately participating, owning and approving every act performed by the presider in the midst of the people. It is concelebrating. For every petition of a liturgical litany, the people all respond with the affirmation. The faithful repeatedly express their agreement with the church's teaching on the Trinity by making the sign of the cross at every mention of the Holy Trinity. They affirm their assent to the creed by all singing it together. When asked to bow their heads, they do so. At the beginning of the Anaphora, the presider calls the people to "lift up their hearts," and they express their assent with the words "we lift them up to the Lord." In other words, they are actually doing what they are being led to do. All of this culminates in the Eucharist itself. This is the center towards which the entire liturgical dialogue aspires and in which everyone is gathered into one. That oneness depends, of course, on everyone partaking. This insistence on catholic participation has been so strong that the canons even require those who simply observe be excluded from eucharistic assembly. There simply cannot be any nonparticipating observers, any spectators at a eucharistic assembly.[4] There is then no place for observers or spectators among the faithful. They, the whole people of God, share in the priestly ministry by actually being physically present in the same place and by celebrating with the presider, that is, concelebrating, watching, affirming, approving, and living into every move he makes, every word he utters.

3. Afanasiev, *Lord's Supper*, 1.

4. According to ancient canon law, "All who enter the Church of God and hear the Holy Scriptures, but do not communicate with the people in prayers, or who turn away, by reason of some disorder from the holy partaking of the Eucharist, are to be cast out of the Church until, after they shall have made confession, and having brought forth the fruits of penance, and made earnest entreaty, they shall have obtained forgiveness." Canon 2 of the Council of Antioch. See also Canon 21 of Elvira. This canon is noted by the council of Sardica (mid-fourth century) in its 12 Canons as well as Canon 80 of Trullo (Afanasiev, *Lord's Supper*).

So has this liturgical discourse been threatened by contemporary pressures? While I believe the Orthodox Church has firmly and effectively resisted these challenges to liturgical dialogue, I can sense the lurking presence of some dangers. Liturgical dialogue could, I suppose, be *mediated* in the form of images and audio (live streamed, recorded, or Facebooked). As is the case of all mediated dialogue, it would effectively divorce the observers from the other members of the assembly, individualizing the recipients and transforming them into spectators. In that case, the recipients of a mediated liturgy would no longer actually be participating or celebrating, would not have communion, be one with the others. This would effectively reverse the fundamental principle of ancient church life—"Always everyone and always together"—and turn it into the opposite—"not everyone and not together"—each one for himself and each one separate. Moreover, this would render those thus separated noncommunicants in a nonliturgy. It would also reduce the reality of the liturgy to a mere representation of the liturgy; not the liturgy in actuality, simply some pseudoreal, synthetic, ineffective substitute.

The concept of *filtering* would seem to have little impact on Orthodox liturgical dialogue since we have resisted the idea that we should change or tweak the liturgy to suit the whims of the participants and their desire for choices. We do not offer various styles of services, such as contemporary, traditional, etc. We do not respond to user preferences with respect to music, vestments, order of service, etc. As I see it, we have been spared some of the negative effects of filtering because the form of worship is part of what has been given, pre-defined, developed within Tradition under the guidance of the Holy Spirit. We have been provided with an evolving yet already-initiated setting in which the diversity of contemporary worshipers can be directly engaged by the catholic consciousness of the church. In this divinely prescribed context of the liturgy, end-user predilections fade into irrelevance, not because they are not to be taken seriously, but because in this assembly, this gathering, all those individual opinions are not to be highlighted or memorialized but rather acknowledged, celebrated, and molded into a oneness in Christ that moves us toward the common mind of the church. So in the absence of consumer choices, there cannot be much in the way of personalization.

Similarly, contemporary challenges to *authority and expertise* have not had much of an impact on the perceived necessity or importance of the presider in liturgical dialogue. From its earliest times, the church has always made provision for a presider who oversaw the orderly celebration of the Eucharist. For that reason the presider is seen as "one of those vital functions, those manifestations of life, without which the church cannot exist on earth as a living organism."[5] There has always been a special ministry of the presider which is made necessary by the very interactive nature of the Eucharist.

Finally, there may be some pressure being put on liturgical dialogue by *multiculturalism and globalism*. This is most likely to be expressed in terms of the various languages in which this discourse can be practiced. In addition to the purely ethnic interests of various groups who find comfort and a sense of belonging when hearing the liturgy done in their mother tongue, there are several transnational liturgical languages such as Slavonic and Greek. These languages are often insisted upon by immigrants even to the second generation and even after they have ceased being widely understood. In the case of these last two, it is not merely a matter of ethnic preference but of the church's conviction that these languages are better suited to liturgical dialogue. Nevertheless, it has been the practice of the church since the ninth century that the liturgy is to be conducted in the language of the local people. This principle was followed by the church as it expanded across central Russia, Asia, Alaska, and America. Each new language that was encountered was immediately used to meet the liturgical needs of the expanding church. So in spite of the pressures of cultural and linguistic diversity, the church's primary concern has been to make liturgical discourse understandable to as many as possible.

DIDACTIC DISCOURSE

This second type of ecclesial discourse takes place within the teaching ministries of the church. Here I am thinking of sermons given during services, teaching done in classes and for catechumens, as well as certain forms of counseling focused primarily on providing instruction (as opposed to crisis intervention, etc.). In their natural settings, all of these involve verbal presentation. Moreover, they are characterized by a cyclical procedure that alternates between presentation, questions, and explanations. The participants are pursuing movement from a lack of knowledge and understanding to a state of being informed, understanding, and application. Often the listeners' responses involve negotiation for questions that further understanding. In any case, all of these activities can rightly be called dialogue given the verbal interaction they presuppose.

So have the pressures being put on secular public discourse had an effect on didactic discourse in the common spaces of the church? What comes to mind immediately is the widespread practice of making much of this

---

5. Afanasiev and Plekon, *Church of the Holy Spirit*, 17.

material available using *mediated* print. This could be the Sunday sermon printed in the bulletin or calendar, or posted on the parish website either as text or an audio file. The same thing applies to teaching materials that can be emailed, posted on Facebook, or sent to class members. These print technologies do change the character of these communicative acts. As mentioned above, a sermon can only actually be a sermon within the context of a liturgy. So whatever the reader is getting, it is divorced from the setting that gives it its special character and divorces the reader from the one sermonizing, eliminating many crucial elements of the sermon's native context. Nevertheless, in terms of simply transmitting information, these mediated formats are fairly efficient. They make it easier for the participants to get the complete text of a quote they missed during the sermon or to follow up with additional information related to a class.

What then of *filtering*? Certainly, the reader can select only those messages he or she prefers to read. That could create special-interest bubbles within the parish or deprive the reader of the grand narrative being presented. Nevertheless, the topical ecclesial common spaces are probably not greatly affected by this dynamic. Yes, individual parishes do generate an amazing diversity of web-based information. But in most cases, it is simply passing along information that applies equally to all members. There is usually no need or opportunity for feedback, discussion, or dialogue. So while these web-based offerings are increasing and multiplying choice, and while the individual can filter them, they don't, at least in the topical common spaces, seem to impact any positions or teachings since they are simply disseminating information and are not directly involved in a difference-overcoming dialogue in search of consensus.

However, in the metatopical common spaces of the church, we do find a multitude of discussions. If we view the Internet as a metatopical space, we see there a practice that parallels the secular public space, a host of chat rooms, blogs, interactive websites that have sprung up, each run by Orthodox individuals and dedicated to promoting particular positions on a variety of topics. On the surface of it, one might hope these diverse outlets could actually contribute to or facilitate true public dialogue. However, a closer look reveals the vast majority of the participants that visit or leave comments at these sites are people who already agree with the site's position. In other words, they are just echo chambers inhabited by the like-minded, and in which little or no actual dialogue is taking place.

So has this print technology helped the church? Has it promoted open didactic dialogue? Unfortunately, no more than it has done in the secular world. It has simply divided, fragmented, and isolated individual members of the church, making real dialogue and learning nearly impossible. Since we cannot forbid or even limit the continual creation of these divisive web-based echo chambers, the only recourse we have is to a) recognize and publicize the danger, and b) encourage our members to curb their web appetites and limit ecclesial discussions to the appropriate, or should we say actual, common spaces of the church. I suspect a drastic drop in site visits, an outright boycott, could go a long way in tempering the divisive emotions generated in these isolation chambers and encourage a renewal of face-to-face dialogue in the public space of the church.

We noted that public dialogue is being challenged by the death of *expertise*. I suspect something similar is happening in our churches when our sermons,[6] catechetical lessons, and marriage counseling are tested against the opinions of Internet experts. For example, Orthodox Tradition has developed outstanding materials on the topic of child-rearing. St. John Chrysostom and Saint Theophan the Recluse have both offered excellent guidance in keeping with the practice and the teaching of the church. Still, many of our members turn to experts outside the church for advice while neglecting, if not negating, the authorities already established. This proliferation of cyberauthorities "accommodates those who wish to 'be' religious outside the control of an organized religious institution."[7] Some Internet voices, for example, claim you don't need official ordained members of the clergy to celebrate the Eucharist. But by what authority are these claims made? There is no appeal to Scripture, no appeal to Tradition, nothing but the individual opinion of an instant expert who happens to have the resources to create a website which translates his opinion, *qua* cyberspace, into an authoritative doctrinal assertion, true simply because he says it is so. In this way the Internet and CMC accommodate and exaggerate the prevailing post-Enlightenment individualism, the conviction that every person has the freedom to form and assert their own opinions, as well as the general belief the whims of the contemporary moment trump the inheritance of historical continuity, giving us the authority to change that inheritance at will.

This shift in the perception of and the appeal to authority is not just a matter of comparing experts or being right; it strikes right at the heart of the ecclesial understanding and nature of pastoral didactic authority. This authority does not rest on the instant pronouncements of unvetted,

---

6. I recently gave a sermon on what I called some muddled and confused thinking on the topic of forgiveness. Even I as a priest and theologian was called into question by a parishioner although I had carefully set out the biblical, historical, and traditional teaching of the church. Why? Because some online reports seem to support a different (the contemporary muddled) teaching.

7. Christopher Helland, cited in Dawson and Cowan, *Religion Online*, loc. 335 of 4045.

anonymous cyberpersonalities but rather is developed and sustained over the course of centuries in the context of apostolic succession, that is, in the ongoing line of bishops, who are the successors of the apostles. This practice provides the church with a structure of authority that is based on the initial authorization of the apostles by Christ and is activated today as part of this continual, canonical succession of bishops. In this way God has given the church a structure that is initiated by divinity and implemented by humanity. Notice how the early church affirmed the dual finite/infinite character of ecclesial authority by equating the bishops with the very presence of Christ. For example, Ignatius of Antioch wrote to the Ephesians, "For even Jesus Christ, our inseparable life, is the [manifested] will of the Father; as also bishops, settled everywhere to the utmost bounds [of the earth], are so by the will of Jesus Christ."[8] It is fascinating to note the use of the word "mind" in this context. It would seem to indicate the consensus (mind) of belief and practice developed in the common places of the church already exists in Christ and in the bishop whose primary responsibility is not administrative but rather is the preservation of apostolic teaching. That authority is also delegated by the bishop to the priest, making him the local repository of authority and what amounts to the resident "expert"[9] on all matters of the faith. This structure obviates the need for external authorities, instant or otherwise, to inform our deliberations. What is needed in the church today is not more Internet fact-checking of everything a bishop or a priest says and does but rather humbly submitting to extensive knowledge of the biblical, Traditional, and Hierarchical expressions of that one common mind, the mind of Christ.

As we have seen, much of this is being thrown over by the Internet experts who claim religious authority for themselves. I fear the general convenience of CMC has led to a glut of expert opinions on just about anything, even things related to the church. I think we need to a) inform our people of the danger, b) reemphasize and actively exercise ecclesial authority, and c) invite and facilitate rigorous dialogue within the common spaces of the church. This effort has to be deliberate, aggressive, and sustained because the forces arrayed against the church are powerful and manifold.

It may also be that some of this teaching is passed along using the *pseudorealities of social media*. I think it is easily demonstrated that Facebook is no more suited to didactic dialogue than any of the other mediated forms of communication. Information can be passed along, creating the illusion of a

---

8. Ignatius of Antioch, "Epistle of Ignatius to the Ephesians," para. 3.

9. Sadly, there are many priests who, by reason of laziness, ignorance, etc., do not live up to this standard. But that does not obviate the principle.

teaching environment. Here, I need only point to the oft-repeated limitations of online education. But in reality, social media cannot establish the natural oral context needed for teaching. With the teacher and the student separated from each other, the didactically required cycle of inquiry is lost, or at best forced into a stuttering delayed sequence of mediated questions and answers. Another aspect of Facebook unreality comes in the form of the recipient's ability to like or dislike the post. This one-word response hardly characterizes discourse. Moreover, if the post happens to be or contain a passage of the Holy Scriptures, then the act of liking is reduced to the inane and offensive act of dismissing with an emoji the very word of God.

Finally, we should ask if the pressures of *multiculturalism* have affected didactic discourse in the church. Short of teaching classes in the native languages of our parishioners, there appears to be little interface between this dynamic and teaching in the church. However, there may be one exception in certain ethnically dominated contexts. Some churches with roots in other cultures may offer instruction in, for example, Russian or Greek schools. In some Greek parishes, for example, this is organized and executed by the American Hellenic Educational Progressive Association (AHEPA). The mission of this group is "[t]o promote the ancient Hellenic ideals of education, philanthropy, civic responsibility, family and individual excellence through community service and volunteerism."[10] This is no doubt a laudable effort, but as far as I can tell, it seems to have little to do with the actual life of an Orthodox parish. It is often an almost external activity in which the participants are not officially connected with the parish. Fortunately, it has little or no impact on the didactic discourse of the parish.

COMMUNAL DIALOGUE

The New Testament uses a technical term (κοινωνία) to describe the interpersonal relationship between the members of the church. *Koinonia* is described as having something in common, such as our faith (Titus 1:4) and salvation itself (Jude 3). In Acts 2:44 and 4:32, the disciples live what is called a "common" life, following the example of Jesus (Luke 8:1). This life in "community is not based on economic theory, legal socialization, or philosophical imitation of nature, but expresses the loving fellowship which renounces ownership (cf. Luke 12:33) in order to help others (Acts 2:45)."[11] Ordinarily, this fellowship takes place within the context of the divine services. Since it has to do with our faith and life in the church, it is not to

---

10. "Promoting Hellenism," para. 1.
11. Kittel et al., *Theological Dictionary*, 448.

be taken as a substitute for secular social interaction. In other words, the church is not in the business of satisfying the social needs of its members. An interesting explication of this perspective is provided by the Russian word *sobornost* (Соборность). The term was used by the early Slavophiles. Drawing on their own Orthodox heritage and idioms of the Russian people, they developed the idea of *integrality* or wholeness—the precondition of which was a religious faith uncontaminated by rationalism. True knowledge and understanding were to be found in the organic fellowship of *sobornost*, in which the individual is connected with the collective (just as the tri-hypostatic God is one, so multihypostatic humanity is one). The individual can comprehend the truth only so far as he or she is united to and physically participating in the life of the church.

Contemporary pressures have certainly affected ecclesial efforts at communion. First, not that much of our interaction takes place in the realm of the *mediated and pseudoreal* context of cyberspace. Tempted by the promises of contemporary platforms of social interaction, it seems our parishes have substituted the technology of social media for genuine *koinonia*. This is evident from random visits to the websites of individual Orthodox parishes. Almost every one of them has a Facebook and/or Twitter link. In this they are, of course, just following the lead of their national organizations[12] in prominently displaying such links. This technology has been incorporated churchwide and with almost no discussion or consideration of the implications or unintended consequences. So aside from the obvious question of having our churches associated with the dishonest, lecherous, manipulative, and near-treasonous activities of these companies (see above pp. 116-20), has this technology helped the church develop communion? Has it delivered on its promise of enhanced social discourse, more intimate fellowship? It really does not look that way.

First, transferring most of our important communication to social media platforms has exaggerated the divisions and groupings within the church by eliminating from this loop those who do not use social media. This is not simply a matter of internet haves and have-nots. It is rather a clear indictment and isolating of anyone who chooses not to participate in the pseudoreality of online communion. For years we enjoyed a close working and personal relationship with a number of colleagues in ministry as well as with our own adult children. During that time, we were among the first to know when a baby was on the way, a child graduated, someone was sick, and so on. However, once these people adopted Facebook technology,

---

12. See https://www.oca.org, https://atlmetropolis.org/social-media, and https://www.dosoca.org.

we who do not use it were simply left out. Now, we only get this kind of family news indirectly, third and fourth hand. Our relationship, our "friendship," (if one can call it that) was summarily terminated by the convenience of the technology. Why does this happen? Osuagwu writes:

> Social Networking Addicts place a higher value on their online community than they do their offline community, or the people they see in person. It is quite common for an addict to forget birthdays and anniversaries. Their main excuse would be that they did not get a Facebook or Myspace reminder. Their entire world revolves around their social networking community.[13]

Second, by providing this technology with ecclesial legitimization, the church has become responsible for the media addiction or at least its exacerbation of its own members. The problem is not a trivial one. Consider the warnings now coming from the creators of Facebook. Sean Parker, co-founder of the service, admits

> [t]he thought process that went into building these applications, Facebook being the first of them, was all about: 'How do we consume as much of your time and conscious attention as possible? That means that we need to sort of give you a little dopamine hit every once in a while, because someone liked or commented on a photo or a post or whatever. And that's going to get you to contribute more content, and that's going to get you . . . more likes and comments.[14]

So even if we promote self-discipline, "there are a thousand people on the other side of the screen whose job it is to break down the self-regulation you have."[15] Parker himself no longer uses the service because it was "too much of a time sink."[16] But then, what of our members now so addicted to friending that they are late to work, not feeding their infants, not completing home-school lessons, not tending to their toddlers (and yes! I have heard all this and more in the tearful confessions of parishioners)?

Third, if the creators of this technology are now saying they do not want their own children using it, then why do we insist on imposing it on our spiritual children? Tim Cook, CEO of Apple, said "I don't have a kid, but I have a nephew that I put some boundaries on. . . There are some things

---

13. Osuagwu, *Facebook Addiction*, loc. 71 of 654.
14. Lee, "Facebook Founding President Sounds Alarm," 1.
15. Alter, *Irresistible*, 1.
16. Lee, "Facebook Founding President Sounds Alarm," 2.

that I won't allow; I don't want them on a social network."[17] Sean Parker wonders, "God only knows what it's doing to our children's brains"[18] and points to a

> growing body of research [that] demonstrates that excessive use of digital devices and social media is harmful to children and teens, making it very likely this new app will undermine children's healthy development.[19]

Finally, the widespread use of these media in the church is having the same harmful effect on us as it has had on the world around us. Gradually, this very convenient medium undermines our willingness to engage in messy, direct encounters with real people. Chamath Palihapitiya, another former Facebook executive, said

> social media was "destroying how society works," adding that he felt "tremendous guilt" for what he helped make. "In the back, deep, deep recesses of our mind, we kind of knew something bad could happen."[20]

What then of the other pressures? Filtering, which is endemic to social media, seems to be responsible for the very narrow political opinions present in the church. Today, we have believers who are willing to accept the word of a dishonest, immoral, treasonous, individual over the teaching of the holy Scriptures. Our parishes seem to have become political filter bubbles. The use of the pseudorealistic realm of social media has also allowed many in the church to question and even reject the teachings of the clergy and even our bishops. We are also being affected by multinational or international issues. Take for example the dispute over the Orthodox Church in the Ukraine. Some take the side of the Russians and others follow the lead of the (Greek) ecumenical patriarch in Constantinople. In any case, the prevailing sensitivities to national and international issues makes this a matter of concern in the church and does shape its internal dialogue.

TRANSFORMATIONAL DISCOURSE

This type of ecclesial discourse involves actively traversing a path from carnality to holiness or deification. This is a process whereby a human being

---

17. Price, "Apple CEO Tim Cook," 2.
18. Allen, "Sean Parker Unloads on Facebook," para. 2.
19. Wakefield, "Facebook 'No Place' for Young Children," para. 5.
20. Price, "Apple CEO Tim Cook," 3.

created in the image and likeness of God is gradually conformed to that divine likeness, i.e., to the holiness of God. We often think of it in terms of a journey or a progression through specific stages of development, purification, illumination, and perfection. This is dynamic discourse that takes place not in isolation from others but within the context of a believing community who together are trying to identify and eliminate passions and replace them with virtues. The lists of passions generally include the practices and technologies of gluttony, unchastity, avarice, anger, dejection, listlessness, self-esteem, and pride. The virtues are things like love, patience, humility, and integrity.

So if ecclesial communal dialogue includes seeking and overcoming our sinful and detrimental structures, devices, and behaviors, what does that look like in today's context? How has contemporary communication helped us? Does *mediated* communication give us any advantage? Probably not, since it tends to separate and isolate the individual members of the church and actually prevents true dialogue and therefore true fellowship. Does it encourage *filtering*? No doubt it does, leading to more of the isolation associated with filter bubbles. Has it undermined expertise? Without a doubt. But the real question for us is this: What, within the process of sanctification, will we do about it? Do we feel any guilt at all for mindlessly embracing a technology that has led to a decline or even a loss of communion and fellowship in the church? What is it about us that prevents us from acting on the obvious? I suppose there are some who do recognize the danger[21] but still think that we are capable of avoiding the pitfalls. Perhaps, we Orthodox believers have some secret advantage (the truth) over our secular contemporaries. Maybe we think a group of people so versed in and familiar with true Spirit-guided communion would never trade that away for the unsatisfying counterfeit of pseudocommunion. Social media might well be dangerous in the wrong hands, but we've got this under control. We can handle this. But this sounds a bit like the famous last words of the Evangelicals who, because they prided themselves on having a corner on biblical truth, entered the swamp of power politics, only to find themselves robbed of their own moral integrity and drained of both truth and spiritual life. But can we Orthodox handle it? Judging by the 2020 pandemic breakdown in the church communion, I would say no. We, like every other religious organization in this country, are being overwhelmed and changed by our complicity in using and promoting this addictive and destructive technology.

21. I suppose it was some sense of the potential danger that motivated the OCA's Guidelines for Clergy Use of Online Social Networking. But the "dangers" referred to in the piece have more to do with the legal implications than with spiritual life or communion.

So do we feel any shame whatsoever for having thoughtlessly condemned our members, our own children, to the isolation and dysfunction of social media? What is it about us that prevents us from seeing that one addiction is as bad as every other one? To date, I haven't seen any indication we are even beginning to rethink this. Quite to the contrary, by officially using and endorsing the use of these technologies, the church has directly contributed to the addiction of many of its own members. We are deliberately and knowingly putting an irresistible, addictive substance into the hands of our spiritual children. Because it is so widely used and endorsed in that environment, most parishioners don't even think twice about it until it is too late:

> In truth, addiction is produced largely by environment and circumstance. Steve Jobs knew this. He kept the iPad from his kids because, for all the advantages that made them unlikely substance addicts, he knew they were susceptible to the iPad's charms. These entrepreneurs recognize that the tools they promote—engineered to be irresistible—will ensnare users indiscriminately. There isn't a bright line between addicts and the rest of us. We're all one product or experience away from developing our own addictions.[22]

Do we have any intention of rectifying that mistake? I think we need to do something. If we think being involved in social media, etc. is something we cannot avoid, if the church is going to continue encouraging its use, then we should, at the very least, be educating our members (especially our children), alerting them to the dangers, and teaching them how to use these tools. Sadly, I have seen little or no evidence of that kind of training in our churches. The closest we have come to that are the "Guidelines for Clergy Use of Online Social Networking," published by the OCA in 2011.[23] Other than that we continue to use it and enthusiastically recommend its use to our people. I find that interesting in light of the fact that even secular groups dedicated to teaching responsible use of social media are being formed. One group called Common Sense Media included the following in its mission statement:

> Media and technology are at the very center of all our lives today—especially our children's. Kids today spend over 50 hours of screen time every week. The media content they consume and create has a profound impact on their social, emotional, cognitive, and physical development. Learning how to

22. Alter, *Irresistible*, 3.
23. See "Guidelines for Clergy Use of Online Social Networking."

use media and technology wisely is an essential skill for life and learning in the 21st century. But parents, teachers, and policymakers struggle to keep up with the rapidly changing digital world in which our children live and learn.[24]

So if these nonreligious groups feel the need for special training in light of the dangers of social media, shouldn't the church be even more inclined and active? Of course, we could go even further. Perhaps we should shut down every parish Facebook page. We could teach our members to fast from friending. Yes! This would be a reasonable response in the face of the real damage being done by this technology. We have nothing to lose, and it might provide a respite during which the church could begin to heal. But again, judging by recent, not to mention official, endorsements of Facebook by the national church, I am not very hopeful. In fact, I fear the battle has already been largely lost because in spite of all evidence to the contrary, social media is still enthusiastically promoted. Facebook

> has served us well as we send a weekly newsletter, which highlights the upcoming liturgical schedule, showcases ministries, and promotes upcoming events, and a newsletter on our Facebook page. People always enjoy seeing pictures of our church feasts, men's and women's group activities, our Catechesis of the Good Shepherd Church School program, and another very powerful tool Father Andre uses is "Facebook live." "Using an app called 'Facebook Page Manager,' one can easily stream an event live from a mobile phone," said Father Andre. "We currently stream the Sunday Epistle and Gospel readings and sermon live, which is helpful for parishioners who may be sick or who live in distant areas."[25]

In an amazing expression of apparent capitulation, the OCA's "Guidelines for Clergy Use of Online Social Networking" clearly states, "The church should not shy away from these new forms of media, but should be actively present in them."[26] If we teach abstinence and moderation in the case of other addictive threats (drugs, alcohol, sex, etc.), then why not here? God help us! In the public sphere of the church, fellowship is being replaced by social media, and the truly public processing of differences in the church, discourse toward consensus, has been effectively throttled.

---

24. "Common Sense Media's Mission" para. 1. See also, "How Tech is Changing Childhood."
25. Paez, "Planting Grant Missions," paras. 9–11.
26. "Guidelines for Clergy Use of Online Social Networking," para. 1.

ECCLESIAL DISCOURSE AND AGENDA-BUILDING

As mentioned above, our common spaces, both secular and ecclesial, are supposed to engage in discussion about questions and differences that arise out of some common interest or problem. One of the mysteries of the public sphere is the way in which these questions or issues are identified. It is probably true that most of these issues are brought into the space from outside, that is, by external powers such as mass media, political debates, or events that have an impact on the general population. Habermas has proposed a model of agenda-building that envisions some "group outside the government structure 1) articulat[ing] a grievance, 2) tr[ying] to expand interest in the issue to enough other groups in the population to gain a place on the public agenda, in order to 3) create sufficient pressure on decision makers to force the issue onto the formal agenda for their serious consideration."[27] These interests are then furthered by institutions of influence such as education, legal (courts) government, church, and commerce (advertising), and come to define the public debate. Take, as an example, the case of the Colorado baker, Jack Phillips, who refused to make a wedding cake for a gay couple on religious grounds. Following the model mentioned above, the aggrieved parties took to mass media to argue their case, that in turn ended up in court where the baker lost, only to have him take it to the Supreme Court, where he was exonerated.[28] In these ways, the issues, not only of this specific grievance or difference, but also, by extension, the more general issue of gender rights as such, were placed on the agenda for public discourse, and it was then widely discussed in the media and in cyberspace.[29] So what began as a relatively private difference on the very edge of the public sphere is by virtue of rapid proliferation and generalization submitted to the public for discussion in the hope of influencing those (courts) who in the end have the power to actually resolve the difference. Moreover, once public discussion has been activated, the debate itself attracts and gives space to any number of related issues, giving the original issue a kind of disputational longevity. In this case, same-sex marriages, LGBTQ rights, and so on.

According to Habermas, this *civil-social periphery* is the source of many contemporary public issues.

> The communication structures of the public sphere are linked with the private life spheres in a way that gives the civil-social

---

27. Habermas, *Between Facts and Norms*, 380.
28. See Anderson, "Colorado Baker Who Refused."
29. This rapid increase in interest is sometimes facilitated by cyberphenomena such as *going viral*, *trending*, and *cascading*.

periphery, in contrast to the political center, the advantage of greater sensitivity in detecting and identifying new problem situations. The great issues of the last decades give evidence for this. Consider, for example, the spiraling nuclear-arms race; consider the risks involved in the peaceful use of atomic energy or in other large-scale technological projects and scientific experimentation, such as genetic engineering; consider the ecological threats involved in an overstrained natural environment (acid rain, water pollution, species extinction, etc.); consider the dramatically progressing impoverishment of the Third World and problems of the world economic order; or consider such issues as feminism, increasing immigration, and the associated problems of multiculturalism. Hardly any of these topics were initially brought up by exponents of the state apparatus, large organizations, or functional systems. Instead, they were broached by intellectuals, concerned citizens, radical professionals, self-proclaimed "advocates," and the like. Moving in from this outermost periphery, such issues force their way into newspapers and interested associations, clubs, professional organizations, academies, and universities.[30]

By way of contrast, in the church, questions placed on the common ecclesial agenda are usually generated at the interface between the givens of Scripture, Tradition, our common practice as believers. Let's call this the *interface of being* (as in being a believer). So generally these issues are not the products of individual aggrievement but of the contrast between individual believers and the given standards. We might say these issues are *native* to the context of the church. Moreover, they will be debated according to the abovementioned constraints and resolved in keeping with ecclesial competencies.

For example, an individual in the topical sphere of an individual parish may observe differences among the members on the question of how to prepare for holy communion and thus feel compelled to pose the question to fellow members. Since this is of vital interest to all, a public discussion ensues, which may include discussions, bulletins, talks, sermons, and even CMC. At some point, a person (bishop, priest, warden, parish council, etc.) with the power to regulate difference will be convinced by the discussion to decide the issue by presenting the teaching of the church and, because of the common discussion, show how we can process individual differences, such as those who, for medical reasons, cannot fast before communion.

---

30. Habermas, *Between Facts and Norms*, 381.

A similar pattern is followed at the metatopical level where an issue, such as giving, percolates from the local interfaces of being. In many cases the discussion is centered on the difference between a dues-based approach and some form of proportional giving (ideally a tithe). Obviously, each parish has a vested interest in promoting biblically based giving. But then, so does that national church, which is funded by the parishes. So in this case the shared interest ranges beyond the parish, even the diocese, to the national church itself. In addition to local and regional discussion, a forum for metatopical debate is provided at the All-American Council. There, the question is formally put on the agenda and discussed by the delegates under the direction of the bishops. Finally, one proposed position or another is then accepted and becomes the official policy of the whole church. Such was the case in 2018, where, after rigorous debate, the assembly and the synod approved the concept of proportional giving.[31] Following the pattern suggested by Habermas, we see that within the limitations set by Hierarchy, Scripture, and Tradition, public debate and resolution of ecclesiastically legitimate issues parallels secular spaces.[32]

Complicating the situation within the church is the fact that some issues rightly generated in the civil-social periphery are now discussed in the church through the interface of being. Because our own members are also participants in the civil sphere, they will be aware of the questions being asked there, and the possibility of conflating the two spheres is certainly understandable. This may not be a reasoned action on the part of church members, but as long as they play a role in civil society and the public sphere, which we all do, they will always be aware of and informed by the content of public debate. Obviously, there is no lack of aggressive discussion of women's rights, gender rights, etc., in the secular public sphere. Every believer who is an American citizen will not only be aware of this but also be involved in and to some extent affected by that general debate. More importantly, as the general public begins to articulate and solidify its own positions, it becomes increasingly difficult for the believer not to transpose this discussion and, more importantly, secular conclusions, onto the common space of the church. When that happens, it is no longer the church's

---

31. See "Boot Camp."

32. Another example of metatopical discourse in the church is seen in the UMC's struggle with the question of homosexuality. Their current position shows the debate has been guided by ecclesial constraints (Scripture) and resolved in keeping with its own competencies. "The practice of homosexuality is incompatible with Christian teaching. Therefore, self-avowed practicing homosexuals are not to be certified as candidates, ordained as ministers, or appointed to serve in The United Methodist Church" ("What is the Denomination's Position?," para. 2).

teaching, nor its members' attempts to actualize that teaching, that is generating these questions, in which case the questions are being asked in or out of an entirely different context. In other words, they are not native to the context of the church, and unlike the civil realm, the church does not possess the kind of authority needed to definitively resolve civil differences. Of course, it does have the power to resolve dogmatic and doctrinal aspects of ecclesial practice. Moreover, a nonnative issue cannot be resolved with native authority. So while the civil issues imported into the church are discussed in the church, that discourse cannot unfold in keeping with the four constraints mentioned above. The difficulty for the church is not just a matter of the context out of which the grievance has come and how the question is formulated, but also a matter of the givens that are supposed to guide ecclesial discussion. The way it looks today, secular issues seem to be setting the agenda for the church where they are now being discussed according to guidelines that are not native to the church.

Returning to the situation with the baker mentioned above: even if the issue were to be discussed extensively in the common spaces of the church, the church has no power to legally resolve the issue as did the courts. From that standpoint, it is not a question that can be legitimately discussed in the church, at least not with a view toward difference-resolution. However, the church does have in its Scriptures and Traditions a number of guidelines that can be brought to bear on these questions if they are posed in ways that are appropriate to the power of resolution that it does have. So in this case, the question, as informed by the faith, would have two components: a) Is what the baker did the loving (as defined by the church) thing to do?, and b) Does the church have any teaching on the general issue of gender interchangeability? On the first part of the question, we have to answer with Christ's example and say the baker did not act within Christian norms of love and should be encouraged to do so. On the second part we can answer that according to our belief God deliberately created human beings as male and female, and those modes of existence are not interchangeable. So we seem to be in the difficult position of having to love under the laws of our land as well as those of our church.

Interestingly, there has never been any sustained ecclesial discussion of gender interchangeability in the church. Theologically the idea of noninterchangeability is rooted in the fact that God intentionally created human beings as male and female. So if this question has not arisen at the Orthodox *interface of being*,[33] where has it come from? Who is asking it and to what

---

33. Although it is merely anecdotal data, I can affirm that in 20 years of serving Orthodox parishes, the very modern, well-educated, professional women in these parishes never raised the question.

end? Obviously, the question was first asked by aggrieved individuals at the *civil-social periphery* with a view toward legalizing the interchangeability of the genders. That was discussed for decades and the courts have clearly legalized the interchange. For that reason, in this country is it now legal to ordain both men and women. This debate has brought many changes to the church in the area of gender equality. In many ways, we are now being forced by law to conform with our own general teaching (Gal 3:28). So it would appear the question, as it is now being asked and discussed in the church, is the result of the changes that have already occurred in the secular sphere. Because gender equality (with which we do not disagree) is now so well established and because the civil resolution of the issue allows, if not requires, the ordination of women, the question is now being forced onto the Orthodox ecclesial agenda from without. However, not only is the civil realm setting the agenda for the church, it is seeking to impose its resolutions of the issues on the church, overriding or causing revisions to the standing ecclesial canons.

Still, the Orthodox church has done remarkably well in responding to these societal pressures. On all the difficult social issues mentioned above, the church has remained remarkably true to its own teaching. By way of example, consider its very consistent teaching on the sanctity of life.

> The teaching of the Orthodox Church is well expressed by canon 91 of the Sixth Ecumenical Council. Those who give drugs for procuring abortion, and those who receive poisons to kill the fetus, are subjected to the penalty for murder.
>
> The willful aborting of unborn children, as an act of murder, is contrary to the will of God. The unborn child is human life with potential, and not potential human life. The church recognizes the existence of certain extreme cases in which difficult moral decisions must be made in view of saving human life, and fully sympathizes with those who must make such decisions. Such an extreme circumstance is the definitely diagnosed danger to the life of the mother at childbirth. The mother must decide whether to lay down her own life for that of her unborn child. Whatever the decisions of human legislatures and courts, the church cannot accept the willful destruction of an unborn child at any stage of its development as anything other than the destruction of life.[34]

But the pressure on the church is intense, and sadly, while not caving in completely, we may be opening the door by means of an intermediate

---

34. "Synodal Affirmations," para. 6.

softening of our teachings that could gradually alter the mind of the church in such a way as to make accepting such change a real possibility in a generation or two, causing it to become the new normal. Take, for example, the very clear statement on marriage and divorces maintained by the church in keeping with its own Canons:

> The perfect marriage can only be one, single and unique. The prototype of marriage, the unity between Christ and his Church, excludes multiple marriages: Christ has only one Church; the church has no other Christ. Even death cannot break the bond of perfect love.[35]

In spite of its clarity, this stance is sometimes softened under the impact of the radical rise of divorce rates in both the ancient and the contemporary worlds. This softening can be seen in the fact that the church "permits up to, but not more than, three marriages for any Orthodox Christian."[36] The main reason for this is the church "recognizes that sometimes the spiritual well-being of Christians caught in a broken and essentially nonexistent marriage justifies a divorce . . . "[37] While I think all of us can sympathize with the sentiment of this position, I wonder what effect this softened position has had on the general population of the church. It seems to me, based on twenty years of pastoral experience, that because we are all subject to the entropy of sin and because divorce is commonplace in our society, divorce is now widely accepted as a normal occurrence in our parishes. I am not saying the Orthodox divorce rate is particularly high; it is, in fact, lower than that of many other religious groups.[38] However, since the national rate is around 50 percent, a significant portion of our members are going to be divorced. I worry the official softening has subtly changed our petitioners' firm opposition to divorce and weakened their defense against the encroaching assumptions of the public sphere. I fear each successive generation will become increasingly tolerant and eventually the position of the church will be brought into line with that of the secular realm. If that is true, then I suggest not that we change our policy of compassion, but that we intensify our teaching on the actual nature of the marriage bond. The same thing could be said of our current approach to so-called mixed marriages.

> Though the church would prefer that all Orthodox Christians would marry Orthodox Christians, it does not insist on it in

---

35. "Synodal Affirmations," para. 2.
36. Harakas, "Stand of the Orthodox Church," para. 4.
37. Harakas, "Stand of the Orthodox Church," para. 14.
38. See "Religious Landscape Survey."

> practice. Out of its concern for the spiritual welfare of members who wish to marry a non-Orthodox Christian, the church will conduct a "mixed marriage." For this purpose, a "non-Orthodox Christian" is a member of the Roman Catholic Church, or one of the many Protestant churches which believe in and baptize in the name of the Holy Trinity. This means that such mixed marriages may be performed in the Orthodox Church. However, the Orthodox Church does not perform marriages between Orthodox Christians and persons belonging to other religions . . .[39]

Again, we see an exemplary compassion, but discover a gradual shift in the attitudes (increased willingness to marry outside the faith, almost unheard of just a generation ago) of my parishioners. Is this a lowering of our defenses? An opening to the forces of the civil sphere? Perhaps. So once again, I recommend increased vigilance and instruction but not abandoning our policies of compassion.

There is, then, a very real sense in which the church is under pressure from within and without to cede the resolution of these common interests to the civil sphere. In some cases, questions are being asked that do not fit the ecclesial context. Similarly, resolutions that cannot be affected by or do not apply to the church are being sought. By seeking to alter the unique nature of the ecclesial common space by bypassing its unique constraints, we are in effect transforming, slowly publicizing the sacred common space of the church.

As we have seen, the common space of the church is circumscribed by a unique set of restraints, or should I say protections. The unique character of the ecclesial common space provides us with an efficient means of resolving issues that grow up in our own context and provides us with several layers of defense against the encroaching secular sphere. The church, not the civil space—the world—sets its agenda. There is a lot at stake in this simple affirmation. Back in the 1960s, there was a slogan popular in certain World Council of Churches circles: "Let the world set the agenda for the church." The thinking embodied in the slogan was accepted by the WCC and fundamentally damaged the ecclesial character and mission of the organization. As Alan Wisdome notes:

> The slogan affirmed God's saving work in all history and all the world, even where the church was not present. It encouraged the church to discern God's providence in contemporary secular movements of human liberation, and to make itself a servant of those movements. This slogan de-emphasized the special

---

39. Harakas, "Stand of the Orthodox Church," para. 16.

revelation of Jesus Christ that has been entrusted to the church. It bypassed the role of the Scriptures, as the authoritative witness to Christ, in setting the agenda for his body. It denied the spiritual poverty of a world that does not know the person of Christ. And it equated secular processes of liberation with the promise of eternal life in Christ.[40]

I think the old slogan illustrates the dangers the church faces. We cannot cede the right to set our own agenda, to ask the questions we think are vital. We cannot, under any circumstances, allow a merge of ecclesial common spaces with secular spaces. The ecclesial cannot be allowed to become secular. Have we been affected by the secular, commercialized environment of North America? Indeed, we have been, but as I am pointing out here, there are some areas in which the church has held its own, has effectively fought off the temptations to conform. It seems this God-given structure can operate almost in spite of us, almost independently of us, by setting boundaries, or should I say erecting protective barriers, that prevent us from falling headlong into the errors of the secular sphere. Let the church be the church!

As I have tried to demonstrate, the church and its members are embedded in both the secular public sphere and the common spaces of the church. For that reason, a certain amount of overlap is to be expected. This seems to have taken two forms. First, the forces that are now challenging the effectiveness of dialogue in the public sphere are creating analogous difficulties within the church. This is not the result of any deliberate importing of worldly structures into the church but rather the simple fact these societal pressures are having the same effects on both the secular and sacred because their respective common spaces share a basic structure and function, that of a public space. And second, what I find much more troubling and threatening is that, being citizens of both the public and the ecclesial spaces, our members may be allowing the agenda of the secular sphere to be transposed onto the church. If we are not vigilant, this comingling will lead to an irreversible secularization of the church.

---

40. Wisdom, "World Council of Churches," 4.

PART IV

A Self-Governing People

The Church and Contemporary Political Structure

12

A Self-Governing People

Nothing is more surprising to those, who consider human affairs with a philosophical eye, than to see the easiness with which the many are governed by the few; and to observe the implicit submission with which men resign their own sentiments and passions to those of their rulers. When we enquire by what means this wonder is brought about, we shall find, that as Force is always on the side of the governed, the governors have nothing to support them but opinion. 'Tis therefore on opinion only that government is founded; and this maxim extends to the most despotic and most military governments, as well as to the most free and most popular.[1]

I COME NOW TO the last of the three areas of social discourse mentioned at the outset. If a society is to function, it will have to engage in a free exchange of goods and services (commerce), it will have to create a power-free common space for dialogue on issues of common interest, and it will have to establish a context of social order based on an agreed-upon system of self-governance. In other words, it will need to agree on a set of norms that will balance the needs and rights of the individual with those of others in order to accomplish a greater good, which no individual can accomplish alone. Moreover, that society will need a group of representatives who are given the authority to create, debate, and implement those norms. I am, of course, not

---

1. David Hume, cited in Morgan, *Inventing the People*, 13.

interested in trying to present a theory of government but rather in looking at the ways in which its underlying principles, in particular the sovereignty of the people, have affected the church. To do that, we will need to have some general understanding of how this self-governance is thought to work.

Agreeing to and implementing a set of norms (laws) for the greater good is said to have its roots in the idea of *popular sovereignty*. According to Taylor, the contemporary understanding of that concept developed along two paths. On the one hand, the idea is inspired by and then adapted from the patterns developed by certain religious groups and institutions.

> The first Puritan churches formed around the idea of a covenant provide examples of this. A new ecclesial structure flowed from a theological innovation;[2] this becomes part of the story of political change, because the civil structures themselves were influenced in certain American colonies by the ways churches were governed, as with Connecticut Congregationalism, where only the converted enjoyed full citizenship.[3]

New England Congregationalism can be taken as one starting point for the development of American democracy. The New England Puritans had come to the colonies to seek out the freedom to live under "a due forme[sic] of Government," both civil and ecclesiastical.[4] This was based on the normative statements set forth in the Cambridge Platform of Church Discipline (1648). That platform began with the assertion that church government is not a matter of simple human improvisation but of God's command as revealed in Scripture. According to these thinkers, "Church polity is based on the New Testament, where there is no mention of popes, or archbishops, or bishops as officers with jurisdiction over other clergy, or presbyteries with authority over particular churches."[5] Instead, the church was seen as a community of spiritually equal individuals which collectively bore the responsibility of the local parish government. This, of course, has the "appearance of a little democracy, and congregationalism has often been eulogized as one of the sources of liberal democratic theory and institutions."[6] Of course, it would be just as fruitful to see the connection in the exaggerated individualism of the Enlightenment, but even if "it is anachronistic to represent the Puritans as incipient democrats, it may be

---

2. So, it was actually a theological heresy that caused the reformation groups to throw off the hierarchical structure of Tradition.

3. Taylor, *Modern Social Imaginaries*, 109.

4. Wright, *Congregational Polity*, 7.

5. Wright, *Congregational Polity*, 7.

6. Wright, *Congregational Polity*, 10–11.

said that they adopted institutional forms into which later generations could breathe a democratic spirit."[7]

On the other hand, the idea of popular sovereignty is the result of "a reinterpretation of a practice that already existed in the old dispensation."[8] We can trace this development by looking at the different ways in which political authority has been claimed and contested. Initially, it was the king who possessed all authority over policy, taxes, and the like. That authority was said to be derived directly from God. "Monarchy has always required close ties with divinity . . . ,"[9] and by the early seventeenth century, those ties were fully articulated as the doctrine of the divine right of kings. Morgan describes the evolution of this idea, which he notes took place as the American Colonies were taking shape and the Counter-Reformation was well underway:

> The pope claimed to be the vicar of God on earth, with sole powers to legitimate secular authority, either directly or by controlling the allegiance of subjects. And the pope was not in the habit of legitimating the authority of Protestant kings. The way to fight divinity was with divinity. And James I, who ruled England from 1603 to 1625, had sallied forth as the champion of Protestantism by demonstrating, to the satisfaction of Englishmen at least, that God had no truck with the pope (who was no other than Antichrist). God conferred authority with his own hand on rightful rulers, including James I, especially James I. Anyone, including the pope, especially the pope, who challenged the authority of a true king was challenging God himself.[10]

Still, according to a practice "holding since time out of mind . . . Parliament [was said to have] its rightful place beside the king."[11] But,

> [s]ince he was God's lieutenant, he could do no wrong, and within his realm his righteousness and the authority that went with it were not to be questioned. He might seek advice and information from his subjects in Parliament, but his was the God-given authority.[12]

This royal power was tempered by the idea of representation. The king saw the members of parliament as "representatives from counties and

---

7. Wright, *Congregational Polity*, 11.
8. Taylor, *Modern Social Imaginaries*, 109–10.
9. Morgan, *Inventing the People*, 17.
10. Morgan, *Inventing the People*, 18.
11. Taylor, *Modern Social Imaginaries*, 110.
12. Morgan, *Inventing the People*, 18.

boroughs [who came] to his Parliament armed with powers of attorney to bind their constituents to whatever taxes or laws they agreed to."[13] However, it did not take long for those representatives to assert their own power. "From early on, they had concocted measures of their own, presenting them as petitions to the king, but nevertheless in effect making governmental policy, making laws."[14] Eventually they replaced the authority of the king. But that raised the question of the basis of their authority. If it was not derived from the king, then was that divinely given right simply transferred to the members of parliament who would then function as a kind of collective monarch? But if that were so, what became of representation? The solution was to invent the idea of a sovereign people. The

> representatives invented the sovereignty of the people in order to claim it for themselves—in order to justify their own resistance, not the resistance of their constituents singly or collectively, to a formerly sovereign king.[15]

But there were still many questions concerning the nature and function of the supposedly sovereign authority ascribed to the people. It was at this juncture that

> [t]his older idea emerges from the American Revolution transformed into a full-fledged foundation in popular sovereignty, whereby the U.S. Constitution is put in the mouth of "We, the people." This was preceded by an appeal to the idealized order of natural law, in the invocation of "truths held self-evident" in the Declaration of Independence.[16]

Initially, it was believed this law was given by God to the king, then to the parliament, and finally to the people, "and the motivation for obeying it was whatever makes us obey God: a sense of obligation to our Creator and the fear of eternal punishment."[17] But "the fear of God is replaced by the idea of impersonal benevolence, or else by a notion of natural sympathy."[18] In other words, both the rights claimed by individuals as well as their willingness to work for the common good were seen to be anchored in the very laws of nature. Of course, the selfish and egocentric tendencies of human beings seem to contradict that idea, yet it was recognized that both good

---

13. Morgan, *Inventing the People*, 39.
14. Morgan, *Inventing the People*, 46.
15. Morgan, *Inventing the People*, 49.
16. Taylor, *Modern Social Imaginaries*, 109.
17. Taylor, *Modern Social Imaginaries*, 117.
18. Taylor, *Modern Social Imaginaries*, 117.

and evil do coexist in the will of individual human beings. They are capable of seeking both their own well-being as well as the greater good. But in order for society to function harmoniously, that dualism would have to be overcome. The two would have to be merged into one will:

> In Rousseau's language, the primitive instincts of self-love (*amour de soi*) and sympathy (*pitié*) fuse together in the rational and virtuous human being into a love of the common good, which in the political context is known as the general will.

This involves a transformation of human will such that "in the perfectly virtuous man self-love is no longer distinct from love of others."[19] In light of narcissistic instincts obviously inherent in human beings, how could such a transformation be accomplished? The only way would be to somehow preserve the individual liberty of each individual and at the same time "[enlarge] and transpose [self-love] into the higher register of morality."[20] In this way, they could be convinced that being actively engaged in the pursuit of the common good rather than being disengaged would be the best way for them to advance their own personal interests. This is what Taylor, referencing Rousseau, calls a journey "from solitude to society."[21] He further writes:

> The passage from the state of nature to the civil state produces a remarkable change in man by substituting justice for instinct in his conduct and giving his acts the morality they previously lacked. . . . In this state he is deprived of some advantages given to him by nature, but he gains others so great—his faculties are exercised and developed, his ideas are broadened, his feelings are ennobled, his whole soul is uplifted—that if the abuses of this new state did not often degrade him below his previous level, he would constantly have reason to bless the happy moment when he was drawn out of the state of nature forever and changed from a stupid, short-sighted animal into an intelligent being and a man.[22]

With the ultimate virtue of individual liberty preserved, the people could exercise their collective sovereignty, that is, each individual would have an equal say in how common concerns would be managed. This was based on an "immediate relation of people and deputy, through the representation of different interests or the undivided expression of a general

---

19. Taylor, *Modern Social Imaginaries*, 117.
20. Taylor, *Modern Social Imaginaries*, 118.
21. Taylor, *Modern Social Imaginaries*, 118.
22. Taylor, *Modern Social Imaginaries*, 119.

will."[23] In this way the people are said to be invested with collective agency.[24] This would then be a system in which the representatives from every class were chosen by the whole, embodying the general[25] will and thus enabling "direct action by the people"[26] where "each [elector] is immediate to the whole"[27] and "equidistant from the center."[28]

However, the implementation of anything approaching direct democratic government raises serious questions. A "committee of the whole"[29] would obviously not work. As Rousseau noted,

> a genuine Democracy never has existed, and never will exist. It is against the natural order that the greater number govern and the smaller number be governed. It is unimaginable that the people remain constantly assembled to attend to public affairs, and it is readily evident that it could not establish commissions to do so without the form of administration changing.[30]

What was needed was a system where representatives were "authorized to act for a group by being given authority prior to taking action," held "accountable for [their] actions on behalf of [the] group," and "rewarded or punished for those actions if they fail[ed] to respond to the group's interests."[31] This was an indirect expression of the sovereign power of the people who "had no actual role in government. Governing is done by delegates who obtain grants of power from voters, through election, and are entitled for a period of time and within certain limits to exercise it on behalf of the people."[32] This became

> the defining feature of indirect rule: the person who takes action—the representative—is not the one source of valuation or preference. He is an executive who acts on the interests, passions, preferences, or opinions of others rather than on his own valuations and he is, for that reason, better able to act rationally.[33]

---

23. Taylor, *Modern Social Imaginaries*, 139.
24. Taylor, *Modern Social Imaginaries*, 76.
25. Taylor, *Modern Social Imaginaries*, 124.
26. Taylor, *Modern Social Imaginaries*, 125.
27. Taylor, *Modern Social Imaginaries*, 157.
28. Taylor, *Modern Social Imaginaries*, 158.
29. Shapiro et al., *Political Representation*, 79.
30. Shapiro et al., *Political Representation*, 93.
31. Shapiro et al., *Political Representation*, 278.
32. Shapiro et al., *Political Representation*, 286.
33. Shapiro et al., *Political Representation*, 287.

However, even if representatives are elected based on their competence and their skill set rather than on the basis of privilege or class, a "government of elected representatives is necessarily aristocratic in some sense."[34] This is true

> whether or not representatives come from a distinct social class, they may themselves constitute a class of a certain kind and would be expected to some extent to pursue their own interests at least some of the time.[35]

In other words, the election of representatives in an indirect democracy leads to an elite of some kind:

> Almost everywhere the representatives get to choose the details of the electoral system by which they get and hold their jobs, and to change it if they think it is working unacceptably. They have nearly universally avoided term limitations and instructions from their constitutions and usually too the institutions of direct democracy. Almost everywhere they have succeeded in gaining or keeping working conditions that make them hard to monitor and control even by the most attentive voters and interest groups. These are "aristocratic" achievements of a sort. But are they traceable to elections as such or to many additional restrictions on the way that election is employed? More importantly, is there any reason to think that the benefits of their achievements are kept by political incumbents?[36]

Still, these democratically elected politicians "enjoy an especially high status because, though they may be our employees, they are expected to 'lead' us, to direct or command our actions . . . so people may psychologically 'elevate' political agents, projecting onto them some undeserved superiority."[37]

So does indirect democracy provide genuine representation for a whole people, or have we simply delegated authority to elected, self-perpetuating assemblies of elites—elite by virtue of the power invested in them? The general election does indeed afford each elector one vote and collectively they determine who is to represent them, to whom they are willing to delegate policy-making authority (unless, of course, if the election itself is called into question as being rigged). Of course, the "competition for office makes

---

34. Shapiro et al., *Political Representation*, 271.
35. Shapiro et al., *Political Representation*, 273.
36. Shapiro et al., *Political Representation*, 300.
37. Shapiro et al., *Political Representation*, 284.

political aspirants dependent on the favor of those who can help them to get it and keep it."[38]

For that reason, elected officials seem to pay close attention to public opinion. There is a sense in which this does influence representatives throughout their terms. Sadly, this opinion does not always represent the will of the people since that collective sentiment is so easily manipulated by outside forces or by the politicians themselves. As we saw above, this has been done by foreign governments using our very vulnerable social media platforms—Facebook, Twitter, etc. It is also being done by the public relations arms of political parties and individual politicians who seek to dictate the narrative of public debate. Consider the obscene amounts of money being spent on campaign advertising. Cook Political projects politicians will spend "$2.4 billion for local broadcast and $850 million for local cable . . . and $600 million of digital ads driven mostly by advertising done on Facebook."[39] All this in an effort to influence individual electors. This is also being done by advertisers and lobbyists seeking their own gain or that of those they represent. In 2017, 11,545 lobbyists spent $3.37 billion in their attempts to influence the outcomes of legislation.[40] It seems then the promise of genuine representation is a myth, and that brings us back to the puzzle stated at the outset: that of the majority agreeing to a minority being granted authority to represent and make decisions for all of them. These

> new fictions, by placing authority and subjection, superiority and inferiority in the same hands, could deprive people, who were actually subjects, of effective control over a government that pretended to speak for them—a form of tyranny that popular sovereignty continues to bring to peoples all over the world.[41]

In what sense does a senator working in Washington, DC actually represent the needs, desires, and wishes of his constituents? On a very practical level, he/she simply cannot be mindful of the people since he/she works at a remove and has no personal understanding of the daily lives of the people they supposedly represent and who are more concerned with their own re-election than anything else. Yes, each elector has the right to voice his opinion directly to the senator, by email, or by letter, but there seem to be only two ways in which the voting public can hope to influence their elected officials. One is through public opinion polls. The other is the general election.

---

38. Shapiro et al., *Political Representation*, 300.
39. Passwaiter, "2018 Campaign Ad Spend," para. 4.
40. See "Lobbying Spending Database."
41. Morgan, *Inventing the People*, 83.

13

Democracy, Politics, and Self-Governance in the Church

All the participants of the assembly together with their presiders constituted a single people of God, the royal priesthood.[1] The royal priesthood became reality and the basis of the life of the church.[2]

As we have seen, the church has, to its own detriment, adopted some of society's commercial practices and presuppositions, and it has sought to create a common space for dialogue, uncritically using many of the structures and technologies of the prevailing culture. In other words, in these two areas of social interaction, the unique imaginary of the church that should be rooted in Scripture and tradition has instead been infiltrated, damaged, or even supplanted by the social imaginary of the prevailing culture (see above pp. 140–43). What then of the third area of interaction, self-governance? Certainly, the church needs to establish for itself a context of order based on an agreed-upon system of governance and laws, a system that allows for and oversees the development and implementation of policies (practices), balancing the needs and rights of the individual with those of others to accomplish a greater good and fulfill the common purpose of the church. In what follows, I will be asking 1) to what extent has the prevailing principle

---

1. Afanasiev and Plekon, *Church of the Holy Spirit*, 18.
2. Afanasiev and Plekon, *Church of the Holy Spirit*, 11.

of the people's sovereignty been allowed to influence the life of the church, and 2) what are the fundamental principles of ecclesial self-governance as dictated by its own unique imaginary?

SOVEREIGNTY OF THE PEOPLE AND THE CHURCH

As we saw above, American democracy is built on the foundation of the sovereign will of the people. "We the people" enshrined in the preamble to our Constitution is now so deeply ingrained in the national psyche as to be above question, beyond any need for defense or justification. It is the default position, the spontaneous response, to questions of social order, of working together as a people. In other words, this people power is an essential element of the modern social imaginary, of everything that is American. That being the case, it is understandable that we do indeed observe this idea's democratizing effect on the church. It can be seen in a) the hyper-individualistic rage to vote, b) the process of making decisions, c) the organizational structure, and d) the ways in which negative forms of politics have crept into and are damaging the church.

The Rage to Vote

One expression of this presumed sovereignty of corporate will is what we might call a general rage to vote, that is, the conviction that we always have the right to vote or have our say on any and every decision or action taken by the church. In the OCA, newly planted parishes are initially designated as "missions." They have no parish councils, and their priests bear the title "priest-in-charge." These priests are the sole authority, the decision-makers in the fledgling groups. They are not hired by the local group; they do not answer to the group, only to their bishops. When I was assigned to oversee such a parish planting project, I remember being uncomfortable with that lack of democracy. So, hoping to involve the laity, I organized what we called a leadership team in which I hoped to tap into the collective wisdom of the group and make decisions by consensus rather than fiat or voting. Sadly, most of the members of that early group were determined to assert their own right to opinion by forcing a vote on almost every decision we made. For example, as a means of outreach and teaching, I wanted to start a few home-based Bible studies. That was rejected as a Protestant practice and the objectors insisted on a vote, even though I was the priest-in-charge. That scenario was repeated *ad nauseum* throughout those early years, causing considerable tension and discord.

This assumed right to choose and to always be able to express one's opinion was also evident in the sanctuary. It is common knowledge that during a divine liturgy the main celebrant has absolute say over who does what, where, and when. Nevertheless, during those early liturgies any number of my altar boys, who were actually young adults, would question my instructions, that is, they would openly argue with me about what I had asked them to do, saying either they did not want to do something or that what I was asking did not conform to the rubrics as they understood them. At one point I remember in my frustration I turned on one of them and asked, "Is this some kind of democracy? Are we supposed to have a debate and take a vote? No! Now please just do what I am asking."

It seems, then, in a very general way, the prevailing secular commitment to the sovereignty of the people embedded in the modern social imaginary quite naturally seeps into the church. This transference is spontaneous and unreflected on since the social imaginary in which we are all steeped colors the way we approach all legislation and morphs into the feeling that voting is the only right way to make decisions in the church. The result is a widespread desire, if not a rage, to transform every ecclesial decision into a referendum that can be decided by voting.

Dual-Realm Decision-Making

Of course, some of these democratic structures and practices are not just the unreflected spillover from the social imaginary but are deliberate, if not necessary, elements of the church's formal interface with civil society. As we saw above (pp. 83–85), certain financial and legal considerations speak in favor of incorporating parishes. If a parish is to be thus recognized by a civil authority, it is required to have a set of by-laws or statutes which define (in terms the state can understand) the internal structure and workings of the parish. For example, the "Uniform Parish By-Laws" of the Diocese of the South, Orthodox Church in America, after defining the parish's name, purpose, and membership, moves into a description of its organizational structure. It begins with the parish meeting, which "is the highest authority of the Parish as a civil corporation. All members of the Parish . . . who have been members for a period of six months and are at least eighteen years old may attend and vote at the Parish Meeting."[3] This statement is followed by a series of articles in which operating principles for additional organizational elements, such as the rector, the parish council, budget committee, auditing committee, and other organizations, are given. Guided by these dictates, our

---

3. "Uniform Parish By-Laws," 4.

annual parish business meetings were conducted according to the strictest parliamentary procedure,[4] and we proposed, seconded, discussed, and voted on practically everything. We could not, it seemed, paint the building, buy new service books, accept a budget, or consider a new bishop without taking a vote. As you might imagine, our members were quite comfortable and proficient using these by-laws-imposed structures and practices. They actively participated with practiced ease, accepting, if not expecting, the mean-spirited and divisive exchanges that occasionally characterized our discussions. And why not? The entire process was clearly in harmony with the prevailing social imaginary. It was exactly what they were used to in every other area of social life.

As effective and perhaps necessary as the imposition of these by-laws are, they do create some intellectual tension, which raises questions at several points. *First*, this arrangement seems to suppress, if not eliminate, the spiritual aspect of business in the parish. When our parish was talking about buying property and building a larger church, I insisted the decisions involved were not just financial and legal but primarily faith-related. However, the idea that accepting the building project as an expression of our faith, something God was leading us to do that we needed to pray about, was mostly lost amidst a discussion of a multitude of mundane concerns. It seems to me the reason for this loss of spiritual focus was we were unfairly asking the people to suddenly switch to a decision-making process radically different than the one they use in everyday life, all the while creating an everyday-like context right there in the parish. What else could we expect?

Second, the by-laws seem to have created overlapping, parallel, or even competing structures of governance within the parish, blurring the boundary between the sacred and the secular. We know Canon law has clearly defined the structures, authorities, and the governing of the church. Indeed, the framers of these diocesan by-laws recognize that and rightly insist "the Parish is governed by Holy Tradition, that is, the whole body of teaching and practice of the One Holy, Catholic, and Apostolic Church."[5] Yet these same authors suggest the "by-laws are issued for the governance of the parishes and local congregations of the Diocese of the South."[6] This presents both a conundrum and a question. On the one hand, we know these by-laws have been derived from and represent secular or civil parliamentary practice. On the other hand, since by-laws are made to control the actions of members, this seems to raise the question of which instruments and which structures

---

4. Such as Robert et al., *Robert's Rules of Order*.
5. "Uniform Parish By-Laws," 2.
6. "Uniform Parish by-Laws," 1.

are to govern the church. The proposed solution to this apparent dilemma appears a few lines later: "The purpose of the regulations contained in these by-laws is to apply Holy Tradition to the organization and daily life of the parish."[7] This seems to suggest we use civil procedures to apply sacred law to the life of the church. Positively, we might say the by-laws serve as a bridge between the church and the secular world, but at the very least this seems to blur the line between the civil world in which we live and life in the church. I am not saying we should ignore the civil law of the country in which we live, but this does at the very least raise the fundamental question of the relationship between civil law and canon law (which I will take up below).

The legislative discontinuity created by this clouded relationship is evident in some of the decisions faced by the OCA's 19th All-American Council, held from July 23–27, 2018. At one point in the deliberations, the holy synod offered an amendment to the statutes on the periodicity of the All-American Council, moving it from every three years to every four years. They did so in keeping with the procedures listed in the *Delegate Handbook*, and it was thus obvious the bishops had already decided in favor of the change. However, after some discussion, a Parliamentarian "noted that Robert's Rules of Order specify that in order for a proposed Statute amendment to be adopted, it must receive two-thirds of the total votes cast and not two-thirds of the total possible votes. . . [a] vote was taken and "the amendment was defeated with 210 votes for and 203 against."[8] In this case, it was the sovereignty of the people, civil law, and not the will of the bishops that carried the day.

Of course, the sovereignty of the people does have some limits within the church. For example, when a new metropolitan is elected in the OCA, the people (council delegates) go through several rounds of voting designed to reduce the list of nominees and finally present a list of two or three to the synod for approval. In many cases, the apparent choice of the people is overridden by the synod of bishops, who choose another candidate. This happened, for example, at the 13th All-American Council (July 21–26, 2002):

> There was no apparent consensus among council delegates concerning who should be the next Primate. With 639 delegates voting, Bishop Seraphim (Storheim) of Ottawa and Canada received 267 votes, far short of the 426 votes needed for nomination on the first ballot. Archbishop Herman (Swaiko) of Philadelphia and Eastern Pennsylvania came in second with 141 votes, and a myriad of other candidates trailed far behind. As

---

7. "Uniform Parish By-Laws," 2.
8. "Council Minutes," 24.

required when no candidate receives a 2/3 majority on the first ballot, a second round of voting took place immediately. On the second ballot, delegates must write in two names for their vote to count. Bishop Seraphim garnered 473 votes while Archbishop Herman received 223 on the second ballot. With the nomination of two candidates by the entire council completed, the members of the Holy Synod proceeded to the sanctuary for the canonical election of the Primate. After the hierarchs had deliberated at length, Archbishop Kyrill of Pittsburgh, the church's senior hierarch, emerged from the sanctuary to announce that Archbishop Herman had been elected the new Primate of the Orthodox Church in America. A Service of Thanksgiving and the vesting of the new Primate in the insignia and accoutrements of the primatial office followed and each of the hierarchs, clergy and laity in attendance, individually, greeted Metropolitan Herman. Thus ended the opening day of the Thirteenth All-American Council.[9]

Still, this does not happen very often and usually the will of the people rules, as happened at the 15th All-American Council (November 10–13, 2008):

> The first ballot produced 233 votes for Bishop Jonah and 212 for Archbishop Job with many other candidates lagging far behind. With no candidate receiving the requisite 2/3 majority (432 votes) in the first round of voting, a second ballot was held immediately. Bishop Jonah received 473 votes, while Archbishop Job obtained 364. These two candidates were presented for canonical election to the Holy Synod. After deliberation and voting by the Synod, Archbishop Dmitri announced the election of Metropolitan Jonah as the church's Primate.[10]

This was "the first time under the current electoral system, which has been in effect since the election of Metropolitan Ireney in 1965, that the Holy Synod had chosen the hierarch with the most delegate votes to be the church's Primate."[11]

---

9. "Synopsis: 13th All-American Council," para. 3.
10. "Synopsis: 15th All-American Council," para. 5.
11. "Synopsis: 15th All-American Council," para. 5.

Organizational Structure

This talk of bishops and metropolitans brings me to the question of the internal organizational structure of the church. Once again, we find a discontinuity created by the fact that we are operating in two worlds, or at least with a dual set of principles. The church has always had a very clear system of hierarchical order, that is, governance. According to Canon law expert Rodopoulos, "the whole system of government of the church is constructed on the fundamental principle of the unity of the divine and human elements in the church and on the unity of the members of the church in one body."[12] Based on that "fundamental system of government of the church, its members are divided into two orders, clergy and laity."[13]

On the one hand, the Lord governs through the hierarchy of higher clergy "which has been constituted by divine right, is also the most important institution in the organization of the church and defines and characterizes the system of government as hierarchical."[14] It follows then that the visible institution of the church is not shaped by the will of the people.[15] While this system can be referred to as a monarchy (headed by God alone), the organization and administration of the whole of the visible church is nevertheless based on basic democratic principles,[16] but not in the usual sense of that word. It is not to be taken as a division or opposition between the faithful, nor a formation of privileged classes, in the sense of greater rights or fewer responsibilities, nor a difference in worth or quality.

It is not to be taken as a division or opposition between the faithful, nor a formation of privileged classes in the sense of greater rights or fewer responsibilities, nor a difference in worth or quality. It is rather intended to emphasize the fact that even though "the laity does not have the special property of the priesthood . . . [they do] participate through baptism in the triple office of the Lord . . . clergy and laity partake of one and the same Spirit." So, the distinction is "external and in no way eliminates the fundamental principle of [the] equality of all the faithful [in] the Spirit."[17]

True, the order of the clergy is the governing order of the church and the laity, the governed. Moreover, "the hieratic authority of the church is based upon divine law, in that the apostles and their successors have the

---

12. Rodopoulos, *Overview of Orthodox Canon Law*, 115.
13. Rodopoulos, *Overview of Orthodox Canon Law*, 115.
14. Rodopoulos, *Overview of Orthodox Canon Law*, 116.
15. Rodopoulos, *Overview of Orthodox Canon Law*, 116.
16. Rodopoulos, *Overview of Orthodox Canon Law*, 116.
17. Rodopoulos, *Overview of Orthodox Canon Law*, 117.

right and the duty to teach, to celebrate the Divine Mysteries, to sanctify and to administer."[18]

On the other hand, the church cannot and does not exist without its members, the unity of a royal priesthood (1 Pet 2:5, 9) which we call the whole body of Christ. In keeping with that orderly distribution of authority, laymen and women assist and affirm the hierarch's work of instruction, participate in the holy mysteries, and take part in the administrative authority in the "wider sense."[19] It is, for example, common knowledge that a priest cannot serve a liturgy without the presence of at least some of the people. The reason, of course, is the laity participate in, or perhaps we need to say actually help constitute the very existence of, the liturgy. This existence-yielding contribution can be seen throughout the divine liturgy during which the people collectively affirm, even enable, that which is being done by the presider. Consent and reception were the people's validation of the presider's acts. This affirmation implies an assumption of active and shared responsibility. It is not just a matter of attending or observing but deliberately participating in, owning, and approving every act performed by the presider in the midst of the people. As Afanasiev puts it,

> [h]aving the charism of discernment and examination the people witness that everything done in the church under the guidance of the pastors is done in accordance with the will of God revealed by the Holy Spirit.[20]

In this manner, in response to the presence of divinity, the people are unified, made to be of one mind and one purpose. The individualism which has so fragmented our society is overcome and replaced with oneness. Thus, united in the presence of God, the eucharistic assembly, clergy, and laity, becomes one church.

This organizational structure—bishop, priest, people—then is the God-given order of authority in the church. It is easy to understand the application of that authority structure requires certain administrative instruments. But again, given the divine point of departure, those instruments will be limited to expressions of the prescribed order. These could understandably include ecumenical councils, local or regional synods, and individual or groupings of patriarchs, metropolitans, bishops, priests, and deacons.[21] But as we have seen above, the church has also given itself another structure,

---

18. Rodopoulos, *Overview of Orthodox Canon Law*, 118.
19. Rodopoulos, *Overview of* Orthodox Canon Law, 119.
20. Afanasiev and Plekon, *Church of the Holy Spirit*, 61.
21. Rodopoulos, *Overview of Orthodox Canon Law*, 135–56.

one imposed by by-laws or state laws, simply on the basis of our location within a secular culture. So if we insist on the primacy of Canon law, we will have to clarify the relationship between ecclesial law and civil law and make the case for the preeminence of the Canons. In discussing law in general, we can observe there are two basic types of law: *private* law (dealing with how the state regulates the relationships between individuals) and *public* law (covering the ways in which the state oversees the interactions between institutions).[22]

That leads to the question of just how church (Canon) law relates to the various realms of state law: "The answer is to neither one nor the other . . . it is a branch of law parallel to, but not subject to the others. The church is complete in itself, it depends on no earthly institution, and therefore, Canon Law occupies a self-sufficient and independent position."[23] In other words, its authority "does not trace back to any earthly power, but the power of Christ. It is a self-sufficient and independent law, parallel to both private and public law of the state.[24] However, it is one thing to affirm the primacy of Canon law in the church, it is quite another thing to define the ways in which the laws of the state in which it is embedded affect or even have jurisdiction over the church. According to Rodopoulos, there are two possible systems of sacred/secular legal relationships, one he calls subservient, the other parallel. Systems of subordination allow one realm to dominate or control the other. The other system of parallelism envisions the two codes existing side-by-side. But what does parallel relationship look like, functionally, in practice? Among several types of relationships, the church in North America is of necessity a system of total separation between church and state: "According to this system, the State regards religion as a purely personal matter and the Church as a legal entity in private law, as an association like any other of the same kind.[25]

There seem to be two overlapping systems within the church. If we are dealing with individual believers' relationships with individual persons outside the church, state private law applies. If we are dealing with the relationship of the church as an institution with other institutions such as banks, taxing agencies, and other organizations, secular public law will apply. However, all relationships within the church, either between individuals, parishes, or institutions, will be governed by the church's own law, Canon law. For this reason, if one priest has something against another priest, it

---

22. Rodopoulos, *Overview of Orthodox Canon Law*, 25.
23. Rodopoulos, *Overview of Orthodox Canon Law*, 23.
24. Rodopoulos, *Overview of Orthodox Canon Law*, 23.
25. Rodopoulos, *Overview of Orthodox Canon Law*, 209.

goes to an ecclesial court, not a secular court, etc. But if the IRS has a claim against a parish, the complaint is handled by a secular court. The challenge here is to know how to keep these systems separate, to enable them to work together without compromising the ecclesial structure. This may be one of the reasons our parishes adopt secular by-laws. They allow us to do our internal business (according to our own Canons) in a way or in a language the secular authorities can understand. This facilitates our interaction with the state at those points in our life where the sacred and the secular intersect, (e.g., finances, taxes). Seen this way, the secular by-laws are not an imposition on the church but simply a bridge to the world in which we live and to which we, at least in some instances, have to give account.

Politics in the Church

Occasionally politics, that is, the practice of self-governance, takes on a decidedly negative tone. The idea is not necessarily negative, as it can, and usually does, refer simply to the "means relating to the way power is achieved and used in a country or society."[26] But it does "mean different things in different contexts, which can be either good or bad based on both the context and their prejudgments."[27] So when we speak of politics in the church, we are most likely referring to very negative behaviors such as "the activities of people who are trying to obtain an advantage [for themselves] within a group or organization,"[28] or to "intrigue [and maneuver] within a political unit or group [church] in order to gain control or power."[29] As a result, ecclesial politics often devolve into partisan obstruction of good order; it is debilitating, and it is counterproductive.

Throughout its history, the church has had its fair share of (negative) politics. You see it at the trial of Jesus during which Pilate and Jesus' accusers play politics by executing an innocent man in order to gain or secure Caesar's favor (John 19:12–17). This was also true of the intrigues that characterized the church-state relationships in the Byzantine Empire, even when ruled by Christian emperors. According to one historian, Byzantine politicians consolidated their own power by carrying out

> ghastly acts of physical mutilation. Many would-be usurpers and deposed emperors were blinded or castrated to prevent

---

26. "Political."
27. "How Do You Define Politics?," para. 39.
28. "Politics," *Cambridge Dictionary*.
29. "Politics," *Wordnik*.

them from leading troops or fathering children, while others had their tongues, noses or lips cut off. Maiming was supposed to prevent victims from challenging for power . . .[30]

More recently, a major American jurisdiction was shaken by equally horrific abuses of ecclesial power. As *The Washington Post* reported,

> [t]he highest officers of [a] 400,000-member denomination, an offshoot of the Russian Orthodox Church, are accused of using the money to cover personal credit card bills, pay sexual blackmail, support family members and make up shortfalls in various church accounts.[31]

While these misdeeds could have and eventually would have been investigated and prosecuted by secular authorities according to civil law, the state tends to defer to the church and its own internal laws (Canons) in such cases. Indeed, the church did conduct its own internal investigation which confirmed the initial allegations. That led to a trial in an ecclesial court, as provided for by the Canons.[32] In the end the miscreants were found guilty. This led to a number of priests (bishops) resigning and/or being deposed. As damaging as these abuses were, the church did recover. It is of note that the church has, and in this case rigorously, applied its own laws. In cases clearly covered by that law, the church is a self-correcting, self-healing entity.

However, as we have seen, that does not seem to prevent politically motivated misbehavior among the ranks of ecclesial leaders. Moreover, we do not have to look for spectacular crimes and scandals at the very highest levels of the organization to find evidence of the negative practice of politics in the church. It seems the desire for power continually haunts the church and tempts many at all levels of leadership, enticing those who acquire it to abuse it. This usually happens when a person holding a position of authority tries to consolidate and expand that power for selfish gain. This often takes place through a series of subtle words, innuendoes, accusations, and half-truths, which are used to intimidate, dominate, and even subjugate others. Because these activities might not rise to the level of overt crimes and scandals, they are hard to detect, and thus escape accountability. Nevertheless, they constitute a clear violation of the basic purpose of these positions, namely service, and amount to an abuse of authority, that is politics.

I suppose the danger of this low-level abuse is particularly intense for those who have been given just a bit of limited authority. But, resisting or

30. Andrews, "10 Things," para. 5.
31. Cooperman, "Accusations," para. 2.
32. Rodopoulos, *Overview of Orthodox Canon Law*, 168–72.

rejecting the limitations of that authority, these individuals are tempted to find ways to expand it. This temptation and its effects are captured in Dostoyevsky's *Notes from the Underground*. In it he relays the confessions of a minor government official who, although he was not a criminal—he did not take bribes—did take pleasure in being a "spiteful official."[33] He openly admits to this behavior, saying,

> When petitioners used to come for information to the table at which I sat, I used to grind my teeth at them, and felt intense enjoyment when I succeeded in making anybody unhappy. I almost did succeed. For the most part they were all timid people—of course, they were petitioners. But of the uppish ones there was one officer in particular I could not endure. He simply would not be humble, and clanked his sword in a disgusting way. I carried on a feud with him for eighteen months over that sword. At last I got the better of him. He left off clanking it.[34]

While all of this was no doubt wrong, these were subtle misdeeds, not crimes. So it would have been difficult for his superiors to accuse him of anything, hold him to account, reprimand him, or even dismiss him. Quite to the contrary, he says he had been getting away with it. He admits he had "been going on like that for a long time—twenty years."[35] It seems this state of mind, this grasping for power, had a corrupting effect on his whole character. Rather than growing into his position and developing the demeanor of a true servant, he became (or already was) a very small-minded, self-serving, and mean-spirited person. At one point he describes himself as a mouse and uses that image to lay out the worst of his "crimes"

> with a smile of assumed contempt in which it does not even itself believe, creep ignominiously into its mouse-hole. There in its nasty, stinking, underground home our insulted, crushed and ridiculed mouse promptly becomes absorbed in cold, malignant and, above all, everlasting spite. For forty years together it will remember its injury down to the smallest, most ignominious details, and every time will add, of itself, details still more ignominious, spitefully teasing and tormenting itself with its own imagination. It will itself be ashamed of its imaginings, but yet it will recall it all, it will go over and over every detail, it will invent

---

33. Dostoyevsky, *Notes from the Underground*, 48.
34. Dostoyevsky, *Notes from the Underground*, 1.
35. Dostoyevsky, *Notes from the Underground*, 1.

unheard of things against itself, pretending that those things might happen, and will forgive nothing.[36]

Obviously, a person who falls prey to this kind of thinking can do a great deal of damage to the church and its members. But given the nature of these "crimes," it would be very difficult to defend against them or refute them, not to mention censure the perpetrators in any official way.

Another group of individuals sorely tempted to play politics in the church are those who have had or still have positions of responsibility in authoritarian or highly structured groups that are outside of, indifferent to, or even in opposition to the faith and teachings of the church. This might include the military, other religious groups, and non-Christian sects and cults. Some clergy who formerly served as officers in the armed forces are easily persuaded to impose a military-style command structure on the local parish, martial law replacing Canon law. While discipline is to be praised, this kind of authoritarianism inevitably leads to abuse. Other clergymen have converted to orthodoxy after having spent significant time in various non-Orthodox religious denominations, cults, and sects. Of the many backgrounds from which Orthodox clergy have come, some include legitimate Christian denominations like the Lutherans, Methodists, etc. The danger is many of them seem unable to completely divorce themselves from the teachings and practices of the groups from which they have come. I know of a number of Orthodox parishes now being pastored by individuals who were once prominent Protestants. Interestingly, their Sunday services still have a distinctly Evangelical flavor. In some cases, their sermons reflect a residual Calvinism. Part of the difficulty seems to be non-Orthodox and Orthodox use the same basic vocabulary, such as Scripture, salvation, sin, and Tradition. But these same terms have distinctly different meanings in each context. Others are actively advancing Protestant church growth practices, tweaking the liturgy, seeking to make everything seeker-friendly, and implementing technologies to make participation more convenient, supposedly in an attempt to advance the church and most of all their own standing in the church.

In the case of individuals with a cultic background, the difficulty of not being able to shed the cult's teaching (brainwashing, programming) is compounded by an undying commitment to the cult's organizational or authority structure. An example of this situation is presented by current Orthodox clergy who were once part of the "Holy Order of Mans."[37] As this esoteric, new-age group moved toward Christianity, hundreds of

---

36. Dostoyevsky, *Notes from the Underground*, 11–12.
37. I personally know four such individuals and the parishes they have led.

its members who converted were baptized and received into Orthodox churches, and many of them became clergy. But as Stark concluded, in doing so "they did not abandon their original cultural content."[38] Another researcher suggests the

> [s]ubstantial embrace of Orthodox doctrines, liturgical rites, and social praxis is not the whole story, however. Even as it underwent its radical transformation, the movement managed to retain several key elements of its original identity.[39]

Of course, one of those elements was the authoritarian nature of this monastic-like cult, utterly dominated by a single person, a director, who, clad in white, considered himself to be, and was revered as, the master teacher,[40] the source of tradition,[41] a shaman of civilization.[42] The internal structure of the group was arranged in a hierarchy of descending levels of authority: director, master-teachers, minister-priests, stewards, disciples, students, and, at the lowest level, novices.[43] If the sociologists studying this movement are correct, the members of this personality cult who became Orthodox brought with them varying degrees of and intensities of authoritarianism, that is, a highly developed sense of hierarchy based on an absolute commitment to a single individual (guru?). Furthermore, those who had been in the upper ranks of that hierarchy and later became Orthodox clergy will have brought with them not only the general authoritarian mindset but an approach to corporate life that arranged or grouped membership according to a structure of ascending authority, culminating in one person. Given the hierarchical structure of the Orthodox church, one can easily imagine these people feeling right at home and interpreting the new authority structures through the lens of their own past rather than the Canons, imposing a nonecclesial ranking on the parish: bishop as a director, clergy as master-teachers, laity as disciples and novices, each with more or mostly less authority (value) within the structure.

Finally, the political abuse of ecclesial power is made all the more likely for those individuals holding positions which have been imported into the

---

38. The five areas highlighted by Lucas are 1) commitment to charitable service, 2) valorization of the monastic ideal, 3) heighten interest in supernatural experiences, 4) dramaturgical and ceremonial tenor, and 5) restorationism, reembodying Christianity's primordium (Lucas, *Odyssey of a New Religion*, 248–51).

39. Lucas, *Odyssey of a New Religion*, 249.
40. Lucas, *Odyssey of a New Religion*, 30.
41. Lucas, *Odyssey of a New Religion*, 22.
42. Lucas, *Odyssey of a New Religion*, 35.
43. Lucas, *Odyssey of a New Religion*, 59–62.

church from the secular world and are not necessarily foreseen by or regulated by the Canons. This is certainly true of the position of dean, which has little foundation in Tradition or Canon law, and is, for that reason, not used by many Orthodox churches. According to one expert on Canon law, the positions of dean or vicar are not of Orthodox origin. In the first millennium (when the Canon law was edited), some of the functions of a contemporary dean were fulfilled by the local priests or by the *chorescopos* (auxiliary bishop).[44] This is not to say the position serves no useful purpose, I am just pointing out it is not something that grows naturally out of Orthodox Tradition. It is rather modeled on extraecclesial practices and has been implemented for purely pragmatic reasons. This is illustrated by the Roman Catholic office of a *vicar forane*,[45] who has essentially the same function as a dean does in parts of the Orthodox world. According to Catholic Canon law (there is no Orthodox Canon law on this subject, but it is mentioned in the national statutes[46]), this person (*vicar*) is simply appointed by the bishop as an administrative assistant. Because this office has no sacramental authority beyond that of the priesthood, it is not a clerical rank, and is not an actual element of the hierarchical structure of the church. According to the OCA statutes, a district dean is primarily an administrative assistant. However, according to Catholic Canon law, this person is charged with a three-fold responsibility: seeing to the *physical* well-being of the priests in his area,

---

44. In a response to my inquiry, Fr. Mehai, a noted Canon Law expert wrote, "You are right to say that the position of dean or vicar are not of Orthodox origin; they incur some administrative authority delegated by the Bishop. In the first millennium (when the Canon Law was edicted) some of those attributions were fulfilled by the local priests or by the chorepiscopos) (auxiliary bishop)." Email dated November 13, 2018.

45. See "Code of Canon Law."

46. However, what is called a "district dean" is described in the OCA Statutes Article XI. According to that statement, the District Dean shall "a) oversee Deanery matters and the activities of its clergy; b) assist the Diocesan Bishop by giving direction and fraternal counsel to deanery clergy in areas of pastoral concern in a private and circumspect manner whenever their personal conduct or manner of discharging their duties indicates the need for such counsel or action; c) receive and investigate complaints against clergy and laity and against the decisions of Parish bodies and submit his report and recommendations to the Diocesan Bishop; d) participate in Parish meetings at the direction of the Diocesan Bishop; e) participate in Parish meetings at the request of the Parish Priest or the Parish Council with the permission of the Diocesan Bishop; f) provide for services during temporary absence of Parish Clergy with the consent of the Diocesan Bishop; g) assist the Diocesan Bishop in the planning and organization of new Parishes within the Deanery; h) convene periodic meetings of Deanery clergy and submit the minutes of the meetings to the Diocesan Bishop; and i) submit an annual report on the Deanery to the Diocesan Bishop and the Diocesan Assembly." ("Statute of the Orthodox Church in America," para. 3).

seeing to the *spiritual* well-being of the priests, and assuring that the services celebrated by those priests *conform* to the rubrics of the church.[47]

Perhaps the fact that the responsibilities of a contemporary dean were originally fulfilled by auxiliary bishops is what has tempted some deans and vicars to view themselves as mini-bishops, as semi-hierarchs, and to assume, exaggerate, and abuse the very limited authority they do have. Indeed, some deans do seem to think their position is integrated into the sacramental hierarchy of the church, positioned just below the diocesan bishop but definitely above the priests (even of the same rank)[48] in their area. They re-create ecclesial structures according to their own misunderstandings, and those misunderstandings deceive them into assuming more authority and responsibility than the position allows for. In any case, the abuse of this semi-canonical position has led to a great deal of confusion in and damage to the church.

On the one hand, these individuals are often so consumed with maintaining and expanding their own power that they neglect many of the responsibilities they have actually been given: failing to look after the clergy's physical and spiritual well-being; seeing if they are discouraged, depressed, have a father-confessor, etc.; never visiting the parishes; attending their services; or making sure they have everything they need for ministry. On the other hand, they actively seek an enlargement of the scope and range of the legitimate responsibilities and authority associated with their position. For example, one dean I knew of barred a priest attached to his parish from even attending. He claimed it was within his purview as rector of [the parish] and as dean to request the priest no longer attend until they could "come to some resolve as to [his] attachment to the altar."[49] But a priest's placement is clearly the sole responsibility of the bishop. I heard of another dean who was asked to keep some information confidential. His angry response was "I can talk to anyone I like, anywhere I like, and anytime I want. I am the dean and you simply do not understand the hierarchy of the church." Yet another dean "apologized" to his bishop for not being able to get a priest in his area under his control, that is, get him to submit to the dean's "authority" and allow himself to be held accountable by the dean.[50] Of course, the priest was

---

47. See "Code of Canon Law."

48. Interestingly, this particular dean and I shared the same priestly rank of Archpriest.

49. ". . . it is in my purview as Rector . . . to request that you no longer attend Holy Apostles until we can come to some resolve as to your attachment to the altar here." Email dated October 18, 2018.

50. "I am concerned that [his] being attached [elsewhere] . . . means he has no one to whom to be accountable locally . . . I pray he finds a Church and clergy that meet his

accountable to the bishop, not the dean, but the apology indicates a bloated view of his own importance, that is, a serious misunderstanding concerning the role and authority of a dean.[51]

This, then, is what we mean by (negative) politics in the church. This dean and many others like him have done everything possible to ingratiate themselves with bishops and metropolitans and have thus advanced their own ecclesial careers at the expense of others, supported and promoted unworthy candidates for clerical office on the basis of friendship, and hindered the advancement of a number of qualified candidates on the basis of personal animus. They use their positions as deans, rectors, and priests to gather information on individuals, which they later used to threaten, intimidate, manipulate, or control others.

Now, all of this is certainly not new in the church. Believers have always been influenced by the political structures and practices of the world around them. Clearly they bring those structures into the church where, when combined with our basic sinfulness, abuses arise within the church, as can be seen from the scandals mentioned above. But in addition to these general influences, some of these anti-canonical teachings are being brought in by individuals who experienced and practiced and became accustomed to political abuse in other professions (military, security) or former religious organizations (cults, sects). Those experiences, combined with the general influence of secular structures and encouraged by semi-ecclesial structures not native to the church, are left with few checks and balances, few natural ways of moderating the political abuse they tend to generate, and are, indeed, damaging the church.

ECCLESIAL ALTERNATIVE: HIERARCHICAL GOVERNMENT BY THE WILL OF GOD

As we have seen, the foundations, structures, and procedures of secular democracy cannot be imposed on the church, at least not without definite limits and modifications, and even then not without the danger of doing

---

expectations and some authority he respects. I clearly was not and am grieved over this failure on my part." Email dated October 28, 2018.

51. In fairness, it must be stated that some of this took place during a lawless time when the diocese concerned had been deprived of the pastoral oversight of a bishop, the bishop having passed away. In any case, jumping into the leadership voids, that is, jumping through the appropriate hoops, these politicians landed for themselves positions on influential committees, from which vantage point he can further obstruct those seeking offices in the church or reward those he favors. In other words, they used their offices for political gain.

damage to the church. Clearly we all share the democratic ideals of our country by virtue of our common social imaginary and, for that very reason, we are indeed inclined to import into the church democratic forms of self-governance based on the principle of the sovereignty of the people. But if that democratic precept is limited and is not and cannot be the foundation of authority and structure in the church, then what is its foundation and just how are we to govern life in the church? What are the Christian alternatives to people power and civil law?

Tradition provides the church with a divinely established visible structure, which is a hierarchical structure established and authorized by God and implemented by humanity according to divine will. Reflecting this reality, the members of the church are divided into two orders, clergy and laity. The clergy (deacons, priests, and bishops) are set apart by ordination and are the instruments of authority though which God governs the church. So the church is not "shaped fundamentally or in the main by the will of the faithful, but the will of God."[52] According to Pseudo-Dionysius, the source of this hierarchical structure and authority is "the font of life, the being of goodness, the one cause of everything, namely the Trinity," or as St. Maximus says, "the true priesthood is in all respects the type of the blessed divinity."[53]

Historically, this Christ-initiated structure has been implemented and maintained by means of what the church calls apostolic succession. This involves an ongoing line of bishops who are the successors of the apostles. Confirming the New Testament pattern (Eph 2:20; 2 Tim 2:2), Clement of Alexandria states "after the Resurrection the Lord gave the tradition of knowledge to James the Just, and John, and Peter, and these gave the tradition to the other apostles, and the other apostles to the Seventy . . . ."[54] Throughout its history, every time the church grew into a new geographic region, new bishops were appointed who in turn ordained priests to represent them by presiding over local parishes. In the bishops, then, we have the continuation of Christ's presence and authority in the church. Ignatius of Antioch admonishes the faithful in Smyrna to "follow the lead of the bishop, as Jesus Christ followed the Father. Where the bishop appears, let the people be, just as where Christ is, there is the Catholic Church."[55] And he writes to the Ephesians: "For even Jesus Christ, our inseparable life, is

---

52. Rodopoulos, *Overview of Orthodox Canon Law*, 116.

53. Pseudo-Dionysius and St Maximus the Confessor, as cited in Scouteris and Veniamin, *Ecclesial Being*, 76.

54. Clement, quoted in Eusebius, *Church History*, 2.1.4.

55. Ignatius of Antioch, "Epistle to the Smyrnaeans," para. 9

the [manifested] will of the Father; as also bishops, settled everywhere to the utmost bounds [of the earth], are so by the will of Jesus Christ."[56] So it is that the bishops and their clergy are authorized, by divine right, to serve the sacraments and spiritually govern the people.

At first glance, this God-given structure might seem to be at odds with the human freedom to self-actualize or with the sovereignty (authority) of the people. However,

> The priesthood is in no way a ministry introducing division or classification within the ecclesial body. Between a priest and a layperson there is no legal distinction, but precisely what we may call charismatic distribution.[57]

As already mentioned, this ecclesial structure does not eliminate democratic principles, at least not as those principles are usually understood, but it does put them into another framework, namely the charismatic structure of ministries. This distribution of responsibilities is rooted in the oneness-in-diversity of the gifts (charism) or ministries given to all the members by the Holy Spirit as described in 1 Peter 2:5, 9–10:

> You also, as living stones, are being built up a spiritual house, a holy priesthood, to offer up spiritual sacrifices acceptable to God through Jesus Christ. . . . But you are a chosen generation, a royal priesthood, a holy nation, his own special people, that you may proclaim the praises of him who called you out of darkness into his marvelous light; who once were not a people but are now the people of God, who had not obtained mercy but now have obtained mercy.

So in the New Testament the entire people constitute a priesthood. For that reason, we cannot think of these gifts as being "possessed individually," nor in terms of "a juridical authority within the ecclesial body, but of a charismatic ministry belonging to all the people of God."[58] In other words, "all the participants of the assembly together with their presiders constituted a single people of God, the royal priesthood."[59] Thus, the gift that every member receives through baptism

> is the charism of royal priesthood. In the church there are no gifts of the Spirit without ministry and there is no ministry

---

56. Ignatius of Antioch, "Epistle to the Ephesians," para. 3.
57. Scouteris and Veniamin, *Ecclesial Being*, 85.
58. Scouteris and Veniamin, *Ecclesial Being*, 81.
59. Afanasiev and Plekon, *Church of the Holy Spirit*, 18.

> without gifts. Through the charisma of the royal priesthood the Christian is called to priestly ministry in the church.[60]

> The priestly ministry of all members of the church finds its expression in the eucharistic assembly . . . The eucharistic assembly was an assembly of the priestly people who offered sacred service to God "in Christ." Sacred service was an ecclesial ministry for the eucharistic assembly itself, was a manifestation of the church of God in all its fullness. The church is where Christ is, but Christ is always present in the fullness of the unity of his body in the Eucharist.[61]

Of course, there has always been the special ministry of the presider, which is made necessary by the very interactive and sacramental nature of the Eucharist. The presider (priest) is "one of those vital functions, those manifestations of life, without which the church cannot exist on earth as a living organism."[62] Seen in this context, when the Eucharist is presided over, it is not being served by a single individual but by the whole assembly, by the people unified in that common ministry. Throughout the divine liturgy, the people are to collectively participate in and affirm that which is being done by the presider. The affirmation of the people shows the presiders serve in the midst of the people and not apart from them.[63] Moreover, the people bear witness to the fact that the presiders act and govern in agreement with the will of God.[64] This affirmation represents the active assumption of shared responsibility, a responsibility that is expressed as an act of the whole eucharistic assembly. So the laity assist the clergy in the celebration of the liturgy. Of course, ministry in the church was not exhausted by this one priestly ministry. "The other fact of life in the primitive Church was the diversity of ministries."[65] St. Paul, for example, speaks of this variety of ministries in Ephesians 4:11–12:

> He himself gave some to be apostles, some prophets, some evangelists, and some pastors and teachers, for the equipping of the saints for the work of ministry, for the edifying of the body of Christ.

---

60. Afanasiev and Plekon, *Church of the Holy Spirit*, 3.
61. Afanasiev and Plekon, *Church of the Holy Spirit*, 4.
62. Afanasiev and Plekon, *Church of the Holy Spirit*, 17.
63. Afanasiev and Plekon, *Church of the Holy Spirit*, 4.
64. Afanasiev and Plekon, *Church of the Holy Spirit*, 6.
65. Afanasiev and Plekon, *Church of the Holy Spirit*, 15.

It is through these divinely given gifts (*charisma*) that the laity find many other opportunities for participating in the overall ministry of the church. In addition to the liturgical setting, Rodopoulos states that Canon law foresees, among other things, advisory lay participation in ecclesial synods, in teaching, and in consultation of the laity over certain matters of ecclesiastical property.[66]

So the Holy Spirit equips (Eph 4:12) all of the members so the church, as a whole, can fulfill its mission in the world. Taken together, we are a nation of priests, lead by a hierarchy of priests and bishops, according to Canons which reflect the will of God.

---

66. Rodopoulos, *Overview of Orthodox Canon Law*, 120–24.

PART V

Conclusions

External Threats to the Church Revisited

14

Lessons and Principles

But for the present age, which prefers the sign to the thing signified, the copy to the original, representation to reality, appearance to essence ... truth is considered profane, and only illusion is sacred. Sacredness is in fact held to be enhanced in proportion as truth decreases and illusion increases, so that the highest degree of illusion comes to be the highest degree of sacredness.[1]

THREAT ASSESSMENT

AT THE OUTSET OF this study, I suggested most of us were captives or prisoners of what Taylor has called a social imaginary or what Michel Foucault referred to as a "regime of truth."[2] This internalized framework is used to guide and evaluate our interaction with the other individuals in our immediate social context. This imaginary, or better yet, its basic operating principles, define the ways in which we view and interpret our surroundings. It is not a set of rules to which we adhere but rather a set of filters that spontaneously color the way we see the world around us. Without requiring much conscious deliberation, it helps us to instinctively know what is American and what is not, which ideas, actions, and behaviors are acceptable, and

---

1. Feuerbach, as quoted in Debord, *Society of the Spectacle*, 23.
2. Foucault, "Political Function of the Intellectual," 13.

even which information is true or false. I also suggested the influence of the social imaginary and its basic operating principles will be evident in three distinct realms of social interaction: commerce, the public sphere, and self-governance. In each case, the imaginary directly influences the meanings, structures, devices, and technologies developed in pursuit of the primary purposes of each realm. Thus, it is individualism, scientism, etc., that drive commerce as they develop tools for the administration, manufacturing, distribution, and consumption of the products given in exchange for other goods and services in order to realize a profit. In the public sphere opinionated members develop technologies to facilitate difference-resolving dialogue with a view toward consensus-based policies that benefit the majority. Efforts at self-governance result in procedures and structures which enable a minority to adequately represent the individual rights and concerns of a sovereign majority for the purpose of establishing public policies, that is, codes of civil and personal law that provide for a stable and ordered context for commerce and public discourse.

Because the members of our churches are also citizens of the larger context established by the prevailing social imaginary, they will be engaged in and thus affected by activities and developments in each of the three areas of interaction. My survey of the interface between the church and culture has shown some understandable overlap and considerable cross-fertilization or borrowing, most of which is one-directional, with the church importing or receiving meanings, structures, and technologies from the surrounding world rather than providing that world with ecclesial alternatives. So the world is in little danger of being affected by the church, but because the church so willingly imports content and practices that conflict with its own teachings and practices, it is being changed, sustaining significant damage to its very nature.

In the case of *commerce*, we see the church is being damaged by the uncritical use of business procedures, tools, and devices on the basis of their availability and effectiveness, regardless of the meanings inherent in those technologies. In some cases, this leads to a second, more serious danger, namely, transforming the parish into a business. There is, of course, a reciprocal relationship between converting the parish into a business and importing business thinking and business-related tools. These devices and structures have been developed and successfully promoted in the world of commerce precisely because they prove effective in advancing business goals. So if we transform the parish into or even just view it as a business enterprise, these tools are going to appear to be effective. But the church is not a business. So can it, a nonbusiness entity, be helped by or advanced through the use of such tools? Definitely not. A mystical, spiritually based, dynamic, and living gathering of individuals whose sole purpose is to glorify God will not benefit from meanings, structures, and devices rooted in the free exchange of goods and services for profit. Of course, if the use of secular tools in the church does appear to be successful, it may be because the church has already been turned into a business. Moreover, if these tools are yielding what you think is success, then you will probably have also bought into an understanding of success that is not in keeping with the nature of the church.

In the arena of *public discourse,* many in the church tempted by free services and alluring counterfeits have largely replaced biblical and Traditional forms of gathering, fellowship, and community with contemporary forms of computer-mediated forms of communication as well as social interaction. In this way, the real elements of ecclesial life, such as worship and fellowship, are being systematically supplanted by simulations, as in so-called virtual churches or worship, and by what philosophers refer to as spectacle,[3] as in the showmanship of some contemporary worship which is no more real than is professional wrestling. Moreover, our fascination with these technologies is subjecting our members and parishes to the dialogue-destroying aspects of filtering and the loss of expertise. In addition, we now know these technologies are highly manipulative and addictive, that their simulated, mediated realities are more appealing than reality itself. Indeed, the general resistance, even in the church, to giving up these conveniences indicates some degree of addiction. All of this leads to the eventual loss of real fellowship and worship, the disruption of discourse, and the creation of ecclesial echo chambers in which we discuss issues not native to the church. If we do not reverse these trends, I fear that soon all we will have left of the church is simulation and spectacle.

Self-governance of the church is today threatened by the same sovereignty of the people, that is, the basis of political power and the resulting legal system in our social order. Since we live in a context of complete separation of church and state, the church has to develop its own internal structure and laws. This it has done in the form of our hierarchy and canon law. Nevertheless, many believers seeking to guarantee their own individual rights insist on an internal structure based on the secular notion of the sovereignty of the people, as well as a parliamentary framework for conducting its affairs. This, of course, leads to some internal discontinuity, as well as potential conflicts with the law of the extraecclesial world. At times this approach allows the laity to override the legitimate authority of the hierarchs.

3. "... the public confines itself to spectacle's primary virtue, which is to abolish all motives and all consequences what matters to this public is not what it believes but what it sees" (Barthes, *Mythologies*, 4).

Reliance on Robert's Rules of Order may make it difficult to be open to or apprehend the divine leading of the Spirit. In addition, the combination of this highly ordered context and individualism also leads to the abuse of power by those in positions of authority, bringing harm not only to the parish but to individual believers. Taken together, these developments threaten to transform the living, Spirit-led body of Christ into a rather mundane association of more or less like-minded individuals.

So yes, the church is in danger, and yes, it has already sustained some damage. There are forces gathering at the gates that could easily destroy the church as we know it, as it has been handed down to us:

> The truth is, today, the world and the church are intertwined, there is a lot of the world in the church. What we mean by this is that the secular spirit has infiltrated our church. There is so much secularization that people who do not have any relationship with the spiritual life of the church are called members in good standing only because they have fulfilled a minimal financial obligation.[4]

We can easily show how it has capitulated in the areas of commerce, social media, and the like. But it must also be noted the church has, at least until now, not been defeated in every area. In other words, there is some reason to hope. We could, for example, show how in the areas of liturgy, hierarchy, and contemporary social issues, it has held its own and has even been a beacon of strength and hope to the world around it. We could point to the faithful priests, bishops, and people who have stood firm in their commitment to the truth of the Scriptures, to Tradition, and resisted the influx of secularism. But even with these positive examples, what I have reviewed in this study causes me to fear we may have already lost the battle, that rescuing or reviving the church is a losing proposition fought for by an ever-shrinking number of defenders while the majority of members actively embrace false teachings and practices. So this warning from Archimandrite Metilinaisos seems particularly apt:

> I want to forewarn you of these things because you need to be aware and prepared accordingly: the enemies of the church, the dark powers, are infiltrating and forever attacking the ranks of vigilant shepherds and guardians of the faith. They slander them. They ridicule them. They revile them because these worthy shepherds impede their catastrophic evil schemes.[5]

---

4. Mitilinaios, *Revelation: The Seven Lampstands*, 135.
5. Mitilinaios, *Revelation: The Seven Lampstands*, 222.

In a recent discussion with an Orthodox Abbess, she stated if you stand up against the lies of the secular world and seek to speak the truth and defend the church, the group of people around you will continually grow smaller. But this reminds us of the biblical concept of the remnant, that small number of individuals who remain faithful to God during times of apostasy and challenge (Isa 1:9; Joel 2:32; Mic 2:12) and thus forestall the complete destruction of God's people. So perhaps there is hope after all. What could that look like today? Listen again to Archimandrite Metilinaisos:

> My friends now I feel that it is my turn to pose this question: Do you have the inner feeling that we belong to the remnant? And if we do, will we continue to belong? Is it possible at a time of weakness, when our self-interests might be at stake, that we too will break and fall apart? Do we know that only few will have remained true when the Lord returns? Let's very clearly understand that the remnant will be saved. Saint Paul is very clear on this, very specific stressing that only this remnant will be saved. Nevertheless, this should not shake us up, it should strengthen us. We only need to be certain that we belong to this remnant. We must develop the consciousness that we are members of this remnant.[6]

But what can this remnant hope to achieve? The forces arrayed against the church today seem invincible. Still, the remnant is called to be faithful. In light of the challenges we face, it seems being faithful involves *refocusing* on an ecclesially appropriate measure of success and maturity, actively *resisting* and *reversing* the enemy's incursions, and then using the treasures of Tradition, seeking to instigate what can only be called *renewal* and *revival* in the church.

REFOCUS: AN APPROPRIATE MEASURE OF SUCCESS

Throughout this study I have expressed concern over the uncritical application of business models to the church. These models embody a very mercenary way of determining success. In the secular world this involves increasing profit, returns on investments, numbers of products sold, and the like. In the church this thinking translates into measuring success in terms of ever-increasing levels of giving, attendance, facilities, etc. This focuses our attention on numbers, rates, and statistics. Of course, the most efficient way to use these external factors to determine if your efforts are succeeding

---

6. Mitilinaios, *Revelation: The Seven Lampstands*, 284.

is to regularly count and record as many of these variables as possible. What troubles me, however, is not so much the counting itself. That is a very natural and understandable human activity and surely there are some aspects of church life that can be meaningfully counted. My concern is rather when we simplistically, or more problematically exclusively, apply business standards and methodologies to the church as if it were a business, the resulting numbers give us an inaccurate picture of the church's health and tend to divert our attention away from standards of ecclesial growth that are more appropriate to the living body of Christ and are, in fact, prescribed for us in the Scriptures. So I'd like to ask what standard(s) of success we ought to be using when evaluating the degree to which the church is fulfilling (succeeding in?) its mission in the world.

The easiest way to define success in general is to do so in terms of the fulfillment or accomplishment of some purpose or desire. Accepting such an objective as legitimate establishes the measure needed to gauge success. So in a capitalistic society the sole purpose of business will be profit. If that is achieved, if there are higher levels of production, increasing sales, etc., it is considered a success. Even so-called nonprofit organizations measure success in terms of funds raised, aid distributed, and so on. In a narcissistic society like ours, the primary purpose of individual existence will be the fulfillment of personal desire. This can be measured in terms of the amassing of material wealth, the prestige afforded by position or education, and of course, the myriad ways in which people amuse themselves. There can be little doubt these two factors—profit and ego satisfaction—are the prevailing aims of our culture and therefore determine the primary means by which the performance of just about anything is measured in North America. It has become understandably difficult for us to even think of success in any other terms than an increase of the desired external aspects of ordinary life.

The other thing that affects our understanding of success is contemporary culture expects and practically demands what it calls progress. The idea is, as our knowledge becomes both broader and more unified, we will experience continued or perpetual progress as envisioned by Enlightenment thinkers such as Condorcet and Kant. This relentless progress is, of course, not limited to advances in technology but includes social, political, and moral progress. Having grown accustomed to the constant evolution of technology, the late-modern individual tends to generalize and project this movement on almost every area of life. For that reason, we think the economy always has to grow, that clubs, schools, sports teams, just about everything has to produce more members, more graduates, more wins, etc. Combined with the profit/loss motive, we have transformed almost every aspect of modern life, including the church, into businesslike entities, measured in terms of uninterrupted gain. Here again, having gotten so used to the truly impressive effectiveness of the techniques used to achieve and measure that profit in the business world, we quite naturally generalize and apply this overall approach even to nonbusiness entities such as the church. A number of authors[7] openly state the church is a business with a product, the gospel, to sell and a mandate to promote that product and generate (demand) profits in the form of converts. By demanding constant growth, we quite naturally turn to counting (in some form) as our chief means of evaluating this performance. While not quite as explicit, most church growth thinking is based on a similar assumption: bigger is better, more is always the goal.

If I were to follow this course, I could tell you that from 2006 to 2016 our average Sunday morning attendance has grown from 62 to 101 (sometimes as high as 130). That is a 63 percent increase in just ten years. But what does this tell us about the growth and the health of my parish? It could mean we are reaching new people with the gospel (in keeping with the Great Commission, Matt 28:18) and/or we are convincing more of our members to attend regularly. Now these things could be important indictors of ecclesial health, but only if they can be shown to be expressions of the spiritual maturity that facilitates active, selfless witness or the progressive sanctification of the members that enflames the desire to be with and worship the living God. The numbers themselves are not important. In other words, numeric growth is not the goal by itself but is rather a side-effect of a completely different kind of growth, a maturing that is commensurate with the fact that the church is a living, multilayered, spiritual reality, the body of Christ, and not a one-dimensional profit-or-loss business. That is precisely why the Scriptures give us a very different standard with which to measure the growth of the church.

The word "success" (ἐπιτυχία) only occurs once in the Bible (Wis 13:19 LXX), and it fits the general definition (see above) of the achievement of some aim. However, the word for "grow" or "increase" (αὐξάνω) does occur in both the Old Testament (39 times) and New Testament (23 times). In most cases it refers to the growth of animals, plants, the hair on our head, the young, and so on. It is also used with specific reference to our faith and to the church. But there we are reminded the growth is caused by God alone (1 Cor 3:6; 2 Cor 9:10), that its object (focal point) is Christ (Eph 4:15), that it involves our witness, faith, spiritual maturity, grace, and good works (Col 1:6, 10; 1 Pet 2:2, 18). In any case, nowhere is this kind of growth, the growth of the church, spoken of in terms of numbers. Some might object that in

---

7. See Reising, *Church Marketing 101*, and Barna, *Marketing the Church*.

the book of Acts (2:41, 4:4) we have reports of growth that indicate how many thousands were added to the church, but we need to remember these are simply descriptive statements, not normative, didactic pronouncements. Here, there is no prescription to grow at a certain rate or to grow (numerically) at all. Here, there is no talk of profit or of ego satisfaction.

Ephesians 4 is a good example of the biblical perspective on ecclesial growth (success). In this chapter, St. Paul refers to several growth-related themes: he talks about children growing into adults, about teaching that leads to increased knowledge, and about the church maturing into the fullness of the knowledge of Christ. So it is this process of maturing into knowledge and not growth rates and numbers, simple counting, that St. Paul sets up as a standard for measuring the growth of the church. If we apply Ephesians 4 to, for example, the command to witness (Matt 28:18), we see the measure of success is our faithfulness to proclaim the gospel and not simply the results of that activity. This also means we will have to measure ourselves not just against one aspect of it but against the commandment taken as a whole, which includes making disciples (not converts), to do so by baptizing and teaching, to do so as you go out into all the world, and to keep on doing that until Christ returns. In other words, the goal of our outreach is not simply an ever-larger number of punctiliar conversions but rather an ongoing, continual ministry of life-long discipleship, which is not really something you can count.

Nevertheless, there is something very appealing about the commercial, numbers-based model, since it is so much easier to count and analyze conversions than to measure spiritual growth or sanctification. If we simply count, we can talk about percentages of increase, trends, and compliment ourselves with detailed reports on who is and who is not being converted, etc. This may even give us a sense of accomplishment, the feeling that we have completed the task. But if conversion is not the end or the actual goal, but just the beginning, then the number of conversions (no matter how high) cannot be a measure of success. Working from the biblical goals-based framework, we will have to look to the state of the ongoing process of facilitating maturity in Christ to find a way of measuring success, not just in mission but in every area of church life. Clearly the various aspects of ecclesial life that St. Paul speaks of in Ephesians 4 are not easily counted and do not readily yield to statistical analysis. After all, how do you count "edifying of the body of Christ" (Eph 4:10), "the unity of the faith" (Eph 4:13), "the knowledge of the Son of God" (Eph 4:13), "the fullness of Christ" (Eph 4:13), "no longer being children" (Eph 4:14), no longer being "tossed to and fro and carried about with every wind of doctrine" (Eph 4:14), and "growing up in all things into him" (Eph 4:15)? Yet these are the very things that constitute success in the life of the church. These are the very things we will need to find a way to assess in order to determine the extent to which we are fulfilling the Great Commission.

SPIRIT-INFORMED RESISTANCE

During this investigation we uncovered many examples of the church importing and using secular devices, procedures, and technologies. How we respond depends on the degree and the nature of the danger posed by the practice. In order to bring sustained healing and ongoing protection to the church, we may have to respond one way to severe threats and damage, and another way to activities that cause minimal disruption. So there will be a range of responses, but whatever we choose to do, we must carefully preserve the active influence of Scripture and Tradition and proceed under the guidance of the Holy Spirit.

If the danger is acute, that is, if we are dealing with a clear-cut violation of scriptural or traditional norms, we have little choice but to eliminate the practice and remove its markers, even if it is an active practice in the church. Money-making schemes that make the parish a node in some huge commercial enterprise simply have to be shut down. The association with evil and criminal enterprises has to be eliminated. Practices that deceive with false promises (fee service) need to be curtailed. I am sure this would be a hard sell since so many of us are already using and already addicted to these services. A concerted teaching effort, exposing the true nature and intent of these services, could lead to believers waking up and seeing the spiritual wisdom of being free of these manipulators, refusing to any longer accept their false substitutes for genuine Christian activities and structure. This movement of healing will take some time and will have to be implemented gradually and sensitively.

If a practice is less dangerous but could still cause serious harm, we may be able to modify the practice and avoid the danger it poses to the church. Again, we have a number of options. Biblical alternatives can be used to replace the harmful practices with the gifts and abilities already given to the church through the gifting of the Holy Spirit. Digital giving, if it is undermining the seriousness of giving as an act of faith, could be replaced with genuine stewardship. This may be difficult since we have become so used to the convenience of online donations. Strategic planning could be replaced with a more deliberate emphasis on spiritual discernment, the absolute sovereignty of the people can be replaced with the active priesthood of all believers, etc. Some of these practices could be redefined in terms of scriptural and traditional norms. With adequate teachings and frequent reminders, digital giving could conceivably be redefined and thus be practiced as genuine stewardship. The cold utility of worship space could be redefined in terms of the biblical ideas of it being a dwelling place of God, a place we are to adorn with the very best we have and with the greatest of respect. In some cases, we might be able to combine the useful aspects of secular procedures with the God-given practices of the church. We can, for example, make good use of the information-disseminating efficiency of all forms of print media. We might even restructure video presentations (of liturgies, lectures, etc.) in conjunction with actual-presence teaching and ministry.[8] We might also repurpose strategic planning by building into it the spiritual aspect of discernment, while taking advantage of its remarkable ability to engage participants and enhance commitment, all while downplaying its promise of control.

Finally, there will probably be some cases in which we can simply accept the use of some practice, especially those that involve the church's overlap with the world around it, such as financial accountability, banking, taxes, adequate compensation, etc. Again, we have to recognize that since we live in two worlds, the sacred and the secular, we will have to, on the one hand, build bridges, legal ones such as statutes or by-laws, and, on the other hand, show ourselves to be deliberate, well-informed, cooperating citizens of both realms.

RENEWAL (ἀνακαίνωσις)

For me, one of the most difficult aspects of this study has been the growing fear that we believers are being overwhelmed by the secular imaginary and robbed of our own heritage, of the invaluable treasures that have been given to us through Tradition. Indeed, many "consider the treasury of orthodoxy antiquated. They seek *renewal*, modernization and progress. . . they try to change the church so that it offers 'more' and becomes more 'useful.'"[9] So we replace the real-presence fellowship traditionally treasured by believers with illusory interaction of social media. We find it more exciting to "gather" in cyberspace simulations or on satellite campuses. Somehow, the big-screen spectacle of some personality is more appealing than the humble reality of a faithful servant standing in front of the local gathering. And so, we lose the blessings of the actual eucharistic assembly. It seems under the efficiency and power of modern technologies, one ecclesial treasure after

---

8. For example, Antiochian outreach with the film *Becoming Truly Human*.
9. Mitilinaios, *Revelation: The Seven Lampstands*, 290.

the other is being lost. Some try to make the divine services more exciting, after all we don't want anyone to be bored. Our hierarchs are reviled, our clergy disrespected in favor of the instant and universal expertise of cyberspace. Sacred spaces are made more comfortable, as much like secular entertainment venues as possible. Icons are replaced with video clips. Church music is replaced with the more exciting strains of popular music mediated by electronic gadgetry of all sorts. Prophetic witness is lost to the path of least resistance since so few are willing to be different or to stand out. The practice of openly standing firm on biblical principles is being lost to the ambivalence of political correctness. I am afraid our experiments at renewal do not lead to new life but to our abandoning of the unique character of our faith and ceding essential elements of the church to technology and convenience. As a result, what we have left today is little more than an empty vestige of the saving treasures we once possessed. What remains is mere spectacle, "a concrete inversion of life, an autonomous movement of the nonliving."[10] If we do not do something to stop and reverse this damage, it will not be long before we have nothing left at all; the church will wither, die spiritually, and have nothing to offer this world.

So what are we to do? The answer, as many have already said, is renewal. But it is neither the church nor its Tradition that needs renewing. Christianity is not old and out of date; instead, "it's the Christians that have withered. The faithful are languishing."[11] So if we speak of the need for renewal, that process must begin with us, "not the Tradition of our church."[12] Indeed, St. Paul calls us to be transformed by the renewing of our minds (Rom 12:2). In general theological terms, the biblical concept of ἀνακαίνωσις refers to "the new and miraculous thing that the age of salvation brings. It is thus a key teleological term in eschatological promise: the new heaven and earth (Rev 21:1; 2 Pet. 3:13)."[13] There we read about a new Jerusalem (Rev 3:12; 21:2). There is talk of new wine in Mark 14:25, a new name (Rev 2:17; 3:12), a new song (Rev 5:9), and a new creation (Rev 21:5). This new creation is the goal and hope of all believers. In anticipation of what is to come, it is expressed in the Christian life (2 Cor 5:17). Believers are to put on the new nature that they are given (Eph 4:24), and so they are constantly called to renewal to vigilance against the deadening effects of legalism.

In this context, St. Paul admonishes us, "Do not be conformed to this world, but be transformed by the renewing of your mind" (Rom 12:2),

---

10. Debord, *Society of the Spectacle*, 24.
11. Mitilinaios, *Revelation: The Seven Lampstands*, 292.
12. Mitilinaios, *Revelation: The Seven Lampstands*, 292.
13. "ἀνακαίνωσις," Kittel et al., *Theological Dictionary*, 3:449.

bringing it into conformity with the "mind" of Christ (Phil 2:5). In other words, renewal involves replacing, rewriting, or overlaying the secular content of our minds with the content of Christ's mind, that is, with his will. So on the one hand, we need to *internalize* the will of God as revealed in the givens of the Christian life. Taken together these givens constitute what we call Tradition (παράδοσις). By this

> we mean everything that was handed to us by Christ, the apostles and their disciples, and the church Fathers. Now this very Tradition is what Christ tells us to hold on to, what Christ tells the bishop of Thyatira: Hold onto what you have until I come back. I gave it to you and you must keep it unaltered until my Second Coming.[14]

God, in his infinite wisdom, has given the church a number of practical tools which define, protect, and preserve the church. These treasures, these good and perfect gifts come down from the Father of lights (Jas 1:17–18), and they include the holy Scriptures, apostolic succession, liturgical structures, councils (dogma and canons), hagiography, and iconography. There are certainly many other gifts given to the church, but these are the ones that are generally associated with the idea of Tradition. In order to move forward, then, we will have to look back to these treasures. For the church to be spiritually renewed

> it must look toward its treasures, towards its deposited Traditions, its life-giving springs. That is where the church must turn, to the Fathers. From there the church will take what is pure, authentic and true, to regenerate itself.[15]

On the other hand, we will not only have to internalize these treasures, we will have to make active, faithful use of them. "We will succeed only if we approach and practice the Tradition of our church: pure, unadulterated, without reductions, without amputations and without modernizations."[16] This renews the mind and gives us the ability to test (δοκιμάζω) everything we do against this known will of God. This is to examine every innovation, new idea, new theory, and new technology, and to determine if it conforms to the "good and acceptable and perfect will of God" (Rom 12:2). Knowing the will of God, then, means being able to actively live according to it. Having determined what is acceptable and thus how we are to act, we

---

14. Mitilinaios, *Revelation: The Seven Lampstands*, 290.
15. Mitilinaios, *Revelation: The Seven Lampstands*, 294.
16. Mitilinaios, *Revelation: The Seven Lampstands*, 292.

can actually commit ourselves to that action by which the cycle of spiritual renewal is continued. That

> does not mean the elimination and alteration of every previous element; the development of new theological theories; or the quest for new ideas, novel methodologies, shapes, or forms . . . True renewal is to search, theologize, and utilize the existing sources. This gold mine already exists; it is deposited and available. I simply need to dig deeper to discover it and to offer it in its pure form. This is the meaning of renewal.[17]

---

17. Mitilinaios, *Revelation: The Seven Lampstands*, 294.

15

On the Possibility and Nature of an Ecclesial Imaginary

Let this mind be in you, which was also in Christ Jesus (Phil 2:5)
For nothing so sustains the great and philosophic soul in the performance of good works as learning that through this one is becoming like God.[1]

OVERVIEW

AT THE VERY OUTSET of this study, I suggested if we in the church have been taken captive by the prevailing social imaginary, we might consider explicating a special version of that imaginary for the church, an *ecclesial imaginary*. Of course, it might be argued it is inappropriate to speak of an imaginary with reference to the church. However, it seems to me that both the origins and the functioning of a possible ecclesial imaginary have obvious similarities with the development and implementation of the social imaginary. As presented above, a social imaginary originates with ideas developed by elite elements of society which are then discussed, disseminated, and adopted by the wider populace. We also noted the current North American social imaginary actualizes itself in the form of several operating principles. In the

---

1. Chrysostom, in Oden, *Ancient Christian Commentary*, 3:236.

case of an ecclesial imaginary, the initial deposit of truth and practice left by Jesus to his apostles is occasionally expanded and rearticulated by individuals we might consider to be the elite of the church, such as apostles, bishops, councils, saints, theologians, etc. Their contributions to the growing deposit of knowledge are discussed in ever-widening circles (the individual faithful, local parishes, metropolia, dioceses, national churches, synods, regional councils) and eventually accepted as the teaching of the whole church, that is, added to the collective conscience of the church. In ecclesial parlance this process, which is superintended by the Holy Spirit, involves the living and dynamically growing mind of the church. All of this is summed up in the term "tradition" (παράδοσις). This body of knowledge, teaching, and practice functions in much the same way the North American social imaginary does. It governs and controls the way people imagine and thus execute their interactions with others. The actual content of this imaginary can be read from its basic operating principles. Tradition, for its part, should govern and control everything we do within the church and its particular content, that is, exactly what it expects, requires, and teaches can be read from its own unique set of operating principles. It might seem strange to speak of such principles in connection with the mind of the church. Nevertheless, I believe we can indeed point to a basic set of guiding precepts that define the basic content of the ecclesial imaginary. As an organizational convenience, let me use the principles I associated with the social imaginary to lay out their ecclesial counterparts.

OPERATING PRINCIPLES OF THE MIND OF THE CHURCH

The Communalism of the Gathering (σύναξις)

It seems much of the contemporary social imaginary has evolved as an effort to guarantee the primacy of individual rights, agency, choices, and opinions. What the ecclesial imaginary offers is a variation on the principle of communalism which preserves the dignity, uniqueness, and identity of each individual while at the same time promoting unity, oneness, fellowship, and communion. This duality is rooted in the conviction that God created human beings in his own image. Here, we have the idea of God releasing something of himself, of his person, in order to create. "God is the creator of his own living images, persons according to his image in its tri-hypostatic character."[2] The church teaches that the one nature (*osia*) of God exists as

---

2. Bulgakov, *Bride of the Lamb*, 87.

three distinct persons (*hypostasis*). So if God replicates himself according to his own image, then each individual human being would have to be an actualization or personalization (*hypostasis*) of human nature (*osia*) contingent upon the divine will of God. This tells us something about who human beings are and not simply what they are. On the one hand, each person is something unique and unrepeatable and, on the other hand, they do not and cannot exist in isolation but rather with in the multihypostatic unity of humanity and in reliance on the Creator's continued good will. As a result, they can only fully reach the God-intended potential of personhood by fully engaging with the world of other human beings or the divine person. The individual, then, was never intended to be an absolutely independent agent but is called, *qua* creation, to self-transcending love for or communion with both God and neighbor.

These strands of interdependency are all brought together in the church, which is constituted by the *gathering* of the faithful. The term refers to the action of a community of believers meeting together for the celebration of the Eucharist. That this gathering is of a personal nature is clear from the fact that the thus-constituted group of faithful is also called the body of Christ, that is, they are unified by the person of the fully present Christ. By partaking of one cup and one bread (1 Cor 10:16, 17), the many become one. In order for that to happen, the faithful have to be physically present in the place where one eucharistic Lamb (bread) is being offered and received. Moreover, individualistic nonparticipation would do great damage to the unity of the body. In the early church, "communion of all the faithful, of the entire *ecclesia*, at each liturgy was a self-evident norm."[3] For that reason, "[t]he Eucharist was both defined and experienced as the 'sacrament of the church, the 'sacrament of the assembly,' the 'sacrament of unity.'"[4] If the church is the gathering of the faithful in order to celebrate the Eucharist, which expresses their oneness, what happens to that unity if some present chooses not to participate? So, if this participation in the gathering is taken seriously, it must under no circumstances be avoided (Heb 10:25). St. Chrysostom asks,

> What is, "not neglecting to meet together"? He knew that much strength arises from being together and assembling together. "For where two or three," it is said, "are gathered in my name, there am I in the midst of them"; and again, "That they may be one, even as we are"; and, "They were of one heart and soul." And not this only, but also because love is increased by our gathering together, and,

---

3. Schmemann, "Confession and Communion," para. 3.
4 Schmemann, "Confession and Communion," para. 3.

because love is increased, the things of God must follow. "And earnest prayer," it is said, was "made by" the people.[5]

The gathering is then a source of strength, teaching, encouragement—in short, the very things we need to appropriately and effectively engage with the world around us. One wonders if a mystical state of *gatheredness* might be extended beyond the actual gathering itself. Am I not still part of the body even when I am not physically present with the others during the liturgy? If so, we would live into the communal nature of our faith at all times. Even when I am physically alone or absent, I need to be aware of the fact that my actions will, on the one hand, be guided by the assembly, and on the other hand will have a direct effect on all the others "gathered" with me. If so, then I will need to evaluate my individual thoughts, actions, and behaviors in light of their possible effect on the gathering.

The Humility of Apophaticism (απόφασις)

The scientism which has grown out of the overestimation of our own rational capabilities has either eliminated much of the church's theological thought or transformed it into a science in its own right. The basic assumption is God and the world are ultimately comprehensible, that is, can be understood using human reason alone. This seems to eliminate all mystery. According to the German Lutheran theologian Wolfhart Pannenberg, "[e]very theological statement must prove itself on the field of reason and can no longer be argued on the basis of unquestioned presuppositions of faith."[6] In this intellectual context, theology is best understood as a form of knowledge or even a science.

The alternative that the church offers is no less rigorous, but it begins with the humble admission that we are not capable of fully understanding everything. The fathers speak of theology as a mystery, not a science, as something that is revealed to our understanding yet never completely revealed because "it transcends our mind,"[7] seeking to express in human language that which lies beyond all human comprehension. "Every theological statement," remarks St. Basil, "falls short of the understanding of the speaker.... Our understanding is weak and our tongue is even more defective."[8] As the Cappadocians remind us, "once theology forgets the

---

5. Chrysostom, in Oden, *Ancient Christian Commentary*, 10:162.
6. Pannenberg, *Theology and the Philosophy of Science*, 162.
7. St. Thalassios the Libyan, "On Love," 330.
8. Basil the Great, *Letter VII*, 8.

inevitable limits of the human understanding, replacing the ineffable Word of God with human logic, it ceases to be *theologia* and sinks to the level of *technologia*."[9] Because the knowledge of God remains a mystery—paradoxical—our theological discourse has to be both negative and positive, both apophatic and cataphatic.

On the path of affirmation (*cataphasis*), one approaches God by assuming he can, at least in some way, be known, and that that knowledge can be expressed by means of positive (logical) affirmations in human language but only to the extent he chooses to reveal himself. This has taken place in what might be called an economy of theophanies.[10] By the mercy of divine condescension, we are granted a series of appearances within the created order, i.e., God revealing something of himself in nature (Ps 19): human beings as the image of God, in the miraculous, in the word of the prophets, in the incarnate Logos through the Holy Spirit, in the church, and in the holy Scriptures. On the basis of these revelations, we are able, by exercise of our rational capabilities, to formulate certain affirmations which express some knowledge about God. This approach is at best incomplete and indirect, and so it requires "completion through a higher knowledge which is an acknowledgment of the very mystery of God"[11]—an *apophatic* or negative path to knowledge.

On the path of negation (*apophasis*), we approach God by eliminating all concepts, definitions, and descriptions which limit the infinity or divinity of God. As Lossky puts it, "the negative way of the knowledge of God is an ascendant undertaking of the mind that progressively eliminates all positive attributes of the object it wishes to attain, in order to culminate, finally, in a kind of apprehension by supreme ignorance of him who cannot be an object of knowledge."[12] The classic statement of this path of negation is found in Pseudo-Dionysius's *Mystical Theology*. There, he suggests if one wishes to understand "the mysterious things," one must leave behind "the senses and the activities of the intellect and all things that the senses or the intellect can perceive, and all things in this world of nothingness, or in that world of being, and that, thine understanding being laid to rest [and] thou strain (so far as thou mayest) towards a union with him whom neither being nor understanding can contain."[13] St. John of Damascus puts it this

---

9. Ware, "Short Theological Education," para. 2.

10. "Now, we cannot know God outside of the economy in which God reveals Himself" (Lossky, *In the Image*, 15).

11. Stăniloae, *Experience of God*, 98.

12. Lossky, *In the Image*, 13.

13. Dionysius the Areopagite, "Mystical Theology," 192.

way: "It is plain, then, that there is a God. But what he is in his essence and nature is absolutely incomprehensible and unknowable. . . . All that is comprehensible about him is his incomprehensibility."[14] In light of this, the only appropriate approach to knowing God involves "the breakdown of human thought before the radical transcendence of God. . . a prostration before the living God, radically ungraspable, unobjectifiable, and unknowable."[15]

The Multidimensional World of Mystery (μυστήριον)

The reductionism of our age has produced a drab, colorless, one-dimensional world with no mystery. It is a world which appears to have no unseen dimensions. Indeed, the ideas of angels, spiritual powers, and divine presence have all been expunged from this world. It is a purely materialistic understanding of both creation and the human being. By way of contrast, the church offers a colorful, multidimensional understanding which uncovers the beauty behind the bare facts of our reality, the richness of our world.

When God created the world, he released the world to *be* on its own. This was not simply an extension of his own eternal being; the result of that would have been something eternal and divine since he is already everything that exists. So the only way God could have created the world would have been to release it into a limited, subeternal, telocentric[16] mode of existence within God. The best way to describe this limitation is to speak of creation's potential or its becoming. In other words, creation is not perfect[17] or complete; it has not yet reached its divinely predetermined destiny, but it is constantly moving toward that goal as evidenced in creation's freedom to self-actualize. This ability to self-actualize reflects the stamp of the Creator, revealing that, like God, creation possess an albeit-limited creative faculty. We note that in the Genesis account the earth brings forth, the waters bring forth, and the animals procreate (Gen 1:12, 21, 22). For that reason, it is possible to see the six days of creation as a progressive self-actualization of creation under God's direction, one unified act of the triune God which continues until creation has reached its appointed end in Christ. It is a living, developing, creative multiplicity.

---

14. John of Damascus "Exact Exposition of the Orthodox Faith," 1.4.1.

15. Lossky, *Orthodox Theology*, 24.

16. A mode of existence centered on the achievement of some ultimate *telos* or destiny, in this case true communion with God.

17. Of course, this should not be taken to mean that the prelapsarian human being was already subject to death and lust. Those came after the fall as the natural consequences of sin.

As I have already mentioned, the human being is a composite entity made up of both created and uncreated elements. On the one hand, a person is going to have a physical or material presence, bound by time and space. But that finitude does not rule out the existence of a divine element. If the divine person is the source of human personhood, having breathed his Spirit into human beings, having created them in his own image, then we must assume the presence of a supramaterial divine element in the human person.

So both creation and the human being are multilayered, composite beings. This fact resists a purely realistic, naturalistic representation, and it helps counter some of modern reliance on its own ability to understand and depict the world. This could help us to recognize the unseen dimensions of life and integrate our lives with them, allowing us to rise above the corrupting influences of secular reductionism.

Submission (ὑποβολή)

The modern imaginary emphasizes individual freedom of choice to the point where an individual's opinion is valid simply because it emerges from personal choice and freedom of expression. The church, on the other hand, offers to restrain human freedom by giving us just one option: complete surrender to Christ in return for forgiveness of sins and eternal life. What is being offered cannot be earned, won in a spiritual lottery, or mediated by any other practice or person. It cannot be demanded as a right, and our opinion about this lack of choice is utterly irrelevant. The terms cannot be negotiated. It is an invitation that is either rejected or accepted by an act of total submission to the person of Christ.

This obviously eliminates the idea of unlimited choice and limits our freedom of expression. In Christ, we are no longer free to formulate personal opinions on every doctrine, every passage of Scripture, every pronouncement of the church; instead, we are to be of one mind with Christ. Rather than expressing our own opinions, we should be tapping into the collective consciousness of the church for the interpretations, explanations, and directions we need. When it comes to witness, we are not free to use any technique we choose to communicate and persuade just because it happens to be effective in the secular world. Any method that is manipulative, designed to gain power over the listener, any method that is depersonalizing, must be rejected since it does violence to the recipient. So rather than putting ourselves in the foreground, we should be highlighting the fathers and the saints of the church, those whom God has graced with his presence, learning from what they taught and from the way they presented Christ. The idea that in some instances our opinions are unimportant, our likes and dislikes irrelevant, is very difficult for the late-modern mind to accept. Yet self-restraint, not unrestrained self-expression, is what the gospel calls us to.

The Sufficiency of Scripture and Tradition (ἀπόδοσις)

The modern social imaginary has focused our attention on the *preeminence of information* as a means of *increased control*. As a result, information has become the most sought-after commodity in our economy. It is paid for, stolen, gathered, stored, and locked away. We retrieve it and use it against those we intend to control and manipulate our fellow Americans "into chasing ever-higher levels of consumption by means of 'motivational research.'"[18]

While most of this secular information has to be generated by human activity and is often unverifiable, what the church has to offer has been given to us as the very word of God addressed to humanity. This is obvious in the case of the sayings of Jesus contained in the gospels. But it was soon recognized, for example, by St. John of Damascus, that the Holy Spirit had superintended the whole process in such a way as to render the entire canon of Scripture divine word. As he put it, "[f]aith comes by hearing. For hearing the divine Scriptures we believe in the teaching of the Holy Spirit."[19] On the other hand, the written form of Scripture preserved the word of God in a form accessible to all. In this way, the unique development of the Scriptures engages the human person in both her infinity (divine word) and in her finiteness (human language). Notice how the words of Scripture convict, console, move, and direct, doing what no other words can do, for these words are the infinite voice of God spoken into the temporal and spatial context of God's own creatures.

Being the word of God, the holy Scriptures also engage human persons in their ability to hold cognitive content to be true. In fact, this is the very basic demand the Scriptures make on the reader, meeting that constitutional need to believe something by telling us what can be believed, informing and building plausibility structures, and enabling us to adjudicate between conflicting claims. So the Scriptures speak to the human faculty of belief by relieving the tension that is caused by having to choose what to believe by showing us what should be believed, and by doing so within an ecclesial context that preserves its true meaning. The word of God helps individuals avoid false "truths" by bringing order and stability to their plausibility

---

18. Berman, *Why America Failed*, 28.
19. John of Damascus, "Exact Exposition of the Orthodox Faith," IV.x.

structures. As such, Scripture is an invaluable asset against the contemporary cacophony of truth claims.

Deification (θεοσις)

As we have seen, the modern imaginary envisions a perpetual movement of improvement in almost all areas of life. This progress is, of course, the result of human effort, rationalism, and the scientific method. Having grown accustomed to the constant evolution of technology, we tend to generalize and project this inexorable movement onto almost every area of life. Moreover, this expectation of relentless progress often leads to a certain restlessness or dissatisfaction with the way of things, a rejection of past practice and thought. However, this attitude does not seem to envision a specific end or *telos* but simply progress as such, nor does it associate the advances with the fulfilment of any particular destiny given to humanity. As such, all this progress seems to be an empty thrashing about, bringing very little in the way of ultimate satisfaction or life meaning.

The church, however, does speak of a progression which involves fulfilling a God-given destiny and which leads to the realization of humanity's full potential as anticipated by their creation. This journey is referred to as "deification," or *theosis*. Having been created in the image and likeness of God, we are tasked with pursuing godlikeness, or what the fathers call *theosis,* which will allow us to fulfill our destiny and become *partakers of divine nature* (2 Pet 1:4) This ultimate deification is defined as a union or communion with God which is so complete it can be that the human being is like God. Adam was not created perfect in an absolute sense, but he was created without sin, in communion with God, and therefore with the potential to achieve that for which he was created: deification. Being created, humans could, of course, never acquire what the uncreated Trinity was by nature. But by God's grace, it was possible for humankind to advance towards Godlikeness.

Self-Transcendence (ἀγάπη)

The individualistic emphasis of the modern imaginary has encouraged what we called a turn inward, that is an extreme reflexivity. Because of the basically sinful nature of human beings, this focus on the self has morphed into self-love with its attendant characteristics of greed and narcissism.

The ecclesial imaginary calls for a reversal of this trend in the form of self-transcendence, a state of being in which self-love has been overcome.

According to the teaching of the church, the soul is a unified whole which possesses three distinct faculties: the intellect, the will, and the emotions. When the soul loves itself, the intellect uses all of its powers to ensure its own desires are fulfilled and its emotions remain pleasurable. To this end, intellect needs to constantly monitor the state of its emotions and its desires. As a result, it is unable to give anything but a passing attention to anyone else while engaged in commerce, public discourse, and governance. On the one hand, overcoming this self-addiction involves disengaging the self from all those things to which it is attached, all those things which bring it carnal pleasure. This includes not only our material possessions but our desires for the sensual, for recognition, and amusement. It is a radical state in which no personal desire can compete with and supplant the will of God. In other words, the focus of the will's desires has been shifted away from the self and is focused on others, initially God.

On the other hand, freeing one's self from this addiction means aligning the self with the will of God such that the intellect directs the will and the emotions to find joy and love in God. It is this path of self-transcendence that enables the believer to be fully present to God and thus to experience divine presence. Moreover, the same dynamic will be at work in the believer's encounters with other human beings. If there are no desires that hold us, we will be naturally, spontaneously free to focus our intellect on the desires of the other. As St. Paul writes to the Philippians (2:3–4), "Let nothing be done through selfish ambition or conceit, but in lowliness of mind let each esteem others as better than himself. Let each one of you look out not only for his own interests, but also for the interests of others." Self-transcendence is the secret of Christian witness, the first step toward building a context of communion through presence.

This, then, is the imaginary that should govern life in the church. These are the principles that should be so well engrained in the fabric of our lives that they enable us to instinctively and instantly evaluate and respond to the threats arrayed against us. If this were the case, we would spontaneously be able to say whether the use of a secular meaning, structure, device, or technology is appropriate in the church. This, of course, presupposes the ecclesial imaginary has been thoroughly absorbed and incorporated into the individual thinking. In the case of the social imaginary, this is, as we saw, certainly the case. We spend enormous amounts of time being exposed to the effects of its secular principles. This is done through endless hours in school, work, and play, as well as being subjected to an endless barrage of manipulative advertising. So it should surprise no one to find that this constant exposure causes the social imaginary to become second nature in the minds of many, even among believers.

That these things are indeed at work in the church was clearly revealed to me during a recent semi-annual business meeting at our church. Because the church is located in the downtown area of a large city, security has become a concern. During the meeting some suggested we surround the property with a six-foot-high fence and hire armed guards to patrol it. What is it that made these Christian people think turning the church into an armed fortress was an acceptable or even good idea? It was the social imaginary, with its emphasis on self-preservation and the protection of investments made. Encouragingly, there were others who instinctively knew this was a bad idea, that it was un-Christian, because the ecclesial imaginary was operating in their hearts and minds. On another topic, finances, one person suggested we open up new channels of revenue by selling off the older parts of our property and transforming the formerly sacred spaces into a venue that could be rented out for secular social events. What was it that, without any discussion or marshalling of facts, made this idea acceptable for a member of a church? Was it not the social imaginary with its mercenary commercialization of almost every aspect of life? Another person, obviously under the sway of the ecclesial imaginary, spontaneously rejected the idea and suggested giving as an expression of our faith was the only acceptable way of raising the parish's income.

All of this took place in the absence of contemporaneous argument or discussion but was rather the spontaneous expressions of internalized imaginaries. In other words, certain data and principles had become second nature, were actually already in the minds of the participants, and dictated the initial response to the ideas presented. It seems reasonable to assert the ecclesial imaginary should dominate the mind of the church and not the social imaginary. For that to happen, we need to, as mentioned above, follow St. Paul's advice by allowing ourselves to be transformed by the renewing of our minds (Rom 12:2). This involves replacing or overwriting the information contained in the social imaginary with the information of the ecclesial imaginary, that is, with the mind of Christ. While it is tempting to think of this in binary terms, that is, as either secular or ecclesial dominance, it seems to me that since the social imaginary is our default position, the transformation will be gradual, and will no doubt involve an evolving mixture of the two, with the relative importance of each changing over time until the social imaginary is successfully supplanted by the ecclesial and the mind of Christ, once again, dominates the believer. But since we have already succumbed to the social imaginary, this transformation is going take time and effort; it is going to be a struggle. But we should not think we can do this on our own, that we can somehow "fight to expel the darkness from the chamber of [our] souls . . ."[20] If we are going to bring the ecclesial imaginary to prominence, we will, instead, have to greatly increase our direct exposure to Christ, the things of the church, our faith, and spend more time with the treasures of Tradition. This will "open a tiny aperture for light to enter, and the darkness will disappear."[21] If we allow that to happen, then our spiritual life will engage in our

> daily contest simply, easily, and without force. The soul is sanctified and purified through the study of the words of the Fathers, through the memorization of the psalms and portions of Scripture, through the singing of hymns and through the repetition of the Jesus Prayer.
>
> Occupy yourself with hymns of praise, with the poetic canons, with the worship of God and with divine *eros*. All the holy books of our church—the Book of the Eight Tones, the Book of the Hours, the Psalter, the books with the Offices for the Feasts and and Saint-day Commemorations—contain holy, loving words addressed to Christ. Read them with joy and love and exaltation. When you devote yourself to this effort with intense desire you will be sanctified in a gentle and mystical way without your even being aware of it.[22]

---

20. Porphyrios, *Wounded by Love*, 136.
21. Porphyrios, *Wounded by Love*, 136.
22. Porphyrios, *Wounded by Love*, 136.

Appendix

The Special Challenges Faced by North American Orthodox Monasteries[1]

My purpose here is not to extol the virtues and benefits of monasteries in some general way. That has already been done by many others who have documented the amazing contributions of monastics to the sciences (mathematics, logic, astronomy); to the preservation of knowledge (the scriptorium, book binding); to the arts (iconography); to theology (Basil, Gregory, Symeon the New); and to the ascetic and spiritual practices (St Theophan, St. Paisios)—all of which has contributed to the survival and the development of the Christian Church. What I am interested in here is a more immediate or local concern, namely the exact nature of the relationship between Orthodox monasteries and the larger communities, the Church and North American Society, of which they are a part. If we can clearly define those relationships, I believe that we will be able to reaffirm with some certainty the good they can offer society, the Church, its parishioners, and its clergy. At the same time, insight into these relationships may give us an understanding of the special challenges and dangers faced by our monasteries, dangers coming from both the Church and the world around us. On the one hand, as I have already shown, the Church has been influenced by secular society, and that thinking and those practices are being passed on to the monasteries by the Churches and their people. On the other hand, the monasteries exist

---

1. These observations are based on extensive time spent in both Orthodox and Catholic monasteries in Europe and the North America. In particular, I rely on several extended periods of full-time service as a priest to two Orthodox Monasteries in the United States.

within society in their own right and as such are constrained to some level of interaction and are subject to the same threats faced by the Church. Before we can speak of specific challenges, I will seek to define the monastery's relationships by asking what monasteries and parishes have in common and in what ways they are different. Aided by that understanding, I will then ask if and to what extent monastic life has been affected by the modern social imaginary and by the damaged imaginary that dominates the Church.

HOW MONASTERIES AND PARISHES ARE THE SAME AND YET DIFFERENT

One way to approach the question of similarity is to say that both monasteries and parishes belong to the same class of objects (entities). When we speak of a class of objects, we are referring to things which, even though they might be different in many ways, do share certain characteristics that allow us to say that they belong together. We are, for example, familiar with the class of objects known as trees. In spite of their amazing variety (an oak is not a willow, is not a maple), that is, even though they are not all the same, they do share certain characteristics (all are plants that have an elongated stem or trunk, supporting branches and leaves, etc.), and thus they all belong to the class of objects called trees.

In the case of most monasteries and parishes, we can also say that they share a number of characteristics and that in spite of some significant differences, they can be considered part of the same group or class of objects. We will call that group or class Church (not a Church, but the Church, Church as such). Of course, there are any number of things that monasteries and parishes share, such as their Christian origins, their teaching, their common tradition, their iconography, their hymnology, and so on. But if there is one thing we know from history, it is that Church has always been defined as a group of believers who, under the leadership of a priest ordained and appointed by a canonically consecrated bishop, gather regularly to celebrate the Eucharist. As mentioned above, the Orthodox Theologian Afanasiev instructs that the Church was established by Christ at the Mystical Supper and actualized at the Eucharist on the day of Pentecost.[2] So, wherever you have these four things (Bishop, priest, believers, regular celebration of the Eucharist), you have what we can call Church. This is, of course, true in parishes and in monasteries that have their own priest/monks to celebrate the Eucharist and, in the absence of a priest, in those monasteries to which the bishop assigns a visiting celebrant.

2. Afanasiev, *Lord's Supper*.

In that case, a monastery is, and again there is no question, as much Church as is a local parish. Moreover, this shared status allows us to speak of unity. St. Paul says that because "we, though many, are one bread and one body; for we all partake of that one bread" (I Cor 10.16–17). This is a commonality, an organic unity of all ecclesial units (parishes and monasteries) taken together as one, the Church. This universal unity is not something imposed onto the local units from the top down. It exists because each Church is united locally as the one Body of Christ, and because the Body of Christ is not divided by multiplicity, all the Churches are united to one another in the oneness of that Body. In that case, the two institutions (the monastery and the parish) are united and actually belong to one another, are joined by the fact that they are both members of and local instances of one and the same Body of Christ. For that reason, one part of the body cannot say to the other, "I don't need you." (1 Cor 12:15–30). The parish can no more say that it does not need the monastery than the monastery can say we don't need the parishes.

If we belong together, then it is our collective responsibility to find out how and in what ways our oneness can be expressed. One word that captures that is communion, by which I mean not only the shared sacraments but also a sharing of life, an intertwining of their very existence. When I speak of communion, I am referring to a self-emptying love for the Other, overcoming one's own boundaries in order to share in the life of the Other, a sharing that can be so complete that it is possible to speak of a fellowship that involves a free, unhindered flow of information, emotions, and desires, and an unmediated participation in every aspect of the Other's being. The characteristics of healthy communion are a) mutual acknowledgment and engagement; b) a participation in or sharing of thoughts, emotions, physical presence, desires; and c) complete absence of any awkwardness or apprehension. When this communion is allowed to exist and not obscured by barriers of privacy or indifference, the monastery and the parishes not only share information, not only pray for and support one another, but actually want to and do spend time in one another's presence: hosting, visiting, sharing in the deep fellowship of a united body.

As good as all of this sounds, it is not without its limitations because there are some profound differences between a monastery and a parish. The monastery is, for example, not a parish. It is not in the business of starting/planting parishes. It does not (must not) serve as a substitute for a local parish. So, even though it is most definitely Church, it is at the same time something quite different. One way of summarizing this difference is to say that a monastery is a community of believers who, having freed themselves from the distractions of their attachments to the world, collectively pursue an ever deeper spiritual life with the help of the sacraments, liturgical services, prayer, the study of the Holy Scriptures, and service. A parish is a place where a group of believers, who have not or cannot withdraw from the world, are given a context within which they receive spiritual nourishment (sacraments) through the services—especially the Eucharist—practical help and instruction on prayer, bible reading, and the spiritual life. As such, the parish is the point of departure for the believers' ongoing encounter with the non-Christian world in which they continue to live. The members of a parish are not of the world but are definitely in the world (Jn 17:15–16). The members of a monastery are not only not of the world, they are largely not even in the world. So, we might refer to a monastery as an oasis and a parish as a harbor.

Nevertheless, reflecting on these differences, I have come to wonder whether the difference is not so much one of substance but rather one of degree or intensity. When a monastic is tonsured, a number of questions are asked and these each refer to a basic virtue. Let me mention just a few of them. Renunciation of the World: "Do you renounce the world and what is of the world according to the commandments of the Lord?"[3] Commitment to the Local Monastery: "Will you abide in this monastery, or that to which under holy obedience you will be sent, and in the ascetic life until your last breath?"[4] Chastity: "Will you keep yourself in virginity, chastity, and piety even unto death?"[5] Obedience: "Will you preserve even unto death, obedience to the Abbess and to all the Sisters in Christ?"[6] Detachment: "Will you remain unto death in non-acquisitiveness and in the voluntary poverty for Christ's sake, which belong to the common life, not acquiring or keeping anything for yourself and then only in obedience and not of your own discretion?"[7]

According to this, a monastic is called (among other things) to renounce the world, to reside in the monastery permanently, to practice chastity, obedience, and detachment. Notice that the commitments being made are almost absolute as evidenced by words "unto death," "until your last breath," etc. What surprises me about this is not the radical nature of monastic commitment but the similarity to what the Scriptures are asking of average parish members. Each one of the five virtues mentioned above

---

3. Russkaiā pravoslavnaiā tserkov', *Great Book of Needs*, I:332.
4. Russkaiā pravoslavnaiā tserkov', *Great Book of Needs*, I:333.
5. Russkaiā pravoslavnaiā tserkov', *Great Book of Needs*, I:333.
6. Russkaiā pravoslavnaiā tserkov', *Great Book of Needs*, I:333.
7. Russkaiā pravoslavnaiā tserkov', *Great Book of Needs*, I:333.

are, in fact, supposed to guide the spiritual lives of all Christians. Let me illustrate using the same five virtues just mentioned.

Renunciation of the World: Jesus said that some people "hear the word, and the cares of this world, the deceitfulness of riches, and the desires for other things entering in choke the word, and it becomes unfruitful." (Mark 4:18–19) Commitment to the Local Parish: Hebrews 10:25 admonishes us not to forsake "the assembling of ourselves together, as is the manner of some . . . and so much the more as you see the Day approaching." Chastity: St. Paul urges the Corinthians to "Flee sexual immorality. Every sin that a man does is outside the body, but he who commits sexual immorality sins against his own body" (1 Cor 6:18). Obedience: In Hebrews 13:1, we read "Obey those who rule over you, and be submissive, for they watch out for your souls, as those who must give account. Let them do so with joy and not with grief, for that would be unprofitable for you." Detachment: Jesus said, "Do not lay up for yourselves treasures on earth, where moth and rust destroy and where thieves break in and steal. . . For where your treasure is, there your heart will be also" (Mt 6:19–21).

In light of this, we could argue that what makes a monastery different is that because it has withdrawn from the world, it is able to pursue the spiritual life without distraction while those in the world, that is, in parishes are called to the same kind of life but can only partially reach those goals because they are burdened by the cares and distractions of the world in which they live. I think that the basic difference is one of degree or intensity determined by the relative proximity to the spiritually damaging influences of the world. So, it is the spiritual life that becomes the point of contact between monastics and the other faithful. The difference, as Archbishop Averky himself, a monastic, puts it,

> consists only in the external forms of life: monks developed for themselves more convenient external forms of life in order more easily and without hindrance to attain the goal of human life, common to all: communion with God. . . However, the spirit of life for both monks and laypeople—as follows perfectly clearly from everything that has been said above—must be, of course, one and the same.[8]

Perhaps we can illustrate this dynamic by pointing to the practice of prayer. It is often said that one of the great contributions that the monasteries make to the Churches is that the monastics offer prayer on their behalf. Apart from the potentially increased volume of prayer, which is probably now what by itself makes prayer effective, the prayers of monastics are no

---

8. Taushev, *Struggle for Virtue,* loc. 212 of 2812.

more effective or beneficial than those of every other believer. The legitimacy and value of prayer is not determined by one's ecclesial position or office but rather by the practitioner's faith and righteousness (James 5.15–16), that is, by that person's level of spiritual maturity and health. However, the monastics do have one potential advantage. If they are indeed detached and therefore undisturbed by the cares and distractions of the world, then they do have an opportunity to develop a level of spiritual maturity that is difficult to attain while in the world. In other words, the monastics can and in many cases have[9] developed to such advanced levels of maturity that their communities become centers of spiritual power that can by example and practice (prayer) radiate truth and teaching out into the parishes. Anyone who visits can sense that strength, learn from it and is sustained by it. Just think of the thousands of pilgrims that have visited these holy places. So, wherever monastics have allowed their advantages to elevate them to genuine piety, they have been able to provide an invaluable service to the Church, and there can be no question that we today are in desperate need of that strength and protection.

However, if my assessment of ongoing, active interaction between monasteries and parishes is even close to the mark, then it becomes obvious that the monasteries are going to be subjected to some of the same cultural forces that have damaged the Church. I have already shown that the Church has been damaged by adopting elements of the modern social imaginary. So, if parishes and monasteries are to share communion, that is, mutually penetrate each other's very existence, then the parishes, already damaged, may exert a corrupting force on the monastery. Moreover, the monastery itself could, as I will show, also sustain damage directly from the world, and depending on the degree of damage, the monasteries could actually harm the parishes rather than benefit them.

So, has the modern commercial imaginary that the Church has not been able to resist also done damage to the monastery? Without pretending to look at all elements of this complex relationship, let me revisit the same three aspects of social interaction (commerce, public discourse, self-governance) I used to measure the Church in order to demonstrate the vulnerabilities and actual damage faced by our monasteries. Let me also assure the reader that this review is not motivated by a spirit of criticism for its own sake but as an appeal to monastics to return to their ancient virtues and once again become sources of spiritual strength for the Church.

---

9. Consider someone like Paisios, *With Pain and Love*.

MONASTERIES AND THE MODERN SOCIAL IMAGINARY

Suggesting that monasteries might be affected by the world around them may seem somewhat contradictory since the whole idea of monasticism was to detach oneself from the distractions of the world, to remove or to minimize those influences and thus gain an advantage in developing the spiritual life. Sometime during the middle of the third century, individual Christians began to withdraw into the desert. Among the first were St. Paul of Thebes (227–340) and St. Anthony of Egypt (251–356) who are said to have left the

> material comforts, worldly politics, and secular social distractions of urban . . . life, for the forbidding solitude of the . . . desert where they hoped to lead an ascetic life of physical mortification and uninterrupted prayer. By the beginning of the fourth century, these solitary eremitics, the so-called Desert Fathers and Mothers, quickly spread into the desert regions of Syria, Egypt, Palestine, and Sinai.[10]

There can be no doubt that they did develop a vibrant spirituality, and the accompanying teaching became the mainstay for instruction in the Church at large.[11]

But the idea of being alone was apparently not sustainable and these pilgrims began to gather in semi-eremitic colonies, such as those at *Nitria* and *Scetis*. Of *Nitria*, Palladius writes

> [o]n the mountain live some 5000 men with different modes of life, each living in accordance with his own powers and wishes, so that it is allowed to live alone, or with another, or with a number of others. There are seven bakeries in the mountain, which serve the needs of both these men and also of the anchorites of the great desert, 600 in all. . . In this mountain of Nitria there is a great church. . . which is occupied only on Saturday and Sunday. . .In this mountain there also live doctors and confectioners. And they use wine and wine is on sale. All these men work with their hands at linen-manufacture, so that all are self-supporting. And indeed, at the ninthe hour it is possible to stand and hear how the strains of psalmody rise from each habitation so that one believes that one is high above the world in Paradise. . . .[12]

Not long after that, another form of monasticism—the cenobium—began to develop. This was a large household of monastics who shared

10. Pennington, "Preface," xxvii.
11. See Stăniloae, *Orthodox Spirituality*.
12. Chitty, *Desert a City*, 15–16.

resources, lived under the direction of an abbot according to a binding set of regulations, a rule. The first of these was founded by *Pachomius* (290–346) at Tabennisi around 320. This arrangement was expanded and disseminated in almost every part of the world by the likes of Basil the Great, John Climacus, Benedict, Symeon, Francis, and many others. Even as some tried quite literall, to keep the idea of living in the desert alive or approximated physical detachment by settling in vast forests and wildernesses, others brought monasticism back into large urban centers and thus into direct contact with the world they sought to avoid. But wherever they located, not all[13] but the vast majority of these communities became fabulously rich with vast financial holdings in gold, gems, rare manuscripts, art, buildings, real estate, and the like. The extraordinary opulence of monastic chapels, refectories, scriptoriums, and rectories has been documented in millions of pictures taken by throngs of tourists not always interested in spiritual things.

So, have the monastics of our day simply abandoned the ancient virtues, like material detachment, and unabashedly accepted the commercialized mentality of our culture? According to the late Father Paisios of Athos this has indeed happened. He writes "Unfortunately, the secular spirit has now entered many monasteries, because Fathers today promote the monastic life through a secular channel, in a secular spirit, and do not lead souls to the patristic spirit of Grace. I detect an anti-patristic spirit prevailing in many monasteries today. . . Thus, they cannot progress in the spiritual life. . ."[14] They still speak of things like detachment, voluntary poverty, chastity, tolerance, and humility. However, under the insidious pressure of the North American imaginary these ancient norms have been warped and the resulting anti-virtues are being hidden behind the cover of pious speak and an almost impenetrable layer of dissembling. I will illustrate the challenge with examples from just three areas of life.

Commerce

When it comes to the influence of commerce, it has to be pointed out that almost all monasteries are in the business of marketing something. It can be anything from faith-related items such as icons, candles, and incense to non-ecclesial items such as soap, honey, or dogs. I realize that, in some cases, the monasteries have to do something to generate income to replace

---

13. I think here of one Carmelite monastery in northern Illinois in which a few gentle monks lived in truly humble simplicity in order to actively serve the disadvantaged of their area.

14. Paisios, *With Pain and Love*, 83.

some of what the faithful no longer donate. However, it can interfere with the actual work a monastery is supposed to be doing such as prayers and services. In one case, when an abbess was offered the possibility of additional Liturgies, she declined, saying that they were simply too busy with other things. I wonder if this is what St. Paisios meant when he warned that too much work makes monastics worldly:

> It is best for those who desire to live spiritual lives, especially monastics, to avoid pursuits or projects that will stand in the way of this goal. They should not take up too many projects because work never ends. If monastics do not learn inner, spiritual work, they will look of escape in all kinds of external activities. People consumed by endless tasks will end their lives with all kinds of imperfections.[15]

But the real damage in this area comes from the perversion of the concept of detachment and voluntary poverty. As pointed out above, the monastics do indeed commit themselves to these virtues when they are tonsured. But what are we to think when they use their resources to buy up large tracts of land? What are we to say to the extravagance demonstrated in the chapels and residences they erect? In one case, when I was given a tour of a new building, the nun proudly pointed out the marble floors, the exotic wood trim, the fine leather chairs in the magnificent sitting room, etc.[16] In another case, I was shown plans of a huge stone edifice replete with marble, stained glass, and elevators. I was also assured that nothing but the finest (most expensive?) materials were being used.

As I mentioned, this behavior is justified by an appeal to what they say is still voluntary poverty because they do not personally own these things. However, that is straightforward dissembling since the issue is not ownership but rather the attachment to these riches. The individual monastics may not personally own these things, but they have complete access to and absolute control of the use of these "possessions." They don't have to own these things, they simply have them, and they certainly appear to enjoy them. On what basis, then, could they call into question the materialism and luxury pursued by non-monastics if they themselves are still attached to material wealth? But that cannot be the monastic ideal. Consider the words of St. Paisios:

---

15. Paisios, *With Pain and Love*, 219–20.

16. I suppose I could also point to the costly, imported materials used to construct the chapel. But in this case one could, perhaps understandably, argue they were simply to fulfill the biblical mandate to beautify the worship space.

> Once I was at a very luxurious house. We were talking and they said, "We live in Paradise, while other people are in such great need." "You live in hell," I replied. . ." If Christ were to ask me, "Where should I put you, in a house like this or in a prison?" I would reply "in a dark prison." A prison would do me good. It would remind me of Christ, of the holy martyrs, and the ascetics who lived in the holes of the earth. It would remind me of monastic life."[17]

It seems that contemporary monastics have substituted a technically correct understanding of non-ownership for the reality of the true spirit of detachment. They amass an almost unbelievable trove of valuable items (rare books, furniture, artwork) donated by others. A great deal of time invested in cataloging these items for sale on eBay, flea-markets, and the like. The profits from these business dealings are not passed on to the poor in any notable way (no help for the hungry, none for the unemployed right in their own neighborhoods) but are rather lavished on themselves, on the extravagances of the massive and enormously expensive buildings they are constructing. Theirs is a vision of grandeur and opulence (the best marble floors, fantastic stained-glass windows, the finest in door fixtures, the most expensive roof, etc., etc.). It is, in short, an attempt at regal splendor (to honor God?). Thus, the simplicity of life to which they have been called is transformed into a form of idolatry, worshiping massive monuments to their own egos. The monastery itself has become their God. So yes, some monastics today have been captured by the spirit of commerce and are obviously subject to greed and materialism. Yet, they tend to hide what amounts to a de facto materialism, living in a way that only the rich can live, demanding, getting, and getting used to the best of everything, assuming (taking for granted) the generosity of the faithful.

Public Discourse

As we saw above, the second arena of human interaction is what is called the public sphere, that space in which we engage in difference-overcoming dialogue with anyone and everyone. On the one hand, this assumes a willingness to actually be open and tolerant and to create a context (in this case the topical public spaces of the monastery) in which discourse can take place. On the other hand, this involves a kind of discourse that reflects the spiritual virtues like humility, love, and patience that monasticism supposedly has an advantage in developing.

17. Paisios, *With Pain and Love,* 191.

With respect to actually creating a public space, some monasteries have chosen not only to close themselves off from the world around them[18] but also to create an island of foreignness that makes engagement all but impossible. In several cases, the monasteries are established as microcosms of another culture in which the flag of that nation is flown, the language of that culture is in exclusive use, especially during the services, and in which everything else from the food to the architecture is imported. While this may have some value as a curiosity, it really does not invite any real interaction with the surrounding people. Perhaps one might argue that they are aggressively resisting any influence from the prevailing context by establishing an alter context based on a very distant culture. Of course, we have observed that the multiplicity of cultural and languages can hinder public discourse, but I rather doubt that a mono-cultural, mono-linguistic isolationism will be any more dialogue-facilitating. In any case, this behavior is, in effect, similar to the filtering referred to above. This physical, linguistic, and cultural isolation allows the monastics to avoid being confronted with individuals and information they don't want to be exposed to. It effectively eliminates discourse and transforms the monastery into an almost impenetrable filter bubble.

Nevertheless, even in these isolated enclaves there are some opportunities for dialogue with "outsiders" which one would expect to be conducted in keeping with the ancient virtues of chastity, holiness, and self-control. While this does involve corporal chastity, one would think a strict discipline of thought and speech would also be involved. But what is left of chastity if it is frittered away with lewd jokes and off-color stories told around the lunch table, making sexually demeaning comments about men, energetically supporting and defending the most immoral of public persons? What remains of holiness if non-believing workers hired by the monastery are treated with disrespect, abusive language, and a lack of justice? What is one to think when the monastics' public behavior earns them a consistently poor reputation in the eyes of so many others—ranks of clergy, legal counsel, and a host of others (fellow believers, contractors, government officials, community leaders, business owners) who were in one way or the other have contact with the monastics and who have all seen and recognized their wrong and unjust actions? What remains of self-disciple if one can yell and shout at will, using crude language to say literally anything that comes to the angry mind? This is self-control transformed into an unlimited verbal and mental freedom shaped only by self-love. What happens when someone in need appeals for

---

18. I can actually understand that some of the ways in which this is done are simply designed to preserve the presence of detachment.

help and is dismissed with the words "our only responsibility is to work out our own salvation"? What are visitors to think when, during meals in the refectory, individuals are singled out and publicly embarrassed? Interestingly, much of what is said often comes in the form of pious terminology and the empty, tired catchphrases, clichés, and slogans that they have been using for decades to cover their own abuses and to intimidate others.

So, yes, some monastics have failed to develop the spiritual maturity and virtues that would make discourse in the public sphere possible. They are, of course, frail human beings like the rest of us and can hardly be expected to attain perfection. But in light of that, one might expect that remorse and repentance would be an important part of their spiritual repertoire. If passion-filled behavior can hinder discourse, then genuine repentance could surely heal much of the damage done. But alas, these monastics rarely feel the need to ask for forgiveness. As one of them suggested after an altercation, "You must ask for forgiveness when you speak sharply to me because you are uncomfortable with that, but I can shout at anyone at any time and because I am comfortable with doing that (I am just being myself) there is no need for me to apologize." Indeed, although I have repeatedly been on the receiving end of unloving, disrespectful verbal abuse, I have never once received an apology. The self-emptying love of Christ is transformed into the "love means never having to say you're sorry" philosophy of 1the 970 film *Love Story*.

One reason for this anti-repentance may be what amounts to the presumption of perfection. Any misbehavior I have witnessed and questioned has been casually dismissed with the words "that is just the way we are" or "we are holy." In other words, we are not doing anything wrong, we are just being ourselves (an Army Brat, a New Yorker, a Greek, an Italian). As a result, no criticism is tolerated or even entertained. Any suggestion of spiritual deficiency is rejected with outright hostility. This supposed state of perfection was even eternalized in the statement, "we are what we are, we will never change, and there is no need to change." The Orthodox understanding of the gradual path of deification, the slow but constant sanctification of the believer, is dismissed as unnecessary and replaced with the arrogant claim to personal perfection. Of course, a rather high degree of dishonesty is required to keep up this illusion of perfection. One monastic, seething with anger, red in the face, visibly shaking, gesticulating, and shouting could still say "I am not angry," and after dishing out such abuse could couch it in pious speak with the words "this is good for you" or "I love you." How can this constitute anything other than severe damage to the monastic ideals?

Self-Governance

The third area of social interaction dealt with above is that of self-governance. In the case of monasteries, this idea takes special significance since they are generally considered completely autonomous or self-governing. As such, they are not in danger of yielding to the democratic principles or the people's sovereignty. But they are in danger of a kind of power politics that does indeed damage or even eliminate community. Even the technicality of "being under" the rule of a bishop is greatly limited by local authority of the abbot or abbess. In that sense, they are isolated from the rest of the Church with no one to teach them or hold them to account. They have become a rule unto themselves, one that allows them to violate the "rules" of both scripture and Tradition without fear of broader ecclesial consequences. For example, at one monastery only baptized Orthodox individuals could participate in the Liturgy even though that is not the Tradition of the Church or in keeping with the current teaching of their Synod. One of the potential dangers of this lack of supervision is a "rock-like" inflexibility which constitutes a serious misunderstanding of the nature and function of authority. While the Abbess has absolute authority and is to be obeyed in everything, even unto death, there are some limits to what that power can affect. For example, just because the Abbot is not pained by the presence of an evil spirit, that does not mean that, by definition, no one else can experience such suffering, that such evil cannot be present. Just because he is not troubled by the worldly meanings of a technology brought into the monastery, his authority does not mean that, by definition, those observations of non-monastics are wrong. Just because an Abbess is in charge, it does not mean that she by extension can obviate the clear statements of Christ's commands. Of course, if you set yourself up as the determinant of all truth and all valid experience, you will never be able to show understanding, compassion, or love for any variant of your own opinions. And so, legitimate authority is transformed into the frightening spectacle of rank tyranny.

ON THE POSSIBILITY OF A NEW-MONASTIC IMAGINARY

Without having gone into too much detail, it seems clear that under the influence of the imaginary-damaged Church and the social imaginary itself, monastics and thus monasteries have been spiritually damaged. While there are probably many ways to categorize and analyze that damage, I think that the most important fact is that the harm done has prevented the monastics from realizing their spiritual potential and rendered the monasteries impotent. Yet, we can hope that even the monastics that appear in the experiences described here could, even though they are not (yet) prefect, be reanimated by the Spirit and show us the way after all. If they would truly renounce the world, reject its corrupting influences, they might still benefit the Church. They do have an advantage, and because they can (could) pursue their ascetic efforts with fewer distractions, they may still experience those higher levels of consolation, peace, and joy that we all so desperately need. In light of the overall goal of this project, reversing some of the damage done to the Church by the modern social imaginary, I think that monastics could make two essential contributions.

They Could Set a Clear Example of Life in Christ

As I have said, because monastics have detached (could detach) themselves from the distractions of the world, they have an advantage over the rest of us when it comes to developing their life in Christ. I think it fair to say that they are able to attain higher levels of or expressions of the basic characteristics required of all believers. Chastity, for example, involves not only corporal chastity but also includes the strict discipline of one's thoughts, avoiding impure feelings. Detachment, that is, "[n]on-possession means that one rejects any attempt to seek richness and temporal benefits. A monastic possesses only that which is necessary for life, while giving the rest to the poor and being never attached to anything temporal so that his mind may be always free from any concern for things vain and temporal but be busy with the concern for the salvation of himself and his neighbors."[19] Obedience is the essential characteristic of monastic life. "'Obedience is the grave of one's own will and the resurrection of humbleness,' says St. John Climacus, "An obedient one, like a dead one, will not contradict or judge either in good things or what may seem evil to him; for the responsibility for everything is borne by the one who piously deadened his soul."[20] If they could truly forsake the cares of this world, they would have time to pray regularly through the day in their cells and during the services, referring to the requests sent in to them by the surrounding parishes and priests. They would gladly begin every day with Matins and end with Vespers and celebrate as many divine services on Sundays and feast days as was possible.

If these things were true of a monastery, then just visiting would expose the believer to the joy, the peace, the quiet of the place, and show the

19. Hilarion, "Importance of Monasticism," 2.
20. Climacus, as cited by Hilarion, "Importance of Monasticism," 2.

way to spiritual growth. So, if you wanted to know about the spiritual life, if you wanted to grow spiritually even while living in the world, then you could spend some time at a monastery like that talking and praying with the monastics.

They Could Teach Us How to Witness

Throughout the history of the Church, successful witness has always been based upon and driven by a spiritual base of power. This power was variously centered in monasteries, the residents of which devoted themselves to ascetic labor of prayer for the salvation of those around them who through prayer and holy living attracted those around them to faith in Christ. Speaking of 14th century revival of hesychast spirituality in Russian monasteries, one author likened their spiritual power to ". . .a magnetic field . . .spiritual energy [which] attracted loose elements and filled the surrounding area with invisible powers" and triggered "one of the most remarkable missionary movements in Christian history."[21]

This close connection between spiritual power and witness is very much in keeping with the way many of us have come to view Evangelism. The basic idea here is that the Gospel is not simply information but is actually the person of Christ. The whole idea is to get people personally connected to Christ and not simply acknowledge the truthfulness of some statement about Christ. If that is the case, then the primary task of the witness is to introduce the person of Christ to others. For that to happen, He has to be present, accessible, or available to us. One of the places that Christ is present in the world today is in the life of the believer. We are repeatedly told that Christ lives in us, that we are the temples of the Holy Spirit, the dwelling place of God. In 1 Cor 3:16, St. Paul asks, "Do you not know that you are the temple of God and that the Spirit of God dwells in you." In a way analogous to the Old Testament passages about the Tabernacle, we find that the individual Christian is both the temple and the altar of divine presence. So, when we ask, "Where is Christ today?," we have to answer that He is in us, the faithful.

St. Paul also takes up the idea that we faithful are a divine building, a temple, (Eph 2:22) "in whom you also are being built together for a dwelling place of God in the Spirit." So, where do you look for the presence of God today? In the lives of Christians. That is where the reality of Christ's person is revealed. How this Christological presence works is evident in the encounter between St. Seraphim of Sarov and the layman Motovilov. After

---

21. Billington, *Icon and the Axe*, 52–53.

failing to get him to understand the ways of acquiring the Holy Spirit, St. Seraphim took him very firmly by the shoulders and said, "'We are both in the Spirit of God now, my son. Why don't you look at me?' I replied: 'I cannot look, Father, because your eyes are flashing like lightning. Your face has become brighter than the sun, and my eyes ache with pain.' Father Seraphim said: 'Don't be alarmed, . . . Now you yourself have become as bright as I am. You are now in the fullness of the Spirit of God yourself; otherwise you would not be able to see me as I am.'"[22]

Now, if what I have been saying about a greater degree of spiritual intensity in monastics is true, then what better place to go looking for Christ? So, if you want to introduce someone to Christ, then bring them to the monastery and let them see Him present and at work in the lives of the monastics. If you want to learn how to help others see Christ in your life, come to the monastery and learn about being filled with the presence of Christ yourself. Remember, in every case, there was recognition of the fact that "those who live always according to the Spirit of Christ are, without the use of words, the best preachers of Christ and the most convincing apostles of Christianity."[23] I think St. Paisios captured these sentiments beautifully:

> Do you realize how destructive [the] secular spirit is? If true spirituality leaves monasticism, there will be nothing left. When salt has lost its taste, it is good for nothing. Garbage will at least turn into fertilizer, but salt will not. If you put it on a plant, it will burn it. Ours is a time when monasticism should shine. It is in these rotten times that we need the "salt." The greatest contribution to society will be made by monasteries that do not have a secular mindset and have reached a spiritual state. Monastics there will not need to say much or do anything else, because they will be able to speak through their way of life. This is what the world needs today.[24]

---

22. "St. Seraphim of Sarov's Conversation with Nicholas Motovilov," para. 2.
23. St. Theophan the Recluse, *Thoughts for Each Day*, 53.
24. Paisios, *With Pain and Love*, 87.

Bibliography

"501(C)(3) Tax Guide for Churches & Religious Organizations." https://www.irs.gov/pub/irs-pdf/p1828.pdf.

"AAC Delegates Pass Funding Resolution." *OCA*, 2018. https://oca.org/news/headline-news/aac-delegates-pass-funding-resolution.

"About Amazonsmile." https://smile.amazon.com/gp/chpf/about/ref=smi_se_rspo_laas_aas.

"About the American Montessori Society." *American Montessori Society*. https://amshq.org/About-AMS.

Afanasiev, Nikolai. *The Lord's Supper*. Translated by Alvian N. Smirensky. Paris: Orthodox Theological Institute, 1952.

Afanasiev, Nikolai, and Michael Plekon. *The Church of the Holy Spirit*. English language ed. Notre Dame: University of Notre Dame Press, 2007.

Ahmed, Usman, and Clam Lorenz. "Understanding the Costs of Charitable Giving." *PayPal*, 2018. https://www.paypalobjects.com/digitalassets/c/website/marketing/global/shared/global/social-innovation/documents/Understanding-the-Costs-of-Charitable-Giving-Final.pdf

Allen, Mike. "Sean Parker Unloads on Facebook: 'God Only Knows What it's Doing to Our Children's Brains.'" *AXIOS*, 2017. https://www.axios.com/sean-parker-unloads-on-facebook-god-only-knows-what-its-doing-to-our-childrens-brains-1513306792-f855e7b4-4e99-4d60-8d51-2775559c2671.html.

Allen, Roland. *The Spontaneous Expansion of the Church and the Causes Which Hinder it*. 1st American ed. Grand Rapids: Eerdmans, 1962.

Allison, Michael, and Jude Kaye. *Strategic Planning for Nonprofit Organizations: A Practical Guide for Dynamic Times*. Hoboken, NJ: Wiley Nonprofit Authority, 2015. Kindle ed.

Alter, Adam L. *Irresistible: The Rise of Addictive Technology and the Business of Keeping Us Hooked*. New York: Penguin, 2017.

Anderson, Benedict Richard O'Gorman. *Imagined Communities: Reflections on the Origin and Spread of Nationalism*. Rev. ed. London: Verso, 2006.

Anderson, James. "Colorado Baker Who Refused to Make Cake for Gay Couple Won't Create One for Gender Transition." *The Chicago Tribune*, 2018. http://www.chicagotribune.com/news/nationworld/ct-colorado-baker-gender-transition-cake-20180815-story.html.

Andrews, Evan. "10 Things You May Not Know about the Byzantine Empire." *History. com*, 2016. https://www.history.com/news/10-things-you-may-not-know-about-the-byzantine-empire.

Appleby, Joyce. *The Relentless Revolution: A History of Capitalism.* 1st ed. New York: W. W. Norton, 2010.

Athanasius. *On the Incarnation of the Word.* Translated by Archibald Robertson. London: David Nutt, 1893.

"Background Check." https://www.definitions.net/definition/background%20check.

Barna, George. *Marketing the Church.* Colorado Springs: NavPress, 1988.

Barthes, Roland. *Mythologies.* New York: Hill and Wang, 1972.

Bartlett, Bruce. *The Truth Matters: A Citizen's Guide to Separating Facts from Lies and Stopping Fake News in its Tracks.* Berkeley, CA: Ten Speed, 2017.

Basil the Great. *Letter VII.* http://www.ccel.org/ccel/schaff/npnf208.ix.viii.html.

Bea, David L. "Should Churches Incorporate and Seek Confirmation of Tax Exempt Status from the IRS?" *Bea and VandenBerk*, 2010. https://www.beavandenberk.com/nonprofits/churches-religious/should-churches-incorporate-and-seek-confirmation-of-tax-exempt-status-from-the-irs/.

Benedict XVI. "New Technologies, New Relationships: Promoting a Culture of Respect, Dialogue and Friendship." (2009). http://w2.vatican.va/content/benedict-xvi/en/messages/communications/documents/hf_ben-xvi_mes_20090124_43rd-world-communications-day.html.

Beniger, James R. *The Control Revolution: Technological and Economic Origins of the Information Society.* Cambridge, MA: Harvard University Press, 1986.

Berger, Arthur Asa. *Ads, Fads, and Consumer Culture: Advertising's Impact on American Character and Society.* Fifth edition. ed. Lanham, MD: Rowman & Littlefield, 2015.

Berman, Morris. *Why America Failed: The Roots of Imperial Decline.* Hoboken, NJ: Wiley & Sons, 2012.

Billington, James H. *The Icon and the Axe: An Interpretive History of Russian Culture.* New York: Vintage, 1970.

Bishop, Joseph. "Beloved in Christ." https://www.cgsusa.org/wp-content/uploads/Metr_-Joseph-Endorsement.pdf.

Blanchard, Kenneth H., and Dan Woren. *The New One Minute Manager.* New York: HarperAudio, 2015.

Blimey Cow. "How to Get Millennials Back in Church." *YouTube*, 2015. Video. 4:56. https://www.youtube.com/watch?v=8np8AN3dkSY.

"Boot Camp." *Orthodox Church in America*, 2018. https://goodnews.oca.org/boot-camp/.

Borgmann, Albert. *Technology and the Character of Contemporary Life: A Philosophical Inquiry.* Chicago: University of Chicago Press, 1984.

Brooks, David. *The Road to Character.* New York: Random House, 2015. Kindle.

Brunson, Russell. *Expert Secrets: The Underground Playbook for Creating a Mass Movement of People Who Will Pay for Your Advice.* New York: Morgan James, 2017.

Bulgakov, Sergei Nikolaevich. *The Bride of the Lamb.* Grand Rapids: Eerdmans, 2002.

Bushman, Richard L. *From Puritan to Yankee; Character and the Social Order in Connecticut, 1690–1765.* A Publication of the Center for the Study of the History of Liberty in America, Harvard University. Cambridge, MA: Harvard University Press, 1967.

Butler, Judith, et al. *The Power of Religion in the Public Sphere*. New York: Columbia University Press, 2011.

Cahill, P. Joseph. "Theological Education: Its Fragmentation and Unity." *Theological Studies* 45 (1984) 334–42.

Callero, Peter L. *The Myth of Individualism: How Social Forces Shape Our Lives*. Lanham, MD: Rowman & Littlefield, 2009.

"Capital Campaigns: The Groundbreaking Guide." *Double the Donation*, 2018. https://doublethedonation.com/capital-campaigns/.

"Catechesis of the Good Shepherd." *National Association of the Catechesis of the Good Shepherd*, 2018. http://www.cgsusa.org/about/history.aspx.

Catholic Church, et al. *The Code of Canon Law, in English Translation*. London: Collins, 1983.

Cavalletti, Sofia. *The Good Shepherd and the Child: A Joyful Journey. Revised and Updated*. Chicago: Liturgy Training, 2014.

"CGS in the Orthodox Tradition." *National Association of the Catechesis of the Good Shepherd*, 2020. https://www.cgsusa.org/discover/cgs-and-ecumenism/cgs-in-the-orthodox-tradition/.

Chitty, Derwas J. *The Desert a City: An Introduction to the Study of Egyptian and Palestinian Monasticism under the Christian Empire*. Crestwood, NY: St. Vladimir's Seminary Press, 1995.

Chryssavgis, John. *Light through Darkness: The Orthodox Tradition*. Traditions of Christian Spirituality Series. Maryknoll, NY: Orbis, 2004.

Clifton, Jim, and Sangeeta Bharadwaj Badal. *Entrepreneurial Strengths Finder*. New York: Gallup, 2014.

"Code of Canon Law." *The Vatican*, 2018. http://www.vatican.va/archive/ENG1104/_P1V.HTM.

"Common Sense Media's Mission." https://www.orange.k12.nj.us/domain/2302.

Coniaris, Anthony M. *My Daily Orthodox Prayer Book: Classic Orthodox Prayers for Every Need*. Minneapolis, MN: Light & Life, 2001.

Conniry, Charles J. "Reducing the Identity Crisis in Doctor of Ministry Education." http://citeseerx.ist.psu.edu/viewdoc/download?doi=10.1.1.855.7758&rep=rep1&type=pdf.

Coolidge, Calvin. "Address to the American Society of Newspaper Editors, Washington, D.C." *The American Presidency Project*, 1925. https://www.presidency.ucsb.edu/node/269410.

Cooperman, Alan. "Accusations of Misused Money Roil Orthodox Church." *Washington Post*, February 25, 2006. https://www.washingtonpost.com/wp-dyn/content/article/2006/02/25/AR2006022501266.html.

"A Cost-Benefit Analysis of Nonprofit Fundraising Software." http://webserves.org/a-cost-benefit-analysis-of-nonprofit-fundraising-software/.

"Council Minutes: The 19th All-American Council." *Orthodox Church in America*, 2018. http://files.oca.org/aacs/19thaac-minutes.pdf.

"Covid-19 Digital Toolkit for Parishes." *Greek Archdiocese of America*, 2020. https://www.goarch.org/-/covid19-parish-toolkit.

Orthodox Eastern Church, and Denver Cummings. *The Rudder (Pedalion) of the Metaphorical Ship of the One Holy Catholic and Apostolic Church of Orthodox Christians or, All the Sacred and Divine Canons . . . As Embodied in the Original Greek Text*. Chicago: Orthodox Christian Educational Society, 1957.

Danilchick, Peter M. *Thy Will Be Done: Strategic Leadership, Planning, and Management for Christians.* Crestwood, NY: St. Vladimir's Seminary Press, 2016. Kindle.
Dawson, Lorne L., and Douglas E. Cowan. *Religion Online: Finding Faith on the Internet.* New York: Routledge, 2013. Kindle.
Debord, Guy. *The Society of the Spectacle.* Sussex: Soul Bay, 2009. Kindle.
"Declaration of the Rights of Man—1789." *Yale Law School.* http://avalon.law.yale.edu/18th_century/rightsof.asp.
de Crèvecoeur, J. Hector St. John "What is an American?" In *Individualism: A Reader,* edited by George H. Smith and Marilyn Moore, locs. 934–56. Washington, DC: Cato Institute, 2015. Kindle.
Denysenko, Nicholas. *Theology and Form: Contemporary Orthodox Architecture in America.* Notre Dame: University of Notre Dame Press, 2017.
de Tocqueville, Alexis. "Democracy in America." http://oll.libertyfund.org/titles/tocqueville-democracy-in-america-historical-critical-edition-vol-4#Tocqueville_1532-04_EN_1034.
Dionysius The Areopagite. "Mystical Theology." https://www.ccel.org/ccel/rolt/dionysius.v.html.
Dix, Gregory. *The Shape of the Liturgy.* New ed. London: Continuum, 2005.
Dostoyevsky, Fyodor. *Notes from the Underground.* New York: Dover, 1992.
"Electronic Banking." *Federal Trade Commission,* 2012. https://www.consumer.ftc.gov/articles/pdf-0109-electronic-banking.pdf.
Ellas, John W. *Measuring Church Growth. A Research-Based Tool for Evaluating and Planning.* Houston: Center for Church Growth, 1997.
Elpidophoros. "A Different Communion in 2020." *Greek Orthodox Archdiocese of America,* 2020. https://www.goarch.org/-/archbishop-elpidophoros-communion-2020?inheritRedirect=true.
Emerson, Ralph Waldo. *The Essay on Self-Reliance.* New York: The Roycroft Shop, 1905.
"Employment and Unemployment Rates by Educational Attainment." *National Center for Education Statistics.* https://nces.ed.gov/programs/coe/indicator_cbc.asp.
"English Bill of Rights 1689." *Yale Law School.* http://avalon.law.yale.edu/17th_century/england.asp.
Farley, Edward. *Theologia: The Fragmentation and Unity of Theological Education.* Eugene, OR: Wipf and Stock, 2001.
Fischer, Steven R. *A History of Writing.* London: Reaktion, 2011. Kindle.
Florensky, Pavel. *Pillar and Ground of Truth.* Princeton: Princeton University Press, 1997.
Ford, Mary. "Catechesis of the Good Shepherd: An Approach to Religious Formation for Children, Integrating the Heart, Mind, and Hand." https://www.cgsusa.org/wp-content/uploads/MCF-Key-points-of-CGS-DCF-2-15-17.pdf.
Forni, Pier Massimo. *Choosing Civility: The Twenty-Five Rules of Considerate Conduct.* 1st ed. New York: St. Martin's, 2010. Kindle.
Foucault, Michel. "The Political Function of the Intellectual." *Radical Philosophy* 17 (1977) 12–14.
Friedman, Thomas L. *The Lexus and the Olive Tree.* Rev. ed. New York: Farrar, Straus, Giroux, 2000. Kindle.
"Fr Noah's Suggested Reading List." https://www.st-philip.net/reading.
Galloway, Scott. *The Four: The Hidden DNA of Amazon, Apple, Facebook, and Google.* New York: Portfolio, 2017.

Gardner, David, et al. *The Motley Fool Million-Dollar Portfolio: The Complete Investment Strategy that Beat the Market*. New York: HarperAudio, 2009.
Gay, Peter. *The Enlightenment: An Interpretation*. 2 vols. New York: Norton, 1977.
"Geschichte Der Hochschule." *Theologische Hochschule Ewersbach*, 2018. http://www.th-ewersbach.de/die-hochschule/geschichte/.
Gibbs, David. "5 Questions on Church Incorporation." *9Marks* (2016). https://www.9marks.org/article/5-questions-on-church-incorporation/.
Gladwell, Malcolm. *The Tipping Point*. New York: Little, Brown, 2000.
Gleick, James. *Chaos: Making a New Science*. New York" Viking, 1987.
"GPS: God's Plan for St. John the Divine Greek Orthodox Church." http://stjohnthedivinejax.org/wp-content/uploads/2015/09/Strategic-Plan-of-St.-John-the-Divine-Jacksonville-FL.pdf.
Graves, Lucas. *Deciding What's True: The Rise of Political Fact-Checking in American Journalism*. New York: Columbia University Press, 2016.
Green, Michael. *Evangelism in the Early Church*. Grand Rapids: Eerdmans, 2004. Kindle.
Gripsrud, Jostein, and Martin Eide. *The Idea of the Public Sphere: A Reader*. Lanham, MD: Lexington, 2010. Kindle.
"Guidelines for Clergy Compiled under the Guidance of the Holy Synod of the Orthodox Church in America." https://oca.org/PDF/official/clergyguidelines.pdf.
"Guidelines for Clergy Use of Online Social Networking." https://www.oca.org/holy-synod/statements/holy-synod/guidelines-for-clergy-use-of-online-social-networking.
"Guidelines on Background Checks." *Orthodox Church in America*, 2017. https://oca.org/PDF/sexual-misconduct/2017-0314-hs-guidelines-background-check.pdf.
Guinness, Os. *The Global Public Square: Religious Freedom and the Making of a World Safe for Diversity*. Downers Grove, IL: InterVarsity, 2013.
Habermas, Jürgen. *Between Facts and Norms: Contributions to a Discourse Theory of Law and Democracy*. Studies in Contemporary German Social Thought. Cambridge, MA: Massachusetts Institute of Technology Press, 1996.
———. "Political Communication in Media Society: Does Democracy Still Enjoy an Epistemic Dimension? The Impact of Normative Theory on Empirical Research." *Communication Theory* 16 (2006) 411–26.
———. *The Structural Transformation of the Public Sphere: An Inquiry into a Category of Bourgeois Society*. Studies in Contemporary German Social Thought. Cambridge, MA: Massachusetts Institute of Technology Press, 1989.
———. *Theory and Practice*. Boston: Beacon, 2015. Kindle.
Hafiz, Yasmine. "Sex Abuse Cost the U.S. Catholic Church Nearly $3 Billion According to Report by Bishops Conference." *Huffpost*, 2017. https://www.huffingtonpost.com/2014/04/04/sex-abuse-catholic-church_n_5085414.html.
Harakas, Stanley S. "The Stand of the Orthodox Church on Controversial Issues." https://www.goarch.org/-/the-stand-of-the-orthodox-church-on-controversial-issues.
Hau, Wingfield. "The World's Most Expensive Universities." *Forbes* (2008). https://www.forbes.com/2008/01/21/education-university-globalization-biz-cx_bw_lh_0121colleges.html#533559893ab8.
Hauptli, Bruce W. "The Enlightenment Project." http://faculty.fiu.edu/~hauptli/TheEnlightenmentProjectLectureSupplement.html.

Hayek, Friedrich A. *Individualism and Economic Order.* Chicago: University of Chircago, 1948.
Helberger, Natali. *Digital Consumers and the Law: Towards a Cohesive European Framework.* Frederick, MD: Kluwer Law International, 2013. Kindle.
Hilarion. "Importance of Monasticism for Orthodoxy Today." *Russian Orthodox Church*, 2010. https://mospat.ru/en/2010/11/19/news30796/.
"History of the Catechesis of the Good Shepherd." *National Association of the Catechesis of the Good Shepherd*, 2020. https://www.cgsusa.org/discover/the-cgs-method-past/history/.
Hobbes, Thomas, and Richard Tuck. *Leviathan.* Rev. student ed. Cambridge: Cambridge University Press, 2017. Kindle.
Holyoake, George Jacob. "Free Thought—Its Conditions, Agreements, and Secular Results." In *Individualism: A Reader*, edited by George H. Smith and Marilyn Moore, locs. 2225–2304. Washington, DC: Cato Institute, 2015. Kindle.
Holy Synod of Bishops of the Orthodox Church in America. "Policies, Standards, and Procedures on Sexual Misconduct." (2014). https://oca.org/PDF/sexual-misconduct/2014-04-PSP-Sexual-Misconduct.pdf.
———. "Resources for the Prevention of Sexual Misconduct." (2018). https://oca.org/about/sexual-misconduct.
Holy Synod of the Orthodox Church in America. "Guidelines on Background Checks." (2017). https://oca.org/PDF/sexual-misconduct/2017-0314-hs-guidelines-background-check.pdf.
"How Did Universities Develop?" https://dailyhistory.org/How_did_universities_develop%3F#cite_note-10.
"How Do You Define Politics?" *Quora*, 2018. https://www.quora.com/How-do-you-define-politics.
"How Tech is Changing Childhood." https://www.commonsense.org/our-impact.
Ignatius of Antioch. "The Epistle of Ignatius to the Ephesians." https://www.newadvent.org/fathers/0104.htm.
———. "The Epistle to the Smyrnaeans." https://www.newadvent.org/fathers/0109.htm.
Illing, Sean. "Cambridge Analytica, the Shady Data Firm that Might Be a Key Trump-Russia Link, Explained." *VOX*, 2018. https://www.vox.com/policy-and-politics/2017/10/16/15657512/cambridge-analytica-facebook-alexander-nix-christopher-wylie.
Ingersoll, Robert G. "Individuality." In *Individualism: A Reader*, edited by George H. Smith and Marilyn Moore, locs. 2307–87. Washington, DC: Cato Institute, 2015. Kindle.
"Introduction to Montessori Method." *American Montessori Society*, 2018. https://www.theivyschool.org/about-ivy/curriculum-2/what-is-montessori-2/montessori-method/.
Jamieson, Robert, et al. *A Commentary, Critical and Explanatory, on the Old and New Testaments.* Hartford, CT: S. S. Scranton, 1877.
John of Damascus. "An Exact Exposition of the Orthodox Faith." https://ccel.org/ccel/schaff/npnf209/npnf209.iii.i.html.
Kampouris, Nick. "Ecumenical Patriarch Announces Halt to All Orthodox Church Services Globally Due to Coronavirus." *Greek Reporter*, 2020. https://

eu.greekreporter.com/2020/03/18/ecumenical-patriarch-announces-halt-to-all-orthodox-church-services-globally-due-to-coronavirus/.

Kant, Immanuel, and Ted Humphrey. *Perpetual Peace, and Other Essays on Politics, History, and Morals.* HPC Philosophical Classics Series. Indianapolis: Hackett, 1983.

Kavanagh, Aiden. *Elements of Rite: A Handbook of Liturgical Style.* New York: Pueblo, 1966.

Kellner, Douglas. "Introduction to the Second Edition." In *One-Dimensional Man: Studies in the Ideology of Advanced Industrial Society,* by Herbert Marcuse, locs. 57–475. New York: Routledge, 2013. Kindle.

Kelsey, David H. *Between Athens and Berlin: The Theological Education Debate.* Grand Rapids: Eerdmans, 1993.

Kenneson, Philip D., and James L. Street. *Selling Out the Church: The Dangers of Church Marketing.* Nashville: Abingdon, 1997.

Kern, Heinrich. "Humboldt's Educational Ideal and Modern Academic Education." http://www.drc.uns.ac.rs/presentations/05_DS/03-Prof.Dr.HeinrichKern.pdf.

Kittel, Gerhard, et al. *Theological Dictionary of the New Testament.* 10 vols. Grand Rapids: Eerdmans, 1985.

Kokkinidis, Tasos. "Greece Overrules Church, Orders Suspension of All Services to Battle Coronavirus." *Greek Reporter,* 2020. https://greece.greekreporter.com/2020/03/17/greece-overrules-church-orders-suspension-of-all-services-to-battle-coronavirus/.

———."Greek Faithful Defy Coronovirus Scare to Attend Church Services." *Greek Reporter,* 2020. https://greece.greekreporter.com/2020/03/15/greek-faithful-defy-coronovirus-scare-to-attend-church-services/.

Lacy, Bridgette A. "Teach the People." *Divinity* 17.2 (Spring 2018) 22–25.

Lautenbach, Geranne. *The Concept of the Rule of Law and the European Court of Human Rights.* 1st ed. Oxford: Oxford University Press, 2013.

Leach, William. *Land of Desire: Merchants, Power, and the Rise of a New American Culture.* 1st ed. New York: Vintage, 2011. Kindle.

"Learn More about Gift Card Fundraising." https://www.shopwithscrip.com/learnmore.

Lee, Dave. "Facebook Founding President Sounds Alarm." *BBC,* 2017. https://www.bbc.com/news/technology-41936791.

Lerins, St. Vincent. "Commonitory." New Advent, https://www.newadvent.org/fathers/3506.htm.

Lin, Ruoyun, et al. "Ambient Intimacy on Twitter." *Cyberpsychology* 10.1 (2016), article 6. https://cyberpsychology.eu/article/view/6186/5916.

Little, Paul. *Witnessing: How to Give Away Your Faith.* Downers Grove, IL: Intervarsity, 2014. Kindle.

"Lobbying Spending Database." *Open Secrets,* 2018. https://www.opensecrets.org/lobby/clientsum.php?id=D000023726.

Locke, John, and C. B. Macpherson. *Second Treatise of Government.* 1st ed. Indianapolis: Hackett, 2011. Kindle.

Lossky, Vladimir. *In the Image and Likeness of God.* London: Mowbrays, 1975.

———. *Orthodox Theology: An Introduction.* Crestwood, NY: St. Vladimir's Seminary Press, 1978.

Lucas, Phillip Charles. *The Odyssey of a New Religion: The Holy Order of MANS from New Age to Orthodoxy*. Bloomington: Indiana University Press, 1995.

Lyotard, Jean-François. *The Postmodern Condition: A Report on Knowledge*. Theory and History of Literature. Minneapolis: University of Minnesota Press, 1984.

Mahaffey, David. "Endorsement Letter." https://www.cgsusa.org/wp-content/uploads/Bishop-David.pdf.

Malphurs, Aubery. *Advanced Strategic Planning: A 21st-Century Model for Church and Ministry Leaders*. Grand Rapids: Baker, 2013. Kindle.

Marcuse, Herbert. *One-Dimensional Man: Studies in the Ideology of Advanced Industrial Society* New York: Routledge, 2002. Kindle.

Marianes, Bill. "Igniting the Flame of True Orthodox Christian Stewardship." http://stewardshipcalling.com/wp-content/uploads/2014/01/Part-7-2014-Igniting-the-Flame-of-True-Orthdodox-Christian-Stewardship.pdf.

———. "It's Not about Me." https://stewardshipcalling.com/its-not-about-me/.

Martin, Areva. "Why Your Brand Plan is More Important than Your Business Plan." *Entrepreneur*, 2018. https://www.entrepreneur.com/article/309188.

Martin, Roger L. "The Big Lie of Strategic Planning." *Harvard Business Review* (January-February 2014). https://hbr.org/2014/01/the-big-lie-of-strategic-planning.

Marvin, Ginny. "Google Marketing Live: Here Come Fully Automated Ads & Campaigns for Local, Shopping & More." *Search Engine Land*, 2008. https://searchengineland.com/google-marketing-live-here-come-fully-automated-ads-campaigns-for-local-shopping-more-301746.

Matz, Sandra, et al. "Psychological Targeting as an Effective Approach to Digital Mass Persuasion." *Proceedings of the National Academy of Sciences* 114.48 (November 28, 2017) 12714–19.

McDougall, Walter A. *Freedom Just around the Corner: A New American History, 1585–1828*. 1st ed. New York: HarperCollins, 2004.

McLuhan, Marshall. *Understanding Media: The Extensions of Man*. 1st ed. New York: McGraw-Hill, 1964.

McNamee, Roger. *Zucked: Waking up to the Facebook Catastrophe*. New York: Penguin, 2019. Kindle.

"Metanarrative." *New World Encyclopedia*, 2018. http://www.newworldencyclopedia.org/entry/Metanarrative#Credits.

Metaxas, Eric. *Seven Men: And the Secret of Their Greatness*. Nashville: Thomas Nelson, 2013.

Mill, John Stuart. "Of Individuality as One of the Elements of Well-Being." In *Individualism: A Reader*, edited by George H. Smith and Marilyn Moore, locs. 516–838. Washington, DC: Cato Institute, 2015.

Miller, Stephen. *Conversation: A History of a Declining Art*. New Haven: Yale University Press, 2006.

"Minutes of the Joint Meeting of the Lesser Synod and the 2012 Spring Session of the Metropolitan Council." *Orthodox Church in America*. https://oca.org/cdn/PDFs/metropolitancouncil/2012/spring-metcouncil/spring12mcdraftminutes.pdf.

"Mission and Vision Statements." *Holy Cross Hellenic College*, 2018. http://www.hchc.edu/about/.

Mitilinaios, Athanasios. *Revelation: The Seven Lampstands*. Orthodox Christian Lessons 1. Dunlap. CA: Zoe, 2016.

———. *Revelation: The Seven Seals.* Orthodox Christian Lessons 2. Dunlap, CA: Zoe, 2014.

"Montessori Philosophy." *Montessori School of Shanghai*, 2018, http://www.montessorisos.com/montessori-philosophy.

Mooney, Sue. "Nurturing Spirituality in a Montessori Classroom." *Gladwyne Montessori*, 2019. https://www.gladwyne.org/about/why/posts/~board/did-you-know/post/nurturing-spirituality-in-a-montessori-classroom.

Morgan, Edmund S. *Inventing the People: The Rise of Popular Sovereignty in England and America.* 1st ed. New York: Norton, 2013. Kindle.

Muller, Steven. "Wilhelm von Humboldt and the University in the United States." *Johns Hopkins APL Technical Digest* 6.3 (1985) 253–56.

"Multiculturalism." https://www.canada.ca/en/services/culture/canadian-identity-society/multiculturalism.html.

Neal, Gregory S. "Holy Communion over the Internet: Reflections on an Experiment in Sacramental Practice." http://www.revneal.org/Neal%20-%20Online%20Communion%20Experiment.pdf.

Negroponte, Nicholas. *Being Digital.* 1st ed. New York: Knopf, 1995.

Nicholas, David. *The Evolution of the Medieval World: Society, Government, and Thought in Europe, 312–1500.* London: Longman, 1992.

Nichols, Thomas M. *The Death of Expertise: The Campaign against Established Knowledge and Why it Matters.* New York: Oxford University Press, 2017.

Nicodemus, Makarios, et al. *The Philokalia: The Complete Text.* 4 vols. London: Faber and Faber, 1979.

Nye, David E. *Technology Matters: Questions to Live With.* Cambridge: Massachusetts Institute of Technology Press, 2006.

"OCA Strategic Planning Committee Holds First Meeting." *OCA News.* https://oca.org/news/archived/oca-strategic-planning-committee-holds-first-meeting.

"OCMC Seeks Development and Marketing Administrative Assistant." OCA, 2018. https://oca.org/news/headline-news/ocmc-seeks-development-and-marketing-administrative-assistant.

Oden, Thomas C. *Ancient Christian Commentary on Scripture. New Testament.* 12 vols. Chicago: Dearborn, 1998.

Ong, Walter J. *Orality and Literacy: The Technologizing of the Word.* New York: Routledge, 2002. Kindle.

Osteen, Joel. *Become a Better You: 7 Keys to Improving Your Life Every Day.* 10th anniversary edition, Howard trade paperback edition. ed. New York: Howard, 2017.

Osuagwu, Nnamdi Godson. *Facebook Addiction: The Life & Times of Social Networking Addicts.* New York: Ice Cream Melts, 2010. Kindle.

"Our History." https://www.svots.edu/our-history.

"Our Mission." https://www.commonsensemedia.org/about-us/our-mission.

"Our Mission, Vision, & Values." *St. Vladimir's Theological Seminary*, 2018. https://www.svots.edu/about/mission.

Overton, Richard. "An Arrow against All Tyrants." In *Individualism: A Reader*, edited by George H. Smith and Marilyn Moore, locs. 1209–62. Washington, DC: Cato Institute, 2015. Kindle.

Packard, Vance. *The Hidden Persuaders.* Rev. ed. New York: Pocket, 1980.

Paez, Andre. "Planting Grant Missions: Digital Tools for the 'Modern Fishermen.'" https://www.svots.edu/voices/alumni/planting-grant-missions-digital-tools-modern-fishermen.
Paine, Thomas. *Common Sense*. Radford, VA: Wilder, 2007. Kindle.
Paisios, Elder. *With Pain and Love for Contemporary Man*. Vol. 1. 5 vols. Translated by Cornelia A. Tskiridou and Maria Spanou. Saint Paisios of Mount Athos Spiritual Counsels. Edited by Peter Chamberas and Eleftheria Kaimakliotis. Thessaloniki: Holy Hesychasterion Evangelist John the Theologian, 2016.
Pannenberg, Wolfhart. *Theology and the Philosophy of Science*. Philadelphia: Westminster, 1976.
Pariser, Eli. *The Filter Bubble: What the Internet is Hiding from You*. New York: Penguin, 2011. Kindle.
Passwaiter, Steve. "2018 Campaign Ad Spend Will Be in the Billions." *Cook Political Report*, 2018. https://www.cookpolitical.com/analysis/national/political-advertising/2018-campaign-ad-spend-will-be-billions.
Pennington, Basil. "Preface." In *The Desert Fathers: Translations from the Latin*, edited by Helen Waddell, xiii–xxiii. Vintage Spiritual Classics. 1st ed. New York: Vintage, 1998.
"Plans and Pricing." *easyTithe*, 2018. https://www.easytithe.com/pricing.htm.
"Political." *Collins English Dictionary*, 2018. https://www.collinsdictionary.com/us/dictionary/english/political.
"Politics." *Cambridge Dictionary*, 2018. https://dictionary.cambridge.org/us/dictionary/english/politics.
"Politics." *Wordnik*, 2018. https://www.wordnik.com/words/politics.
Porphyrios, Elder. *Wounded by Love: The Life and Wisdom of Saint Porphyrios*. Edited by Sisters of the Holy Convent of Chrysopigi. Evia, Greece: Denise Harvey, 2005.
"Post-Gospel Stichera Entrance of the Theotokos into the Temple—November 21." *Orthodox Church in America*. https://oca.org/PDF/Music/MajorFeasts/TheotokosTemple/11.21.post-gospel.common.pdf.
Postman, Neil. *Amusing Ourselves to Death: Public Discourse in the Age of Show Business*. New York: Penguin, 1986.
———. *Technopoly: The Surrender of Culture to Technology*. New York: Knopf, 1992.
Powerpoint Presentations, 16th All-American Council. Syosset, NY: Orthodox Church in America, 2011.
"Preface to the Standards of Accreditation." https://www.ats.edu/uploads/accrediting/documents/preface-to-the-standards-of-accreditation.pdf.
Price, Rob. "Apple CEO Tim Cook: I Don't Want My Nephew on a Social Network." *Business Insider*, 2017. http://www.businessinsider.com/apple-ceo-tim-cook-doesnt-let-nephew-use-social-media-2018-1.
———. "George Soros Calls Facebook and Google a 'Menace' to Society and 'Obstacles to Innovation' in Blistering Attack." *Business Insider*, 2018. http://www.businessinsider.com/george-soros-calls-facebook-google-menace-society-obstacles-innovation-2018-1.
Prigogine, Ilya, and John Holte. *Chaos: The New Science: Nobel Conference Xxvi*. St. Peter, MN: Gustavus Adolphus College Press, 1993.
"The Process of Developing Immediate and Long-Term Outcomes for Strategic Planning." *Universal Class*, 2020. https://www.universalclass.com/articles/

business/the-process-of-developing-immediate-and-long-term-outcomes-for-strategic-planning.htm.
"Promoting Hellenism." *American Hellenic Educational Progressive Association*, 2019. https://ahepa.org.
"Pros and Cons of Online Education." *NC State*, August 19, 2015. https://www.ies.ncsu.edu/resources/white-papers/pros-and-cons-of-online-education/.
Purnell, Timothy J. "AMA Seeks Assistant Manager of Membership." https://amshq.org/Educators/Community/Announcements/All-Announcements/1010-AMS-Seeks-Assistant-Manager-of-Membership.
Rath, Tom. *Strengths Finder 2.0*. New York: Gallop, 2007.
Raz, Joseph. "Multiculturalism." *Ratio Juris* 11.3 (1998) 193–205.
Readings, Lea. "Online Giving for Churches: 5 Donation Tools to Grow Your Contributions." *Capterra*, 2018. https://blog.capterra.com/online-giving-churches-donation-tools/.
"Realm Church Management Software." https://www.acstechnologies.com/realm/.
Reichelt, Leisa. "Ambient Intimacy." *Disambiguity*, 2007. http://www.disambiguity.com/ambient-intimacy/.
Reising, Richard. *Church Marketing 101: Preparing Your Church for Greater Growth*. Grand Rapids: Baker, 2006. Kindle.
"Religious Landscape Survey." *Pew Research Center*, 2018. http://www.pewforum.org/religious-landscape-study/religious-tradition/orthodox-christian/.
Rigby, Darrell K. *Management Tools 2015. An Executive's Guide*. Boston: Bain & Company, 2015.
———. "Management Tools." http://www.bain.com/publications/articles/management-tools-strategic-planning.aspx.
Rigby, Darrell K., and Barbara Bilodeau. "Management Tools & Trends." http://www.bain.com/publications/articles/management-tools-and-trends-2017.aspx.
Robbins, Anthony. *Money: Master the Game: 7 Simple Steps to Financial Freedom*. New York: Simon & Schuster, 2014.
Robert, Henry M., et al. *Robert's Rules of Order, Newly Revised*. Philadelphia: Da Capo, 2011.
Robichau, Bernard Peter. "Author, Speaker, Consultant. Peter Robischau." https://robichau.com.
———. "Building a Startup?—Be Prepared to Get Dirty." https://www.robichau.com/building-a-startup-be-prepared-to-get-dirty/.
———. *Stop Climbing that Ladder and Build Your Own! Leverage Your Skills, Excel Professionally, and Love What You Do*. Wilmington, DE: Category 3, 2015. Kindle.
Rodopoulos, Panteleimon. *An Overview of Orthodox Canon Law*. Rollinsford, NH: Orthodox Research Institute, 2007.
Rogers, James R. "The Meaning of 'the Pursuit of Happiness.'" *First Things* (2012). https://www.firstthings.com/web-exclusives/2012/06/the-meaning-of-the-pursuit-of-happiness.
Rommen, Edward. *Being the Church: An Eastern Orthodox Understanding of Church Growth*. Eugene, OR: Cascade, 2017.
Rosen, Christine. "Virtual Friendship and the New Narcissism." *New Atlantis* (Summer 2007) 15–31. http://www.thenewatlantis.com/publications/virtual-friendship-and-the-new-narcissism.

Rousseau, Jean-Jacques. *Essay on the Origin of Writing*. Translated by John Moran. New York: Frederick Ungar, 1966.
Ruoyun Lin, et al. "Ambient Intimacy on Twitter." *Cyberpsychology* 10.1 (2016) 1–16. https://cyberpsychology.eu/article/view/6186/5916.
Russkaiā pravoslavnaiā tserkov'. *The Great Book of Needs: Expanded and Supplemented*. 4 vols. South Canaan, PA: St. Tikhon's Seminary Press, 1998.
Scharrer, Lisa, et al. "When Science Becomes Too Easy: Science Popularization Inclines Laypeople to Underrate Their Dependence on Experts." *Sage* 26.8 (2017) 1003–18. https://doi.org/10.1177/0963662516680311.
Schmemann, Alexander. "Confession and Communion." https://www.schmemann.org/byhim/confessionandcommunion.html.
———. *The Eucharist—Sacrament of the Kingdom*. Crestwood, NY: St. Vladimir's Seminary Press, 1987.
Schmemann, Aleksandr. *For the Life of the World: Sacraments and Orthodoxy*. 2nd rev. and expanded ed. Crestwood, NY: St. Vladimir's Seminary Press, 1973.
Scholz, Heinrich. *Schleiermachers Kurze Darstellung Des Theologischen Studiums*. Leipzig: A. Deichert'sche Verlagsbuchhandlung, 1935.
Schwarz, Christian A. *The ABC's of Natural Church Development*. St. Charles, IL: Churchsmart, 2001.
Scouteris, Constantine B., and Christopher Veniamin. *Ecclesial Being: Contributions to Theological Dialogue*. South Canaan, PA: Mount Tabor, 2005.
Searle, John R. *The Construction of Social Reality*. New York: Free Press, 2010. Kindle.
"Secure Online Giving at St. Basil." http://wilmingtonoca.org/author/admin.
Self-Study Handbook. The Association of Theological Schools. The Commission on Accrediting, 2020. https://www.ats.edu/uploads/accrediting/documents/self-study-handbook.pdf.
Senge, Peter. *The Fifth Discipline*. New York: Doubleday, 1990.
Shapiro, Ian, et al., eds. *Political Representation*. Cambridge: Cambridge University Press, 2009.
Simerick, Michael. "A New Era of Evangelistic Fervor." *Orthodox Church in America*, 2002. https://oca.org/parish-ministry/witnessmission/a-new-era-of-evangelistic-fervor.
Simkovic, Michael. "A Value Added Perspective on Higher Education." *UC Irvine Law Review* 7.1 (2017) article 6. https://scholarship.law.uci.edu/ucilr/vol7/iss1/6/.
Smith, George H. "Introduction." In *Individualism: A Reader*, edited by George H. Smith and Marilyn Moore, locs. 60–401. Washington, DC: Cato Institute, 2015. Kindle.
Smith, George H., and Marilyn Moore. *Individualism: A Reader*. Washington, DC: Cato Institute, 2015. Kindle.
Smith, Marc A., and Peter Kollock. *Communities in Cyberspace*. New York: Routledge, 1999.
"Speech Circuit." http://www.oxfordreference.com/view/10.1093/oi/authority.20110803100522510.
Spooner, Lysander. "Vices are Not Crimes: A Vindication of Moral Liberty." In *Individualism: A Reader*, edited by George H. Smith and Marilyn Moore, locs. 1340–99. Washington, DC: Cato Institute, 2015. Kindle.

Stambor, Zak "Google Doubles Down on Shopping Ads." *Digital Commerce 360*, 2018. https://www.digitalcommerce360.com/2018/07/10/google-doubles-down-on-shopping-ads/.

"Standards and Notations." *ATS*, 2018. http://www.ats.edu/accrediting/standards-and-notations.

"Standards of Accreditation." https://www.ats.edu/uploads/accrediting/documents/standards-of-accreditation-161130.pdf.

Stăniloae, Dumitru, et al. *The Experience of God*. Brookline, MA: Holy Cross Orthodox Press, 1994.

———. *Orthodox Spirituality: A Practical Guide for the Faithful and a Definitive Manual for the Scholar*. South Canaan, PA: St. Tikhon's Seminary Press, 2002.

Stark, Rodney, and William Sims Bainbridge. *The Future of Religion: Secularization, Revival, and Cult Formation*. Berkeley: University of California Press, 1985.

"The Statute of the Orthodox Church in America." *Orthodox Church in America*, 2015. https://oca.org/statute/article-xi.

"Strategic Management—History and Development." http://vijaykumarbhatia.weebly.com/strategic-management-history-and-development.html.

"Strategic Plan for the Greek Orthodox Metropolis of Atlanta." https://d2y1pz2y630308.cloudfront.net/12343/documents/2019/5/FINAL-STRATEGIC-PLAN-6-6-15.pdf.

"Strategic Plan for the Orthodox Church in America." https://oca.org/PDF/NEWS/2011/2011-strategic-plan-v6.pdf.

"Strategic Plan for the Ukrainian Orthodox Church of the USA and its Parishes." *The Ukrainian Orthodox Church of the United States of America*, 2016. https://www.uocofusa.org/files/strategy/ABSOLUTE-FINAL-UOC-of-USA-STRATEGIC-PLAN.pdf.

"Strategic Planning Workshop #1." *OCA*, 2009. https://www.dowoca.org/PDF/Assemblies/2009/OCA-Strategic-Plan-Workshop-1-Slides.pdf.

"St. Seraphim of Sarov's Conversation with Nicholas Motovilov." *Orthodox Christian Information Center*. http://orthodoxinfo.com/praxis/wonderful.aspx.

"St. Vladimir's Seminary Trustees Implement New Governance Model, Seek CEO." *St. Vladimir's Theological Seminary*, 2016. https://www.svots.edu/headlines/seminary-trustees-implement-new-governance-model-seek-ceo.

St Vladimir's Theological Seminary. "Our Mission, Vision, & Values." https://www.svots.edu/about/mission.

Sunstein, Cass R. *#Republic: Divided Democracy in the Age of Social Media*. Princeton: Princeton University Press, 2017.

"SVS Press Receives Major Gift to Establish Endowment." *St. Vladimir's Theological Seminary*, 2017. https://www.svots.edu/headlines/svs-press-receives-major-gift-establish-endowment.

"Synodal Affirmations on Marriage, Family, Sexuality, and the Sanctity of Life." *Orthodox Church in America*. https://oca.org/holy-synod/statements/holy-synod/synodal-affirmations-on-marriage-family-sexuality-and-the-sanctity-of-life.

"Synopsis: The 13th All-American Council." *Orthodox Church in America*. https://oca.org/history-archives/aacs/the-13th-all-american-council.

"Synopsis: The 15th All-American Council." *Orthodox Church in America*. https://oca.org/history-archives/aacs/the-15th-all-american-council.

Synovitz, Ron. "Coronavirus vs. the Church: Orthodox Traditionalists Stand Behind the Holy Spoon." *Radio Free Europe*, 2020. https://www.rferl.org/a/coronavirus-vs-the-church-orthodox-traditionalists-stand-behind-the-holy-spoon/30492749.html.

Szabó, András "The Impact of the Internet on the Public Sphere and on the Culture Industry: A Study of Blogs, Social News Sites and Discussion Forums." Master's thesis, University of Vaasa, 2007 (p87336).

Taplin, Jonathan T. *Move Fast and Break Things: How Facebook, Google, and Amazon Cornered Culture and Undermined Democracy*. 1st ed. New York: Little, Brown, 2017. Kindle.

Taushev, Averky. *The Struggle for Virtue: Asceticism in a Modern Secular Society*. Jordanville, NY: Holy Trinity, 2014. Kindle.

Taylor, Charles. *Modern Social Imaginaries*. Durham, NC: Duke University Press, 2004. Kindle.

———. *Secular Age*. Cambridge, MA: Belknap of Harvard University Press, 2007.

———. *Sources of the Self: The Making of the Modern Identity*. Cambridge, MA: Harvard University Press, 1989.

———. "Why We Need a Radical Redefinition of Secularism." In *The Power of Religion in the Public Square*, edited by Judith Butler, 34–58. New York: Columbia University Press, 2011.

Taylor, Frederick Winslow. *The Principles of Scientific Management*. New York: Harper & Brothers, 2012. Kindle.

Thalassios the Libyan, Saint. "On Love, Self-Control, and Life in Accordance with the Intellect." In *The Philokalia: The Complete Text; compiled by St. Nikodimos of the Holy Mountain and St. Markarios of Corinth*, edited and translated by, G. E. H. Palmer, Philip Sherrard and Kallistos Ware, 307–33. Boston: Faber and Faber, 1979.

Theophan the Recluse, Saint. *Thoughts for Each Day of the Year*. Platina, CA: St. Herman of Alaska Brotherhood, 2010.

Tolkien, J. R. R., et al. *The Silmarillion*. London: Houghton Mifflin Harcourt, 2012. Kindle.

Tom. "5 Disadvantages to Consider about Online Education." *Peterson's*, 2018. https://www.petersons.com/blog/5-disadvantages-to-consider-about-online-education/.

Turkle, Sherry. *The Second Self: Computers and the Human Spirit*. 20th anniversary ed. Cambridge, MA: MIT Press, 2005. Kindle.

"UK Hits Facebook with Maximum Fine over Cambridge Analytica Scandal." *Pontiac Tribune*, 2018, https://pontiactribune.com/2018/07/uk-hits-facebook-with-maximum-fine/.

"The Ultimate List of Online Giving Statistics." *Non-Profit Source*, 2018. https://nonprofitssource.com/online-giving-statistics/.

"Uniform Parish By-Laws." *Diocese of the South, Orthodox Church in America*. https://static1.squarespace.com/static/58b44e83f5e2315970185fbe/t/58b62bb4d1758e628 70aa274/1488333749378/DOS-Bylaws-7-23-09.pdf.

"The U.S. Bill of Rights." *Bill of Rights Institute*. https://billofrightsinstitute.org/wp-content/uploads/2018/12/Bill-of-Rights-for-Website.pdf.Van Alstyne, Marshall, and Erik Brynjolfsson "Electronic Communities: Global Village or Cyberbalkans?" http://web.mit.edu/marshall/www/papers/CyberBalkans.pdf.

Van Alstyne, Marshall, and Erik Brynjolfsson. "Electronic Communities: Global Village or Cyberbalkans?" http://web.mit.edu/marshall/www/papers/CyberBalkans.pdf.

Vinogradov, Alexis. "The Vernacular in Church Architecture." *The Wheel* 5 (Spring 2016) 24–30.

Vrame, Anton C. "Endorsement from Rev. Anton C. Vrame, Ph.D. Director Department of Religious Education Greek Orthodox Archdiocese of America." https://www.cgsusa.org/wp-content/uploads/Vrame-CGS-Endorsement.pdf.

Waddell, Helen. *The Desert Fathers: Translations from the Latin*. Vintage Spiritual Classics. 1st ed. New York: Vintage, 1998.

Wakefield, Jane. "Facebook 'No Place' for Young Children." *BBC*, 2018. https://www.bbc.com/news/technology-42872603.

Walicki, Andrzej. *A History of Russian Thought from the Enlightenment to Marxism*. Stanford, CA: Stanford University Press, 1979.

Ware, Kallistos. "Theological Education in Scripture and the Fathers." Paper presented at the 5th International Consultation of Orthodox Theological Schools, Halki Theological School, Halki, Turkey, August 14–20, 1994.

Warrillow, John. *The Automatic Customer: Creating a Subscription Business in Any Industry*. New York: Penguin, 2015.

Watts, Clint. *Messing with the Enemy: Surviving in a Social Media World of Hackers, Terrorists, Russians, and Fake News*. New York: Harper, 2018. Kindle.

Webster, Douglas D. *Selling Jesus: What's Wrong with Marketing the Church?* Downers Grove, IL: InterVarsity, 1992.

Weinmann, Gabriel. *Communicating Unreality*. Thousand Oaks, CA: Sage, 2012. Kindle.

"What is a Background Check?" *Protect My Ministry*. https://www.protectmyministry.com/background-checks/.

"What is Montessori?" *The Ivy School*. https://www.theivyschool.org/about-ivy/curriculum-2/what-is-montessori-2/montessori-method/.

"What is Scrip?" *St. John the Evangelist Orthodox Church*. https://www.stjohnaz.org/parish-life/giving/what-is-scrip/.

"What is the Denomination's Position on Homosexuality?" *United Methodist Church*, 2019. http://www.umc.org/what-we-believe/what-is-the-denominations-position-on-homosexuality.

"What is the Rule of Law?" *ABA Division for Public Education*, 2018. https://www.americanbar.org/advocacy/rule_of_law/what-is-the-rule-of-law/.

Wilde, Oscar. "The Soul of Man under Socialism." In *Individualism: A Reader,* edited by George H. Smith and Marilyn Moore, locs. 839–70. Washington, DC: Cato Institute, 2015. Kindle.

Williams, John. "The Basics of Branding." *Entrepreneur*, 2018. https://www.entrepreneur.com/article/77408.

Wilson, Edward O. *Consilience: The Unity of Knowledge*. New York: Vintage, 1999.

Wilson, Henry. "Archbishop Temple on Betting." In *Individualism: A Reader,* edited by George H. Smith and Marilyn Moore, locs. 1401–20. Washington, DC: Cato Institute, 2015. Kindle.

Wisdom, Alan F. H. "The World Council of Churches: Time for Jubilee?" *Theology Matters* 4.6 (1998) 1–14. https://theologymatters.com/wp-content/uploads/2020/03/98Vol4-No6-TM.pdf.

Wood, Andrew F., and Matthew J. Smith. *Online Communication: Linking Technology, Identity, and Culture*. 2nd ed. Mahwah, NJ: Lawrence Erlbaum Associates, 2004. Kindle.

Wright, Conrad. *Congregational Polity. A Historical Survey of Unitarian and Universalist Practice.* Boston: Unitarian Universalist Association, 1997.

Young, Richard D. "Perspectives on Strategic Planning in the Public Sector." http://www.ipspr.sc.edu/publication/perspectives%20on%20Strategic%20Planning.pdf.

Zell, Thomas. "The Trail of the Tithe." *Antiochian Orthodox Christian Archdiocese of North America*, 2018. http://ww1.antiochian.org/node/16719#.

www.ingramcontent.com/pod-product-compliance
Lightning Source LLC
Chambersburg PA
CBHW071233230426
43668CB00011B/1409